From Ex-Wife to
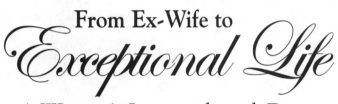
Exceptional Life

A Woman's Journey through Divorce

Donna F. Ferber, LPC, LADC

PURPLE
LOTUS
PRESS™
LLC

Purple Lotus Press, LLC
Farmington, CT

Purple Lotus Press, LLC
Farmington, CT
Second Printing, January 2006

"Questions about your Relationship," from REBUILDING: When Your Relationship Ends, 3rd Edition © 2000 by Bruce Fisher and Robert E. Alberti. Reproduced for Donna Ferber by permission of Impact Publishers, Inc. P.O. Box 6016, Atascadero, CA 93423. Further reproduction prohibited.

Although the author and publisher have made every effort to ensure the accuracy and completeness of information contained in this book, we assume no responsibility for errors, inaccuracy, omissions, or any inconsistency herein. Any slights of people, places or organizations are unintentional.

In order to protect the confidentiality of the women who shared their experience, the names and identifying circumstances have been altered. The women described herein are composites.

The author's intent is to offer information of a general nature to help in your quest for well being. It is published for general reference and not as a substitute for independent verification by users when circumstances warrant. The advice contained herein is not to be substituted for the advice of a professional. The publisher and author disclaim any personal liability, either directly or indirectly, for advice or information presented herein. The reader should consult psychotherapists, attorneys, accountants, financial planners, nutritionists, and other appropriate professionals for advice on your specific situation. The author and publisher assume no responsibility for your actions.

Cover Design: Lisa Reilly and Nancy Marshall
Text Design: Nancy Marshall
Printed in Lowell, MA, USA

Ferber, Donna F.
From Ex-Wife to Exceptional Life: A Woman's Journey through Divorce
Includes Bibliographical References and Index.
Library of Congress Control Number: 2004097747
ISBN 0-9761133-0-9

Discounts are available on bulk purchases of this book for training purposes, fund raising or gift giving. For information, please contact:

Purple Lotus Press
P.O. Box 811 • Farmington, CT 06034-0811
860 674-0855
www.donnaferber.com

Acknowledgments

This book started about seven years ago. It took two years to make it from my head onto the paper. It took three more years to find its way into this format. Like divorce itself, writing a book is a process. It takes you on an incredible journey – sometimes an easy straight road where everything is clear and just when it all seems as if everything will fall neatly into place, you find wild and crazy hairpin turns with no shoulder and a long drop off the edge. The journey seems to go on like that forever – up, down, and all around. There are big, quick starts and big dead ends. It seems as if it will never work out. Then suddenly, it all begins to settle down and your life is forever changed by the process.

Thank you to all who contributed and supported both my emotional health and my literary process along this path. Molly Hinchman, Marion Durant, Barbara Grunwerg, my "Four Agreements" Group, and Noreen Collins, kept me going even at those moments when I thought I had lost it (my mind and my confidence). To Barry Armata, Holly Abery-Wetstone, Wendy Rosen, Pat Froberg, Angela Mazur, Laurie DeNigris, Bonnie Robson, Carol Pekrul, Judith N., Mary Lou Costanza, and Nancy Fidler, who contributed their wisdom and caring to these pages. For Joey, my ever wild puppy, who kept reminding me not to take myself so seriously, as he camped out under my desk chewing on socks for hours while I wrote and wrote. A special thanks to my editor, Nancy Simonds, and to Chris Murphy and Kathleen Berube. Thank you to Cheryl Jones who helped steer me into the right hands. To Richard D. Pomp who said "Why not?" and to Kent Jamison who always asked the "hard" questions.

Thank you to Marilyn French who told me years ago to "write what you know about." To Anne Lamott, who encouraged me through *Bird by Bird* to keep writing "even if you don't want to."

And last but certainly not least, a giant thank you to all of the women who honored me with their stories of heartbreak, insight, humor, wisdom and courage. Thank you for your trust and confidence. Your stories and struggles touched me to my core. I hope this book does justice to you and your journey.

Forward by Marilyn French

In the fall of 1967, I was teaching at Hofstra University. Faculty taught four courses a semester, and one of mine was freshman English. Among the 25 to 30 students in that class was a young woman named Donna Ferber. As teacher and student, we did not have personal conversations; we spoke only about course work. But in speaking to Donna, I had the sense that this young woman needed help, but of a kind I could not give. She could have had the same perception about me.

In fact, both of us were suffering from terrible personal problems.

I had two major problems: one was that I had been writing for some years, but had achieved no success. Since I believed I wrote well, I did not know why I was not being published: I had written a number of short stories and a novel; an agent had believed the novel showed promise, but no publisher took it. It never even occurred to me that my point of view was radically different from that of American (and European) publishers, that I was coming from a place they were unfamiliar with. There was no way to foresee that a decade later, I would publish a novel that became a best-seller in over twenty languages...

My second, and far more pressing problem, was that for years I had felt imprisoned within an extremely unhappy marriage. I married in 1950; by 1957, I had realized that the marriage was unsalvageable. My husband had a split personality (I am not sure how it would be described by a professional; I am describing his behavior). In public, he was the man I married - the most amiable fellow imaginable, sweet and funny and self-effacing. He deferred to me and was physically affectionate. In private, he withheld affection and was often punitive, regularly slipping into a "Mister Hyde" self (as I called it). He threw terrifying rages for little or no cause, rages that could last for several days, and always went on for many hours. Yet if the front doorbell rang while he was in the midst of a rage, he would instantly revert to his charming self, while I and my children still shook with fear and trembling. I had tried to talk to him about this problem, urging him to see psychotherapists. He preferred, however, that I go. Of course, that had no effect on him. Under threat of divorce, he did go briefly to a couple of therapists - one woman and one man - but because he remained his sweetest self with them, no one ever realized his problem.

At that time, everyone I knew was married. People mentioning divorce whispered the word, as my mother did, when she spoke of a scandalous uncle. Like the word rape. It was unspeakable in polite society, even in the intimate conversation of mother and daughter. But my unhappiness grew great enough that I was willing to risk the opprobrium of divorce. At that time, however, achieving it was near impossible. The laws of New York State, where I lived, allowed divorce only for adultery. My husband was not unfaithful and he was fiercely opposed to a divorce: he insisted he loved me and dismissed his rages as inconsequential. (Indeed, I was not sure he really remembered them afterwards.) I had no money beyond my tiny instructor's salary (which was not enough to support me alone, much less my children and me). My parents did not want to take me and the children in, reluctant to wreck the pleasant lives they had finally achieved. Nor did I think it was fair to them, who had sacrificed everything for my sister and me while we were growing up. I felt strongly that this was their time for leisure and pleasure. But that left me with no place to go and no way to survive. I could have left and vanished, if I had been willing to leave my children behind - but I was not. The brunt of my husband's rage fell on them, and without me there to try to shield them, I feared for their well-being.

The marriage moved to a crisis point when my husband, in a fit of pique at my son, kicked out at him and slipped and broke his leg. He was then at home all day, every day; screaming demands at me (but laughing and joking with the nurses who helped him in the hospital). He sat all day in a wheelchair, drinking manhattans and peering through his binoculars at couples who parked near the bay at the foot of our street to have sex. He was invariably drunk and abusive when the children came home from school and more so later, when I got home from teaching. It was unendurable. In the summer of 1967, I borrowed money from a friend, found a lawyer willing to help me (my husband was a lawyer, so it was difficult), and flew to Mexico for a quickie divorce.

Once he knew I was planning to divorce him, my husband embarked on a campaign of harassment. Almost every day or evening, he would appear - at the Hofstra Faculty club, where I had lunch, at our house, on the beach near our house where I would go in my misery to walk and think - to beg and cajole, to curse and rage, to search my desk, my mail, my waste paper basket, to count the plates in the dishwasher - whatever occurred to him. Why he thought these actions would restore me to him, I don't know. But they were terribly hard on me because I did love this man, and understood that he loved me, in whatever odd, sick way. I knew he was falling apart, but I also knew that if I didn't leave him, I would kill myself and my children would be left in a hideous turmoil.

It was in this frame of mind that I taught Donna's English class.

One of the worst things about being tormented by someone who is larger than you and fiercer and who enjoys being physically threatening, is being unable to talk about it. I could not talk to my mother, who could not understand why I wanted a divorce; no matter how I described my husband's irrational rages, she couldn't comprehend them, never having seen him like that and unable to imagine such ferocity in the sweet fellow she knew. She believed that unmarried, I would fall into poverty, and that terrified her. Nor could I speak to my sister, who liked my husband better than she liked me. Most of my friends simply could not imagine the amiable fellow they knew behaving like a monster.

But one friend, an extremely perceptive woman, who later became a psychotherapist herself, did stand by me. Having glimpsed my husband's hateful side, she took me in when I needed shelter, and protected me from him. She listened to my griefs and sympathized and offered advice. She kept me sane. Partly because of her, I got through those years.

So did Donna Ferber, whose problems, very different from mine, were equally difficult and challenging. I cannot describe the courage and intellect it had to take for her to work her way through the maze of her situation, and I would not even know about it except that thirty years later, she wrote to me. Somehow, she found my address, in my house in the Berkshire mountains, and asked if I remembered her. I did, but vaguely. She asked if she could take me to lunch. When I saw her, she instantly returned to my memory. She was that troubled young woman struggling to write well. Over lunch, she told me her story.

I was deeply impressed and moved by this young woman who had faced many obstacles but had fought her way through to happiness, achievement, and a lovely useful life. And here she was, sitting there telling me that remarks I had made in class, in freshman English all those years ago, had helped her through her ordeal. Had I known that at the time, it would have made those dismal days brighter.

It seems to me utterly fitting that Donna should have written a book dealing with the greatest problem of my life - achieving a divorce. What a difference for women of today! Divorce, no longer unspeakable, is common and not at all shameful. There are people to help you through it, not just lawyers, but counselors like Donna, especially trained in the subject. Such a person in my life would have lightened my anguish immeasurably. Not only that, but she sees you through the days, one by one, days that were for me, punches on my heart. She does this clearly, understandably, concisely - all a writing teacher could ask. If you are thinking about divorce, this book will guide you well. I only wish I had it thirty-seven years ago.

Marilyn French

It will take you one year to read this book.

If you are reading this book, I assume that you are either considering a divorce, or are in the throes of one. Undoubtedly, this is one of the hardest events you will ever experience. With the right frame of mind, appropriate knowledge, and a reliable support system, it can also be a life-affirming and positive experience.

Divorce is a life-changing event. It can wreak havoc on your life. Like any crisis, it also provides the opportunity for change and growth.

The goal of this book is to provide you with information, inspiration, support, laughter and to encourage creative thinking. These tools can help assure that your divorce changes your life for the better, which can happen if you use this opportunity to challenge yourself. Think of your divorce as a marathon – it will take time, concentration, exerted effort and, most importantly, patience. As you prepare for the inevitable ups and downs inherent in the divorce process, patience is mandatory: Set a pace that will take you the distance. By learning to accept that divorce is a *process* rather than an *event*, you can begin to take better care of yourself, prepare as needed, and acquire the knowledge that is critical in making the informed decisions that will affect you for *the rest of your life*. If you rush through the marathon, without training and adequate equipment, you will run into problems. If you don't pace yourself, you will burn out. Without building stamina, you can get injured. So, for all you over-achievers out there who want to rush through this process quickly, please, please, *relax*.

There are short-term marriages, long term marriages, marriages that you ended, marriages that he ended. There are marriages with children and marriages without children. There are in-laws, friends, property, finances, legalities, and settlements to consider. In truth, divorce is one of those experiences that touches every part of your life! It is a profound event, which can shake you to your core, yet strengthen and empower you. My goal is to help strengthen and empower you!

Regardless of the unique circumstances surrounding each divorce, every woman going through this process finds herself short on both time and concentration. Often when a woman is faced with divorce, she runs to the local bookstore and purchases a pile of self-help books that end up collecting dust or serving as coasters on a night table. Many women are so exhausted at the end of the day that they just tumble into bed, unable to put one more thought into their already spinning brain. The goal of this book is to support you, not overload you. To that end, it is divided into one-page chapters. Every day you will read only one page. That's it. Use the book preferably in the morning so you can allow it to resonate with you all day. If that is not possible, read it the night before and carry the message with you throughout the following day.

Three hundred and sixty five days: one year of topics, thoughts, ideas and advice. As often as you can, follow the suggestion at the bottom of the page. Like anything that works effectively, it must be practiced. We can read exercise books, purchase workout videos, and join a gym, but nothing happens if we don't follow through. There is no magic formula to make change easy, but there are methods and strategies to make it less painful. While the format of this book may resemble a meditation book, it is also a workbook and guide. Read the pages in order or use the index to pick a topic for the day, or simply let the book open to any page. However your choice is made, date that page. That way, the book will serve as a journal for you to review when you need to affirm all that you have done, or when you need to revisit a specific subject.

You may think, "Well, I will be divorced in three months. I don't need a year of this stuff." While it may be true that the legal divorce takes only a few months, the emotional divorce often takes longer. One year from start to finish is a good rule of thumb. If your process takes less time, that's fine. And if it takes more time, well, that's fine, too. This marathon is about getting to the finish, not being the first one there. It is about you, your life and your choices. You are in charge of how you run this marathon, as long as you remember to care for yourself, emotionally, physically, and spiritually. Don't try to turn it into a sprint. Don't try to rush through this process. Pay attention to details, speak up for yourself and do your research. Listen to your intuition, but make sure you enlist support. You want to avoid mistakes and pitfalls that could cause regret later on in your life. You also want to maximize the gifts that can be inherent in the process. These include self-awareness, self-confidence, and assertiveness. Enhancement of each of these traits, along with new knowledge, skills, and basic information about yourself and how you relate to others, are some of the achievements that can be yours. It takes time, hard work and commitment, but you can do it!

Some of the pages may not apply to you and you may want to skip those. For example, you may want to ignore the pages on children if you don't have children. I would suggest you read them anyway. Reading about issues which are not problematic for you, provides you with a more global view of the process. This is not so you can gloat, but to change your outlook a bit. Reading about issues that aren't specifically yours can give you a moment of gratitude and a different perspective on your own pain. Use the book consistently. Make room for it on your night table, or where it is visible and likely to be picked up. Make it a part of your daily regimen, like brushing your teeth. After a while it will become a habit. You won't see the results right away, but this is a process; like letting your hair grow out from a bad haircut, the process is happening whether you are aware of it or not.

Approach your divorce with resolve, conviction, and determination. Rather than have the focus be on winning, try to concentrate on using this time for growth. Use your fear and anger to energize you, not for revenge. Be aware of the feelings, the challenges, the disappointments, and the pain. But, most importantly, allow yourself to feel the joy, exhilaration, and excitement that results from becoming your own person!

...but they are still beating."

These are the words spoken by New York City's mayor, Rudolph Guiliani, as he hosted the first Saturday Night Live show after the September 11, 2001 attacks on our country. Just as the September 11 attacks changed a nation, divorce will change you. Although it may not feel like it now, you will laugh; find joy, love, and experience happiness again in your life. Right now you don't have to feel it or think it. You just need to believe that it is possible. Every day, people experience crises and tragedy of all kinds and they survive. Human beings have a wonderful capacity for healing and we can bounce back from adversity stronger and more courageous. This can happen to you.

Where were you the day of the September 11, 2001 attacks? Can you remember your fear? Did you ever think there would again be laughter, hope and joy in your life? Mayor Guiliani gave us all permission to laugh again. He also acknowledged it would take time and effort and that it would feel uncomfortable at first. We found a way to move past the horrific experience of September 11. From tragedy emerge many stories of hope, courage, and humanity. I have counseled people who have experienced horrendous things and most of them tell me that the experience made them stronger, braver and more grateful for this life.

You are probably having a hard time believing that you will ever feel that way, but you will. It will take time but it will happen. One year from now, you will look back with amazement at how far you have come. At first, the pain feels so unbearable you cannot imagine that you can go on, but you do. Then, the pain dulls a bit and it becomes manageable. What a nice surprise! With effort, insight and support, you will feel better daily. Sometimes you may feel like you are moving backwards; trust in your strength and spirit. You can handle more than you ever thought. You will turn your agony into victory, empowerment, and freedom. There will be many new discoveries about yourself this year. This is the beginning of your journey. This is the beginning of a whole new life.

Today I acknowledge this acute pain, but I also have faith that it will not last forever. I will heal and I will become a stronger individual. I will uncover aspects of my self, which have been hidden. I will reconnect with the woman I am. I will love her. Daily, I will discover her fortitude, courage, humor, and caring. This is a time of heartbreak but it is also a time of rebirth.

"*I never thought this would happen to me.*"

Many women share that sentiment. No one walks down the aisle thinking about splitting up. (At least in their first marriage!) So, when a marriage falls apart, it can be more difficult in some ways than a death. Death is inevitable, but divorce, well, everyone likes to think that it happens to "somebody else." With divorce there are many feelings and among them is anger.

Divorce anger can be very positive, especially if you feel like a victim. Anger has energy and can create movement. It can be empowering and help a woman detach from an unhealthy relationship.

When you think of your relationship, and you think about your anger, what are you **most** angry about? This question opens the door for an inner dialogue. When you think about how you felt a month ago, how has your anger changed? It may be the same, it may not. One thing is certain; over time what you are angry with and the depth of that anger will change. Some women identify their anger as completely self-directed and others as completely directed at their spouse. With their new insights, they may begin to see the issues differently. Congratulate yourself on any changes you feel. Even the slightest change is positive, as it signifies growth and a shift out of the rut.

You have a right to your anger. It is healthy to feel angry when one is betrayed, violated, or abandoned.

DO not feel "bad" about anger. Many women equate anger with the behavior of aggression and are terrified to acknowledge the feeling in themselves. There is a difference between feeling angry and the behavior of angry. It is important to learn assertive ways to express anger rather than bottling it up or behaving violently.

Anger – the *feeling* of anger – is not *bad*. It is the negative behaviors associated with the feeling, such as aggression and violence that are destructive. As we become more comfortable with our ability to separate the feeling from the behavior, we learn that:

- We are entitled to our anger.
- We do not have to act on every feeling.
- We are responsible for controlling our impulses to act on those feelings.

Today I understand that my anger does not have to be a problem. I can use it to grow and detach from my pain. However, I will be mindful that my behavior is my responsibility. I will pay attention to how I express my anger, knowing that violence is never acceptable, either from my partner or myself.

There will be days when you will have doubts about whether you can make it on your own, about the children, about your decision, about finances. Thoughts of reconciliation may occur as you travel along this path. Sometimes reconciliation can work; however, without couples' therapy and lots of hard work, couples frequently fall back into old habits and patterns.

Imagine the marriage you would like to have with this person. Imagine the changes you would like to see. Now ask yourself... is it possible? Really possible?

Of course, anything is possible, provided the other person is willing. Let's assume that he is willing and you go to couples' therapy, you work hard, you both change. Now ask yourself... Would it be enough? If your answer is no, then you are on the right path. Many women who have reached this point say that nothing would be enough. The pain, deception, betrayal, and loss of trust are so great that nothing could change those feelings. If you are one of those women, honor your decision to divorce and realize you are on the right track. You aren't a failure or a quitter; you have merely learned when to cut your losses.

The desire to reconcile is often the desire to return to a known entity, to a familiar way of being. It is often the fear of the unknown rather than a true desire to reconcile your marriage. Some women change their mind and try again—not because they think it can work out successfully, but because they are afraid of the unknown of the future. The future is always unknown, whether you stay or you go. However, making decisions that are based on truth rather than fear is always healthier. It puts us in charge of our lives and our destiny.

Today I recognize that nothing he could do at this point would be enough and that closes the option of going back to the marriage. While that is sad, it also frees me to look ahead to my future without complicated "what ifs."

Use an attorney who specializes in family law. While a general practitioner may charge less per hour, he/she will not have as much experience with and knowledge of divorce, as a family law attorney. It may take the general lawyer more time to learn the nuances of your case. He/she may need to consult with other attorneys. This translates to more fees for you to pay. Consequently, while he/she may charge less per hour, you may pay for more hours. Don't hire a lawyer just because she is a friend of the family. Expertise counts for much more than family connection!

The divorce rate is estimated at fifty percent (Krieder & Fields, 2002), so chances are you know someone who has been through a divorce. Ask them about their lawyer. But remember that each divorce is different, so while they may have had a good experience, it does not necessarily mean that you will, too. Here are some resources to help you find a reputable attorney:

- Check with the Bar Association in your state.

- Web sites, such as Divorcesource.com.

- Use Martindale-Hubbard, which you can find on-line or in the library. Every lawyer is listed with all pertinent information, such as specialty, years in practice, special awards and rating.

- Ask your therapist.

Once you have THREE referrals, set up appointments with ALL three. Yes, three. We spend more time picking out a winter coat than selecting an attorney. Your attorney is someone you will be working with closely, so this person's expertise, and the chemistry and communication between you, are critically important. The financial and legal decisions you make as a result of your divorce can affect you for many years to come.

Today I will begin to research good divorce attorneys in my area. I will take my time and do my homework. While my divorce may seem like a simple matter to me, I will be mindful that there can be negative legal and financial ramifications from not being thorough in my search. Taking my time to get referrals is part of taking care of myself.

Day 5   *Identify Problem Areas in the Relationship*

Are you open to looking inside? Are you ready to go a little deeper? The following list of questions about relationships is adapted from *Rebuilding: When Your Relationship Ends,* an excellent book by Bruce Fisher. Take your time reading the list.

- Were you friends?
- Did you share responsibilities in ways that were mutually agreeable?
- Did you each make sacrifices for the sake of the marriage?
- Did you agree on child rearing?
- Did you share similar, moral and ethical beliefs?
- Did you laugh at the same things?
- Did you allow each other separate time?
- Did the relationship make room for individual growth?
- Did you share friends?
- Did you share long term goals?
- Did you fight fairly?
- Did you share a mutually satisfying sexual relationship?
- Did you agree on issues regarding money?
- Did you have successful methods for problem solving?

When you're finished, sit with your thoughts for a few minutes. Then read it again. Do you see areas of deficiency? Focus on each item and how it contributed to the success or demise of the relationship. By letting yourself fully acknowledge the deficits in the marriage, you can begin to recognize that your relationship has probably been unfulfilling to you in many ways for quite some time.

Now reread the list and ask yourself how your partner would have answered those questions. This can add to your insight as to what went wrong. Remember that this is not about blame, guilt, or recrimination. It is about insight and growth and acceptance of the end of your relationship. Sometimes seeing it for what it was helps us realize that it was over a long time ago.

Today I am committed to understanding everything I can about my relationship. I will do this without self-punishment. I will allow myself to grieve for the loss of the good things, but also admit that many of my needs ceased to be met many years ago.

The decision-making process when choosing to divorce is a complex one. Finally reaching resolution with their decision, some women feel ready to proceed, then find themselves absolutely paralyzed at the prospect of filing the papers. As the plaintiff or petitioner of the divorce suit, other women report feeling empowered when they actively take action to end the marriage. Why is there such a disparity in feelings? Some women doubt whether they are doing the right thing. They may find themselves backpedaling and struggling with decisions they have already made.

More often than not, this indecision is really not doubt about the decision, but self-doubt. Doubt and fear are usually related to self-esteem. Low self-esteem contributes to the difficulty one has in making decisions, and then sticking to one's convictions. There is also the fear that people will be disapproving or angry with you, as well as fear of the future. More than likely, it is not your decision that needs more work; it is your sense of self. How, you ask, do you work on that?

Just recognizing that the issue is self-doubt, and not doubt about the divorce, can be very helpful. It can help you focus on what is really going on. The real fear is "I can't handle this." Focus on the most difficult things you have encountered thus far in your life: the death of a loved one, a job loss, an illness, an accident. How did you handle each crisis? Try to look at the ways you behaved and felt and thought. Examine them objectively as an outsider would. You got through them, didn't you? Otherwise, you wouldn't be reading this! Most of us are capable of handling far worse than we can imagine.

Now, take a moment to affirm how much inner strength that took. It doesn't matter whether you went through your crisis with grace or kicking and screaming. You went through it and made it. That is what you need to remember. You will make it through this as well.

Today as I proceed through my process, I will remember the difficult things I have gone through and I will draw strength from those experiences. If I feel fear, I will not let it disable me. I know I can handle whatever comes my way. My experience has taught me that this is so.

My yoga teacher always starts the class by asking us to close our eyes and "create an intention" about what we want from the class that morning. I found that if I took a moment and considered what I wanted from each class, I enjoyed it more and felt more fulfilled when it was over. That feeling of well being stayed with me throughout my day. Recently, a friend was telling me how she created intention each morning in the shower. Creating intention is about being mindful of what you want in your day.

Try this: As you step into the shower, imagine that the water actually has the power to take all of your worries away. Wash yourself with awareness and gentleness and as you rinse, close your eyes and imagine all the worries, anxiety, and negative thoughts being washed down the drain. Open your eyes and observe the water going down the drain. Your problems are being rinsed away. Step out from under the water and watch them disappear down the drain. Now close your eyes again and as you step back under the water, create your intention for yourself. What do you want to accomplish today? How do you want to feel when the day ends? As the water washes over you, imagine that it is your intention washing over you. You are being bathed with your mindfulness. It will stay with you all day. Imagine the sun is able to reach through your ceiling and warm you. Feel the radiance and warmth of the sun on your body as you turn off the water and gently towel yourself off. The heat is sealing in the intention, making it a part of you.

Tonight as you prepare for bed, think of your morning shower, the intention that was created and how you spent your day. Amazing things can begin to happen!

Today as I prepare my body to face a new day, I will also prepare my soul. I will begin to practice creating the life I want to have. I honor myself when I create intention. It is a way to care for and respect myself.

If you have never been to court, notification of your first court appearance can be terrifying. The legal system, the acrimony of divorce, the adversarial posture of attorneys all can trigger anxiety. Here are some things you can do to make the day a bit easier and less intimidating.

- Have your lawyer brief you in detail as to where to go and what to expect. Many women are concerned about having to testify. Your attorney, or perhaps her/his legal assistant, can fill you in on what to expect.

- Know where you are going. Take a trial run the week before so you know where you are going, where to park, how long it takes to get there. It helps to go in to the building and walk around. Familiarizing yourself with the surroundings helps diminish the unknown and, consequently, minimize some of your fears.

- On your court date, take a friend/relative with you. The moral support is invaluable. Having someone you know and trust at your side will make the process less daunting.

- Bring a good book or your knitting. This will help pass the time.

- Wear something you are comfortable in, but not necessarily something you like a lot. Sometimes we associate different outfits with different events. You may not be able to look at that outfit without thinking, "Divorce Dress."

- Use visual imagery. Ellen envisioned all the court players as animals in a barnyard. Just thinking of her husband's attorney as a donkey helped diminish her anxiety.

- Make believe you are a reporter or a critic, sitting in on someone else's divorce. The emotional distance can help you keep perspective and listen without as much emotion.

- Don't lose your cool. You will feel better about yourself if you act with dignity. Remember, we can't control the behavior of others, but we can control our own behavior.

- Confronting our fears makes us stronger. When your day in court is over, you will feel many things. One thing you will feel is the conviction of your own courage.

Today as I prepare for court, I will acquire the necessary knowledge, quiet myself, and ask for support. I will do everything I can to diminish my anxiety. Today is another opportunity to learn that just because something scares me, that doesn't mean I can't do it.

The decision to end a marriage is not any easy one. We can become obsessed with saving our marriage. To that end, we may have seen numerous counselors, marital therapists, physicians, and clergy. We have gone to seers, had our cards read, had our astrology charts done. We have read volumes of self-help books. Now we are exhausted and may feel utter despair. "When," we ask, "is it okay to say this marriage is over?"

Without even realizing it, most women take half the life of the relationship to make the decision without even realizing it. For example, if a woman was married twenty years, she would say she has been unhappy for about ten years. Ask yourself how long you have been unhappy and you will probably realize that you have been struggling in your marriage for longer than you even thought.

The opinions of others can shake our confidence in our decision. "You always seemed so happy" can fill us with doubt. Why is it that we are so quick to take an outsider's perspective of our marriage? They weren't the ones living in it day to day! This ease with which we acquiesce our personal power may be due, in part, to the way we were raised. We were taught to compromise and sacrifice for the good of our children, our parents, our co-workers. It is a trait often admired by the culture because it makes us compliant and, therefore, malleable. But does it help us like ourselves? What about the need to honor our own opinion?

Nobody wants to divorce. We long to be happy. The Dalai Lama points out in *The Art of Happiness* that we often confuse pleasure with happiness. Pleasure comes from immediate gratification, such as that extra piece of cheesecake, a new outfit, a winning lotto ticket, drugs, alcohol or great sex. Although these things provide a quick "high," the feeling doesn't last. Happiness is not achieved through ingesting or acquiring. It is a state of being that comes from living one's life in a way that is congruent with one's belief system.

It is not surprising that many women in unhappy marriages find pleasure in food, shopping and alcohol. They are seeking an outlet for their sorrow, trying to put a Band-Aid on a bigger problem. Often when they divorce, the weight comes off without effort, and the abuse of money and substances ceases.

If you think about your own journey, you will realize how long you really have been struggling. Trust your gut instinct. It will tell you when enough is enough!

Today I will think about what I want from my life. I will think about all I have done to try and make my marriage better. If I am through, then I am through. I will trust that I know what is best for me.

As we go through divorce, it is important to understand why we got married, as well as why our marriage ended. This is not about assigning *blame*, but about responsibility. When we take responsibility, we can see we have made choices. Recognizing those choices helps us recognize our own personal power and learn about who we are. Why did you get married?

- To get out of my parents' house.
- Everyone was doing it.
- I was afraid to be alone.
- I was afraid no one else would ask me.
- I wanted to have children.
- I was pregnant.
- I wanted to take care of someone.
- I wanted to have someone take care of me.
- I was in love.
- I wanted a wedding.
- I wanted someone to complete me.
- I was tired of doing it all myself.

Although not all women marry for the above reasons, most women can identify with at least some of the reasons on the above list. Take time to explore why you married. This can be both exhausting and energizing. These insights help us see the influences in our lives and help us look beyond the obvious for the subtler messages. Only when we can decode those messages and their meanings can we change.

Melinda married right after college. She moved from her parents' home to her husband's house without ever having lived on her own. Now she is forty-five and her husband has decided he wants to end the marriage. As Melinda studied the above list, she saw that many of the issues pertained to her. She wanted to leave home because of her father's drinking and temper. She could have gone to college, as her grades were good and her parents encouraged her to do so. But she was afraid she couldn't make it on her own. Her desire to leave home and her fear of being on her own contributed to her haste in getting married. These are issues Melinda will work on in therapy so that her fear does not impact her decisions in the future.

Today I will honestly explore my motives for marrying, without self-criticism or self-blame. I do this to gain information that will help me understand this marriage. It will also help me make healthier choices in my future relationships.

Women going through divorce often use their anger and sadness to mobilize their resources to make positive changes. Often, appetite for food diminishes when one is experiencing the stress of divorce. It is not unusual for women to lose weight during the process. This weight loss may make them feel differently about themselves. They may purchase new clothes, which often spurs on the desire for a new hair style. These changes are fun and empowering and help women feel more confidence as they see their external transformation. Many women also consider re-entering the workplace or beginning school. These changes can be daunting and anxiety-provoking, but at the same time, the challenge can ultimately contribute to one's self of self-reliance and value.

Changing our marital status, our appearance and our work situation are significant changes! We can get on a roll and want to change everything. I have seen divorce impel women into incredible action-changing professions, cosmetic surgery, relocation, a new romance, buying real estate. Sometimes, we can do too much too quickly or make a major decision on impulse. Taking action can make us feel valuable, in charge and in control, but it is also a way to distract us from our pain. In our desire to empower ourselves, we may find we act in haste, making decisions that we later regret. We may be reacting to our situation rather than pro-acting. (For example, you may cut your long hair as an act of defiance to your ex, who insisted you keep it long. If that is the only reason you cut it, you are still reacting to him, not to your own opinion or need.)

Experts agree that while change is inevitable and good, in stressful times we should not implement too many changes. There are enough changes to deal with as you go through divorce. It is not the time to begin medical school or to move across the country. Delay big changes for a year. Your hair will grow back, but other changes are harder to undo. Take the time you need to adjust to the changes inherent in your situation. Make sure you have settled in to this new life before you move on to something else.

Today I ask myself why I rush to make change. Am I running away from my feelings? Some changes are okay to make now, but others can wait until the divorce dust settles. Meanwhile I can dream. Dreams are the beginning of living my life in accordance with my authentic self. I honor those dreams by creating a life that is thought out and carefully planned. This will help minimize regrets in the future.

The following information is from a PBS special entitled *"The American Frontier"* that was broadcast in the summer of 2002. In 1873:

- One in fifteen marriages among homesteaders ended in divorce.

- The women cited abandonment, cruelty and drunkenness as the predominant reasons.

- The men cited the women's inability to submit.

Given the hardships of life on the frontier, it is apparent why more women did not leave. The work was physically demanding and challenging. Every set of hands was necessary to live. It was clear that many women would have perished if they were alone on the prairie.

Today many more marriages end in divorce. Over the past twenty years, women have frequently been the initiators, possibly because they are now more economically independent and they are freer to leave. But is that the real reason for breakdown of the American marriage? Having economic options merely frees women from having to tolerate the intolerable. The breakdown of the American marriage is not due to economic freedom, but to the same issues that plagued us more than 100 years ago: the inability to treat each other with respect, to uphold the vows of commitment, and the epidemic of substance abuse.

Today women are better able to advocate for themselves when they are mistreated. Still, this is not consistently true for all women. Some struggle with economic dependency and the fear that if they leave their marriage they will not be able to economically provide for themselves and their children. If you are a woman struggling with the economic realities of divorce and this is the reason that you stay in an unhealthy abusive marriage, there is help. Contact your church or synagogue, your local women's shelter, the Salvation Army, the YWCA, or call a Hot Line. Some divorce attorneys will do pro bono work, which means they will not charge you if there is economic hardship. Call your local college or university and ask for someone in the women's studies department or in social work. Call your local mental health association. There are funds and programs available. The reality is that there is help!

Today I acknowledge that sometimes I feel trapped in an intolerable situation. However, I do have many options. I will seek out all the information available. Nothing will change unless I reach out and ask for help. Today I will make one phone call. My situation is not hopeless. I will stop thinking of it as such and in doing so, I will begin to act with hope. I deserve a better life and with the help of others, I can make it happen.

Experts disagree on how much sleep one needs. Many say seven to eight hours of sleep are required, others claim as much as nine. Gregg D. Jacobs, Ph.D., states in his book *Say Good Night to Insomnia,* that five hours is enough sleep and it is only when we have less than five hours that it impacts our lives adversely.

Each person requires a different amount of sleep. Often, we think we need more than we really do. In truth, most of us can get by, at least for a couple of nights, on less sleep than we really need. One or two sleepless nights will not hurt you. However, an accumulation of sleepless nights begins to take its toll, both emotionally and physically.

When going through a divorce, one is bound to experience some sleeplessness. Insomnia often accompanies the shock, grief, anxiety, worry and fear that are inherent in the divorce process.

Let's take a moment to talk about things you can do to improve your sleep habits.

- Cut out ALL caffeine – if you drink a lot of coffee, decrease your caffeine gradually mixing decaf and "high test." This will reduce the chances of developing those nasty caffeine withdrawal headaches.
- Cut out alcohol – a drink at bedtime will not help you sleep.
- Go to bed at the same time every night – routine helps!
- Keep the room quiet and tranquil, with soothing colors, blinds drawn, soft music, scented candles.
- Do not watch violent or anxiety-provoking television for three hours before bedtime. If you really must watch ER, tape it and watch it in the morning while you are exercising.
- Have a bedtime ritual.
- Take some time to read in bed – boring or monotonous material – crossword puzzles work for some.
- No paperwork should ever be done in the bedroom.
- Try sipping warm milk or chamomile tea to help you feel sleepy.
- Do not exercise or eat for three hours before bedtime.
- Do not nap during the day.
- Avoid upsetting conversations after dinner.
- Try progressive relaxation or imagery tapes.

If you follow the above suggestions for a few nights and still aren't sleeping, talk with your doctor about over-the-counter or prescription sleeping aids. Talk to her/him about herbs as well. "All natural" doesn't necessarily mean "without risk." Even if you are taking a sleeping aid, follow the above guidelines to help you learn to sleep better on your own. Sleeping aids are useful for the short term, but over the long haul, it is better to learn to sleep without them.

Today I will remind myself that making sure I get enough sleep is part of taking care of myself. I will begin a bedtime routine today.

Do you know the difference between responding and reacting?

Example: Your estranged husband tells you he cannot take the kids to his place for the weekend as planned. Before hearing his explanation, you become furious because he can "never be counted on, always does this, is unreliable" and so on. You scream at him that he is a loser and get upset because your plans will have to be cancelled. He then explains that he will take them to his mother's house because he is having the kids' bedrooms at his house repainted and he doesn't want to expose the children to the paint fumes.

Example: On Friday, your boss tells you he wants to see you first thing on Monday morning. You spend the whole weekend worrying that you did something wrong. You convince yourself that you will be fired. To spare the humiliation, you write a letter of resignation, which you are prepared to hand him at the meeting. On Monday morning, he commends you for a job done well and mentions a possible raise.

Did you react or respond? In both situations, you reacted to your feelings about what you thought was happening. Rather than respond to the information (or lack of it) in an appropriate way, you *assumed* certain things and then *assumed* they would result in certain negative events. You *reacted* to what you perceived to be true, rather than *responding* to the information with which you were actually presented.

As a marriage unravels, we all become reactive. Our emotions are raw. We begin to assume the worst and then try to protect ourselves from further wounding. Our own reactions can create additional stress and heartache. In the above scenarios, your feelings were based on assumptions, not on facts. You did not have enough information before you made a judgment. You became anxious and stressed without due cause. This kind of behavior distorts communication. People just end up yelling at each other, feeling misunderstood and resentful.

When we **respond**, we hold our feelings at bay and only deal with the facts. We deal with what is *actually happening or being said*. This increases cooperation and results in more constructive communication. Here are ways to reduce reactive behavior and become more responsive:

- Slow down your reaction.
- Ask questions.
- Clarify what you heard.
- Listen to the speaker's words, not what you think he meant.
- Don't assume anything.

Today I acknowledge that I have an investment in being as responsive as I can be. I will practice responsiveness, knowing it is not easy to change old patterns. I will be gentle with myself, remembering that change happens slowly. I do not expect miracles from myself. I will do the best I can, knowing that may change daily. I will remember that responsive behavior encourages resolution.

Getting all "A's" is not about your grades in school. It is about how we live our lives. We all need to work to receive these "A's" in our lives. They are:

Attention – This is about receiving caring, compassion and concern. When someone pays attention to us in positive ways, it reinforces our sense of value. It lets us know we are on the right track.

Acceptance – In relationships, we always seem to want to change each other. Is there a place in your life where you feel affirmed for who you are? That whatever you say and feel is okay? Acceptance affords us a different experience than having to "walk on egg shells." Rather than being self-conscious and restricted in our expression, when we are accepted, we feel a freedom to be ourselves. When we are free to be ourselves, silly and spontaneous or introspective and philosophical, we are more creative, more spiritual and more authentic.

Appreciation – Being appreciated includes praise, compliments and pats on the back. Appreciation tells us that our contribution has value and means something to others. It acknowledges that our behavior and our effort have meaning.

Assertion – People do not always behave as we would want. Sometimes we don't tell them clearly what our needs are. Of course, it works both ways. Those in our life need to feel free to tell us when they agree or disagree with us. In any relationship, it is vital to ask for, and express clearly, what it is we are feeling and what it is we need. Without this kind of communication, relationships begin to unravel and eventually crumble.

Affection – Affection includes gentle play, loving acts and gentleness, not just physical gestures of touching. We express affection through greeting cards and flowers as well as hugs and caresses. If you find that your life is lacking human affection, do not diminish the importance of stroking your cat or petting your dog. Research has shown that physical contact with your animal companion can be helpful to your health in many ways.

Today when I think of getting all "A's" as an adult, I realize that it is important to have love in my life. These "A's" are not about romantic love, but about the love that contributes to well being and self-esteem. Today I will be aware of my needs. I will look at my life and see where I might want to work on bringing more "A's" into my life. I will also take a moment to feel grateful for the "A's" which already exist.

What is mediation? A trained mediator, who is also an attorney, facilitates the couple negotiating their divorce. The goal of mediation, especially when the divorce involves children, is to minimize the amount of acrimony rather than escalate it. Mediation offers the couple an opportunity to work together in a congenial atmosphere that usually continues in the post-divorce relationship. Many experts contend that *how* you divorce has more impact on the children than the actual divorce itself.

In mediation, clients negotiate their own issues and design their own divorce settlement. The mediator is like a referee. Mediation costs less and takes less time than a traditional divorce. Rather than requiring multiple trips to court, mediation usually requires only one court trip to finalize the divorce.

When possible, the costs of mediation are split, giving each party an equal investment in the process. This diminishes any sense of the mediator being biased to the paying party. Mediators also encourage that separate attorneys review all mediated divorces. The mediator offers support and advice when it is appropriate. Many women who participate in mediation feel empowered. It helps boost their self-confidence and sense of competence. However, in situations with a history of domestic violence or when a woman is fearful of her partner harming her or her children, mediation is not appropriate. Here are examples of how mediation might be structured:

- The consultation where the couple becomes acquainted with the mediation process.

- Individual meetings with each party so they may share information they feel uncomfortable sharing in front of their spouse.

- Marital history is taken. Filing for the divorce occurs. Temporary financial agreements are established to maintain and keep the family financially stable throughout the process.

- A parenting plan is discussed. Often this includes a structured visitation, which may change as the children grow older.

- Finances are discussed and a plan is created.

- Visit to the courthouse to finalize their settlement.

Today I don't know if mediation is something that will work for us. However, reducing time, cost and acrimony is very appealing. I can call the local Bar Association or some women's groups in my area. Doing the research helps insure that I make the right choices, thus protecting the future of myself and my children.

If you are thinking about divorcing, there are some things you can do to prepare yourself both practically, legally, and financially. Before filing, take a look at the following financial and legal areas. This will help contribute to your peace of mind and help you in your emotional journey as well.

- **Start to build a nest egg.** This can be done in many different ways. One suggestion is taking a little extra money each time you use the ATM and putting that aside. As the amount grows, use traveler's checks which are both safe and untraceable. Keep them at a friend's house. Another suggestion is to change the number of dependents you are claiming at work. This will give you more money in every paycheck to put aside.

- **Take care of all repairs on your car.** A vehicle in working order assures you have reliable transportation.

- **Develop credit in your own name.** This is essential for buying a car, a home or anything on your own. Even if you rent an apartment, the landlord will check your credit history to see if you are reliable. If you have a joint credit card now, call the credit card company and tell them you would like one in your own name. If your husband's credit is not good, chances are they will refuse you. In that case, start with a credit card from a gas company. Often they are more lenient when offering credit. Use it, but pay your bills promptly. Credit is worthless if your credit rating is poor.

- **See an attorney and learn the laws in your state before making decisions and proceeding on your own.** For example, in some states, moving out of the family home can result in your losing your equity in the home.

- **Check on health insurance laws in your state.** Many women who are covered by their husband's health insurance are concerned that they will have no access to health insurance after the divorce. COBRA is a federal law, which entitles you to have health insurance coverage under your husband's policy for thirty-six months after the divorce. There are still out-of-pocket expenses to be considered. Make sure your health exams and dental needs are up to date before you divorce. This can prevent lots of expenses in your first year of being single.

- **Please, *please* do not date.** This can hurt your case legally, which can impact you financially. It can also lead to emotional confusion. As tempting as it may seem, it simply isn't worth the risk. If a guy is really worth it, he will wait for you.

- Don't quit your job.

- Don't build debt.

- Don't sign anything without first conferring with an attorney.

Today I will think about the things I need to do for myself. I am eager to begin this process, but I will make sure I have my "ducks in a row." I will make sure I protect myself and I will take the time I need, so that I may do this right.

A marriage takes more than love to make it work. When analyzing why your marriage ended, consider the three-legged stool theory (TLST). The TLST says that a sturdy marriage is like a three-legged stool. Imagine that one leg is chemistry, one leg represents common interests, and the last leg comprises similar values and belief system. The TLST suggests that unless all legs are solid, the relationship will tip over and crash.

Chemistry refers to the attraction two people feel for each other. It includes sexual attraction, yet it also includes other aspects of the person and relationship. Ann dated a great guy in law school but she ended the relationship because of the way he smelled. Cheryl rejected a man she met at a party because although she found him physically attractive and easy to talk with, his voice was extremely irritating. Chemistry is our total visceral experience of the other person.

Common interests refer to what you have in common. Do you enjoy similar activities? Mutual friends? The same kind of lifestyle? Clearly the more similar your interests, the easier it will be to get along together. When a couple pursues most activities separately, this leg may be shaky.

Similar values and belief systems comprise the third leg of the stool. It is often an area that young couples overlook in favor of chemistry and common interests. At that time in our life, our values and belief systems may not be fully developed. Couples who break up in later years often site this area as problematic. Couples who marry later in life often place a greater emphasis on this area.

Clearly, all three areas are critical. Look back on your marriage and other previous relationships. Do you see patterns? Did all of your relationships seem to have one leg that "wobbled" more than another? Was it consistently the same leg? Do you frequently respond to chemistry and ignore the other areas? Or was the emphasis on common interests only? How important were values? Which leg was most solid in your relationship? Knowing which areas you have valued more than others can assist you in making more mindful, balanced choices in the future.

Today I ask myself, what was the wobbly leg of my marriage? Was this consistent in all my relationships? Do I value one leg as more important than the others? Today when I examine my relationship, I will use the TLST as a way to gain insight. This will be helpful as I consider both my choice of spouse and the demise of the marriage. My goal is insight and growth, not blame and regrets.

When a relationship ends, we find ourselves grieving. Even in the light of unacceptable behavior, we find ourselves rationalizing it by saying, "But he really loved me." I am often amazed when intelligent women make excuses for unacceptable or abusive behavior. When I ask them, "How do you know he loved you?" they respond with, "Well, he told me so."

We are taught the skills to nurture, to compromise, to be compassionate, and to forgive. These are positive attributes, but not when they lead to an inability to advocate for ourselves. Love is a verb. It is a behavior that needs to be expressed in action throughout the day, even when we are upset or angry. Treating a woman cruelly by calling her names or hitting her and then saying "I love you" does not make the behavior acceptable. Men who treat women abusively are NOT being loving.

You are worth more. You deserve the right to be treated with respect, dignity, honesty, and integrity.

Today *I will close my eyes and imagine my whole relationship on videotape in my mind. Before I play the tape, I will press the mute button so there will be no words to hear, only actions to see. As I play the tape, I will ask myself, "Are those the actions of LOVE?"*

Why is chocolate so irresistible, especially to women? There are scientific reasons why we yearn for chocolate. A chemical found in chocolate called phenylethylamine, or PEA, is a natural amphetamine. This chemical is similar to serotonin and dopamine which are found in our brain. These chemicals contribute to our sense of well being. Because of the PEA, chocolate may serve as a kind of self medication.

When we fall in love, our body secretes PEA in large doses. When we speak about the "chemistry of love" or feeling "high as a kite," we are not taking liberty with the language. (Spink 1996) Literally, chemistry is involved and we do feel euphoric. We are suddenly energized, needing little sleep or food and feel on top of the world. At the beginning of a relationship, the secretion of PEA is very high. This vast output of the chemical lasts a couple of years (Friar 2004) and many couples marry during this time period. When the PEA "rush" ceases, many feel disillusioned or "fall out of love." This may be one of the reasons the divorce statistics are so high during the first few years of marriage.

We crave chocolate when we are depressed, angry, lonely, or pre-menstrual. During divorce, our feelings may be quite erratic. We frequently feel down in the dumps. Our craving for chocolate is enhanced by our desire to feel – if not madly in love – at least a feeling of well being. Chocolate cravings can be episodic and fluctuate with hormonal changes just before and during the menses. This may explain why women are more likely to experience chocolate cravings. The combination of chocolate's sensory characteristics, nutrient composition, and psychoactive ingredients, compounded with monthly hormonal fluctuations and mood swings, provides an explanation for chocolate cravings. (Bruinsma, K.,& Taren, D.L. 1996)

Both cheese and salami contain even higher doses of PEA, but most of us still opt for the chocolate. What is more satisfying than a cup of hot chocolate on a cold dreary night, or a huge piece of chocolate pie while watching "Love Story" for the zillionth time?

Today ah, chocolate! Unlike a man who may leave, chocolate will always be there for me – first in my mouth and then forever on my hips and thighs.

Most women talk about a hole in their lives left from the other person's absence. When you divorce, you are without a partner, and no matter how you may feel about it, there are adjustments to be made. Dealing with this reality is part of the process of evolving into a single woman. Although you may not have a choice about the divorce, you **do** have choices about what comes next in your life. Let's look at the "hole." It offers opportunity for growth and change.

Think about things you gave up during the marriage. It can be something as simple as watching a "girl movie" or as drastic as sky diving. The reality is that while marriage affords us lots of opportunity, it also involves compromise. When you are single, you do not have to compromise as much. You have more options. Look at the hole as an opportunity for self-fulfillment. It can empower you in ways you may not have thought possible. Here are some simple and fun suggestions from other divorcing women on filling the empty place in your life.

- Redo your bedroom the way you always wanted it to be.

- Sleep in the middle of your bed.

- Change your seating arrangement at meals or remove the extra chair.

- Make a list of things around the house that need to get done, that he would usually do. When you are feeling bored or lonely, tackle one of these projects. Home repairs and cooking are very similar. If you can follow directions, you can fix **anything**!

- Make long term plans – buy two tickets to a show you always wanted to see. Buy the tickets six months in advance. Don't worry with whom you will go. You can always ask a friend. It will give you something to which you can look forward.

- Plan a special event each weekend to do by yourself. It can be a quiet bath or something more elaborate. The point is to foster and encourage enthusiasm about time spent with yourself.

- Plan something social each weekend. This can be visiting a friend or family. It cuts down on the isolation and gives you something to which you can look forward.

- Plan a "chick flick" weekend. This is when you just hunker down with all the girl movies he refused to see, and of course, a big bowl of popcorn.

- Put away all the mementos and things that remind you of *him*. "Feminize" your living space.

- Do something he never would have approved of – anything from eating Oreos in bed to dying your hair green!

Today I will look at the "hole" as an opportunity to bring new experiences into my life. I will begin to consider that I have infinite choices! While there may be losses in my life, today I will focus on the opportunities and options I have.

One of the most difficult things you will ever have to do as a parent is tell your children that their parents are breaking up. It is important that you shift your focus from your loss to your children's loss. Divorce is about the *dissolution* of a husband-wife relationship. It marks a *change* in the parent-child relationship. Awareness of this difference will support you in supporting your children. In talking with your children, stay focused on their feelings about this experience. If you focus on the spousal relationship, your own feelings may get in the way of good parenting.

Here are some tips for explaining the divorce to your children:

- If possible, both parents should be present. This illustrates to the children that you will still be able to co-parent.
- Tell them close to the time that one of the parents is planning to move out. Telling them months in advance doesn't "prepare them." It only makes them anxious and worried.
- Tell them calmly.
- Keep it age appropriate. Don't give them information that is over their heads.
- Keep it short and sweet.
- Explain that divorce is between the adults and that parents do not divorce children.
- Ask for questions. Answer honestly with age-appropriate information. Don't be afraid to say, "I don't know the answer to that. When I do, I will tell you."
- You don't tell your children about marital issues, like your sex life or money problems. The details of divorce should also stay between the two of you.
- Explain to your children the ways the divorce will affect them directly, i.e., will you move, will they stay in the same schools, and so on.
- Remember that divorce begins for the children the day the living situation changes. On the day one parent leaves, that is the day their parents' marriage ends.
- Let your children cry if they need to do so. It is important to let them grieve.
- Reassure them that you will not leave them, even if you are angry (which is some children's biggest fear).
- Reassure them that you will always love them.
- Notify their teachers, scout leaders, karate instructor and anyone else who has contact with your children, so they can be aware of and sensitive to your children's needs.
- Be prepared for any and all reactions from, "That's too bad, what's for dinner?" to crying and yelling. Stay calm and be reassuring.
- Remember your children will be as healthy about this as you are. They will take their cues from you.
- Continue to talk with your children about the process. One conversation is only the introduction. As uncomfortable as this may be for you, your children need your guidance and support.

Today when I tell my children that their parents are divorcing, I will focus on their needs. I will keep my feelings and thoughts about my spouse to myself.

Divorce is a life-changing event. It can impact your work, health, self-esteem, and relationships. A therapist can provide you with the support, clarity, and insight needed to move forward through the financial, legal and emotional aspects of the divorce. A therapist can facilitate healing and growth and help minimize the devastation.

In your search for a therapist, your friends, insurance company, divorce attorneys, and local mental health associations are good referral sources. Take time to choose wisely. You are going to make a commitment of time, energy and money. Trusting ANYONE when going through divorce is difficult, so it is imperative that you pick a therapist with whom you feel a good rapport.

After you have a few names, call them all and ask about their fees, their schooling, and their experience in dealing with divorce. Notice how quickly they return your call. This will give you some idea of how receptive they will be if you have an emergency. Ask whether they are licensed, about their philosophy and their specialty. Don't fall for a therapist who claims you can be "cured in a set number of sessions." No therapist can promise you that!

Many divorce attorneys strongly encourage their clients to work with a therapist. With a therapist in the picture, you will not be tempted to misuse your attorney to support your emotional issues. Your therapist can also help you clarify what it is you really need and want from your settlement.

If you find a therapist with whom you have rapport, but who is not covered by your insurance, do not hesitate to contact your insurance company and explain to them that this therapist specializes in divorce and is geographically desirable. Some HMOs make exceptions and allow patients to access health care outside of the network when there is no one in network who is suitable. There have been a number of lawsuits from patients who were denied proper health care due to HMO limitations. Advocate for what you want! If, however, your pleas are not fruitful, or if you choose NOT to use your health insurance (some women prefer that their husbands NOT know they are in therapy), then be candid with the therapist about your financial limitations. Many therapists will work on a sliding fee scale. Do not be embarrassed to ask!

Today I know even if I am not sure I need a therapist, it can't hurt me to access the additional support. So, I will begin the process of finding one. Asking for help is a good thing to do for myself. I might find that the support and insight are invaluable in my growth process.

Many women who live with abuse don't even recognize it as such. They have grown so accustomed to these behaviors that they may be numb to them. Do you answer YES to any of these questions?

- Does he put you down?
- Has he ever called you names?
- Does he make fun of your family, friends, interests, and so on?
- Does he try to keep you from seeing your family and friends?
- Does he control the money?
- Is he overly jealous?
- Does he make fun of you in front of other people? Insults? Put-downs?
- Does he demean you?
- Does he say inappropriate things about you to the children?
- Does he threaten to leave you?
- Does he threaten to take the children away from you?
- Does he force you to do sexual things that you do not want to do?
- Does he make demeaning sexual remarks about you or other women?
- Does he have affairs?
- Does he drink too much?
- Is he involved with drugs?
- Is he sarcastic and then tells you that you don't have a sense of humor?
- Does he demean you physically, emotionally, or intellectually?
- Does he yell?
- Does he push, hit, and punch you?
- Does he restrain you?
- Does he prevent you from leaving?
- Has he ever broken a bone, given you a bruise or hurt you physically?
- Has he threatened to hurt/kill you?
- Has he threatened to hurt/kill your family/children/friends or other people you love?

Any one of the above behaviors is abusive and does not belong in a marriage. You may be thinking, "Well, yeah, he has done some of those things, but he would never hit me, punch me, kill me." Really? Think again. More women are hurt or killed by their partners than by strangers. Many of them became victims because they were in denial. It is important to know that abuse usually escalates. Always, always, err on the side of caution.

Domestic violence can occur in all homes, regardless of race, religion, and socio-economic status. Do not minimize the seriousness of the situation. Denial and minimization are a woman's way of colluding with violence. It can have life or death consequences.

Today I will admit to myself that my situation is worse than I wish it was. I will confide my concerns to one person whom I trust. What has happened is NOT my fault. NO ONE ever deserves to be abused, no matter what my husband says. In telling one person, I break the silence, which breaks the guilt and shame. I am on the road to getting the help I need.

Friends offer us support, validation, and a connection to our past, our present and our future. They laugh, cry, mourn, and rejoice with us. Our friends are most vital to us when we are going through a life-changing event such as a divorce. However, when we are married, our friends are frequently made up of couples. So we socialize as couples. These friends are thought to "belong" to the marriage. Often, we grieve the loss of friends that can occur as a by-product of divorce. Some friendships are unable to sustain the enormous burden of divorce. It is not unusual to find that suddenly you feel alienated from your married friends. This occurs for a number of reasons.

Some married couples feel uncomfortable around a newly single person. In the 70's and 80's, the newly-divorced woman was seen as a temptation for married men. (Happily we don't see much of *that* stereotype anymore.) More common is the following scenario: the newly-single woman presents a life that may seem enviable to the unhappily married woman. This may threaten the husband on some level. Also, married couples may not know what to say or how to behave – clearly your interests are different. They may feel awkward, especially if trying to also maintain a relationship with your estranged spouse.

Frequently, they may feel caught in the middle.

One of the inevitable facts of marriage is that our relationships with friends often become secondary to the primary relationship. For adult singles, our friendships *are* the primary adult relationships. Friendship adds to our lives regardless of our marital status. But for the newly-divorced single adult, friendships take on a new importance. Some newly-divorced persons, especially women, say that they have no time for friendships, that working and parenting take up all their time. Friendship will support your parenting by offering you validation, community, companionship, and compassion. These attributes will enhance your parenting rather than detract from it. Friendships will provide you with the adult companionship that the estranged spouse no longer provides. Utilize and encourage your friendships. They are never more important than in this time of need.

Today I will recognize the need to have a support system in my life. I will consider the connections I already have and how they offer me support. I will allow myself to grieve for the connections that I have lost in the divorce process. I will examine areas in my life where I feel I need more support and begin to act on my own behalf to fill those gaps.

If your husband is leaving your marriage for another woman, it can be devastating. Even if you were aware that the marriage was stale and perhaps even had a fling of your own, you may feel knocked to the ground. Betrayal and violation of trust play a huge role in your pain, but, even more devastating is the sense of being rejected and replaced. That pain goes beyond the marital relationship and can strike your core in the most personal way. The feelings of inadequacy and self-doubt often plague the victim of betrayal.

When infidelity is exposed in a marriage, the wife often becomes obsessed with the other woman: who is she, what does she look like, is she younger, thinner, smarter, sexier than me? Do you imagine she is getting something that you didn't? Do you imagine he treats her like a queen? Do you imagine their life together is idyllic? Notice how each question contains the word "imagine." One of the most painful things women do to themselves is imagine something and then believe in it. When we do that, no one is hurting us but ourselves. Doing this is a form of self-torture.

He did not replace you with her. He replaced feeling middle-aged, ignored, and insecure with a different, headier feeling. Yes, your marriage was probably in trouble. People usually don't cheat unless that is so. But cheating is the symptom, not the reason for the break-up. While both partners may be at fault for the demise of the marriage, be clear that the infidel is solely responsible for his own behavior. Not every unhappy person goes outside of their marriage. There were other choices. This is his choice alone.

By focusing on *her*, you let him off the hook and feel badly about yourself. His behavior is not your fault, nor is it hers. She did not break her solemn vows to you; he did. She is not a replacement, she is a symptom. He was looking for an antidote to feel better about himself. He could have gone to therapy, taken a class, changed jobs, gotten hair plugs. Don't imagine she is getting the new-improved version of your old worn out husband. She's not.

Today I realize that when I focus on her, I let him off the hook. I will ask myself honestly do I really want this man back? Can I trust him, or respect him? Would I ever feel safe with him again? I may still have loving feelings for him, but that doesn't mean he can be/ will be/ or was a good partner for me. Allowing myself to stay focused in the reality may feel painful, but in the long run, it will help me heal and grow.

When we are hurt or attacked, our first instinct is to defend ourselves much in the same way a cornered, wounded animal does. We long to strike back. We think if we hurt the other, then our pain will stop.

"He did it to me," we rationalize. Well, yes, he behaved terribly, but do you want to allow him to set the standards for your own behavior?

Laura knew her all husband's passwords. She had access to all his bank transactions, e-mail and voice mail. When she tapped into these resources, she found information that could hurt him, but information that hurt her terribly. At first she felt as if she was getting him back by violating his privacy. In truth, she was seriously hurting herself. Being a person of high standards and morals, she also felt ashamed of her behavior. Guilt, shame and pain were what she reaped from her "sleuthing," nothing more. When she realized this, she stopped accessing all his accounts. As her focus turned from him to herself, she began slowly to heal from the pain she had experienced. She stopped hurting herself.

Carol's husband left her and she wanted him to pay, so she methodically and systematically turned his children against him by sharing intimate details of his transgressions and flaws. When the children wanted to see their father, she would act out, become sick or cry. Eventually, they gave up trying to see him as they didn't want to deal with her behavior. Today in their late twenties, these children have a cordial, yet limited relationship with their father. The son is angry and drinks too much. The daughter flits from one relationship to another. Both treat their mother with contempt and scorn. She is unhappy, guilty, and filled with remorse. If Carol had taken the high road, we don't know if her children would have faired differently, but she would have less guilt and remorse and feel better about herself as a mother, as a woman and as a person.

Taking the high road does not mean being a doormat and caving in to his every wish. It means standing up for yourself, but not in a way that compromises who you are. It means behaving ethically and with dignity. In the end, taking the high road leaves you with feelings of peace and pride. That makes you a survivor and a winner! It helps build good self-esteem and it lets you sleep at night!

Today when I fantasize about making his life miserable, I will ask myself, "Will it really help me feel better?" How is lowering myself going to help me? Will it improve my sense of self? Will I be proud of myself? When I match someone else's bad behavior, I let them define who I am and consequently, run my life.

What does that mean?

Most of us, at one time or another, have mistaken feelings for facts. An illustration of this is when we are premenstrual, bloated and feel like beached whales. We know we aren't beached whales, but we sure feel that way. In this case, we know the feeling will pass in a few days, so we don't decide it is time to live in the ocean. That would be silly. That would be acting on the *feelings*.

Sometimes, though, it is not clear what are feelings and what are facts. When the attorney doesn't return your phone call, you may feel that she/he is avoiding you. An old friend declines an invitation and you ask yourself if she siding with your ex. Your kids come back from a weekend at their Dad's all excited that they had a great time and suddenly you feel like they don't love you and they want to go live with him.

We all have those moments when it is hard to discern feelings from facts. The important thing is to make sure you do so before you act. Acting on our feelings often gets us in trouble. In a divorce situation, it can fuel the acrimony that can result in more litigation and therefore be more costly, both legally and emotionally.

Today I will attend to my feelings and then back them up with good hard facts. I am entitled to my feelings, but acting out on them can be damaging. Part of taking care of myself is acting on my best behalf. I will take time to process and honor my feelings, but I will allow the facts to decide my course of action.

It is a tendency of many women to withdraw when they are in pain, because they feel:

- Embarrassed.
- Like a burden.
- They do not want to "give him the satisfaction."
- Depressed.
- Shame.

Withdrawal from friends, family, colleagues and activities can lead to isolation. Then, we are alone with our thoughts, which can become distorted and may magnify our fears. When we isolate, our only companion is our painful thoughts and feelings. Objective input and positive emotional support from others helps us debunk the distorted messages of those who have hurt us.

Have you ever noticed that in the middle of the night, pain seems worse than during the day? If we wake up sick in the middle of the night, we think that the headache is a brain tumor, or the heartburn is a heart attack! The same is true with emotional pain. In the night, we are isolated and our sole companions are our pain and fear.

Coming out of isolation may feel overwhelming at first, but you can do it in baby steps. For example, join a support group, or, if that feels too exposing, then make an individual appointment with a therapist or counselor. Talking with a friend can be helpful. We lighten our load when we connect with another being. When we share our pain with a friend, we are not burdening them. We are acknowledging their importance in our lives and we honor that relationship by risking emotional intimacy.

Of course, if you do not spend any time alone, then you have no time to really get to know yourself. Some women, out of fear of being alone, do just the opposite of isolators. They are always out and about, joining everything, talking to everyone, never allowing themselves time to process everything they are learning. As with most things, it is about balance. Finding balance is not easy. It takes time and conscious awareness of one's needs.

Today I will think about striking a balance between my need to spend time alone and my need to be connected. To that end, I will be mindful not to isolate, knowing that sometimes my own introspection can create additional pain. Each weekend, I will try to do one thing that connects me in an emotional way to others, and one solitary activity.

One of the most renowned pieces of sculpture in the world is Michelangelo's statue of David. Supposedly, Michelangelo was asked about how he created the magnificent statue David from a block of stone. He replied that he did not create David from the stone; rather, he saw David in the stone and merely chipped away at the unneeded pieces until David emerged. Human beings are like that. Underneath all the things we were taught to feel and think about ourselves, our relationships and the world, lies our authentic true self.

When coming out of an unhappy marriage, many women feel as if they have lost themselves. They are entombed in the roles of the family culture and the larger, societal culture. After years of acquiescence and trying to bring harmony to the marriage, many feel as if they have lost themselves. Having put the needs of others first for so long, they are amazed to find they do not feel connected with themselves. When I ask, "What do you like to do?", many women report that they simply do not know. It has been so long since they had the opportunity to attend to themselves, their wishes and desires, that they stopped listening to their own emotions.

Start listening again. Like Michelangelo chipping away at the stone that encased David, you must chip away at those things which keep you trapped. Criticism, negativity, fear, and abuses of all kinds are what entomb us and prohibit us from being our beautiful, free, authentic selves. Divorce can be the chisel to chip away at those unwanted pieces that impede our growth and joy. The process of divorce is difficult and painful, but it can be the opportunity to free you from the stone. Divorce can provide you with answers to questions that keep you stuck; it can strengthen your voice; it can free you to be yourself.

Like the freeing of David, this does not happen overnight. It takes patient dedication, attention to the task and focus. Michelangelo's determination and vision were what freed David, along with his belief that he could make it happen as he envisioned.

Today I will acknowledge that this process is difficult. But like Michelangelo, I can stay focused on the absolute belief that I am hidden underneath all this weighty excess of guilt, self-doubt, and fear. Little by little, I will work to chip away at those unwanted pieces. I will close my eyes and affirm that I am becoming the woman I want to be— the woman I have always been.

A relationship doesn't go from wonderful to terrible overnight. Over time, there is a breakdown in communication, affection, respect, caring and consideration. Loving feelings are frequently replaced with feelings of inadequacy, rejection, fear, anger, low self-esteem, betrayal, and self-doubt. No one who has gone through a divorce does so with their ego completely intact. Divorce brings up feelings of failure, shame, guilt, and low self-worth. We can not look to another person to rebuild our sense of self—we have to look inward. Often our husbands stopped doing those little romantic things they had done in courtship, like bring us flowers, or candy. Over time we began to resent being taken for granted. We felt invisible and unworthy.

Feeling better begins with treating ourselves better. The first thing we can do is treat ourselves with gentleness, affection and compassion. Start in small ways, one step at a time. For some, that means eating healthier, quitting smoking or starting an exercise program. For others, it means paying attention to the negative messages we give ourselves such as, "You are so old, who will want you" or "You really blew it." It means tending to ourselves with gentleness and love. It means parenting ourselves as we would our children. It means being nurturing and encouraging rather than criticizing and scolding.

Today I will buy myself flowers. I will take time choosing them. Whether a single-stem rose or a huge bouquet, I will choose the flowers I love, in the colors I love. I will bring them home and lovingly arrange them in a special vase. I will put them in a place where I can see them and enjoy them frequently. Every time I look at them I will be reminded that I am lovable and good and caring and that I will treat myself in exactly the ways I need to feel special.

Month Two

Once upon a time, in a town not unlike your own, there was a princess who met a prince. They met in school and fell instantly in love. They were the perfect couple! How in love they were! So, they decided to marry! How excited the princess was! She and the Queen shopped, read *Bride Magazine*, interviewed caterers, fought over flowers, chose invitations, and worried about the centerpieces. This was a dream come true for the Princess, who would have her fairy tale wedding!

As the day approached, the happy couple was focused on the wedding. They didn't worry about the marriage, as they just knew everything would be perfect. True love, they agreed, would conquer all. Unlike many around them, they would never fall prey to that evil monster, Divorce.

The big day arrived. As the couple stood in front of the minister, he handed the young couple a plant and said solemnly, "It is very important that you take good care of this plant. This is your relationship. In order for it to grow, be healthy and vital, it needs care, water, sun, food, pruning, and love. It will need this on a daily basis. It doesn't matter how you divide the tasks of making sure the plant stays vital; that will be up to you. But tend to it daily if you want it to grow and be sturdy."

The couple reached for the plant. The Princess said, "Oh my love, you have so much to tend to. I will take the plant and care for it. If you have time, you can help, but do not fear. It is in good hands." The Prince was a little surprised. Why, he thought, would she want to take on this responsibility? But he was a young prince, with many things to do, so he was a little relieved not to have to care for this plant.

Years passed. The couple lived in a big castle with their three children who all played soccer, piano, and tennis. The princess realized that it was impossible to have her own career, take care of the children and cart around that plant. She had to admit to herself that taking care of the plant was far more work than she had expected. But she said nothing to the Prince.

More time passed. The couple fell into a rhythm. He worked, played golf, and watched football. She carted the kids around, planned the family vacations, decorated the home, cooked the meals, and attended school functions. And she took care of the plant. She was exhausted.

One day she said to her beloved, "Hey beloved, I really need some help with this plant." He stopped in his tracks. "Why? You are doing a great job and I don't really have a lot of time." She continued taking care of the plant, but with growing resentment. She fed it and watered it, but less often. She hoped he would notice its wilting leaves, he did not. On rare occasions when he did try to help, she screamed that he wasn't doing it right. "Fine," he screamed back, throwing down the clippers and the watering can, "Do it yourself. You are so controlling!" "All I want is a little help here," she pleaded. "But when I try to help, you just criticize. Make up your mind!" he retorted angrily.

And so it came to pass that the plant died. It stopped blooming and then it lost its leaves. Soon there was nothing left but two dried-up stems. Frantically, the couple tried to revive it, but it was too late. And there was no happily ever after.

Today I will think about my marriage. Who tended it and how did it die? Looking at my role in the marriage is not assigning blame, but a way to help me understand my own behavior.

Day 2   Is There Such a Thing as a Good Divorce?

Imagine a marriage where both parties are unhappy and bickering all the time. Their values and goals are different. There is no chemistry between them. The children are exposed to awkward silences and all-out battles. There may be emotional, verbal or physical abuse. Everyone in the family is miserable. Should this couple stay together for the sake of the children? Most of us would agree they would be better off apart.

Now what if those two people, without the stress of trying to get along in this marriage, found that they were happier separately? What if they could get along on parenting issues? What if, outside of the rigors of the marital relationship, they were able to consistently exercise respect, and clear communication? As separate individuals, they could thrive, perhaps remarry and experience good viable relationships. The children would also thrive, as there would be no stress between the parents. The children would be exposed to two different, yet high-functioning marriages. That would be a good divorce.

Sometimes there *are* good divorces. There could be more good divorces, if we would stop seeing divorce as anti-marriage or anti-family. Without the negativity our culture imposes on divorce, people would feel less stigmatized and less like failures. There would be less hurt feelings and acrimony. Divorce could be a good solution to a bad situation.

Marriage is not going out of style, but it is changing. Some say this is in response to the women's movement, increased life expectancy, the sexual revolution or economics. Whatever the reason, we are marrying just as often, but divorcing more frequently. We try again and again. We keep trying because loving, connection, and commitment have not gone out of style. They merely look different.

No one takes divorce lightly. It is a decision we wrangle with. Often, we take more time considering divorce than we do marriage. Divorce is not always a negative thing. It can be an opportunity for all parties involved to have a better, healthier life. It can be a gift to our children and future generations as well.

Today when I think about my divorce, I will consider the possibility that we will all be better off and that maybe my divorce is a good divorce. To that end, maybe we can work at improving our post-divorce communication in a way that was not possible in the marriage. A bad marriage doesn't necessarily have to lead to a bad divorce.

Jane was married for twenty five years. Her husband filed for divorce and Jane is struggling to understand what happened. "Disappointed," was Jane's response when I queried as to how she felt. Over and over she spoke of her disappointment.

Jane was diagnosed with depression during the marriage. She shut down emotionally. She was not accessible to her husband or children. I asked her if she was happy in the marriage. "Not really, but life is hard." Her husband, a dominant, verbose guy, didn't like to hear of Jane's complaints, so after a while she learned to keep them to herself. She tried to minimize them ("This is not that important") or rationalize them ("He really didn't mean that"). Years of minimizing her own pain and trying to hold it in turned into depression for Jane. She wasn't just disappointed. She was really, really angry.

Jane had not had any positive experience with anger. Growing up in a volatile family, Jane did not learn that anger was a feeling. She saw it as a behavior, and a frightening one at that. The times she had allowed herself to feel angry resulted in her spanking her children a little too hard. Feeling guilt, regret, and shame, she saw no other option than to suppress her feelings. She became depressed.

Minimalization is a technique we employ, often unconsciously, to help us deal with those issues in our life that simply feel too overwhelming. We may have both the strength and courage to deal with life issues, but we may not have the tools. When we learn the tools and how to implement them, we can move forward and look life squarely in the eye without undue fear.

One of these tools is self-esteem. With healthy self-esteem, we know we deserve to be happy. That knowledge provides us with the energy of conviction that can be utilized to combat our fear of change. Minimalization often accompanies fear of change: "If it isn't so bad, then things won't have to change." This is a common form of minimalization expressed by women who are in terrible marriages. Their self-esteem is so damaged by the relationship that they have no tools to bring about change. So they rely on minimalization as a way to avoid change and maintain the status quo.

Today I ask myself, am I making excuses for other people's bad behavior? Am I trying to adapt constantly? Am I tip-toeing around everyone? Do I feel trapped, unheard, powerless and really angry? Do I suffer a lot from physical ailments or depression? I have other choices. I just have to acknowledge what is really happening.

Assuring that your child gets the care she/he needs is part of good parenting. Many parents worry that bringing a child to therapy will make them look like unstable, bad parents. Quite the contrary, taking care of and being sensitive to your child's emotional health is as important as taking care of her/his physical health. When you take your child to the dentist, you are not being a bad parent. To not take her/him could be considered neglectful.

Some parents fear the therapist will blame them for the child's problems. The therapist's role is to support both you and your child, to offer information, affirmation and insight. They will not judge you as a mother. They will evaluate and discuss your child's needs. It will not be a punitive experience for either you or your child, but one that heightens your awareness and validates that this is a difficult time in your life as well as in your child's life.

Choosing a therapist for yourself may seem easier than finding a competent child therapist. You can interview them, but how do you know if the therapist will "click" with your child? How do you know that the therapist is reputable? Ask your pediatrician or your friends for a referral. Ask your therapist, consult with the school psychologist or social worker. A referral from a reputable source is better than selecting a name out of the phone book. Angela Mazur, LCSW of Farmington, Connecticut, is a therapist who specializes in children. She offers these guidelines in choosing a child therapist:

- Don't be afraid to ask questions before setting up an appointment.
- Ask about credentials and experience.
- How long have they been in the field?
- What is their experience with children?
- How much expertise do they have with regard to divorce issues?
- Ask about length of treatment, costs, style and so on.
- Ask how the therapist will utilize parents. Will they be part of the treatment? Will they will utilized as a "co-therapist"?

If the child is an adolescent and doesn't want the therapist to talk with the parent, the parent needs to understand the child's right to privacy. If there are issues that are possibly harmful to the child, the therapist will involve the parent. Adolescents are very concerned about privacy and are slow to trust. The parent of an adolescent has to be (as usual) especially patient.

Today I will begin to pursue finding a good therapist for my child. It may feel overwhelming. I may even feel a little scared and resentful. However, I may be heading off bigger problems in the future. Having another person involved in our lives may at first feel daunting, but in truth, it will lighten my load.

Nothing can build confidence more quickly than taking the risk to do something outside of our comfort level. This does not mean something dangerous or death defying. It can be just a simple step outside of our comfort zone. Many women have fears about doing things alone, such as going to the movies or out to eat by themselves.

Some myths associated with doing these activities alone are:

- It is dangerous.
- I will look like a loser.
- Women alone always get the worst seat.
- I will feel lonely.
- People will feel sorry for me.

What are your myths? Write them down, then look at them one by one and debunk those thoughts that keep you stuck. For example:

- **It is dangerous.** Well, at night it could be dangerous to go to that part of town alone, so I will go during the day when I can feel more comfortable.

- **I will look like a loser.** Is everyone really looking at me?

- **Women always get the worst seats.** That is not so. If I call first and reserve a table, I can specify where I want to sit.

- **I will feel lonely.** I will only feel lonely if I go with that frame of mind. If I am open to the idea of enjoying myself, then I will. Besides, which is worse – staying home and feeling lonely or going out and doing what I want and maybe having such a good time, that I forget about being lonely. How many times did I go somewhere with him and feel REALLY lonely?

- **People will feel sorry for me.** When I see a woman out by herself having a good time, I don't feel sorry for her. I see her as having courage and confidence.

Fear of doing things by ourselves keeps us from experiencing new situations. Identify something that you want to do, that feels risky for you, and challenge yourself to do it within the next week. If you are a procrastinator, you may put up lots of roadblocks. Keep reminding yourself that making small changes will help you feel better.

If you continue to have difficulty with this exercise, you may want to think about what is holding you back. Sometimes women are so focused on trying to change others, we forget about changing ourselves. When we try to change others, we are almost always met with defeat. When we work on changing ourselves, then success is imminent.

Today I will make a date with myself to do something I have never done before. I will write it on the calendar and I will be true to my commitment. I will look forward to my commitment with excitement and then rejoice for the changes I am making! I am becoming the woman I want to be! Hooray!!

Once you have the names of three attorneys, begin interviewing them. Remember this person is going to be a critical part of your divorce team and will work for you! Rather than accepting the first name you are given and hiring that person, you need to do a little more research. Here are some criteria to use in helping you make your choice:

- Call all three. Before you even speak with them, you can get a sense of the way they do business. Do you get a voice mail or a live person? How soon is your call returned? Does the staff sound courteous? Is it a one-person office or a large firm? Does it matter whether the attorney is male or female?

- Set up your initial appointments at least two days apart. Make a list of questions to bring with you to each consultation. Don't forget to ask if there is a fee for the initial consultation. At each consultation, ask your questions and write down the answers, but also pay attention to the "feel" of the office. For example, were you kept waiting? Does the attorney continue to take telephone calls during your consultation? Does the attorney seem genuinely interested in your case? Does the attorney seem interested in educating you or does he/she seem more interested in impressing you? Don't forget to ask about fees. Retainers are usual and customary for divorce attorneys. However, the amount can vary greatly from lawyer to lawyer, case to case, town to town, state to state. Other questions include:

- If the paralegal does work on my case, what is his or her hourly rate?

- Are there things I can do to keep costs down?

- How do they bill for telephone calls?

- What happens if you or the attorney is not available on a court date?

- How much does the attorney estimate the whole divorce will cost?

- Does the office have provisions for a payment plan?

- What do you think my settlement will look like?

Remember, the lawyer works for YOU! We tend to be intimidated by professionals. Sometimes, we see them in a position of authority and have a tendency to either turn over all control to them or be anxious about appearing stupid. Of course, you are going to ask naïve questions. You are hiring an attorney for her/his expertise for the things you do not know. Don't be afraid to ask for what you want.

Today I will do my homework, ask the proper questions and not forget to follow my intuition. I will begin to listen to my inner wisdom. I will advocate on behalf of myself because I know I am worth it. I will select my attorney with confidence, knowing that I can make big decisions on my own. Then, I will take a deep breath and hire my attorney. I am on my way!

Admitting you might have a problem with alcohol or drugs is a difficult thing to do. Since denial is a major symptom of a problem, it is difficult to assess what is factual and what is denial.

To help figure out if you do have a problem, ask yourself these questions:

- Do other people have concerns about my drinking? Or drug use?
- Do I hide how much I drink or use drugs?
- Have I made promises to myself or others that I will quit or cut back, and then broke that promise?
- Have I ever missed work because of drinking or drug use?
- Have I ever had a memory lapse when I was drinking or using drugs?
- Have I ever been in trouble with the law due to drinking or using drugs?
- Do I sometimes feel remorse about my drinking or drug use?

Honest answers may feel uncomfortable, even frightening. If you answer yes to even one of these questions, you may have a problem. Without professional help, there is no way to tell how severe the problem is, or how severe it may get. Alcoholism/drug addiction is a progressive disease and it will get worse if untreated. Over time the abuse of drugs/alcohol will effect your health. Eventually irreversible damage occurs and, if left untreated, the results are fatal.

If you only drink or use drugs on weekends, that doesn't mean you are out of the woods. You can have a problem and not be a daily drinker. You can be high functioning in your work and with your family, but because of the progressive nature of the disease, over time, impairment will become evident.

There is no shame in being an alcoholic/addict. The shame comes from not getting the help you need. Help is available in many forms and anonymously. Professionals who work in the field are extremely sensitive to the need for privacy. An assessment by a professional drug and alcohol counselor will let you know if you have a problem with abuse or addiction. Together with your counselor, you can find strategies to deal with it. Alcoholics Anonymous (AA), Narcotics Anonymous (NA) or Cocaine Anonymous (CA) are fellowships for people with addictions. They offer support with the goal of sobriety. They are free and anonymous meetings, held all over the world. If you think you may have a problem, look up AA, NA or CA in your yellow pages and call the toll free number. The voice on the other end will not ask you personal questions, but will offer support, information, and a list of meetings held in your area.

Be aware that prescription drug use can also lead to addiction. These include some medications prescribed for insomnia, anxiety, and depression. If you feel you are becoming dependent on your sleeping medication, painkillers, or tranquilizers, call your doctor and discuss your concerns. If you have a family history of drug abuse or alcoholism, you will have a greater tendency to develop a problem.

Today I will ask for help if I answer "yes" to any of the above questions. I will not let my denial, stubbornness, or pride get in the way of doing what is best for me. I do not have control over everything that happens in my life, but I do have choices about how to handle problems as they come up. Paying attention to my concerns about alcohol or drug usage is one of the ways I take control of my health and my life.

Think about what you have been taught about marriage. Look at the messages you were given from your parents, your culture, your religion, and the media. What messages did you receive about the role of women? What did you learn from fairy tales? Did you play house as a child? Were you the bride or the Mommy? Think of the love songs you listened to as an adolescent. All of these influences contribute to our expectations about love and marriage. Make a list of all the messages you received about marriage. How many of the losses and negative feelings listed here can you identify with? Are there other losses not mentioned in this list?

- Loss of a dream.
- Loss of the ideal.
- Loss of future dreams.
- Loss of co-parent.
- Loss of handyman.
- Loss of built-in date.
- Loss of two incomes.
- Feelings of failure.
- Feelings of guilt or doing something wrong (i.e. religious convictions).
- Feelings of shame.
- Loss of friends.
- Loss of Happily-Ever-After.
- Feelings of inadequacy as a woman.
- Loss of in-laws, extended family.
- Loss of status.
- Loss of financial security.

Exploring all the losses that are peripheral to the divorce can help you understand why you are feeling so much pain. Often, women who want the divorce can't understand why they feel so badly. They start to question their decision, thinking that if they feel so badly, then they must be making a mistake. It is helpful to see that even in the worst marriage, there are losses. As you explore your own losses, you gain insight into why divorce is so devastating.

Today I will let myself grieve. Allowing myself time to heal is critical to my recovery. I will honor my pain as if it were physical by being nurturing, gentle and accepting of myself. I will let myself be patient, knowing that in time I will heal and be stronger than ever.

A lively debate recently ensued as a group of divorcing women discussed whether the retelling of their story was helpful in their healing process. Ethel emphatically stated that it was not. The retelling flooded her with emotion. Her greatest fear was that she would fall apart in court and collapse into a flood of tears. This was especially problematic as her ex-husband was trying to prove she was emotionally unstable. Sally said that when she told her story, it used to be accompanied by uncontrollable tears. Now she finds she can tell the story without tears, although she experiences some sadness. Patti noted that when she told her story, it felt as if it was someone else's story. She has little emotional attachment to it. Patti's legal divorce was final some time ago.

Our stories are part of our history, which is a major contributor to creating the person we are becoming. Our stories hold the keys to opening the doors to our own self-awareness. All of us have experienced the telling of stories which at one time held great emotion and now can be told with so much detachment that, in some ways, the story feels as if it belongs to someone else.

Time affords us distance from our story so that we can develop objectivity. How we use that time can make all the difference in how quickly we move through the emotional process. We come to terms and deal with all the emotions and practical challenges. We evolve from a wife to a single woman. Dealing with hurt, anger, betrayal, abandonment, and fear helps us move away from our pain. Time even affords us some closure: in time the children will adjust, we will know what the final settlement will look like, and we will have some experience of living on our own. Many of our fears will be resolved or greatly diminished. Absence of fear will help our ability to detach.

Finally, the greatest single aid in the ability to detach is to *want to*. Sometimes we hold onto our pain because we are anxious about what it will feel like without it. Our pain can keep us connected, get us some attention, and keep us in a victim role. Some women think that their pain serves as testimony to his bad behavior; if they let it go, he will in some way be exonerated.

Today I ask myself what happens to me when I tell my story. Do I experience the same level of pain that I always did, or is that pain starting to dwindle, even a little bit? Are there elements of my story that make me proud of myself? That make me laugh? If so, then I am beginning to detach. While I will never forget what happened or the valuable lessons that I learned, it is good to know I won't have this pain forever.

Alexis commented, "The most important thing I learned going through my divorce was to ask for help."

Frequently, women feel they have to prove themselves by doing everything themselves. Some women are afraid that if they ask for help, they may not get it. Others feel that enlisting assistance is giving up control. Some are afraid they will be perceived as a burden or as weak if they ask for help.

Our families gave us clear messages about "help." As you look back on your life, what did you learn about asking for help? In your family of origin, did people help each other? Did you receive assistance or support from others, or were you the one who always helped everyone else? Were your parents there for you? Were they reliable and dependable? Or were they busy dealing with problems of their own? Were you the one everyone relied on? Did you feel let down a lot? If you relate to some of these questions, then you might believe something like this: "If I can't count on my family, who can I count on?" Some lessons you may have learned are: "Do it yourself," "There is no one to rely on," "We are all too busy." Or your family may have made it difficult for you to make your own decisions. If everyone had an opinion and tried to press them on you, then you may be afraid of losing control. Some families, in their zest to help, can become controlling and overbearing. When we think about asking for help, we must remember that not all people are like our families whether they were under-functioning and unreliable or overpowering and controlling.

Often when we ask friends for help, they are grateful for the chance to assist us and to make a difference in our life. Think about times when you have been asked for help and the feeling of accomplishment and value you felt in being able to make a difference in the life of a friend. Sometimes asking someone for help is giving a gift. It is a way to let someone know they have value and meaning in our lives.

Today I will think about messages that I received from my family of origin regarding asking for help. I will be aware of my tendency to expect others to react to me in the same way as my family did. But my friends are not my family. I will realize there are people I can count on, who will be happy to help me. I will ask for help. Then I will allow myself to fully experience what it feels like to have someone come through for me!

What does it mean to express anger in a healthy way? Divorce anger is important. It is energy. It helps you detach from your spouse. However, there is also a time to let it go. Holding onto your anger for too long can have negative effects. Physically, it can contribute to health problems such as high blood pressure, gastrointestinal problems and headaches. Emotionally, it can contribute to anxiety and depression. Socially inappropriate anger can create distance and acrimony in your relationships. So, it is vital for your well-being that you tend to your anger in positive ways.

Remember that anger is a feeling. Aggression is the behavior we often associate with angry feelings, but you do not have to be aggressive to express your anger.

Here are some suggestions for expressing anger that I have gathered from other women going through divorce:

- **Talk to a friend.** A good idea, but be aware of over utilizing one person. After a while, she may think "No wonder he left her – she never stops!"
- **Write letters.** These letters are **not** the ones you mail, but rather the ones you write without censorship, to help you get your feelings out. Date them, save them and every month or so take them out and read them again. You will be amazed at how your anger evolves.
- **Talk to the chair.** Sit across from an empty chair and imagine your partner sitting there. Say all the things to him you would like to say. Scream, yell, and throw things. Get it out!
- **Get a punching bag.** Women have a difficult time with this at first, but once they let go, the physical release can be amazing!
- **Take Kickboxing** (or Karate) Same as above, with the added asset of feeling empowered by learning to defend yourself!
- **Write his name on the bottom of your sneakers.** Then go work out. There is nothing like a good run when you are thinking of grinding him into the pavement!
- **Imagine his face on your golf ball or tennis ball every time you swing.** This is not limited to sports. Mop the floor with him or vacuum him up!
- **Cry.** A big one. Needs no explanation.
- **Scream.** Really. At the top of your lungs. In the car, with the windows rolled up, seems to be a favorite place. Passersby will think you are singing.
- **Clean.** As you do, imagine cleaning him out of your home and your life. Then empty the trash into your garbage cans. Imagine throwing him out with the trash!

There are a number of good books on the market that can explain how to positively and assertively address anger. The one I most recommend is *Your Perfect Right* by Alberti and Emmons.

Today I will think of my anger as energy. I will use that energy as a resource to create power for myself. I will pour all of that energy into an activity that helps me feel unburdened and lighter.

"Am I going crazy?," you ask yourself.

You were a good sleeper and now you are not sleeping. You are losing weight without trying. You are forgetting things. You are having accidents. You are bumping into things. You can't concentrate. You cry. You get angry. You get anxious. The symptoms feel terrible, but in truth, you are having a *normal reaction to an abnormal situation*.

Sometimes medication is recommended and is useful and necessary. However, when we medicate our normal reactions, I think we give women a message they ARE going crazy. Most of the time when life stresses are present and a woman is feeling miserable, she is having a normal reaction. Medication is appropriate when the symptoms are present but the stresses aren't. When a woman says, "I have everything anyone would want, yet I am so unhappy," that is when we consider using medication. That woman's chemistry is not letting her feel happy. She is *not* having a normal reaction.

We also consider medication when a woman's symptomatic response to a stressful situation is extreme in depth and duration. An example is when a woman has lost hope, feels constantly overwhelmed, can feel NO joy and is even having thoughts of suicide. When these types of symptoms are present, medication may be useful and even empowering as the woman is doing all she can to help herself.

However, when the reaction is normal and appropriate, even though uncomfortable, we need to forgo the pills and find other tools to deal with the grief and pain. Masking the symptoms does not help us learn. If we did not feel pain when we put our hand on a hot stove, we would do it over and over. Pain is a great teacher; it serves a purpose and it also empowers. When you look back on this time in your life, you will be humbled and amazed at your own strength and courage. Use medication as a tool to foster your growth and healing, not as a crutch to numb what is normal and necessary.

Today I will consider how much distress I feel. What day was the worst? Is today better? Do I see ups and downs, but progress in my healing? I will honor that my feelings are normal. Are my symptoms as severe today as they have been throughout the process? If this is true, I will ask for help from my physician or therapist to assess my need for medication. If they decide it will be helpful, I will see the medication as one more tool I can use to help myself heal. I will respect my reactions, whatever they are, because they reflect who I am and what I need.

Relationships take time. Time is short. You are stressed to the max. Yes, I know.

However, you need your relationships and so you need to nurture them. Paying attention to your relationships is like watering the lawn – a huge return for a little bit of effort. You need your relationships for support. They validate you and give you strength. That strength builds confidence that will help you meet each day's challenges.

Here are some things you can do that don't take a lot of time and can go a long way in letting the people in your life know they are important to you.

E-mail, voice mail, e-cards, greeting cards, balloon-a-grams, singing telegrams and tins of popcorn are some of our culture's tools for reaching out and letting people know we are thinking about them. Use these tools. Isn't it nice to come home to a blinking light on your voice mail or to hear that computer voice inform you, "You've got mail"?

To have a friend is to be a friend. Don't expect anything from your friends that you yourself don't give. If you have not heard from a friend in a while, rather than write her off, think about the last time you called her. Let friends know they are important in your life. Often, friends distance from divorcing friends, as they feel awkward and unsure of what they should say. Let your friends know you are okay, what is going on with you, and what you need from them. Remember, even the closest of friends cannot read your mind. Friends can be very helpful and supportive, but be cautious not to over-utilize your friends. After a while, it can become difficult to listen to someone in distress. We all have our threshold. Some ways to manage your need to talk and still care for your friendships are:

- Join a support group. You can go on and on about your divorce and they will listen attentively.

- Utilize more than one friend – rotate the burden so one person is not feeling the entire weight of your situation.

- Make a deal with yourself to only talk about the divorce to your friends at certain times and for a limited time.

- Check in with your friends to see if they feel burdened.

- Use a journal to vent instead of a friend.

Today I will look at the friend that I have become. Have I neglected people who are dear to me? Am I relying too heavily on one person? Am I constantly focused on my problems? Do I make time to listen to my friends' problems with empathy and compassion? Am I doing my part?

Love is the subject of poets, novelists, songwriters, playwrights, and filmmakers. Fairy tales tell us the most wonderful, magical thing that can happen in our lives is for the handsome prince to come to us, on his white stallion, and whisk us away to happily-ever-after. From childhood, we are bombarded in our culture by the words of romantic love.

We do everything we can to be loved. But sometimes we get confused. We want so desperately to be lovable, we will believe we are loved even when someone treats us badly. When I hear horrific stories of women being neglected or abused, I ask, "Why do you stay?" They say, "Because he loves me." "How do you know that?" I ask. "Because he says so," they respond.

There is a problem with this kind of thinking. What good are the words of love without the behavior? He must *show* you that he loves you. He must treat you as lovable. That means with tenderness, respect, consideration, honesty, fairness, and caring.

We are seduced by the words and the symbols. Why is it that women will accept an occasional bouquet of flowers or a box of chocolates as love? These are the gestures of love but not love itself. In order for love to have meaning and value in one's life, it must be manifested in actions every minute of every day. Certainly there will be angry times, but there should be kindness even underneath the anger.

Women who stay in relationships where love is not shown in actions sometimes end up in a therapist's office. First they have been to see their physician for a myriad of ailments, including stomach, neck and back problems, migraines, or anxiety. Staying in a relationship in which you are not treated in a caring way will take its toll on your health. Like a plant that needs sun, water, and tender care to grow and thrive, we need the same. Just saying to the plant, "I will water you" isn't enough to keep it happy and healthy. Just saying "I love you" won't allow you to thrive, either.

Today I ask myself, was I seduced by the words and gestures? Did I want to be loved so badly that I overlooked abusive behaviors? Did I think that "the words" were enough? How do my body and spirit feel? Did this relationship nurture me? Did I get to grow and thrive? Or did I accept the words and not get anything else?

Children going through divorce have emotional work to do that is very different from that of their parents. As a good parent, it is your responsibility to be able to separate your anger and disappointment from that of your child's. Divorce is the termination of a marriage. It does not signal the termination of the parent/child relationship. Even if your children's father is deemed an unfit parent by the court, your child will still love his father unconditionally and need his love and support. Whether he/she gets it or not is another issue. As a good parent, it is your job to be mindful of the child's needs, which includes supporting your child's relationship with the other parent. Just as you will have emotional work to do as you go through your process, your child will also have emotional work to do. The five major issues for children as described by Dr. Judith Wallerstein are:

1. My parent is not divorcing me. Many women are unaware that they give the child the message that the father is leaving both the wife AND the children. It is important to explain to your children that while Dad has moved out, the relationship he has with his children is not being terminated. The relationship will change but not end. It is critical for the child's ability to develop future relationships that the child does not feel abandoned. By pointing out that families live in separate homes, you can help children more readily accept this concept. Two examples of this can be grandparents living in another state or town, or an older sibling being away at college. Geography alone does not make or break a relationship.

2. The divorce is not my fault. Many children, regardless of age, think they should have been able to do something to keep their parents together or they may feel that because they did something "bad", they drove the parent away. These feelings need to be discussed in detail. Guilt for something that is not your responsibility is a terrible burden for anyone, especially children.

3. Scary thoughts do not make things happen. This is called magical thinking. Small children are apt to do this. They may think because they were mad at a parent and wished to "make Daddy go away" that somehow their wish was granted. Explain to your child that thoughts do not have magical powers.

4. My parents will not remarry each other. Children, regardless of the age, often hold onto the fantasy that their parents will remarry. They misconstrue the smallest civil interchange between the parents as a romantic gesture. That is one of the reasons children can have a difficult time with remarriage – it signifies the end of the fantasy of their parents' reconciliation.

5. Having two houses to live in. Children have to get used to going back and forth. Depending upon the adults' attitude toward this experience, it can be either positive or negative. Many children enjoy having two homes, with two sets of toys, friends, holidays. It also gives children an opportunity to experience different ways of being in a family. You can make the transition easier if on visitation days you are prepared, cordial, enthusiastic, and on time.

Today I will begin a dialogue with my child to see how the adjustment is going. I will be mindful to the fact that my child's issues are different than mine and therefore his/her feelings will be different as well.

One evening a couple of years ago, I was flipping through the channels and a program on riptides caught my eye. I love the ocean but have never been a particularly good swimmer, so I decided to watch.

The narrator explained that when caught in a riptide, most people try to swim directly toward the shore. What happens is that they get absolutely nowhere. They only wear themselves out and begin to panic. Many become exhausted and they drown. The way to manage a riptide if you are ever caught in one, the narrator continued, is to swim parallel to shore. The tide will be with you and you can even float along as you get tired. Eventually, the tide changes and then you can swim into shore.

How many times do we plunge headfirst into something and struggle valiantly to reach our goal, only to end up exhausted, frustrated, and back where we started? When we are faced with a crisis, the challenge is to meet it with grace and not panic. Our first instinct is not always the best. Our impulses can get us into trouble.

Divorce is a kind of riptide that pulls us down, dragging us along, making us feel out of control and crazy. To control our impulse is to use our intellect to our advantage. It also means to exercise patience and faith that the tide will eventually turn and we will again find ourselves safely on the shore.

Today I will think about times when I feel out of control and ways that I have behaved in the past. Have I been happy with those results? Have I exercised patience and self-control? Have I acted prudently and advocated for myself in a way that was healthy and would bring me the results I yearned for? Today I will remember that sometimes it is okay to go with the tide and relax a little and float along. That way, I can save my strength for the swim into shore.

At one time, most women received alimony in a divorce. Now, only one woman in six receives alimony. Not only is it no longer a given, but it is not assumed by gender. This means if your husband makes less money than you, he can possibly request that you pay *him* alimony. Furthermore, in most states marital misconduct plays little to no role in granting alimony.

However, temporary spousal support is fairly common. If not agreed on by the couple, the court will usually award temporary support until final orders are issued. The goal of temporary spousal support is to keep the family economically stable as it moves through the divorce process. Trying to support two households on the same amount of money is difficult. The standard of living of both parties tends to decline.

Furthermore, if alimony is awarded in the final settlement, it is rarely awarded for life. It is usually limited and known as compensatory (lost income and professional growth), or rehabilitative (based on the costs of training the spouses to be able to support themselves). Usually alimony is terminated when the receiving partner remarries or cohabitates.

Some factors considered in awarding spousal support include:

- Ability and time for each party to gain employment.

- Employability of each spouse.

- Future earning capacity of each spouse.

- Custody of the child(ren).

- Length of the marriage.

- Ability of one spouse to pay another.

- Tax consequences for each partner (alimony is usually tax deductible to the party who is paying and taxable income to the recipient).

- Age of spouse.

- Length of time support is needed.

Today I will discuss with my attorney if and how alimony applies in my particular case. I should not make assumptions about any legal issue until I am fully educated. I need to be aware of all of the nuances of my particular situation. I also will not panic about finances. Until I have all the information I need, I will resist the temptation to make assumptions.

How about those thoughts that go round and round in your head, never leaving you with a peaceful moment? They may be about his behavior, your fears, self-criticism, or a myriad of other issues. We all get them at times of stress. Those thoughts stop us from sleeping, concentrating at work, paying attention to our kids, and getting on with our life.

Do you know which thoughts cause you the most distress? Instead of trying to banish them or solve them, really listen to them. Then write them down and say out loud, "YOU DON'T BELONG IN MY HEAD!!!!!!!"

Take the piece of paper you wrote on and rip it up and throw it in the toilet. Then flush. Or toss it in the fireplace. As it disappears, say out loud, "YOU ARE GONE FOREVER!" Sometimes we have to repeat this exercise more than once until the thought is gone. If you find you must repeat the exercise, each time say, "YOU ARE GONE FOREVER!" Say it a bit louder and with more conviction.

Sometimes the things that hurt us the most are the things we do to ourselves. Listening to our thoughts, we are often surprised that the cruelest things said to us are the ones we say to ourselves.

Today I will pay close attention to my thoughts and to negative and hurtful things that I say to myself. Although I can't control what others think or say, I can control my own thoughts and feelings. I will not let negative self-talk undermine my growth and blossoming self-esteem. I will NOT tolerate abusive behavior from anyone, especially myself. When I start to think hurtful things, I will take a stand and shout, **"YOU DON'T BELONG IN MY HEAD!"**

- Make an appointment for a physical. It doesn't matter if you never get sick or don't feel sick. Do it anyway. Don't be embarrassed to tell your doctor what is happening in your life. Doctors know stress affects health. In order to treat you effectively, they need as much information as you can give them. If you feel you can't talk to your MD, then find another. Now is not the time to withhold information. Your life is depending on it!

- Most people experience difficulty sleeping and eating when they are faced with crisis. Divorce is definitely a crisis. Make sure you discuss all your symptoms with the doctor and she/he can help you decide if medication is necessary.

- During periods of stress, we tend to drink more alcohol than we normally would. Under no circumstances is this the time to increase your drinking. (In fact, I can't think of a time when you should!) The first drink can feel relaxing, but alcohol is a depressant and, contrary to a common belief, it does not help you sleep better. It can interrupt sleep. Mixing alcohol with certain medications can be dangerous. A good rule of thumb – decrease your alcohol intake when going through a stressful period.

- Exercise. If you haven't exercised before, start gradually, but get up and do something. Exercise is an excellent way to work off the stress and anxiety that accompany divorce. It can help you sleep better, which in turn will help with your concentration and focus. You will need these as you go through this process. If you feel you haven't got time to start an exercise program, then work a little exercise into your life. Take the stairs instead of the elevator or park further away from the grocery store. Gardening, cleaning your house, washing your car, these are all ways to incorporate exercise into your life. It doesn't really matter whether you run, dance, kickbox, play tennis, or wash floors – just get up and *move*. If you already work out, then keep it going. Many women say, "I feel too tired or too stressed to work out." Some women report that imagining their estranged husband's face on the bottom of their sneakers is a good way to stay motivated to exercise!

- Try to eat healthy. Even if you can't eat a lot, be mindful of what you do eat. Go for the yogurt instead of the donut. Think of your body as a machine. The higher-grade fuel you put in, the better the performance.

- Incorporate a relaxing regime into your life, such as massage, yoga, meditation, or prayer. Pay attention to the mind-body connection. Learn stress reducing techniques or self-hypnosis as ways to manage anxiety and stress. Inexpensive programs are available in most communities. Contact your local hospital, continuing education program or YWCA.

Today I will make an appointment for a check up and do something to improve my health. Every day I will be conscious of taking care of my body, how I use it, what I put into it, and making sure it has enough rest. Taking care of my body is part of loving myself.

Today is a holiday! You have been working really hard and you need a break!

So today just laugh and enjoy. Here are a few of my favorite divorce jokes. Hopefully, they will bring a smile to your face.

- "Divorce – from the Latin word to pull a man's genitals out through his wallet."
  – *Robin Williams*

- "I am a good housekeeper; every time I leave a man, I keep the house."
  – *Eva Gabor*

- "A woman needs a man like a fish needs a bicycle."
  – *Gloria Steinem*

- "Everytime I date a man, I think, is this the man I want my children to spend weekends with?"
  – *Rita Rudner*

- "I don't believe man is woman's natural enemy. Perhaps his lawyer is."
  – *Shana Alexander*

- "Whenever you want to marry someone, have lunch with their ex-wife."
  – *Shelley Winters*

- "I don't think of myself as single. I think of myself as romantically challenged."
  – *Stephanie Piro*

- "I rely on my personality for birth control."
  – *Liz Winston*

- "A man's home may be his castle from the outside; inside, it is more often his nursery."
  – *Clare Booth Luce*

- "If the world were a logical place, men would ride sidesaddle."
  – *Rita Mae Brown*

Today I will give myself permission to take a holiday from all my worries, conflicts, problems and anxieties. I declare this day "off limits" for any stress. I will allow myself a break from all the emotional work. I will eat take-out in front of the television, or picnic with my kids in the park, back yard, or even on my bed. Maybe we will make tents out of blankets and "camp out" in the living room. We will have dessert for breakfast and pancakes for dinner. Just for today, I want to play!

When your husband decided to leave, you may have panicked. You may have tried to get him back. You may have cried, screamed, called him repeatedly. You may have even threatened him. Your fear and pain were so strong that your entire focus became "getting him back." You may have found creative and dire ways to try to manipulate the object of your desire. When you continue to pursue someone and they continue to rebuff you, you may be headed for trouble. When does "love" go too far?

If you have begun to consider dire behaviors, then you need to stop for a minute and think about what you are doing. This is no longer about love, but about control, fear, or revenge. When you lie, or manipulate and scheme, you set yourself up for feelings of shame and embarrassment and more rejection. You may even get arrested. This behavior won't make him come back to you. In fact, it may make him loathe you and, in the process of behaving this way, you will begin to loathe yourself. If you recognize any of these behaviors, then you have gone over the line to obsession. Get help from a trusted friend or therapist. Contact a support group or an anonymous hotline that can help you deal with this problem. Make no mistake: this IS a problem. Obsession means that your thoughts are dominated by one single idea. There is a major difference between "He's important in my life" and "He is my life." Being obsessed is serious and dangerous. Are you mixing love with obsession? Do you:

- Change yourself to get him back?
- Lose your focus and interest in anything else?
- Hear friends or family suggest you are too wrapped up in him?
- Feel you would die without him?
- Let him be abusive toward you?
- Have fantasies of hurting him or someone he loves?
- Call his friends/girlfriend?
- Plan your life around seeing him?
- Secretly take pictures of him?
- Continue to try to force a relationship with him?
- Misinterpret his behavior, look for signs of returned affection?
- Drive by his home or place of work daily or park there?
- Spy on him?
- Read his personal e-mails, listen to his voice mail, break into his home?
- Call him over and over?
- Fantasize about getting rid of his girlfriend?

Today I will realize that anytime my thoughts are dominated by a single person to the exclusion of anything else, I risk becoming addicted to that person. If left untreated, the problem will escalate. If I think my behavior is even possibly obsessive, I will ask for help immediately. I am too important to allow my thoughts of another person to dominate and ruin my life.

Do you have days when you fantasize about him? Are there times when you question if it really was that bad? This is not an uncommon phenomenon. Women who are struggling to detach from their husbands and women who are long past even wanting their husbands back, find themselves fantasizing about "the good times."

There is a saying, "Pain is inevitable, suffering is optional." When you fantasize/dream about your ex, you are increasing your suffering. The pain of divorce is inescapable, but the choice of how much to suffer is yours.

Try this:

- Write down the five most hurtful things your husband did. Write as much or as little as you want.

- On a smaller piece of paper, as tiny as possible, write down one or two words that best represent each situation. For example, if he cheated with your best friend, you may want to write cheating and betrayal. It doesn't matter what words you write. What is important is that they are significant to you.

- Fold the piece of paper and stick it in your bra over your heart.

- When you go to sleep each night, put the tiny piece of paper under your pillow.

- Do this for two weeks.

Most of the time, you won't even be aware of the paper, but your unconscious mind will know of its presence and will absorb and hold the information. The effect of this will surprise you. This exercise will help diminish your painful fantasies and reduce your suffering.

Today like Nellie Forbush in the musical "South Pacific" who "washed that man right out of her hair," I will wash that man right out of my heart!

- The divorce rate in the United States has remained fairly stable since 1988, and provisional data for 1993 show the rate to be 4.6 divorces per 1,000 population. The divorce rate had risen steadily from 2.5 in 1966 to a peak of 5.3 in both 1979 and 1981. The rate declined in the early and mid-1980's and leveled off at about 4.7 during 1988-93.

- First marriages ending in divorce lasted an average of 11 years for both men and women, while remarriages ending in divorce lasted an average of 7.4 years for men and 7.1 years for women. Nationally, all marriages ending in divorce lasted an average of 9.8 years, ranging from a duration of 8.2 years in Alaska to 11.6 years in Maryland.

- Divorce numbers are highest among men aged 30-34 years and women aged 25-29 years.

- The average age of men divorcing after the first marriage was 35 years; for women the average age was 33 years. The average age for men divorcing from their second marriage was 42 years; for women it was 39 years. For the thrice or more divorced, the average age of men was 46.5 years; for women it was 42 years.

- The largest proportion of divorces were granted to men and women who had married between the ages of 20-24 years. First-time male divorcees on average were 24 years of age when they married; for women, the average was 22 years.

- In 27 reporting States and the District of Columbia, young white persons aged 15-24 years had substantially higher divorce rates than young black persons the same age. Among people aged 25 years and over, the black population had higher divorce rates than the white population.

- Divorce rates ranged from 2.7 in Massachusetts to 10.8 in Nevada. Because of differences in reporting between States, there is no means for accurately ranking all 50 States.

- Divorce had varying impact on family structure from State-to-State. A greater percent of children were involved in divorces in Nebraska and Utah than in other reporting States. Sixty-four percent of divorces in Nebraska and 63 percent in Utah involved at least one child. Meanwhile, the greatest percent of divorces involving no children occurred in the District of Columbia and Maryland.

- In 19 reporting States, 72 percent of custody cases were awarded to the wife, and 9 percent of custody cases were awarded to the husband. Joint custody was awarded in 16 percent of the cases. (Advance Report on Vital Divorce Statistics 1989-90). (*The collection of detailed data was suspended beginning in January 1996. Limitations in information collected by the States as well as budgetary considerations necessitated this action.*) †(*National Center for Health Statistics,2004*)

Today when I look at the above statistics, I know that I am not alone. Rather than see myself as an anomaly and a failure, the statistics help me recognize that I am not alone in this growing phenomenon.

"Yesterday is history, tomorrow is a mystery, today is a gift. That is why it is called the present."

Spending too much time reminiscing about what was, or thinking about what can be, only creates more suffering. We cannot change the past and we cannot predict the future. Doing either is a colossal waste of time. The only thing that counts is the present. Living each moment to its fullest is the only way you can enjoy life. I have met people who spent their whole life grieving for what they had and what they lost. They are filled with regrets and resentments, and feel their hurts and disappointments as fresh as the day they occurred. I have also met people who live completely in the future, strategizing and obsessing about what can go wrong. They are so caught up in what **might** happen that they miss what **is** happening.

How do you learn to live in the present? It takes practice to discipline the mind. "Mindfulness" is about staying in the moment. So many times, in our hurried lives, we are doing one thing and thinking about another. For example, when you are driving to work, chances are you are not noticing the scenery and the color of the sky, but are focused on the things you need to do at work, or the things that were happening when you left home. When you are taking a shower, are you thinking about your day and what lies ahead rather than allowing yourself to enjoy the water cascading over you?

Try this: take one simple activity you do every day, like driving to work or showering and pay attention while you are doing it. Engage all your senses – smell, touch, sight, sound and taste. Take the time to notice how your senses react. Let your brain register each detail and let yourself fully feel the experience of the blue sky, or the feel of the water. What pleasure your senses will experience! Eventually joy and gratitude for your life will begin to emerge in these small mindful tasks. You will be surprised at how many of the simple pleasures of everyday life you are missing by thinking about the past or worrying for the future.

Today I will learn from my past and plan for my future. But most importantly, I will learn to allow myself the joy of living in the present. I will work at developing "mindfulness" and I will be amazed and overjoyed at the gifts I will receive.

In her mid-forties, Sandra's executive husband left her for his twenty-two year old secretary. Sandra was left to deal with two pre-teen children and a disability that made it impossible for her to work. As one could expect, she was bitter, hurt, and enraged. Her life had changed in a way she had not chosen. Sandra's husband faithfully paid his child support and alimony and paid to keep Sandra living in the big house they had just built in a stylish neighborhood. Sandra took him to court for every small thing and belittled him without mercy. The children, stunned by their mother's pain and their father's behavior, rallied around her and refused to see their Dad.

Time passed and the father remarried. Eventually, the children missed their father and began seeing him, first without his new wife and then with her. Sandra's outrage grew and grew. When she dated men, they never called her back because she so badly assailed her ex. She began losing friends. When her children were in their late teens, her son came to her and said, "No wonder Dad left you. You are the most miserable person in the world. I can't stand it anymore." With that, he packed his stuff and went to live with the father and his new wife. Two years later, the daughter followed suit. Sandra lives alone in her big house, still embittered, years of her life wasted and her relationship with her kids in shambles. Don't make the same mistakes Sandra made. Here are a few tips on helping your children cope:

- The details of divorce should stay between the two of you.
- It is not your children's job to comfort you, no matter how old they are.
- Children are entitled to be free to love both their parents.
- Do not keep your children informed about when you go to court or what the documents say.
- Do not discuss child support and alimony with your kids.
- Never ask kids to transport money/check from parent to parent.
- Never pump children for information.
- Never make children feel guilty about visiting the other parent.
- Always be on time for pick up and drop off.
- Never use the "exchange" time to battle with your spouse.
- Let your children transport their things freely between the houses. This gives children a sense of connection and continuity rather than feeling split between "what things belong at what house." Once you give something to your children, it is theirs. Not letting them take it to the other parent's house is just plain childish. And selfish.

Today *I realize that as hard as it is to support my child's relationship with his/her father, I do it because it is the right thing to do. My child will be emotionally healthier if he/she has a good relationship with us both. And I will feel good about myself, knowing that I did not let my anger get the better of me.*

Are you a woman of great creativity and vision? Can you see a broken-down chair at a garage sale and know with a little elbow grease it can become a treasured heirloom? Are you a woman who loves challenges, solving puzzles, or figuring out how to make things work? Are you resourceful, successful, and creative? Those are all wonderful traits… unless your passion for fixing things extends to your relationships. Do you find yourself saying things like, "I don't know what else I can do. If only he would try, he has so much potential"? Do you look at a man and say, "If he only didn't have this alcohol (drug, job, family, gambling) problem, he would be so wonderful"?

Does this sound like your ex-husband? The guy who almost "had it all"? Think back to when you met him, there were probably some warning bells trying to alert you to the current problems. You may have forged ahead thinking they didn't matter, or that you could fix them. Women who love the fixer-upper men see them more as a project rather than a relationship. The fantasy is that with a little work, you can turn him into a gem of a partner, just as you restored that old broken-down chair. Unfortunately, relationships don't work that way. What you see is what you get. People only change if they want to, not because we want them to. On some level, you probably know that. So, what is it that keeps bringing you back? What keeps you in it for so long? The clues may lie within the messages you received about relationships from your family of origin.

- Was care-taking reinforced as a positive attribute by either parent?

- Was your mother a fixer-upper?

- What was your parent's relationship like?

- Was one clearly more "high functioning" than the other?

- Was one (or both) of your parents suffering from mental or physical illness?

- Was one (or both) of your parents alcoholics?

- Are you the oldest child?

- Are you the only girl?

- What messages did you receive about how women should behave?

- Was approval granted for what you did rather than who you are?

Awareness is the first step in changing this pattern. While it is not easy, it will take you closer to realizing the relationship you want and deserve.

Today I know that I cannot finish this work in a day. I will be content and accept whatever insights I receive from this exercise. When I am ready, I will commit time and effort to changing my unhealthy attraction and patterns.

Day 27   Would You Recognize This as Abusive Behavior?

Sometimes when we think of abusive behavior, we think of physical violence. Here are some forms of abusive behavior that are not physical, but are still considered abuse:

- Criticizing you, your friends, family, job, or anyone or anything important to you.
- Blaming you for everything.
- Making fun of you in front of other people. This includes remarks about your looks, family, job, or sex.
- Demanding that you account for all your time away from him.
- Listening in on your phone conversations.
- Reading your mail.
- Isolating you from your friends and family.
- Yelling, throwing things, slamming his hand on the counter, slamming doors, punching walls.
- Using sarcasm.
- Ordering you about.
- Controlling money issues.
- Discussing you behind your back.
- Demanding he have everything done his way.
- Controlling what you wear.
- Forcing you to have sex or to do sexual things you are not comfortable doing.

Some women have commented, "Well, he *does* some of those things, but don't all men?" No, not all men behave this way! It is not normal to hurt the person you love. This is abuse. Standing up to your spouse lets him know that this behavior is unacceptable. You do not have to be abusive back, only state calmly that it is not acceptable. Don't threaten or yell. That only challenges the abuser to try to control even more. Underneath the bravado, abusers are weak and insecure. By intimidating you and making you feel bad about yourself, they make themselves feel powerful. By knocking you down emotionally ("Who would want you?"), they think they make it impossible for you to seek options. Seeing the behavior for what it is can help fortify you to take a stand. Don't try to analyze him; he will only guffaw and act worse. Don't talk about him. Talk about yourself. This is not acceptable to ME!

One important word of caution. If he lays a hand on you – a slap, push, or punch – it is time to leave. Maybe not forever, but until he gets help. Physical abuse escalates. When he has crossed that line from hitting the counter to hitting you, then it is time to go. Without help, it will only get worse. Don't think, "Oh, she doesn't know him, he would never do that." Many women who lost their lives to domestic violence said the exact same thing.

Today I will no longer accept unacceptable behavior. I need to be treated with dignity, respect and love. If my partner is unable to do that, I will make sure I treat myself that way. When I accept the unacceptable, I begin treating myself abusively. I cannot stop his behavior, but I can certainly work on my own!

Day 28   If the "Other Woman" Was Your "Friend"

One of the most difficult scenarios that can occur in a divorce is when your husband leaves you for a woman who was your friend. Of course, if that happens, she wasn't really a friend to begin with! While this is not a common scenario, it does happen and it is incredibly painful.

Our relationships with our women friends are sacrosanct – they are our sisters, mothers, daughters, aunts, nieces, grandmothers. In our women friends, we see ourselves – as we are, as we want to be, and how we have grown. The bond between women friends can be among the strongest connections we have in our lives. When they betray us, we are shattered. When they betray us with our husbands, even our estranged ones, it feels as if the world is collapsing. When a marriage ends, we usually turn to our women friends with our fears of trusting men again. When our friend becomes our betrayer, it feels like there is no one left, man or woman whom we can trust.

It is easy to take that experience of pain and mistrust and generalize it to all our relationships. We must be cautious about doing that, as it will only leave us isolated and bitter. So, how do we deal with a betrayal so huge that it feels insurmountable?

- Be mindful of the nature of your betrayal and anger. Do not condemn a whole gender for one person's misdoing. When we globalize our pain, we make it larger than it need be.
- Recognize that time really does help heal all wounds, no matter how deep they may be.
- Turn toward other women for comfort and solace.

Turning to women after the betrayal of a woman friend is different from turning toward a man after the end of a romantic relationship. The investment is different, because our agenda (AND THEIR agenda) are different. Women can offer you support, guidance, insight, and a sense of hope. They will not need nor want anything but your friendship in return. Turn toward other women to help heal both wounds. It will renew your trust in women and help restore your confidence. No one can understand what you are feeling like another woman who has experienced it. When we share our trust, intimate thoughts, and feelings with other women, they become the mirrors of our own souls.

Today I will allow myself to grieve for what I have lost. But I will also be conscious not to let these betrayals embitter me; I will not allow them that much power. I will not allow them to deny me other intimate and caring relationships in the future. I will turn toward my women friends who stand, arms outstretched, waiting to hold me and comfort me. I know I will find safety in their love and nurturance.

Collaborative divorce offers an alternative to the adversarial "win/lose" mentality of a traditionally litigated divorce. Unlike mediation, it allows counsel for each party. All four parties involved (the couple and their attorneys) agree that the goal is to "look at the big picture"; that is, a family going through divorce still has emotional and financial ties to each other, but they are redefined. Experts have long pointed out that divorce itself is not what causes the long-term emotional damage. Rather it is the acrimony, fighting, hostility, and resentment that sets up the long-term scenario of turmoil. By committing to a process that reduces this kind of acrimony (and financial expenditure), collaborative divorces are more cost-effective, address issues of long-term consequences, and result in far less resentment down the road. The goal is to reduce conflict, which sets the stage for an ongoing commitment of working together.

Atty. Barry F. Armata, a family lawyer in Bristol, Connecticut, who handles both collaborative and traditional divorces, cites many advantages to collaborative divorce. They include:

- Future needs such as college costs and visitation schedules are addressed and custom made for each family.

- Because collaborative divorce encourages the use of the same professionals (appraisers, accountants, and the like), the cost to both parties is greatly reduced.

- The agreement is reached in private.

- It sets the stage for transition into a more collaborative post-divorce relationship.

- It can be a more detailed agreement.

- It can greatly reduce legal fees.

Collaborative divorce offers an opportunity to see divorce as a problem to be solved, rather than an opportunity to "do the other one in." With collaborative divorce, post-divorce litigation is reduced and co-parenting skills are enhanced. The children suffer less than in the traditional adversarial divorce. Expensive court proceedings and endless litigation do not eat up the family's funds.

Collaborative divorce is an important and useful option if the spouses can deal with emotional issues separately from the business of dissolving the legal marriage. If they can do this, then collaborative divorce is a win-win for all involved. After all, would you rather use your money to pay for your attorney's children's college bills, or save it for your own children?

Today I will consider collaborative divorce. I will research this avenue on the Internet, or perhaps ask a few local attorneys if they participate in the process. If my partner and I are willing to see the big picture, this option might work for us. I would much rather have a problem to solve than a war to fight.

Day 30   Was He Your Safe Haven in The Storm. . .

. . . or The Storm?

When you look at relationships and try to ascertain whether or not they are healthy, you need to examine what role the relationship plays in your life. Some questions to ask yourself are:

- Does the relationship provide stability and security?
- Is this relationship the place you feel the safest?
- In this relationship, are you free to be yourself?
- Does the relationship provide you caring and support?
- Is he the first person you think to call when there is good news?
- Is he the first person you call with bad news?
- Are you ever afraid of his reaction?
- Do you feel constantly misunderstood?
- Do you feel diminished in the relationship?
- Do you feel inadequate most of the time?
- Do you worry about how he treats your kids?
- Do you worry about his drinking/drug use?
- Do you worry that he will humiliate or embarrass you in public?

When you worry constantly about what he is thinking/feeling/behaving/reacting, then you aren't really feeling safe. When you find yourself incessantly thinking about how to fix the relationship, then he is no longer your port in the storm. He is your storm. Deciding whether the storm is temporary is difficult to do in the middle of the downpour. All relationships weather storms. The duration, frequency, and intensity are what make them unmanageable, dangerous, and impossible to sustain. Unfortunately, some storms keep on raging without letup.

Each of us needs to decide for ourselves how many storms we can handle in our lives. Some of us will probably be able to handle only a few really rough storms. Others will sustain stormy weather for years. There is no right or wrong. What is healthy for you and your children? Ask yourself how often has he been your safe haven. Does he frequently provide you with shelter – or is it more often the destructive storm? Knowing this can help you decide the healthiest path to take.

All of us need a safe harbor in life, whether we find it in a spouse, a friend, a colleague, or a family member. The desire to feel safe and loved is part of our desire to be happy and to find connection. There is no shame in wanting and needing a safe place.

Today I will ask myself what I get from this person. Is he the source of my worry and anxiety or is he the place I go to gain support for my feelings? I will listen attentively to my answer and I will make my decisions accordingly.

Notes

Month Three

While there is never a simple reason for a marriage breaking up, we can often find clues when we look back and examine the history of the relationship. Frequently, the seeds of problems were sowed in the dating years, but may have laid dormant. Or perhaps they had already sprouted but you said to yourself:

- He will outgrow that.

- That's just part of being single.

- It's just a phase.

- Everyone does that.

- I can change that.

- I can live with that.

- It's no big deal.

- He has so many good qualities.

For example, his drinking is a problem now. Maybe he drank a little too much in school, but he was the life of the party! You may have said to yourself, "He'll change when we are married." Or now you find him uncommunicative and resistant to discussing what is bothering him, but he may have just appeared shy when he was younger. The point is this: problems in relationships do not just occur overnight. The doubts you had that day walking down the aisle were your intuition telling you that this behavior was a warning sign.

Some women say, "No, I didn't see it then." I would suggest that you look a little deeper. What did you argue about? How did you argue? Look at the substance of your arguments (or lack of) and the style of interaction you had for solving those arguments. You will probably see that little seed was taking root even then.

So, why is this important now? It reminds us to trust our instincts, to heed the voice within, to turn up the volume and respect it above all others. You know deep down inside what is healthy for you; you just have to listen harder. For some women, who have gotten so used to hearing everyone's voices over their own, it means listening for the first time in a long time.

Today *I will listen to what I know to be my truth. When unsure I will ask myself this: "What is the healthy thing for me?" Again, not what is right or accepted, or what others think, but the healthy thing. I will listen to myself. I know what is best for me. I will get beyond all the other voices and LISTEN!*

By now you probably have begun to realize the importance of support in your life. Many women going through divorce do not have many friends on whom they can rely. The reasons for this are varied. Some women had put the needs of their family first. Often, they threw themselves into the activities of everyday life with such a fury that there was little time left for themselves. Other women withdrew from friendships, as they may have felt ashamed of their situation. Still others have surrendered friendships because their husbands required it and, out of fear, they had no choice.

Support systems are important and they have many faces. We need support in the emotionally intimate way, someone we can call in the middle of the night and cry with. But we need other supports as well, such as someone who will be your back up if you are late picking up your kids from school. Some husbands provided a support system. As one woman put it, "He didn't do much when he was here, but at least, when I had to run to the store for milk, he would be there to watch the children. Now I have to bundle them up and take them with me. Just getting milk is a major ordeal."

Supports necessary for a single mother fall into these categories:
Emotional support
- Personal – this is a friend, support group, therapist, your Mom, someone with whom you can share your feelings without fear of judgment or criticism. It helps to have more than one person in this category as you don't want to "over utilize" anyone.
- Practical – this includes parenting issues. Your ex-husband may still be available for this role, although if he wasn't during the marriage, he probably won't be now. Friends, school personnel, your child's therapist are all people you can utilize for support in these areas.
- Work related – someone you can vent to about your professional life. May be a friend or co-worker.

Practical support
- Personal – someone who will give you a ride to the airport, help you hang the wallpaper, move heavy furniture, and so on. Some of these services you can hire; but another option, especially if money is tight, is to swap services with another single parent. You could offer to baby-sit for your neighbor's children in exchange for his cleaning your gutters.
- Children – a back up person(s) so when you do have to run out to get milk, you don't always have to take the children with you. It may be babysitters, grandparents, neighbors, the children's father.
- Work related – colleague, co-worker, mentor on whom you can rely if you get in a jam and need a little support. When going through a divorce, you may have to take time off from work. An example of practical support is an understanding boss or a co-worker who fields your calls when you are not available.

Accessing support isn't a sign of weakness. It is a sign of a good manager.

Today I ask myself, where am I lacking support? Rather than wait until there is a crisis and I am desperate for help, I will plan ahead and anticipate where I will need help. I can use the above list as a guide to bring necessary supports into my life. If I am creative, my finances will not limit me. In truth, the only thing that limits me is my fear of asking. I refuse to let that stand in my way.

When women are experiencing divorce, their thoughts sometimes return to their first love. They wander down memory lane and create various scenarios involving another time in their lives when they were perhaps happier, confident, younger, and filled with optimism.

Time has a tendency to soften the edges on even the most acrimonious of these past relationships. This, coupled with the acute pain of the present, can result in a very favorable comparison between your present spouse and this ex-partner. Suddenly, you see many good attributes that you may have missed.

Going back to find an ex-love is neither bad nor good. Sometimes it works out, sometimes it doesn't. But don't do it while you are in the throes of recovering from another relationship. The desire to minimize the loss and pain is strong and you may feel desperate to again feel loveable (happy, attractive, desirable). One woman found herself contacting an old love even before her separation. When he responded enthusiastically, she found herself high as a kite. He was also in the midst of divorce. They immediately had a connection: their pain. However, as they wrote, she was able to see that he had not changed and her decision years ago to leave him was the right one. She was aware this man was not good for her, yet she was delighted with the confirmation she could feel "that way" again. She realized how unappreciated she felt in her marriage and that she did long for a healthy connection. However, not now and not with her old love. Her ability to maintain healthy boundaries and to assess him so objectively is a difficult thing to do. She put herself in a vulnerable situation but was able to recognize the pitfalls of getting involved with this man.

If you decide to seek out an old love, wait until you're through with your pain, loss and grief over this marriage. Otherwise, it is almost impossible to tell what is real, and what is merely a panacea for your pain.

Today if I have been fantasizing about an old love, I will allow myself the fantasy. However, I recognize that doing anything about it now may result in a disastrous outcome. I will not act impulsively, but will allow myself to heal from the great wound I have suffered over the loss of my marriage. I owe that to myself. When I am whole and strong, if I decide to seek out my old flame, I will do so. Then I can proceed with an open mind and a healed heart.

Do you know the difference?

Some women say they are "better" and that they are ready to "move on." They say the divorce is no longer an issue in their life. However, when they continue to be revengeful, rageful, suspicious, cynical and negative, have they really moved on?

"Oh, I am over that bastard," they say. "And I won't ever get married again. In fact, who even wants to date? They are all the same, right?" When our experience with one man turns us into man haters, we are not over anything. We are not better, we are bitter. When we take the actions of one person and use them against an entire gender (or race, or religion) we are spreading contempt, negativity, and even hate. Sweeping generalizations are unfair, and can be harmful and even dangerous. Bitterness and the resistance to let go of anger eventually decays the human spirit. When we are filled with revenge, rage, spite, or any of the other feelings that come with bitterness, we are not nurturing our inner life. Our emotional health, spiritual well being, and even physical health are often sacrificed. Like years of inhaling cigarettes, or eating food that is high in fat and cholesterol, we do not see the negative effects immediately. Toxic feelings, like nicotine and high fat, will eventually take its toll on our whole well being.

Bitterness keeps us a victim and it also serves to keep people away. Even those closest to us begin to avoid us, wondering when we will get on with our lives. They begin to lose patience with our bitter tirades. Where there once was empathy and support, now there is impatience and even disgust. Bitterness simply is not an attractive trait. It does not attract people to us.

Being better is about moving on with acceptance and serenity. It is making peace with your pain and about letting go of your anger. You do this not for him, but for you. Holding on to your anger makes you hard, cynical, and suspicious. Being better is about self-growth and awareness. You experience insight and a renewed sense of self. Bitterness only impedes that process.

Today I will ask myself, "Am I better or am I bitter?" When I consider my feelings and my inner thoughts, I will honestly look at myself. Do I experience a renewed sense of hope or am I still ruminating on all the horrible things he did to me? Is my heart filled with thoughts of a future of opportunity and hope, or is it about revenge and rage? What stands in the way of my letting go of my bitterness? Can I imagine how acceptance would feel?

How do you rebuild self-esteem? Consider if you really want to rebuild or you want to reconstruct. Rebuilding implies that you want your life to be exactly what it was before your marriage. In reconstruction, we consider taking the best of what was and adding the best of what can be. Close your eyes and imagine how you would like to be. The first things you may think of are physical changes. Gently guide yourself inward and look at how you would *like to feel, think, and behave.* While we are often very clear about what we don't want, we often haven't spent time looking at what we do want. We stay stuck in disliking something (or many things) about ourselves. Few of us ever think about how to *change* that.

Just entertaining the idea of change can be powerful. Many women, particularly victims of domestic abuse, have gotten used to being passive and feeling hopeless. Part of turning a victim into a survivor is seeing the choices. In choosing, lies power.

Try writing down some ideas or talking it over with a friend. Keep the discussion in the present or future. If you have trouble imagining yourself differently, the following may be helpful.

Imagine – You have just been chosen to be in a movie. You get to play your favorite character. Who is that character? What do you like about her? Can you imagine what it would feel like to be her?

Use your imagination; it gives you the opportunity to stretch into realms you may not have thought possible. Many women with low self-esteem have lost the ability to dream and consequently have feelings of hopelessness. Use your imagination to reopen the door of possibilities.

Today I will think about what I want in my future. I will imagine how I want to live my life. When negativity comes up, I will remind myself of my goals. This will be my "future rehearsal." The more I rehearse, the easier the role will be.

If you are like most women going through divorce, you are overwhelmed with childcare, work, the mechanics of divorce and so on. What do you do for yourself? Women, especially divorcing women, often do very little for themselves. Usually, they put themselves last. The importance of taking care of your health cannot be overstated. You may have a lot of excuses for not doing so. Some of us take better care of our cars than ourselves. Like the car, you need fuel, maintenance, and most importantly, preventative care. If not, you will break down.

So, what are some things you can do for yourself? Write down one big change you want for your physical or emotional health; get more sleep, get a check up, etc. and one smaller change: add a five minute walk at lunch time, a relaxing bath before bedtime. Make a silent commitment to do one of the small changes starting today and one big change by the end of the month.

Do not set your goals so high that you will not experience success. Make sure you pick things that are manageable. Getting a Ph.D. or losing fifty pounds are much too big. It is important to build success. Perhaps taking one class or losing five pounds are more appropriate goals. We often take on more than we can do. Then we feel overwhelmed, abandon our goal and experience failure. Try…

To improve physical health
- Add a bit of exercise.
- Cut down on fats.
- Sleep a little more.
- Get your teeth cleaned.

To improve emotional health
- Join a support group.
- Do one nice thing a day for yourself.
- Ask for help.
- Substitute negative messages with positive ones.
- Laugh daily.
- Have dinner with a friend.

To improve spiritual health
- Meditate.
- Pray.
- Practice Yoga.
- Go to sleep each night thinking of one thing in your life for which you are grateful.
- Join a spiritual community.

Today I will allow myself to take care of myself. I will begin to think about what my needs are and how I can improve my health. I will begin to be as good to myself as I am to others.

Divorce is a time of transition and a time of many unknowns. We feel in flux, delicately balancing on a tightrope of decisions. Each step feels precarious and uncertain. These unknowns can feel overwhelming and perilous. One decision blurs with another and you feel out of control. You feel as if any minute you might slip off that tightrope.

What frightens you the most? "Everything" or "the fear of the unknown" are common responses. Let's push that a little bit. What specifically frightens you the most? What feels like the most terrible thing that could happen? Think about your fear. What really "kicks you in the gut"? Once you name that fear, rather than run from it or negate it, spend some time exploring it.

- **Is your fear realistic?**

Many times our fears are unrealistic. For example, many women have a fear that they will end up homeless. While that may be a possibility, and I am sure you could make an argument for how that could happen, let's look at the other side. What kind of work have you done? Who supports you now? What would your family do to help you? Your children? Your friends? If you truly feel as if you don't have a safety net, then the next step is to create one. Do you want to go back to school? Can you check out what kind of public assistance is available? When we dwell on our fear, we enlarge it. Focus on the reality of the situation and then possible solutions.

- **Is your fear something that has been a theme throughout your life?**

Sometimes fears are thematic. That means we experience the same emotions in different situations. Another way of putting it is that even though the circumstances change, our perspective is always the same. For example, let's say you were a middle child and only daughter and that your brothers received all the attention and you were shortchanged in every circumstance. Your greatest fear may be of being overridden and not heard by the court system. You may fear that your husband will "win" everything. This is not a feeling based on the experience of the court system, this is an experience from childhood. It may feel the same, but feelings aren't facts. Really look at your fear. Is it about what is happening now, or does it seem vaguely familiar?

- **Is the thing you fear irreversible?**

Let's say your fear is about making a mistake. First of all, accept that sometime in your life and probably in this process, you will make mistakes. It is part of being human. Secondly, most mistakes are reversible. Thirdly, all mistakes offer us chances to learn. Think of a mistake as an opportunity to learn something new.

- **What would you do if your greatest fear came true?**

Really, what would you do? Think about it this way, the Dali Lama says problems either have a solution or they don't. If they have a solution, then there is nothing to worry about. And if they don't have a solution, then there is nothing to worry about either. The point is, worrying won't make it better. Do the best you can with what you know and let the rest of it go.

Today I name my greatest fear and I found that it is not so scary after all. I can handle anything that comes my way and if I can't, then why worry about it? Living my life in fear only robs me of precious moments of life. I have named my fear, I have stared directly into its eyes and I will go on and live my life to its fullest.

Even young children are aware that they are part of both parents. We tell them the story of our courtship, our wedding and of their birth. We show them baby pictures. "You have Daddy's smile and you have Mommy's eyes," we tell them. This is part of being in a family. This is one of the ways children develop a sense of belonging.

Sometimes, in anger, we give clear messages to the child that there are things about Daddy that we don't like that are also in the child. As acrimony between the parents escalates, these remarks become sharper, taking on new significance for the child. The child of divorcing parents who is told, "You remind me of your father," hears a painful rejection of himself. The thought process goes something like this: "If you divorced Daddy, because you didn't like him, and I am like Daddy, will you divorce me, too?" The child is suddenly confused and frightened. At one time, being a part of both parents was a positive thing, affirmed and supported. Now, suddenly, it is a major crime to be anything like him. The child feels torn, and needing to feel good about himself, he may gravitate away from the verbally negative parent and staunchly defend the other parent. Or he may distance himself from the father, in order to gain mother's attention. Either way, the child is damaged. He is denied access to his feelings to freely love both parents, and he is denied the freedom to accept himself completely. The result may be a child who is alienated from a parent, or even worse, is filled with self-doubt and self-loathing.

Be mindful of your child's need to love both parents. Your husband might be the worst person on the face of the planet, but it is your child's right to find that out for himself, based on his experience, not yours. Talk with a friend, support group, therapist, or relative about your negative feelings. But do not share these feelings with your kids. If you continue to let them know your deep disapproval for their father, you can do irreparable damage to your child and your relationship with him.

Today I ask myself if I give my child signals about how much I dislike his/her father. I will be careful not to hurt my child. When I am angry with my husband, I will not express it to the children; rather, I will call a trusted friend or family member and VENT! That way, I can get my needs met, and still meet the needs of my children.

Day 9   The Destructive Power of Negative Self Talk

Negative self-messages erode self-esteem. Long after our husbands are out of our lives, the critical and abusive words they said to us linger in our minds. We give them power when we begin to believe them and doubt ourselves.

Women going through divorce, particularly those whose husbands left the marriage, may experience lots of negative self-talk. Think about some of your negative self-messages. Writing them down helps. Saying them out loud helps. We debunk the power of the messages when we face them and deal with them.

Some of these self-messages are:

- If I had been younger, prettier, thinner, funny, smarter, he wouldn't have left me.

- He changed for her, why can't he change for me?

- I will never feel better.

- He will do better alone than I will.

- He drank, fooled around, hit me, gambled, took drugs, cheated, because I wasn't good enough.

- He had a tough childhood. I should have made more allowances.

- I got the worst years, she will get the best.

- I don't know anything about money, taxes, mortgages, car repairs— that is his domain.

- Divorce means failure.

- He is doing just fine without me.

- No one will ever want me.

- I can't make it on my own.

As you go through the list, consider how you would feel if a friend was saying those things about herself. How would you respond to *her* negative self-messages? What positive things would you say to debunk her negative self-talk? Use those same arguments to debunk your own list. It will take some time to do this. Sometimes, we find that the source of one or more of the negative self-messages is not from our marriage but from prior childhood experiences. It can be helpful to talk these over with a counselor or therapist.

Today I will make a list of all my negative self-messages. Then I will go through them one by one and write positive self-messages next to each. I will say them out loud to a friend, a therapist, or to myself. I will learn to believe the positive and stop the negative from continuing to haunt me. I will learn to believe in myself.

From Ex-Wife to Exceptional Life

Kenny Rodgers sings "Know when to hold them, know when to fold them," a song about the game of poker. In some ways, life offers us the same options. Knowing when to hold onto her marriage and when to walk away from it is probably one of the most difficult decisions a woman will make in her lifetime. Sometimes, even when women divorce, they still hold onto their ex-spouse. The reasons women hold on are varied: some hold on out of fear, some out of hope, some out of resentment, some because they don't know how to walk away.

Whatever the reason, staying emotionally connected to a spouse through the divorce and after it can be damaging to you. It can diminish the possibility for personal growth and new relationships. It can result in your feeling rejected over and over. It can lead to bitterness that erodes all parts of your life and all other relationships.

Many women say, "I wouldn't want that creep back." They think that because they are angry, they are moving on. However, when you are constantly taking him back to court, or thinking about what he is doing or who he is with, then you haven't moved on. You are still sitting in the rubble of your ended marriage. The following questions will help you sort out how attached you still are:

- Do you think about him every day?
- Do you spend a good deal of time reminiscing?
- Do you think a lot about what he is doing now?
- Do you imagine how your future could be with him?
- Do you ask friends about him?
- Do you pump your children for information?
- Does your stomach "flip flop" when you hear his name or see him?
- Do you feel revengeful toward him?
- Do you have conversations with him in your head?
- Do you drive past his house, call him, follow him?

Each attachment is a thread that connects you to your past. Those threads weave a web that keep you stuck. You will move on when those emotional threads are broken. Otherwise, you can stay floundering and stuck for a long time. The result will be no growth… and without growth, life withers and eventually dies.

Today I will take a hard look at each of the questions and explore my feelings and thoughts. If there are areas where I am still holding on, then I will be conscious of working on those areas. I will be gentle and supportive of myself. I will remember that divorce is a process, and it doesn't so much matter where I am, as long as I continue to move along.

Often, when dealing with divorce loss, women are able to relate it to other losses in their life.

Close your eyes and think about the greatest loss or difficulty you have experienced thus far in your life and how you grew from it. Maybe you want to write it down or maybe you just want to sit with your thoughts and feelings. Allow yourself to see how powerful you are, how you survived that difficult time, and how you became a stronger, wiser person because of the experience.

While you may not be able to see how you will grow from divorce, crisis always offers opportunity for change. Think about the other difficult things you have survived. Imagine how you want to feel when this ordeal is over. Allow yourself to imagine how it will make you a stronger individual.

Today I will think about how I will grow from this time. I will allow myself to imagine the person I am becoming. I will tap into the excitement and empowerment I want to feel. I will laugh with the joy of knowing such a strong, wonderful woman!

Joel Goodman of the Humor Project in Saratoga Springs, New York says, "Humor is what lubricates life." Humor can help you deal with stressors in your life. Humor cannot erase the situation, but it can take the sting out of many things, thus reducing their negative impact. In order for humor to be curative in your life, you need to find your own laugh button. Remember, divorce is one part of your life; don't make it your whole life!

Jennie remarked recently how surprised she was that she could still feel joy taking a walk on a beautiful autumn morning, even though she felt devastated by her divorce. Nurture those feelings of joy, laughter, and wonder. Laughter is not just a luxury; it is a vital piece in the healing process. It is especially important during times of stress. It provides our body, heart, and mind with a welcome and necessary reprieve.

Creating humor from a stressful situation gives you the opportunity to experience a shift in perspective. No one is suggesting that you become a stand-up comic. In fact, no one else has to think it is funny. What is important is that you create a scenario or image that feels funny to you. If putting donkey ears and a big mustache on photos of your estranged makes you feel better, then go ahead and do it! (Of course, no one has to see it).

Tips for bringing humor into your life:
- Read the funnies, watch a television comedy, rent a funny movie.
- Keep a humor journal.
- Tell a joke.
- Laugh at yourself.
- Look for the funny side.
- Exaggerate.
- Try humor instead of anger.
- Use humor to handle anxiety.
- Make up a comedy routine.
- Hang out with happy people.
- Smile.

Bill Cosby said, "If you can laugh at it, you can survive it."

Today I will make a conscious effort to bring laughter back into my life by trying one of the above suggestions or one of my own. I will do this just for the fun of it!

...You've Got Everything!

When you are going through a divorce, this is especially important. Imagine yourself going into battle and not having gone to boot camp. You would be ill equipped to deal with the rigors of war. Divorce is a kind of war – there is acrimony, hostility and confrontation.

During divorce, we eat junk food (if anything at all), hardly sleep, and sometimes abuse alcohol or sedatives. Even if we exercised before this crisis, often we are too tired to do so now.

To avoid illness and other complications in your life, taking care of your health is a priority. Remember you are going to make decisions now that are going to affect you for the rest of your life. You will have to make difficult legal and financial choices, often about things you may feel ill-equipped to handle. So, you will need to concentrate and stay focused throughout the process. Taking care of your health can result in making better, more informed decisions. Consequently you will experience less regret later on. (Yes, there is a life after divorce, I promise!)

Today I will think about ways I can take better care of myself. It makes sense that I need to be in the best shape I can be in, not only in this difficult time, but always. It is part of having a good life and being good to myself.

Thanksgiving marks the official beginning of the holiday season. Although usually less fraught with anxiety than Christmas, if it is the first "big holiday" since your estrangement from your spouse, you may be dreading the day. It also may be your first holiday without your children.

Going through a divorce can give you the perfect "excuse" to break with tradition and forge your own way of celebrating. Spending the holiday home by yourself watching videos and eating Chinese take-out (yes, they are open on Thanksgiving) may be just what you need to do! Evelyn prepared a complete Thanksgiving dinner for herself of her favorite foods. She set the table with linen and candles and put on music she liked. Then she enjoyed the day celebrating by herself. Divorce gives you the opportunity to listen to what you want and what works for you. It can be a time of loss of traditions, but it also can signal liberation from those traditions, rituals, and obligations that no longer have meaning for you.

If you decide to spend the holiday alone, some people may feel uncomfortable with your decision. Stand your ground. Know what is right for you. If you need to spend the day cleaning out the basement or making cookies, then do it! Pay attention to your own needs. If you have your children for the holiday, you may want to discuss alternate plans with them. Some families go to the movies on Thanksgiving Day, eschewing the big turkey for a big bag of popcorn. You can make new choices to fit your life. Above all remember, every holiday is only twenty four hours. You can get through twenty four hours. Next year won't carry the same weight as this year. You will be surprised when you look back on how far you have really come. You will be able to affirm that the journey was tough, but worth it!

One final word on Thanksgiving—whatever you decide to do, set aside a few minutes to express and feel your gratitude. You can do this in prayer, with your children, in a letter to yourself, or in volunteering. There are good things in your life. When you neglect to honor them, you give divorce too much power. Divorce is not your whole life, but rather something that happens in your life!

Today Thanksgiving will be as I want it to be this year. I can forge ahead and make new traditions, limited only by my imagination. I can even decide to forego the holiday completely if I choose. Whatever plans I make, I will take a few minutes to express my gratitude for all that is good and healthy and meaningful in my life.

...Are the Gifts of the Future

So, what have you learned so far?

Regardless of where you are in the divorce process, it is never too early to take stock and figure out what lessons you have learned thus far. I know at this point you might have the urge to say something like, "I will never get married again, that's what I have learned!" Look a little further into yourself and the process. True, there are lessons gleaned from the external experience about finances, relationships, and the legal system. But the real lessons, the ones that will make the most difference in your life and in the choices you make from here on, are the lessons that you have learned about yourself. Can you begin to figure out what you have learned? Here is a list of questions you can ask yourself.

- What was it like to be married to me?
- What things would I do differently if I could "do it over?"
- What things would I do again?
- Am I a good and fair fighter?
- Do I work toward resolution or do I try to win?
- Can I agree to disagree or do I always need to be right?
- In what ways did I over-function?
- In what ways could I have participated more?
- Was I fun to be with?
- Was I attentive?
- Did I expect my partner to read my mind?
- Was I tolerant?
- Did I make problems out of our differences?
- Did I make my partner responsible for my self-worth?
- Did I behave in a way that was lovable?
- Was I a person who could be trusted?
- Was I a person who kept my promises?

The goal is not self-blame, but self-exploration. Use your experience, pain, disappointment, and sadness to fuel your quest for understanding and insight. That will foster self-growth. The suffering you are experiencing now is not futile when you find the gifts that are hidden underneath.

Today as I ponder these questions, and so many more, my intent will be to gather knowledge rather than judge and criticize. I will acknowledge that these insights are not easy ones, but as I acquire more insight about who I am in the world and in my relationships, I come closer to being the person I want to be.

Moving Day symbolizes the first real change in the status of the couple. Usually, it is fraught with tension for all involved. There are the practical questions: what is he taking, who is helping with the move, where is he going, should I be there, should the kids be there? How will I feel after he leaves?

In dealing with the actual move itself, you and your spouse should decide in advance what furniture is staying and what is going. Divide the household furnishings when the children aren't around. Children's rooms should remain intact and not be split. It is too confusing and disruptive for the child. Later, children may choose to bring things from one house to another, but for now their lives are changed enough without having to deal with rearranging their bedrooms.

One of the complaints frequently voiced by women is when men move out a little at a time. It just prolongs the hurt. If there are reasons that all his possessions cannot be moved out at one time, then store the remainder in the basement or the garage. This allows the family to readjust and rearrange the furniture, *one time*. If the move continues for weeks, it disrupts everyone over and over. This only adds to feelings of instability and chaos. Furthermore, leaving belongings, can be misread by children as a chance for reconciliation.

On moving day, children should not be in the house. Years later, many remember moving day as the most painful event in their parent's divorce. For children, the divorce actually takes place the day the parents physically separate. All of the children's adjustments to the divorce begin at this point. Tell your children a day or two before the move, so they won't worry about it for months.

On the actual moving day, make arrangements for them to be absent from the house. After the move, arrange your furniture to fill in the existing gaps, so the loss doesn't "hit" the children when they walk in. Don't worry how it looks, just fill it in. In days to come, your children can be part of rearranging the rooms in a more orderly and permanent fashion. Remove whatever photos you have of your spouse from the common living areas. Put them in your children's rooms. This signifies an end to your relationship with him, but honors their relationship with him. It sets the tone for how the single parent family will evolve. As for your own needs, when the move is complete, add personal touches and feminize your space. Start with small things immediately. This will help create an environment that reflects your personality and tastes. It will help recreate a home.

Today I acknowledge that Moving Day can be traumatic for all involved. I will prepare to meet the needs of my children and myself. I will remember that as difficult as this feels, I will get through it and ultimately I will have a sense of independence, confidence and pride.

One of the most important adjustments children have to make is living in two homes. Even if a child visits one parent for a few hours a week, the child should feel at home there. This helps foster connection with the non-custodial parent and helps the child to recognize that the non-custodial parent didn't "divorce " him/her. Issues of abandonment and rejection are paramount for children of all ages, although the young ones can't express it and the older ones won't. Creating a sense of belonging in both homes assists the child in making a healthy transition. Many children actually enjoy having two homes because they get special attention, and often two birthday parties and two sets of Christmas or Chanukah gifts.

Here are some ways to help children adjust:
- The child should have her own room. If this isn't possible, she should have her own space in a room – her own dresser drawer, a toy bin, some shelves.
- He should be allowed to keep his things in that space and arrange them as he wants to.
- Let the child help decorate the space. By picking out her own sheets or a poster to hang on the wall, she personalizes the space.
- She should have clothes in both spaces.
- He should be allowed to carry his things back and forth between two houses. This helps with the transition.
- Parents should cooperate in returning clothes and toys.
- Pick up and drop off should always be cordial, on time and upbeat. Save your hostility for court.
- Children should go with the non-custodial parent even when sick. This reinforces both parents' ability to care for the child. It helps the child feel he is safe with both parents and part of a household. When we only send children when they are healthy, the message is that one parent is really the "reliable one." It undermines the other parent and creates a Disneyland Dad.
- Rules and consequences should exist in both homes. Many non-custodial parents are afraid they will "ruin" visitation if they discipline the child. Parenting involves both discipline and respect. If you don't want to feel like an outsider, don't act like one.
- If possible, rules in both homes should be similar. If they aren't, keeping them consistent within each house minimizes problems. Children learn at a very early age that there are different rules in different places – school, camp, church, grandma's house. They can handle another difference, as long as the rules are reliable and consistent in each environment.
- The child should be allowed to call the other parent, but should not be made to do so.

Today I will think about ways to make the transition easier for my child. I will consider showing this page to my child's father as a way to open a dialogue on how to make this happen. I will put aside all my hurt and angry feelings about the marriage and I will deal with him as my child's father, knowing that when my child has a good relationship with both of us, he/she will thrive.

There are friends we share a history with, friends we share common interests with, friends we share space with, and friends we call kindred spirits.

The friends we share history with – These are people we feel like we have known forever. Often they are friends from elementary school or high school; they provide a link to our past and serve as a yardstick to measure our development and growth. They are the ones "who knew us when." Sometimes we find we have grown apart and that our present lives have gone on very divergent paths. These friends, in some ways, are like family. We may not have much in common with them and sometimes we may not even like them. But they offer shared memories of our past and are representative of the continuum of our life.

The friends we share common interests with – These friends offer us an affirmation of our strengths and talents. Whether this friend is the one you love to shop with, or the one you work out with, it is the similarity of goal that connects you. These friends validate and support our emerging self. To a person experiencing divorce, others experiencing divorce provide this grounding and affirmation. It is one of the reasons that divorce groups are so valuable and successful.

The friends we share space with – These are the friends with whom we share our day-to-day lives. They are our neighbors, roommates, co-workers, and all others we meet and connect with in our daily routine. They provide a sense of community and belonging.

Our kindred spirit friends – These are friends of our heart, our intimates, our "families of choice." They may start out as friends of history, interest, or space, but the relationship takes off and grows beyond those parameters. These are friends that can last a lifetime.

When our marital status changes, so do our interests, sometimes our space, and sometimes even that feeling of kindred spirit. Our friendships may change. Some friendships may not survive and others will grow and flourish. Divorce will provide you new opportunities if you stay open to the challenge. These opportunities will allow you to grow and flourish. If you focus on what is lost, you will miss what can be found.

Today I will celebrate the people in my life, both past and present and know that from every relationship I have learned something about life, myself, and relationships. My relationships are important for my personal growth.

Even if you are the one who chose to end the marriage, you weren't looking forward to divorce. No one wants to get divorced. We don't walk down the aisle thinking, "Aw, what the hell, if this doesn't work, I can always get a divorce." You probably thought more along the lines of, "I don't care how many people I know who got divorced. This is not going to happen to us." Yet here you are. It is awful and it hurts more than you could have ever imagined.

Divorce is a process, with many issues, facets, twists, and turns. Your emotional well being, along with your financial and legal assets, will all be called into play. Where you live, how you live, how you define yourself, and what you want from life are all going to be examined, evaluated, and possibly changed. As the process unfolds, the most important thing you can do is learn to pace yourself. You will learn many new things about life, finances, the legal system, your husband, and mostly yourself.

Right now, you are focused on the fear and the loss. But that will change. In one year you will feel better than you do now. In fact, you may feel better than you have ever felt in your life! But, for today all you need to do is to let yourself feel whatever you are feeling and to know this: feelings change, like the wind. It is critical to learn that just because you feel something today doesn't mean you will feel it tomorrow. Learning that and accepting it will help you not act on impulse. It will diminish the possibility of your making any foolish mistakes. Everything in this process can wait one more day. This includes acting on what you feel. So, learn to sit with your feelings and observe yourself. Feeling something won't get you into trouble. Acting on it will!

You will laugh and cry along your one-year journey. You will meet many new people. Some you will like, some you won't. Some of these people may stay in your life for a long, long time. Others will simply pass through your life. As the process evolves, you will encounter new thoughts and new ideas. You will grow. You will find strength, and you will survive!

Today *I know I have a long road in front of me. I will try to focus on pacing myself and having patience. These two attributes will serve me in all my affairs. With patience and pacing, I can pay attention to all that is unfolding and learn everything I need. I will emerge stronger and more confident for having gone through the experience. In one year, I will revel in the joy that comes from surviving a difficult challenge. For the rest of my life, I will be able to face every new challenge with confidence, knowledge and experience. I will learn I can survive anything!*

As girls, we might have received messages that "good girls" were not supposed to get angry. It was seen as inappropriate or unacceptable. We may not have been allowed to show any feelings, especially anger. In some homes there was so much anger and violence that everyone "walked on eggshells." We may have grown up fearing anger. Early childhood messages, either implicit or explicit, tend to stay with us throughout our life and into our adult relationships.

Explore your messages and lessons about anger. An example might be, "Girls were expected to be quiet and compliant." Then ask yourself, "How was anger expressed in my family?" Do you equate anger with aggression or withdrawal? For some children, anger was experienced as a withholding of love, or anger may have been expressed as violence. Can you be angry and feel love at the same time? This self-exploration may give you insight into how you parent your own children and help you see patterns of similarity between you and your parents. Insight is not about judgment; rather it is about how one learns and, therefore, how one grows. You can't fix something unless you know what is wrong with it.

Anger is like vomiting (sorry for getting gross here!) We hate the feeling, but when we get it out, we feel so much better. Conversely, if we do not "let it go," we continue to feel sick. Where do you feel the anger in your body? Many women feel it in their "gut" or in their head. Imagine what the inside of your gut or head will look like in twenty years if you continue to hold on to your anger. Take a deep breath, close your eyes and imagine the inside of your body when it is free of anger.

There are four major reasons to work through divorce anger:

- If we hold onto our anger, it can make us sick, both physically and emotionally. Depression is often anger turned against the self.

- If we hold onto our anger until we explode, we can hurt others and damage our relationships.

- If we continue to hold onto our anger, we become stagnant, unable to grow beyond this point in our development.

- If we continue to hold onto our anger, eventually family and friends will distance from us.

Today I will begin to consider the role anger plays in my life, both now and as a child. I will do this without judgment. I will not turn away from my anger. It is a part of me. I must know it to know myself. I must accept it to accept me.

Some women who have been hurt in the process of a deteriorating marriage fantasize about revenge. When we experience pain, it is not unusual to want to lash out. But hurting the other person doesn't make our pain easier to manage. If you broke your leg, seeing another person with a broken leg would not help you ease your pain. We know that is true, and it sounds silly when we say it, but when it comes to matters of the heart, our intellect goes right out the window.

Revenge is often about wanting to ease our pain, but it is also about *wanting to be understood*. Frequently, women lament that "he doesn't understand what he did to me and how much this hurts." They fantasize that if he could feel their pain, then he would be punished and feel remorse. Somehow his feeling pain would alleviate their own pain.

Still another aspect of revenge involves our need to feel validated. If the other person has the same painful experience and reaction, then we will feel that we are not overreacting. Needing that affirmation from our ex is still a form of connection. When we seek someone's approval, we still give his opinion great status and value. Furthermore, when we continue to ask for validation from those who cannot give it, we run the risk of inflicting more pain on ourselves through repeated rejection and lack of empathy for our feelings.

If you stay in "revenge mode," your thoughts will be filled with anger, resentment and meanness. Living your life filled with bitterness only makes you bitter. You may feel as if you "gave him the best years of your life." When you continue to have thoughts of revenge you stay connected to him. And in doing that, you are just giving him more of your time. If you do that long enough, you will find you gave him ALL of your life. He will be getting on with his life and you will be stuck in a bitter, angry place. Is that who you want to be? Is that how you want to live your life?

Today while I am aware of my hurt, my anger, and my pain, I will make a conscious decision to work toward freeing myself from revenge. Thoughts of revenge keep me stuck, prevent growth and eventually destroy happiness. I will take all of the energy it takes to think mean thoughts and redirect it to think of ways to make myself a more content person. He is not worth my effort. I am worth my effort!

An exit affair is the extra-marital relationship that is seen as the catalyst for breaking up the marriage. However, it is not the exit affair that breaks up the marriage. The exit affair occurs in response to the relationship's demise. It is often what provides the motivation to break the status quo and move on to seek a divorce.

Many couples stay in marriages where the relationship is almost non-existent. They merely function, day-to-day, walking through their lives without much passion or enthusiasm. When one of the couple (let's say the husband) becomes involved in an exit affair, complacency is no longer possible. The husband is often being pressured by his girlfriend to leave the marriage. When the wife finds out, she often demands that a change must take place as well. Some wives file for divorce upon learning of the affair. When this happens, the woman makes the choice to change the situation.

Exit affairs happen for many reasons. As I said, often both members of the couple are already very unhappy, but no one has done anything about it. Exit affairs also serve to provide at least one spouse with a "guarantee" that they will not be alone. (This is a false guarantee. Exit affairs carry much baggage and often do not survive beyond the divorce).

Exit affairs serve as an anesthetic to the pain for one partner. If your husband had an exit affair, it is critical to recognize that the affair did not end the marriage; it just served as a catalyst to dissolution. Do not focus all of your energy on the affair. If you focus all your pain on "the other woman," you let our spouse off the hook. Even if she seduced him, your husband is a big boy. He was the one who broke the vows and he is responsible for his own behavior. No matter how unhappy he was, an affair is not the answer. And if you focus all your attention on what he did, you deny yourself the lessons that are inherent in the process of divorcing. It would be a shame to go through all this pain without learning anything. Most importantly, without learning the lessons inherent in the demise of this marriage, chances are you will go out and repeat the same mistakes again.

Today I acknowledge that an exit affair is a symptom of a marriage in deep trouble. I will try and keep my focus on what I need to learn about relationships and myself. This may be hard, but if I keep my energy focused on myself, I can grow and heal and be healthier in the future. If I focus my attention on what "he did to me," I will feel like a victim and the only things I will learn are hurt, bitterness and mistrust.

Family, friends, therapists, co-workers, and your support group will offer you an opinion on your life, whether you want it or not. When trying to make a big decision, how do you know what the right decision is? Getting advice and perspective from others is helpful, as is taking our time to mull over our dilemma. However, deep down inside of us, in our core, we know the answer to all our questions. But we don't always trust ourselves. Other people's opinions get in the way and we begin to waffle.

Growing up means trusting oneself. After you gather all the information and think about all facets of your choices, it is time to go into yourself and ask, "What is the healthiest thing for me to do?" Notice the question doesn't include what is "right" or "nice" or "approved" or even "wanted." Only "What is healthy?" When you ask yourself what is the healthiest thing to do, your answer usually comes to you fairly quickly. You may not like the answer, because it is not what you want or think you need, so you may try to dismiss it. You may try all kinds of distractions to avoid looking at the healthy thing. Rationalization, denial, and minimalization all can help you stay away from the healthy answer. But you will keep coming back to the same resolution, if indeed it is the healthy one. When it comes to your health, emotional or physical, it is important to pay close attention to the answer.

When we make the healthy choice, then all conflicting voices simply fade away and we see our path clearly. Whatever obstructions – perceived or real – that existed are suddenly in perspective. Staying focused on our health gives us fortitude and direction. When we begin to question or waver, we need to bring our attention back to our original request. The answer will be the same. Our health requirements do not change daily, even though our mood, our wants, and our desires might.

You know the answer to all the hard questions. The goal is to trust yourself. Trust that whatever fear you have is manageable. Know that conquering your fear will empower you to move ahead and make any other necessary changes in your life. Trust that you know yourself better than anyone else and move ahead. Don't be held back from your bliss.

Today when a hard decision presents itself, I will ask myself, "What is the healthiest thing for me to do?" Then, as scary as it may feel, I will trust myself and move toward what I know is healthy for me. Ultimately, if I act with this mindfulness, then no decision will ever be the wrong one.

It's a misconception that divorce doesn't affect older adult children. One of the things we forget is while our children may be adults (and even may have experienced divorce themselves) they are still our children. In going through divorce, many women "lean" on their children, making them into confidantes and sometimes, surrogate spouses. Children, even adult children, are uncomfortable with details of their parents' personal life. Confiding to a child about a parent's indiscretions puts the child in a no-win situation. Many of the adult children I have spoken with say that they are shocked and angry by their parents' behavior. But as the child, they continue to want the relationship. Giving adult children inappropriate information puts them in a quandary – how to have a relationship with a parent who behaved so terribly in marriage without feeling disloyal to the other parent? Children are entitled to have a relationship with their parents which is not based on the parents' performance in the marriage.

Older children are also affected in practical ways. Dividing visiting time between the two parents, possibly even grandparents, is a huge problem. The pressure of being "fair and equal" becomes enormous. As parents age, children often find themselves in the role of caregiver. If parents are divorced, this role can fall to them twice. Juggling their own lives and their children's lives is difficult when a parent or both parents become ill. Some adult children feel resentful, especially when a marriage has been bad for a long time. They may wish that the divorce had taken place earlier, so as to have been spared the fighting and bickering. Many adult children feel the divorce will only be a liability to them now at this stage of their lives.

Then there is the issue of remarriage. Many adult children who have adjusted to one or both parents having a new significant other, wince at the idea of their parents remarrying at this stage of life. Issues of inheritance and jealousy with regard to step-siblings and their grandchildren are difficult issues for adult children. The best way to help our adult children is to pay attention to our conduct during the divorce and remember to be aware of their issues and feelings.

Today I will think about how much I tell my children about my husband and my divorce. Am I crossing boundaries? Am I discussing marital issues that will hurt my children? Am I relying too heavily on them for support? I will consider what other support systems I have in my life and be more conscious of my children's needs and feelings.

The single most dangerous element in living with an abusive man is your denial of the problem. More women are killed by their domestic partners than by the hands of strangers. If your spouse has shown any of the signs or symptoms of being abusive, it is extremely important that you get help. Depending upon the situation, help comes in all forms from seeking counseling to calling the police. The way to find out what intervention is most appropriate for your situation is to call the women's shelters in your area. If you do not have a shelter in your area, chances are the closest big city will have one. All of the shelters have toll-free lines, so it doesn't matter which one you call. All calls are kept anonymous for your safety. The caseworker at the shelter can assist you in figuring out what you need to do to be safe. Some women feel embarrassed to call the shelters; they believe they should be able to handle it themselves, or their problem is not as bad as other women's. They may believe that because they are middle class or professional women, the shelter is not for them. This kind of thinking is a form of minimization, which adds to denial. It can be lethal. The shelter is for any woman who thinks she may be abused. No one is turned away.

Until you can access help from the outside, there are some things you can do in the house to make yourself safer:

- Keep an extra set of car keys hidden somewhere that your husband doesn't know about. Abusers often trap their wives by preventing their leaving.
- Entrust one friend with your story who will let you come to them in an emergency. This should preferably be a person your husband doesn't know.
- If you have a cell phone, keep it with you whenever he is around.
- If you can, sleep in separate rooms and keep the door locked.
- Some abusers have patterns; if you suspect your husband will be violent, leave the house.
- Keep extra clothes for your kids at a neighbor's.
- Always keep a full tank of gas.
- If there are firearms, try to get them out of the house; or at the very least, keep the ammunition in a separate place.
- Never argue with your husband when he is under the influence of alcohol or drugs.
- Keep some money in a place where your husband can't find it.
- Have a get-away plan in place.

Today *even if I think this doesn't pertain to me, I will consider doing some things to make myself safe, even if it feels like a silly over-reaction. I would rather be safe than sorry. I owe that to my children, my family and friends. Most of all, I owe it to myself. Maybe one day I will look back and laugh at being overly cautious, but maybe one day I will look back with gratitude that I was prepared.*

"What will you miss the most about your husband?"
"What will you miss the most about your marriage?"

Consider these two questions separately. It will help you clarify the many different losses. Defining the losses and breaking them down helps put language to our pain. In defining it, we have the opportunity to look at our situation in terms of the specific rather than the global.

This "honing down" makes the elements of pain more manageable. By breaking down any problem into manageable pieces, it becomes less overwhelming. Breaking down our feelings gives us perspective and clarity and keeps us from feeling overwhelmed.

As you reflect on these two questions, you may be surprised to learn that the answers to the two are very different. Many women, especially those who chose to leave their marriage, finally have the opportunity to resolve their confusion. That is, if I chose to leave, why do I feel so badly? This exercise can help you get in touch with your conflicted feelings and identify more precisely what your losses are. Then you can begin to grieve.

Some of the more obvious losses are loss of a spouse, financial security, a full time co-parent, in-law relationships, and the family home, career changes, and marital status. Other losses women have mentioned include issues regarding family pets, vacations, sleeping alone, the garden, traditions, someone to take care of you if you are sick, retirement, companionship, sex, friends, etc. The list is infinite. Although we all experience pain and loss with divorce, we all have different losses, as varied and diverse as the marriages themselves.

Today I will work on defining my losses. I will look at what losses involve my spouse and what losses involve my marriage. That will help me be clear about what I have lost. It will help me grieve and heal with insight and clarity.

According to Dr. Herbert Benson, M.D., chronic insomnia is a national epidemic, with more than 30 million Americans affected. Our stressful, fast-paced lives, with continuing pressures from work, family, friends add to our wakefulness at night. We use these precious sleep hours to obsess about what we didn't handle during our waking hours.

During divorce, it is very common to have difficulty sleeping. If you are the person who initiated the divorce, you have probably spent many sleepless nights agonizing about your decision. If you were the "recipient" of the news, then most likely your sleep problems began that very day.

Sleep is critical to our emotional, physical, psychological, and intellectual functioning.

- **Emotionally:** We are more sensitive and impulsive when we are sleep deprived. Continued sleep deprivation can lead to signs of depression. We are less able to handle negative emotions, which can contribute to stress-related symptoms such as headaches, gastrointestinal problems, and anxiety.

- **Physically:** Sleep strengthens the functioning of our auto-immune system, making us less prone to illness from the common cold to even cancer. This may explain why we sleep more when we are ill.

- **Psychologically:** Our sense of well being is affected by lack of sleep. We feel empowered and more in control when we are rested.

- **Intellectual Functioning:** We feel less able to concentrate and slower at figuring things out. We are more forgetful, make more errors, and are more easily distracted. When we are sleep deprived, we do not pay attention to things as we should, hence we have more accidents.

As you look at the above list and think about the things you need to do as you tend to your divorce, you can see that with extended periods of sleep deprivation, you are going to suffer. This is a time in your life when you are called on to make decisions that will affect you for the rest of your life. In order to make the best decisions and have no regrets, pay attention to your sleep!

Today in order to be the best I can be for my children, family, friends, and co-workers – and especially to me – I have to take care of myself. This starts with something as simple as making sure I get enough sleep.

1. **Money, gifts, sweets and indulging don't "make up" for anything.** Your child is going to have TWO Christmases. No need to feel guilty. Most kids say the dual holidays are the best thing about being a divorced kid.

2. **If possible, make your plans with your ex-spouse ahead of time and *stick to them*.** Let the kids know where they will be and when. It helps them feel in control. Let them make only age appropriate decisions. A good rule of thumb: if it is not a decision you would let your children make while you were married, then don't let them make it now. Let your kids be kids.

3. **Be flexible.** No, this is not a contradiction of #2. It means that S—T happens. So if your ex is two hours late because of an ice storm or because cousin Joey showed up late, try to let it go.

4. **Keep your anger, resentment, annoyance, disgust about your ex, his sports car, his girlfriend, his family, to yourself.** Remember, your kids are part of both of you and when you slam him, your child feels slammed as well.

5. **Do not make your children responsible for your happiness.** "Go have a good time with Dad in Jamaica, while I sit here miserable and all alone," only breeds resentment and guilt in your child.

6. **Don't compete.** If he can afford more than you – fine. Rather than resenting his/her father, appreciate that your child can experience things you can't buy him. Don't overspend to keep up. *Make* memories by doing fun things together – bake cookies, read a Christmas story, build a snowman. Money does not buy love.

7. **The new girlfriend can not and will not take your place.** Children are unbelievably loyal. They can love many people, but the title and honor of parent is yours and will be only yours, forever. Relax. Deal with your jealousy without making your kid responsible for your feeling threatened. This is simply not the job of the child.

8. **Divorce is the severing of the adult relationship and should not be the termination of the parent-child relationship, no matter how much you really can't stand him/her.** If your child is not in harm's way, the relationship needs to continue. This is the CHILD's right. If you really feel the child is in danger, then get a lawyer, prove it and have supervised visitation. Never keep a child from being with a parent based on your own feelings!

9. **Lastly, remember that you are the adult.** Suck up your anger toward your ex and make the holidays wonderful for your kids.

Today I know my children have their own issues to deal with as they go through this first year of holidays without their parents being together. I will do what I can to make it easier for them, even if it means biting my tongue at times. When I look back on this time, I will be proud of myself for behaving in a healthy way. By my behaving in a positive way, my children will have fond memories and not feelings of resentment.

At the end of each hectic day, as our head hits the pillow, we often review the day's events and think about the tasks, errands, and obligations we have to do tomorrow. When we are experiencing a divorce, much of our thoughts are devoted to managing all the aspects of the process as well as all the new adjustments with which we must deal. With all that "stuff" whirling around in our brain, no wonder our sleep is often restless and disturbed.

Make the last thing you think about before you fall asleep something nice that happened to you during the day. This helps clear and relax the mind, helps to promote better sleep, and, most importantly, helps you see that there is always something for which to be grateful. If you are having difficulty finding something, then you aren't looking hard enough. The smallest experience, a beautiful sunrise or a baby's laughter, can fill us with joy if we just open ourselves up to the experience. This exercise assists in widening perspective and encouraging optimism. You may find this difficult at first. We become so used to thinking about the negative, we don't even see the positive. Keep trying. Like any change we make, it may seem uncomfortable at first. You may not see the benefit. But what is the benefit of ruminating over all the negative things, or things you have to do? It will only increase your anxiety and contribute to sleeping poorly.

You have choices about how to live your life. Being aware and choosing thoughtfully can empower and improve your life. You can choose to bring joy into your life everyday, just by allowing yourself to appreciate the joy that is already there!

Today I will look forward to getting into my bed. I will close my eyes and think of all the wondrous things that happened today. I will pick one and focus on it, allowing myself to re-experience the joy. I will allow my breathing to slow and deepen as I focus on that wonderful experience I had today. I will drift off into a calm, relaxed sleep and awaken refreshed and eager to face another day!

Bringing women together creates a family of choice, a place where you can be comforted without fear of criticism. It is a place to exchange ideas and advice regarding issues such as legal, financial, visitation, co-parenting, dating and housing. It is a place where women can laugh and cry together. It is a safe place where shattered self-esteem can be healed and growth can take place.

Sometimes potential group members are worried they will not have enough of the facilitator's time. Each member becomes a facilitator, a guide for the others, and in this mutual support they find their own strength and are empowered. On a practical side, facilitator-run groups provide women with affordable counseling, quality support and education. While the groups are not therapy groups per se, they are therapeutic. Facilitator-run groups make affordable, quality care a reality.

There are many self-help groups without therapists leading them that are successful and healing. Certainly, the twelve-step model proves this is possible. However, my experience has led me to have concerns about self-run divorce groups, or even groups run by non-professionals. Often the trauma of divorce unmasks an earlier trauma. It is imperative that there be a trained person present to cope with this kind of phenomenon. Also, it is not unusual to become depressed during a divorce. A trained facilitator is able to identify when grief becomes depression and when a participant needs further care, whether it be individual therapy or medication.

Coed groups are trouble. Even if the strictest rules against dating are set, people frequently date other group members. You are vulnerable and wounded when a marriage splits up and a soft, gentle, supportive listener can feel wonderful. It is not unusual to "fall in love" with someone who treats you with dignity, value, and respect. It is easy to mistake loving the person for loving the behavior. I have seen too many romances that began in coed groups end disastrously. The focus of a support group should be just that –SUPPORT! There is time later for dating.

Today even though I have friends and family who are very caring, I will consider a divorce support group. Being with other women who are going through this difficult transition can give me a sense of camaraderie and hope. Perhaps I can learn something from someone else and maybe they will learn something from me.

Today, take time to think about what has happened in your life over the last months since you became involved in the divorce process. The reason for doing this is not to evaluate your progress but to acknowledge your strength and fortitude. This is hard because we tend to be our worst critics!

In some ways the process may be more difficult than you expected and in some ways it may be easier. Just noticing that can help you realize how far you have come. Think about the questions below as you take stock of your life today:

- When I look back to the beginning of this process, who I was then and how am I different now?

- What things did I learn about myself that surprised me?

- What things did I learn about the process that surprised me?

- What are my strengths as I go through this process?

- Where do I need to pay more attention?

- Am I utilizing my support system effectively?

- How can I improve on my self-care?

These are some questions that can help you reflect on your growth. Add your own questions to the above list. Do this exercise without self-blame, criticism, or negativity. The focus of this is to relax, and to take a day to honor your inner strength and resolve. Doing so in a conscious manner reinforces your growth and your positive sense of self.

In a journal or a letter to yourself, record your observations and date them. You will come back to them and add to them during this process. The Chinese symbol for crisis is also the one for opportunity and this makes sense. It is in crisis where the opportunity for change, growth, and self-awareness takes place. While divorce is a crisis, it is also an opportunity to learn about yourself and to develop and hone new skills. Divorce can be a life-affirming transition filled with hope, optimism, and joy for the future. This can only happen when you take the time to explore your inner world and become truly familiar with who you are and what makes you happy. The day of reflection offers you the opportunity to formally continue your inward journey.

Today *I will reflect on my growth and the changes I have endured. I will applaud my resolve and my tenacity. I will honor the way I have taken care of things. I will not compare myself to anyone else. This is my journey and I will do it my way and I will rejoice in who I am and the woman I am becoming.*

Month Four

Nothing toys with our emotions like the break up of a relationship. Elizabeth Kubler-Ross describes the six stages of grief as:

- Shock
- Denial
- Bargaining
- Anger
- Sadness
- Acceptance

When one is going through divorce, add one more category: **FEAR.** When a woman experiences divorce, she often feels all of these things at the same time. This can complicate how she sees, thinks and feels about things. On top of all of this, she may also feel:

- Relief
- Joy
- Empowerment
- Exhilaration
- Freedom

These feelings change frequently, sometimes in a day, sometimes in a matter of minutes. Think of your process as a roller coaster of emotions that starts out with really, really deep lows and hardly any highs. Then moderate highs will appear but probably will only last a short time. As your process advances, you will notice a change in the ride; the lows will be less deep and of shorter duration, and the highs will be higher and last a bit longer. Certainly it is unrealistic to believe the highs will last forever, but when you are through the process, your roller coaster ride will feel more like a gentle undulating wave. There will still be highs and lows, but they will be less drastic, less emotionally upsetting. Women ask me all the time, "Am I going crazy? How can I feel all these things, many of them conflicting at the same time?" You are not going crazy. You are going through transition. Your life is changing. A transformation is occurring. These feelings are normal.

How to get through it? Sometimes all we can do is hang on, knowing that whatever we are feeling will pass with time. Just knowing that these feelings will not last forever can offer reassurance and encouragement.

Today *if my roller coaster ride takes me into the depths of despair, I will take comfort in knowing this feeling will pass. And when my roller coaster takes me to the pinnacle of joy, I will allow myself to feel that feeling fully, to rejoice and experience my life to its fullest.*

- What if I decide to leave him and I don't meet anyone else?
- What if I have to spend my life alone?
- What if I decide to leave and he "gets better"?
- What if I can't support myself?
- What if my family is angry with me?
- What if this messes up my kids?
- What if I regret this?

Decision-making would be so much easier if we had a crystal ball. We could simply consult it to find out what our futures hold for us. Decision-making is always challenging because it holds within it so many unknowns. We complicate the process when we introduce the "what ifs." The "what ifs" are our fears screaming at us. If we allow them to enter our thought process, then we are making decisions based on our fear of what might be, rather than what is.

In making a decision to leave a marriage, or a job, or a neighborhood, it is always less stressful if you make the decision based on what is rather than on what will be. Making a decision on what might happen is not "fact-based" but "wish-based." We are not using our cognition as much as our emotions. When leaving a marriage, there are many unknowns. In order to facilitate making the best decision you can make, try to gather as much information prior to moving ahead. This includes seeing a lawyer (or two), an accountant, and a therapist. These professionals can give you information on what to expect.

Once you have your information, you are in a better place to make an informed decision. It helps to have faith in yourself. Without confidence in yourself, you might not choose anything. That means you may stay in your marriage, not out of choice, but by default. You will avoid making a decision by maintaining the status quo.

Making decisions helps us feel good about who we are. Some women wish their spouse would leave so they wouldn't have to decide. It is true that if he leaves, the result will be the same; you will get divorced, but you will not have experienced the growth that comes by trusting yourself and taking responsibility for how you want to live your life.

Today I accept that all possibilities for a happy life lie in the faith and confidence I have in myself. Decision-making requires a leap of faith – in myself. Am I ready to make that investment?

Negative messages from our family of origin can diminish self-esteem. On top of that, a bad marriage can reinforce those messages. This can result in self-talk that is filled with negative messages.

Some of these self-messages are:
- This is ALL MY FAULT.
- If I had only tried harder, this wouldn't be happening.
- It is the woman's job to keep the family together.
- My family was right when they said I was lazy (stupid, fat, cranky, bad, undeserving).
- If I were smarter (prettier, richer, funnier, thinner) this would not be happening.
- Everything always happens to me.
- Why do I have bad luck?
- Am I being punished?
- I will never feel better.
- I deserve this.
- My parents will be humiliated (ashamed, broken hearted, furious, etc.).

Confront those negative messages. Saying them out loud helps debunk their power. Or you write them down and talk about them with a trusted friend. Doing a reality check with a caring individual, can help you see how your negative self-talk gets in the way of your recovery.

For every negative message, think of a positive one. For example, "I will never feel better" can become "I can feel as good as I allow myself to feel." You might be saying to yourself, "Well, I don't *know* that I will feel better for sure." That is true, but you don't know that you will always feel this bad, either. So, if you have to believe one way or the other, doesn't it make sense to take the positive approach? Sometimes, we do have to "fake it until we make it."

Knowing you have choices about negative self-thoughts can help you begin to retrain yourself to think differently. This helps reclaim a part of yourself. It isn't easy, but with practice it is very do-able.

Today I will make a list of all my negative messages. Then, on another piece of paper, I will make a list of positive self-messages. I will throw away the old, negative messages and hang the list of positive messages, where I can see them every day; for example, on the bathroom mirror. And every night before I go to bed, I will repeat those messages with strength and conviction!

The bedroom is our most personal space and this is where to begin creating your new home. You might be thinking there is neither time nor money to begin such a project. I am not suggesting a major renovation, but some small changes – some of which cost no money – that can have a large impact on your well-being.

- If you haven't already done this, remove all your husband's clothes/personal items from the bedroom/master bath. Put them wherever you want, but remove them from the bedroom. This is your private space, where you need to relax, renew and rejuvenate. It is where you come to get away from the world.

- Don't leave those spaces empty. Fill them up immediately with your own stuff. Most women are always complaining that there isn't enough closet space. Well, now there is. Same thing in the bathroom – fill his old space with your stuff. It will amaze you how this can change your outlook!

- Buy new sheets, in your favorite color. If you can afford it, go for all new bedding. Everyone has a "signature smell" and it lingers, especially in bedding, for a very long time. Get rid of it and make the bed your own.

- Rearrange the furniture, move the bed to a different wall, if possible. The new arrangement and new perspective will help eradicate those intimate memories.

- Sleep in the MIDDLE OF THE BED! It amazes me how many women tell me that they just pile junk on that side of the bed! Think about how many nights you wished you had more room to stretch out. Now take all that space for yourself!

- Buy a scented candle. Okay, that may sound corny. But do it! Pick a scent you find particularly pleasing. Light it while you get ready for bed. When we find a fragrance soothing and appealing, we breathe deeper. This puts us in a calmer state which will lull us into a deeper, healing sleep.

- Bring music into the room. Listen to music while you prepare for bed. Music that pleases YOU, that you connect with. Ally McBeal, the television character, was famous for having a theme song. Clients over the years reported finding one song that signified their journey through their divorce. They claim that playing it over and over had a healing effect.

- Paint your room your favorite color. Wendy painted her room a deep purple, got rid of all the furniture, took her mattress off the frame and placed it in the middle of the floor. She put tiny phosphorescent stars on her ceiling to create a whole galaxy in her bedroom. Then she surrounded herself with books she always longed to read, placing them all around the bed. She spent most of the next few months in that bed reading. She said she was hibernating until the pain lifted. Every day after work and tending to her kids, she retreated to her hideaway and read and read. Because her husband always watched television in bed, she never had the opportunity to read, undistracted. It was her way of reclaiming her space and attending to her own needs.

Today I will plan to do one thing different in my bedroom and I will commit to a date to do it. By doing this, I say to myself that I can move ahead, I am not afraid of changes and I want to value my own preferences. I am important. I deserve to feel pleasure and comfort.

As you glance through the mail, one white envelope slides away from the others. The fancy writing and the heft of the envelope are the biggest clues that you have just received your first wedding invitation since you have been separated. Suddenly, there is a thud in your midsection like you have been kicked.

Weddings are difficult for newly-divorced or separated women. We come together as a community to share the experience of the couple vowing their endless love and commitment for each other. When your marriage has deteriorated into various degrees of hostility, infidelity, betrayal, and mistrust, weddings can stir up feelings from great sadness to extreme bitterness.

Should you go? If this is a family wedding, it may feel difficult to renege. You can talk with the mother of the bride and explain the situation. You can ask to bring a friend. You can also opt to attend just the ceremony and forgo the reception if that feels easier. If the wedding couple is on his side, then you may want to think about NOT going.

Many women hope their relationship with their husband's family can continue. The intensity of the connection and frequency of contact will change over time, especially when either of you have another love interest. While it may feel like another loss to grieve, you may save yourself a great deal of hurt if you choose to sit this one out. Going to the wedding won't erase the reality that things have changed. You may just diminish your discomfort by deferring.

The big question is, will he be there? If the answer is yes, then definitely bring a friend. Ask to sit in a different area at both the ceremony and reception. Watch your alcohol intake! Excessive alcohol can increase the possibility of an unpleasant confrontation. If you do go and find it too painful, you can always leave early.

Today I know that weddings are a part of life and life goes on. Someday I will enjoy going to weddings, even if I don't feel that way now. I will take time to consider whether I want to go to this wedding. Making decisions that involve others can be difficult, but I also know that with every hard decision I make, I am growing stronger and more confident.

If you haven't already gotten a day planner, run right out today and get one! A day planner is a combination calendar, appointment book, to do list, address book. It is mandatory for women going through divorce! It will help you sort out appointments and keep telephone numbers and messages in order. It even has sections for financial records. In our busy lives, we all forget some things. When we are under pressure, we tend to forget more things, lose more things, mix up and misplace more things. Keeping your papers and schedule in order in one place is one less thing you have to think about. Write down every appointment, divorce related or not. This will help minimize scheduling conflicts, confusion and stress.

Keep all telephone numbers relevant to the divorce in your day planner. Also keep the numbers of people who are relevant in your life and your children's lives. These include their school, emergency numbers and close friends. Having that information with you at all times prepares you to deal with all kinds of situations; it offers security and helps avoid a crisis. When we record our thoughts on paper, we no longer have to keep them in our head. When we organize our legal and financial documents, it is far less likely we will make a mistake or leave out something critical. The most important reason for writing it all down is that you won't lose sleep worrying whether you have forgotten anything. A final benefit is that it can serve as a kind of journal. When the year is over, you will have a record of all the events that took place during the year you divorced. You may actually want to look at that someday!

Today I will buy a day planner. Since this day planner will be my constant companion for the whole year, I will take my time picking one that suits my needs. I will like the color and texture of the cover and the sections will be big enough and clear enough to suit my needs. Like any other purchase I make, I will take the time to make sure that I feel comfortable with my choice. Then I will take it home and begin putting all my information in it. Perhaps I will even buy a new pen. Maybe when I write my name in it, I will write it differently, or include my maiden name or leave off my married name. I will allow this book to reflect the me I am becoming. This day planner will be testimony to my hard work, my courage and the payoff that will result. This book is a record of one of the most important years in my life; I will personalize it and make it mine.

You are probably aware of how valuable your support system is in the divorce recovery process but you may find that it has changed since the divorce process began. It is not unusual to have relationships with friends and family members alter during this time. So, we need to maintain important relationships and build new ones.

When we were children, we had "best friends" and often the relationships were based on geography or similar likes and dislikes. Friendships and life are more complicated now and we have lots of needs. It is unrealistic to believe one person can fill all those needs. It is like saying one outfit can be appropriate in all social occasions.

Keeping the Friends You Have

- Make a commitment to yourself to think and talk about the divorce for only a certain period of time each day.
- Don't forget to be a good listener.
- Ask friends about their lives.
- Find a way to show how much you appreciate your friend.
- Talk about *other* topics.
- Don't ask friends for legal or financial advice.

Making New Friends

Expand your idea of friendship. Having friends from different generations can broaden your perspective. Young people can add joy and spontaneity to your life. Older people can add wisdom and support. It is okay to have a friend that is not an intimate, but rather an "activities buddy." For example, a friend can be someone you just play tennis with, but have no other connection outside of the game. Do not minimize these relationships. Soulmates may represent the house, but our other friends add the furniture, making it a well-rounded and secure environment. New friends can be very important as they only know you as single. They don't see you as half of a couple! They are a reflection the current "you" and the "you" that you want to be!

Reconnect with Old Friends

Reconnect with an old friend. There are always people with whom we have lost touch. A letter from an old friend is always welcome! Do not be afraid to reach out and reconnect. Old friends offer a perspective that can have value in the healing process.

How to Find New Friends

Every stranger is a potential friend! Everywhere you go – work, school, the grocery store – offers the opportunity to make a new friend.

Today I will do one thing to expand my circle of friends. I will nurture an old connection and attempt to create a new one. Maybe I will send a card, or an e-mail, or leave a voice message. Maybe I will talk to the person next to me on line at the grocery store. When I reach out, I will find that my options are infinite!

Do you know the difference? The victim has no choices and cannot advocate for herself. She is helpless and trapped in a hopeless situation. The volunteer, on the other hand, has choices, but chooses not to exercise them. Having a choice is the BIG difference. The survivor is the person who sees the choices and, as hard as they may be, *chooses*.

Women who are in unhappy marriages, especially those that are abusive or neglectful, may not see they have choices. Economic, social, and religious mores may result in their feeling trapped. They see no options. They are victims. They are victims as recipients of their spouse's inappropriate behavior. However, they are also victims of their own resistance to change. Their own thought patterns can be more dangerous than their husband's behaviors! A woman who is unable to see or exercise her options denies herself the key to open the door to freedom and safety.

The choices are not easy ones and can have serious consequences. For example, calling the police when your husband beats you may result in his going to jail. Or calling the Department of Children and Family Services, because your husband is beating or molesting your child, may also result in his being removed from the home. Putting a stop to the abuse frequently puts an end to the good stuff as well. If you decide to divorce an abusive husband, you may free yourself and your children from being victims of violence, only to find yourselves victims of economics. Don't misunderstand me, I am not saying there are circumstances in which a woman or her children should put up with violence, abuse, or neglect, just that the choices are always hard. But there are choices and they are yours.

One choice you do not have is this: you cannot change another person. Accepting this makes it easier to focus on yourself. You cannot consider what is possible when you are still obsessed with the impossible. Your choices begin with accepting the reality of your situation.

Today I will begin to see that I DO have options. Not exercising my options, I become a volunteer for abuse. Today I will consider what it would feel like to be on the other side of this, to get away to a more serene life and to stop "walking on eggshells." I vow I will be a survivor!

We all have our "buttons." They are the issues, expressions, remarks, feelings, or behaviors of another that result in our feeling as if we have been punched in the stomach. When a marriage is healthy, loving, and supportive, it is filled with trust and respect and emotional intimacy. Our partner knows our buttons and respectfully avoids them. Our partner is trusted with the most vulnerable part of us and honors that trust by recognizing those places are simply "off limits." We, of course, do the same. When marriages start to deteriorate, and tempers flare, anger and hurt begin to transform us into warriors. We feel undefended. We search for weapons that can inflict damage and pain. We launch emotional weapons of mass destruction—remarks so devastating that we remember them for a lifetime. Violation and betrayal complicate and increase our pain. Our great ally is now our most toxic enemy. Suddenly we are at war!

While we have no control over another person's behavior, we have control over our own. When emotional missiles are fired at us, we need to take cover in safe places. Just physically hiding out will not keep you safe.

Do you know what pushes your buttons? Is it remarks about your family? Your appearance? Your intelligence? What are those tender, vulnerable places in your heart? Knowing those places can help protect you. Recognizing they are being deliberately sought out to inflict pain, can help you emotionally distance from the attack. Remember, the buttons are being pushed to hurt you, not because the message is true.

Linda, married 30 years, is going through a divorce. She lamented that her weight was the core problem in her marriage. Her husband always harangued her to lose weight. She gained more. Weeping, she said that if she had only lost the weight, the marriage would not have ended. I asked her to create a videotape in her mind of her marriage and substitute a thinner self in the movie. Then I asked her to run the movie through her head and see if the outcome would have been any different based on a svelte self. She closed her eyes and ran her tape. When she opened her eyes, she said with amazement, "Everything was the same. My weight had nothing to do with his behavior. He would have found something else to pick on." In that moment, she identified a button, challenged its veracity and then let it go. Now when her husband launches attacks about her weight, they will have no effect. This insight gave her more confidence in her divorce negotiations. It removed a major piece of artillery from his arsenal. While he continued to launch those missiles, they created no further damage.

Today I will think about those places where I bleed so profusely. What can I do to protect them? How can I be less vulnerable and less exposed to his attacks? I must remember I can't stop anyone from behaving the way they choose. But I am not helpless and I will continue to focus on making myself stronger and more impenetrable to attack.

The degree of documentation you need for your divorce will vary greatly, depending upon the state you live in, the length of your divorce, the amount of your assets, and whether you have children. Here is a list of documents you should have copies of:

- Checking and savings account information including account numbers, addresses, ownership, balances.
- Loan and credit card information including account numbers, addresses, ownership, balances.
- Marriage license.
- Birth certificates.
- Social security numbers for you and your spouse.
- Employment information for you and your spouse.
- Retirement and pension information.
- Prenuptial agreement (if there is one).
- Wills and trusts.
- Insurance policies.
- Business information.
- Tax returns for the last five years.
- Children's birth certificates and social security numbers.

Your attorney will let you know if she/he needs any further documentation, depending upon how complex your situation is. If you are the petitioner and it is possible, obtain copies of these documents prior to filing for divorce.

Today I will begin to take an inventory of what documentation I have and what documentation I will need. Rather than be overwhelmed by the task, I will consider it a vital part of creating a new life where I am competent, confident, calm and in charge of my financial matters.

Holly Abery-Wetstone is a Family Court Judge in Connecticut. Prior to her appointment to the bench, she maintained a private practice specializing in family law. Here is Holly's list of the eight biggest mistakes women make in court during their divorce:

- Whining on the witness stand.

- Giving too much detail about an incident that is not relevant.

- Not listening to the question asked before answering.

- Going off on a tangent, or anticipating a question.

- Trying to squeeze in the answer before the question is asked.

- Giving an answer when there is an objection pending.

- Asking for inappropriate custody arrangements, such as custody of only one of your two children.

- Filing false allegations of sexual abuse, physical abuse or failing to act on a real allegation of either.

- Not sharing appropriate information about your child's well being.

- Not staying with the BIG PICTURE. Too much detail about minutiae just takes up time and bores everyone.

You may find some of your own behaviors listed herein. While you cannot change the past, you certainly have control over your behavior in the future. Being aware that you are behaving inappropriately is half the battle. Don't be too hard on yourself if you do recognize yourself in some of the ten items listed above. You simply didn't know better. Now that you do, you can choose to make different decisions regarding your behavior. If you find you have some difficulty seeing the merit or logic in any of the above items, check with your attorney or therapist or support group. They can offer support and insight. You are not in this alone. Utilize your resources!

Today as I read the above list, I will be careful in the future not to indulge in any of those behaviors. If I have done so in the past, I will forgive myself and move forward, noting that changing my behavior is the best, most effective way that I can make amends.

If you really want to heal from this breakup, don't get emotionally entangled in a new relationship just yet. A new romance is just a band-aid; underneath, the wound will still fester. Sure, it would feel great to experience the excitement of falling in love. And it wouldn't hurt your self-esteem, either.

However, there are dangers in getting involved too quickly. First, you really aren't in a place emotionally to choose a new partner. Frankly, anything is going to feel good, considering what you just went through. Second, with everything that is happening right now, how much energy do you have to devote to this relationship and still manage the affairs of the divorce? Thirdly, if it doesn't work out (and most transitional relationships do not!) you will have two lost relationships to deal with.

For right now, a romantic relationship is risky and can complicate matters. When Marcia was going through her divorce, she applied the following acronym to a transitional relationship.

Really
Exciting
Love
Affair
Turns
Into
Outrageous
Nightmare
Sanity
Hangs
In
Peril

New romantic relationships will not always be off limits. However, right now, you have enough to handle!

Today I will begin a romance with myself. I will respect myself, value and nurture myself. I will learn to listen to my heart, tend to my needs, and pay attention to my own inner voice. I will not be afraid to speak up. I will learn that I am enough as I am. I will learn how to be with myself, not just by myself.

Sometimes we have second (third and fourth) thoughts about whether divorce is really the right thing to do. One technique you can use to assess whether the marriage is viable is to think about it as if it was somebody else's marriage. Imagine your child was an adult in a marriage just like yours and she came to you for advice. How would you advise her?

Often, taking a different perspective helps us get clarity with regard to a decision we need to make. By changing your perspective, you give yourself some emotional distance and objectivity. Most of us find when we change our perspective we have the obvious answers to the difficult choices. Too frequently, our inner wisdom gets clouded and distorted by unhealthy emotions of fear and guilt and dependence. These emotions can distort our truth and make our decisions even more complicated.

If you examine this marriage as if it were your child's, and the conclusion you reach is that you would tell your child to leave the marriage, then you know your answer. If you would be outraged and protective if your child were in this situation, then you must be as firm and supportive and encouraging with yourself as you would be with your child. Many of us can clearly see what needs to be done in another's difficult situation. We are great at giving advice. But following advice, especially our own, is a different matter.

Part of growing as a person is paying attention to your inner wisdom. This helps your self-esteem to flourish. When we nurture and support the healthy choices we need to make, we are being respectful to ourselves. Many of us have lived in marriages where we were not respected. Ignoring your own inner wisdom will result in you treating yourself with the same disrespect. Getting healthy means treating yourself with honesty, dignity, and self-respect.

Today if I am struggling with doubts about my decision, I will create a different perspective. I will imagine this is my daughter's marriage, or that of my sister or my best friend. How would I advise them? My strength will come from following my own wisdom and knowing that I can trust my judgment. When I trust myself, I am building confidence and self-esteem.

Everything is <u>Not</u> about you!

Example: When you are driving in your car and someone cuts you off, or honks their horn, or screams epithets at you, do you immediately think you did something wrong?

Example: You are making a pork tenderloin for dinner and unbeknownst to you, one of the guests has become a vegetarian, and declines to eat the pork. Do you feel hurt and interpret her behavior as insulting?

Example: You roll over in bed and put your hand on your sleeping partner's shoulder. He grunts and shifts his weigh and moves away. Do you interpret his action as a rejection of your affections?

None of these has *anything* to do with you – not the driver, the guest or your partner. All of these people had agendas that seemed to collide with yours. You may feel maligned, insulted, misunderstood, rejected but in all these scenarios, the "perpetrators" weren't even thinking about you! They are merely doing what felt right to them. They were not interfering with your personal rights, yet you might have taken their behavior personally. When we take things personally, we give away our personal power; we make the other person in control of how we feel. That gives them a lot of power and diminishes our own. Going through divorce, you may look at your husband's bad behavior and blame it on yourself. If your husband had an affair, you might think you drove him to it because you weren't sexier, thinner, heavier, younger, a better cook, a better lover, a better something.

We blame ourselves. That is, *taking it personally*. His infidelity is not your fault. Your husband may have been unhappy in the marriage, but he had lots of other choices for how to behave. When we take things personally, we let the other person off the hook. We take responsibility for their bad behavior and blame ourselves.

Not taking things personally keeps us from taking responsibility and blame for someone else's behavior. It helps us focus on the things we are responsible for and on the things we need to change. It reduces our guilt and it gives us clarity. It helps us be more assertive and encourages healthier interactions. When you don't take things personally, manipulation no longer becomes a key element in your relationships.

Today I will make a mental note of every time I take something personally. Later, I will reflect on each instance and allow myself to see that I am taking things personally that have nothing to do with me. Ahhh, I can let those things go. My, that feels good!

Day 15 What Was It Like to Come Home to Me?

Sometimes we are so angry at someone else's behavior that we do not see our own. However, it is critical that we are aware of, and understand our own behavior. The goal is insight, which fosters growth, and supports change. Without the ability to change, we cannot grow into the best human being we can be.

Women have terrific recall about their partner's behavior. Many also have great insights into why their men behaved as they did. As nurturers, we are also acute observers, sensitized to everyone's moods and needs. We become experts on our partner's behavior.

All of that focus on the needs of others takes the focus off of ourselves and we may not be aware of our own behavior, or if we are, we dismiss it or we rationalize it. Ask yourself this, "What was it like for my husband to come home to me after a day of work?" You may answer something like, "Well, I was rushed, annoyed, tired. After all, I have so much to do, do you expect me to be *nice* also?"

Well, it isn't about what I expect. It is about what <u>you</u> expect. You expect him to walk in chipper, upbeat, helpful, considerate. Why shouldn't you do the same? Have you ever noticed that some people are nicer to strangers than to their partner?

What was it like to come home to **me**? Here is a list of things to consider about **your** behavior:

- Did I jump right on him with a list of what went wrong during the day?

- Did I acknowledge that he even walked in?

- Did I smile? Or did I acknowledge him with a scowl?

- Did I make an effort to listen?

- Did I offer a kiss or a hug?

- Did I ignore him?

- Did I make time for us to talk with each other?

- Was I critical?

- Was I glad to see him? Did I show it?

Today when I think about my behavior, I will do it without self-blame or self-anger. Rather I will examine my behavior with curiosity and a desire for self-growth. I will explore how I behave so I can make changes where needed, and applaud my strengths. I am determined to use this experience to grow and be the healthiest person I can be!

Does the thought of telling your parents about your divorce fill you with apprehension and perhaps even dread? Depending upon your prior relationship with your parents, unresolved issues may resurface, some going all the way back to your childhood. For example, if you always felt that your parents were disappointed in you, then there may be trepidation that, once again, you will have to face their disappointment. If they disapproved of your choice of spouse, the fear may come from wanting to avoid "I told you so."

Regardless of your prior relationship with your parents, most divorcing adults have found that when they actually tell their parents, they get more support than they thought they would. Here are some thoughts to keep in mind when you "break the news."

- **There is never a "right time."** Bite the bullet and just do it. You certainly don't want them to hear it from someone else.

- **Let your parents know that you need emotional support.** This helps them focus their energies on what you need and also helps them feel valuable to you.

- **Insure them that their relationship with their grandkids will continue.** Many fear the divorce will effect their connection with their grandkids.

- **Don't try to "protect" your parents.** They are likely not to be fooled by your charade. By censoring your feelings, you may feel devalued and shut out.

- **You no longer need their permission.** While we all need support and approval, remember that you are not asking for their permission. This is your life and your decision. Be clear about your decision. Guard against giving your parents too much power and influence over your decision and how you feel about it.

Today when I tell my parents that I am getting divorced, I will remember that I am no longer a child. And while I am still their child and would like their approval, I no longer need or require it to be happy in my own life. I will not try to protect them or convince them or feel defensive. I will ask for their help and support. Regardless of their reaction, I will remember that the most important supporter of my decision is myself.

A wise friend once said to me, "For everything sad that happens in your life, you will cry buckets of tears. You will either cry them now or you will cry them later."

There is much truth in that simple statement! We have a right to cry buckets of tears if we need to do so. And if we don't permit ourselves to cry them now, then the pain stays inside us until we do.

Rather than try and hold back the tears, allow yourself to cry. Of course you can't force this process so that you can get through it quicker. Grief is a process; tears are part of how we work through that process. We cannot rush or deny or ignore what is inevitable. Our tears are not signs of weakness; rather they stand as testimony to our commitment, our disillusionment, our sadness, and our loss. Our tears are one way we honor our loss, and in doing so, honor ourselves.

There is no predetermined time, intensity, or duration for the tears that one cries through divorce. The number of buckets varies for each person. Some women cry a lot. Some don't. Tears are a personal expression and we cannot assume that the quality and quantity of tears will be similar in every person and every situation.

If you broke your leg, you would allow yourself some bed rest. It would be appropriate and healthy to do so. After a while, you would begin physical therapy, actively working to heal the damaged bone. As difficult and trying as it would seem at times, you would begin to use the leg again, struggling at first, but knowing that using it would make it stronger. You would not lie in bed forever, nor would you get up the day after the break and run down the stairs.

There is a process in healing a broken leg or a broken heart. Move along at your own pace, but make sure you move along. Just like the broken leg can heal to be even stronger than it was before, you can also find that in healing your broken heart, a new strength emerges.

Today my process of healing is as unique as I am. I will take as much time as I need, making sure I do the emotional work I need to do to heal completely. Wherever I am in my process, I will treat myself with gentleness rather than self-judgment.

Like many of us going through divorce, your husband has probably shed those extra ten pounds he has been carrying around. Living alone, without so many responsibilities of the family, men have more time to focus on themselves. Many men begin a regular exercise routine, buy some new clothes, and get more frequent haircuts. It may look as if he is positively thriving, while you feel as if you are becoming completely unglued.

Because women are usually the ones with primary custody of the kids, we tend to feel overworked, under-supported, sleep deprived and at our wit's end. When we look at how good our estranged spouses look, it can stir up a lot of resentment.

The truth is, you probably look better now than you even realize. And while you may be feeling stressed to the max, it is a different kind of stress than when he was still at home. Gone is the tension of living in a "cold war" or amidst a raging battle. True, there are a ton of things to do and take care of. However, you are no longer living in a decaying marriage with hostility and conflict. That stress is gone.

Most important, never compare your insides with someone else's outsides. Whenever we compare how someone looks ON THE OUTSIDE to how we feel ON THE INSIDE, we are always going to come up short. We assume if someone looks good, then they feel good as well. We make lots of assumptions based on how things look and those assumptions often result in our creating a glowing fantasy. We then feel inadequate by comparison. It is one more way we set ourselves up to feel badly about ourselves.

Today rather than compare myself to anyone else, if I need a yardstick, I will compare myself to how I was. Then I will think about how I want to be. This life isn't about competing with others; it is about doing the best we can for ourselves. I will set goals for myself based on what I need, not in comparison to anyone else. I will be aware of how I set myself up to feel badly when I compare myself to others. That is counterproductive and now that I am aware that I do that, I will simply refuse to do it to myself anymore!

During the divorce process, it is not unusual to experience the resurfacing of other losses in your life. These can include death or losses of childhood, parents, relatives, friends, or pets. You will feel this happening if you find yourself suddenly filled with thoughts and grief over an event that happened long ago. You may dream about the loss or have the desire to contact someone from your past. Pay attention to the feelings. Don't try to deny them. Keep a "loss list" and, if and when you feel like doing so, write a letter to that person or situation (not to mail) about how you feel. Journal about your feelings and share them with a trusted friend or therapist.

What is critical is that you do not act on these feelings. For example, you might find yourself pining about an old love; perhaps regretting you didn't marry your high school sweetheart. Experiencing regrets about past choices when going through divorce is common. It is a way of reevaluating our choices and also a way of imaging how we could have avoided pain. Maybe you and your high school beau are destined to be together, but now is not the time to find out. Your urge to contact him is not about moving toward a new relationship, it is a desire to distance from the pain you are experiencing.

Grief has to be felt. When you are done, you will know it. That may sound fairly obvious, but when we are experiencing our pain, we feel as if it will never stop. It is important to remember that even though it FEELS as if this pain will never end, the FACT is that it will. Remembering this opens us up to grieve, to heal, and to grow without fear. Crying for past losses is our body's way of telling us we are not through grieving.

Today I will let myself cry if I need to cry. I will remember that my tears are cleansing and healing and that eventually I will stop crying. Crying honors my losses, my pain, and myself.

What is worrying? It is excess concern about what will happen in the future. It is fear that what will happen will be something we either don't want or don't think we can handle. Recently, Jane told me that her 16-year-old daughter was diagnosed with a serious illness. The young woman, who apparently is wise beyond her years, told her mother, "You know, worrying is like a rocking chair. It gives you something to do, but doesn't get you anywhere."

Why do we worry? Do we think that somehow worry will change the outcome? How is it useful? If there could be a study that suggested that worrying could change the outcome of some unknown event in our lives, then there would be workshops on worry given at famous universities and reams of books written that would highlight tips for becoming a better worrier. Until that happens, I suggest a more conservative approach which includes the following:

- Get all the information you can.

- Consider your options.

- Recognize what you can change and what you can't.

- Find a method of relaxation that works for you.

- Use your worry time more effectively.

Sometimes when we worry, we become so focused on our fears that we cannot see our options. Fear gives us tunnel vision and clouds our judgment. By not allowing our fear to overpower us, we can be more in control and therefore be more effective in our decision making.

Workout, visualize, meditate, laugh a lot. Try all the techniques available until you find the one that works for you. But don't give up. Relaxing takes practice. Learning to relax will make a HUGE difference in your life, not only in this particular situation, but also in everything else that happens in your life.

Finally, rather than using the energy to clench your teeth or stiffen your muscles, or think obsessively, try refocusing that energy on something you love to do: crafts, a sport, music, reading, gardening. Do what brings you pleasure. Do it now. When we are stressed and we do something we love, we are taking care of ourselves and encouraging growth.

Today I will look at my worry patterns and decide whether I want to continue rocking and getting nowhere!

Day 21 Sometimes I Don't Even Know What I'm Feeling

Divorce brings with it a myriad of feelings. It may be difficult to tell what you are actually feeling at any given time. Furthermore, just when you think you know, then BAM! another feeling rushes in and overshadows the first. Basically, there are four major feelings. Breaking them down into categories can help you identify what is going on.

- **Mad** – includes angry, frustrated, annoyed, pissed off, rageful and furious.
- **Sad** – includes mopey, blue, under the weather, teary, grieving.
- **Glad** – includes happy, cheerful, upbeat, hopeful, optimistic.
- **Scared** – includes fearful, anxious, nervous, terrified.

These are just a few examples of which feelings fall into what categories. This can get complicated because you can feel more than one feeling at a time. Remember since there are only four main feelings, you don't have to struggle and search too hard—anything you feel fits into one of these categories.

- Usually we are **mad** because we haven't gotten our way. Some one has done or said something we don't like and we react strongly.
- Usually we are **sad** when something has happened that results in some sense of loss. We feel something is taken from us or is missing and we grieve it.
- Usually when things go our way, we feel **glad.** We like that!
- Usually **fear** is related to the concern that somehow we are threatened by an unknown, or feeling out of control. For example, fear of driving your car can be fear of getting stuck, crashing, dying, or merely being late. Regardless, these are all outcomes we would like to avoid. When we are powerless over the outcome, we sometimes feel fear.

Feelings are neither good nor bad; it is what we do with them that counts. As a girl, you might have been taught that all anger was bad. If you use your anger in an aggressive way that hurts yourself or others, we can call that "bad." If you use your anger as fuel to energize you and motivate change, then that is "good." What about guilt, you might ask? Guilt is not so much a feeling, but the conflict of feelings.

An example of conflicted feelings: you may be glad you have an excuse not to go visit your mother on Christmas, but you may also feel sad about not seeing the rest of your family, or scared that other family members will get angry with you. You probably will feel uncomfortable with the conflicting feelings and you might label that discomfort; guilt.

Feelings just *are*. The behavior or expression of these feelings is what we need to be mindful of. The more we are mindful of what we feel, the more accurately and appropriately we can communicate those feelings through our own behavior. When we are aware of what we feel, we have insight into how we behave.

Today I will reflect on what I really feel. Why is it so difficult for me to identify my feelings? Maybe it is because I never understood them or was afraid of them. Today I can accept that my feelings simply are expressions of what I like and I don't like. I will accept what I feel without judgment.

You don't. If you decide your child needs to see a therapist, you simply tell them they are going! Asking a child if he/she wants to go to therapy is like asking if they want to go to the dentist, or to get a flu shot. These are not decisions a child makes. When we ask children to do something that is a parenting decision, we give the child too much power. They may seem to like it, but it makes them feel unsafe. They will wonder if you have what it takes to take care of *them*. Furthermore, it will erode their respect for you. That can really get sticky in adolescence and teenage years when the real wrestling for power and control escalates.

You calmly explain to the child, in a non-judgmental way, what behaviors you see that are of concern to you. For example, "You seem to being having increasing difficulty with your studies." Or, "You seem to be sleeping a great deal and acting very lethargic. I am worried about you," are remarks that state your concern without judgment. On the other hand, "You are turning into a lazy slob, just like your father and I won't put up with it!" is an example of a punitive and critical statement. This will not enhance your relationship with your child nor will it lay a positive groundwork for the introduction of a therapist!

Explain what a therapist is and that he/she is there to support and validate. His/her goal is to help fix the problem, not judge it. Be supportive and assure the child that you are going to participate in the process as much as is needed. Your attitude will convey a great deal. If you feel anxious or guilty, then your child will respond negatively. If you are upbeat and matter of fact about therapy, the response will be far more positive. Some children may threaten not to talk. Do not argue with them. It is the therapist's role to establish rapport and get the child to open up. Your job is just to get them there.

To adolescents or teenagers you can say, "If you can pull up those grades and there is a change in your energy in the next two weeks, then I will reconsider." This should not be a threat, but rather an opportunity to give the child a chance to modify and control his/her own behavior. If you see no change at all, then follow through. This exhibits parental leadership and consistency. However, there are times when the child is <u>not</u> given a choice. When a child is talking about not wanting to live anymore (suicidal thoughts), or is engaging in self-destructive behaviors such as self mutilation (cutting), drugs, alcohol, sex, then this child is in crisis and immediate treatment is vital.

Today I will accept the responsibility for the decisions regarding the health and well being of my child. I will not equivocate on my decision. When I take control, it lets my child know he is safe and loved.

"I am in the divorce process up to my elbows. I have paperwork for my lawyer, deadlines for my job, parent conferences for my kids, friends coming for dinner. I have a birthday party to plan, a lawn to mow, a dog with fleas. I haven't slept more than five hours a night for months. My grey hairs are coming in with a vengeance and my skin is breaking out. Most of the food in my refrigerator looks like science experiments. I have no idea of world events, latest movies, or current songs. I have to get my kids to soccer practice, karate and guitar lessons. I have grocery shopping, vet appointments, orthodontics appointments, child therapy appointments, ob-gyn appointments. I have appointments with my lawyer, my accountant, my therapist. I have appointments with my children's lawyers and therapists. I have an appointment to sit down and talk with my husband about vacation schedules. I am planning a vacation. I am planning to get the house painted. The car broke down. The dishwasher is leaking. My kids came home with head lice. The dog vomited on the carpet."

So, how *are* you doing? It is hectic and overwhelming, but you aren't an emotional wreck anymore, are you? This may be a scary, overwhelming time, but it is your time and while there are things to do and worry about, there is no one threatening you, blaming you, hurting you, holding you down. There is no need to "walk on eggshells."

The bad news is that you are on your own.

The good news is that you are on your own.

Today I will take my emotional pulse and recognize that while things are difficult, they are easier than they used to be. I will have my up days and down days, but gradually, there will be more up than down days. Life will always have those rough moments, but I know now that I have options and choices about how I live my life, and therefore, my life can be the one I choose it to be. I will remember to stop frequently throughout this process and take my emotional pulse. If it feels out of whack, I will work to improve my situation. Sometimes that means just waiting until tomorrow and things will improve on their own.

Time management and practical support are two areas in which single Moms need to be resourceful and creative. Below are some tips that address both these areas.

- **Learn to prioritize.** Make a list of everything you need to do, ranking the tasks on that list in terms of importance. Accept that at the end of the day you will probably only accomplish fifty percent. Celebrate that you could do that much!

- **Take time out for yourself.** When the sink is full of dishes and the lawn needs to be mowed, the most important thing you can do is climb into a warm bath or snuggle down in a cozy chair with a good book.

- **Make time for a social life of your own.** Having your own support system and interests helps avoid parentifying your children; that is, using them as sounding boards for inappropriate information regarding the divorce.

- **Swap help.** For example: you love to cook, your neighbor is available to drive your kids to activities. Make an extra casserole in exchange for their driving your kids. Or try asking the elderly couple down the street to help out with your kids after school in exchange for your mowing the lawn or shoveling their snow.

- **Delegate.** Children should be assigned age-appropriate tasks. It builds a sense of responsibility and teaches them they are a vital part of the family. This is important whether there are one or two parents in the home.

- **Hire help.** Babysitters, au pairs, housecleaners. If you can afford to do this, then do it. Sometimes high schools offer programs for their students to work in the neighborhood. Call your local schools to see if they have such a program.

- **Access community resources.** YMCA's often offer babysitting programs, as do church groups and school programs. Some nursing homes have grandparent programs. Find the resources in your community and use them.

- **Get organized.** Clean out your closets. Get rid of stuff you don't wear. Throw it out or donate it. If it feels too difficult to part with all those fabulous yet outdated clothes, then box them and store them in the basement, garage, or attic. Have your kids do the same thing with their toys. Donating toys is a good way to teach children about the importance of giving and of gratitude. If they can't part with their stuff either, then at least box up the stuff that is not used and put it away.

- **Multi-task when you can.** Throw in a load of laundry before you start dinner and you can fold it later while you watch television. You can unload the dishwasher in the three minutes it takes to heat something in the microwave.

- **Cut down on kitchen time.** Cook for more than one meal. Freeze it and next week, it isn't a leftover!

- **Leave five minutes early for work** and do one errand on the way into the office. Go to the cleaners, the drugstore or return the library books. This way you aren't left with a pile of errands to do on the weekend!

- **Make an effort to connect with other single Moms** for support and ideas.

Today I will think of other timesaving techniques I can incorporate into my life. I will ask friends what their favorite timesaving tips are and will try them out. I will discard those that don't work, and embrace those that do. I will focus on streamlining my life. In doing so, I will spend less time doing chores, worrying about doing chores, and more time enjoying my life and my loved ones.

"The arrival of a good clown exercises more beneficial influence upon the health of a town than twenty asses laden with drugs."
                    —Thomas Sydenham, seventeenth century physician

There are numerous studies of the curative powers of humor. One well-known case is of Norman Cousins. In 1979, when diagnosed with a crippling form of arthritis, he utilized laughter as part of his treatment. Mr. Cousins believed that negative emotions have a negative effect on health and therefore theorized that the opposite might be true; that is, that positive emotion would have a positive effect on health. He believed that the experience of laughter could open him up to feelings of joy and happiness. After his diagnosis, he spent many hours doing fun things, especially watching Marx Brothers films and reruns of *Candid Camera*. It is said that he laughed himself back to good health!

Laughter helps us gain new perspective. Laughter encourages women in pain to relax. Humor is a way to get a break from the pain. A really good belly laugh is relaxing and life affirming. Remember that things that may feel devastating today are the fuel for humor tomorrow.

Humor is often the product of embarrassing or bizarre situations. Often these situations occur at serious times. It is the juxtaposition of these events that often creates humor. Humor also gives us the wonderful opportunity to laugh at our mistakes, our foibles, and ourselves. I am not talking about sarcasm, scorn, contempt or ridicule. Humor becomes harmful when remarks sting us and are deemed funny by others. ("Gee, can't you take a joke?" or "I was only kidding") Good, healthy humor carries no resentment or disdain, only gentleness and acceptance. It is the difference between laughing *at* someone or laughing *with* them.

By seeing humor in a stressful situation, we can change our response to the threat. When one laughs, it is impossible to feel stress. Physiological changes occur in the body when we laugh. These changes are numerous and documented. Laughter triggers the release of endorphins and can help numb pain. One study showed that while watching a Richard Pryor tape, participants had a boosted level of antibodies in their saliva, which help us fight against colds. People who reported using humor frequently as a way of coping with stress had higher baseline levels of these protective antibodies.

Today I will do one thing every day this week to make me laugh a little bit. I will plan to do one thing every week to make me laugh a lot.

... to Help You Sleep Better at Night

It rarely occurs to us that there are things we can do during the day which will improve the quality of our sleep. Most of us fret about our lack of sleep but don't see how it relates to our daily lives. Here are some things you can incorporate into your daily regimen that can facilitate a more satisfying sleep:

- **Eliminate caffeine.** Minimize caffeine and nicotine. They are both stimulants and can keep you from falling asleep. Caffeine is found in coffee, tea, soda, chocolate. If you continue to have difficulty sleeping, you may consider cutting out caffeine completely until your sleep improves.

- **Reduce Alcohol.** Alcohol can cause waking in the night and interferes with sleep quality.

- **Exercise more.** Even a fifteen-minute walk daily can help improve the quality of your sleep. Do not exercise too vigorously too close to bedtime or it can interfere with your sleep. Experts say not to exercise within three hours of bedtime.

- **Take quiet time.** Set aside a period of the day, even ten minutes can be beneficial, for relaxation: meditation, listening to quiet music, a warm bath, or reading a book. These all can help you sleep better in the evening.

- **Stick to a schedule.** Exercising, eating and going to bed at the same time daily can help your body get into a routine so that it begins to expect to sleep at a certain time.

- **Don't eat a heavy meal late in the day.** A light snack before bedtime, however, may help you sleep.

- **Keep a sleep routine.** Try to go to sleep and wake up at the same time each day, even on the weekends. This helps set your "internal clock." Trying to "make up" sleep doesn't help your body fall into a routine. Get up at the same time daily, even if you didn't sleep well the night before.

- **Get as much natural light as you can.** Natural light helps reset our body clock.

- **Do something nice for yourself.** This can help reduce the amount of stress you are feeling and consequently help you relax for sleep.

Today it is difficult to find time to nurture myself especially because my life is so hectic. I can implement the above suggestions with little effort, but with a great payoff. I honor myself by attending to what my body needs.

Alexis reports that her marriage has been in serious trouble for quite some time. She prays for "good" days and tries not to look at the "bad" days. Recently, she reports they are "getting along better." She reports there are fewer arguments and hardly any full-fledged battles being waged. I inquire how this change came about. "Oh, you know," she commented, "We stay away from each other. It is only when we have to talk to each other that we fight. I have learned to stay clear of him and then he doesn't get as angry. Things in the house are bearable."

This marriage reminds me of two skaters on a pond of ice that is not quite frozen solid. The surface looks smooth and sturdy, but it cannot hold the weight of the two skaters. As long as they stay on opposite ends of the pond, they can skate about without mishap. Should they move toward each other and try to skate together, the surface will give way and they will both fall through to the icy water.

Staying on opposite ends of the pond is no way to have a marriage. Without intimacy, respect, trust and conflict resolution, the surface may look good, but it will not sustain the skaters for long.

Alexis resists going to couple's counseling, although her husband is willing. She is afraid she will not be able to "be honest" with him. She doesn't want to "hurt his feelings." This fear results in maintaining the status quo. Not wanting to be seen as the "bad one" or to risk his anger makes it difficult, if not impossible, for this marriage to improve. Most likely, they will end up in divorce court.

Even if the marriage eventually ends, this couple could benefit from therapy by learning what went wrong and what part they were each responsible for. And in this particular case, they could learn conflict resolution skills. Without those skills, these individuals are doomed to skate on separate parts of the ice through all their future relationships.

Today I will ask myself, "If my husband is willing, what harm can there be in attending a few sessions of marital therapy with a skilled therapist?" If we do go our separate ways, a therapist can help make that less acrimonious and I could learn skills that may help me in future relationships.

We frequently feel out of control as we proceed through the divorce process. We worry about the outcome of financial distributions, child support, visitation, retirement funds, house equity and so forth. There are countless decisions to make, and while you will have advice from your attorney, therapist, friends and family, ultimately you alone are making the decisions. For some women, this is the most difficult part of the process. After years of making decisions as a couple, many women are fearful and unsure of their own capabilities. By tapping into our creative side, we have an opportunity to:

- Experience risk.
- Learn to see things a different way.
- Be in charge.
- See a dream become reality.

In our creative process, we find solutions we may have overlooked and alternative ways around once insurmountable obstacles. Success is about enjoying the process and the opportunity to do something in a different way. Some ideas to tap into your creative side include:

- Keep a journal. This is healing and cathartic and can be a wonderful way to preserve all you learned during this time. Writing down your thoughts and reviewing them gives you an opportunity to maintain an ongoing dialogue with yourself. This can foster self-awareness and changes in perception.
- Draw with your non-dominant hand. Use big paper and colored magic markers. Ask yourself "What am I feeling today and what would it look like if it were a picture?" What it actually looks like is unimportant; it is the self-expression that matters. Date your drawings and save them.
- Paint a room.
- Take photographs.
- Knit, crochet, needlepoint, cross-stitch.
- Rearrange your furniture.
- Cook something new, without a recipe.
- Try karaoke, in a club or in the tub (keeping the radio a safe distance away from the water!).
- Dance around the house or take a class. One of my clients belly dances and finds the experience good exercise and great fun. Learning to coordinate her body and control its movement gives her a sense of competence and new self-confidence.
- Take a class through adult education in your neighborhood.
- Learn a new language. Buy tapes or borrow them from the library and listen to them in your car.
- Do a crafts project with your kids. Let them choose it.

To create, to stretch, to take risks, to leave your comfort zone of your own accord – these are all ways to facilitate your road to recovery and reduce the painful effects of divorce.

Today I will begin to look for my inner muse. I will find her, let her speak to me and guide me on my creative path. The excitement of doing something new will affirm my feeling alive and enthusiastic. I will embrace all of my hidden talents. Nurturing them will foster my competence and support me in all arenas in my life.

Day 29   Visitation: How to Insure a Smooth Transition

Most of us experience anxiety mixed with anticipation prior to vacation. Did we remember to stop the mail, get the dog to the kennel, cancel the newspaper, finish that last report at work? Do we have directions, tickets, reservations? Did we pack the right stuff? Did we forget anything?

Children experience those feelings every time there is visitation. These feelings are further complicated by leaving one parent to see another. So while there is joy, there is also sadness. This doesn't mean visitation is bad for children; quite the opposite. It teaches children skills such as flexibility, planning, and dealing with anticipation and anxiety. It also exposes them to different life styles, which can help foster a more global concept of the world. However, we need to help the child transition. Here are some tips to assist in a smooth visitation transition:

- Have a calendar in the child's room. Clearly mark visitation days in bright colors. This visual aid helps even the young child see a pattern to visitation, which will help diminish anxiety.

- Allow the child to do some of his/her own packing. Help the child pack the night before he/she goes.

- Allow the child to bring a special toy or stuffed animal with him. These transitional objects help the child feel grounded and secure during travel and in the other home.

- Pick up and drop off times should NOT involve discussion about anything spousal, including money, the divorce, child support. Parents should not use this time to yell at each other.

- Be punctual with pick up and drop off times.

- Unless there is a HUGE emergency, never cancel at the last minute. It is very hurtful and if you do it enough, your child will learn not to trust you.

- Do not call your child a million times when he is with his father. The child should feel free to call if he wants to do so, but it shouldn't be mandatory.

- If your child becomes home sick, he should be allowed to call. Reassure him but do not take him home. He needs to learn that he is safe and at home with both parents. Giving into the child's fear can set up a negative precedent.

- Visitation should not be canceled because the child is sick. To cancel or send a child back to his mother when sick, says to the child that Daddy is not as capable. Both parents need to participate in all aspects of parenting, including caregiving the sick child.

- Neither parent should "pump" the child about the other parent's life. This includes questions about dating, money, and people who come to the house. Open-ended questions such as "What did you do this weekend?" or "Did you have fun?" "Do you want to talk about it?" will let the child know you are interested in his/her experience and not merely using him/her as a little informant.

Today I will try to allow for fifteen to thirty minutes of quiet play before transition and after arrival at the other home. I will give my child some time to acclimate and adjust before having food, activities, choices, thrust upon him/her.

From Ex-Wife to Exceptional Life

Remember when you were a little girl and you would go for a car ride with your parents? Whether the trip was 3000 miles or three miles, it seemed interminable. "Are we there yet?" is the universal cry of kids, as they question whether the trip would ever really end.

Divorce is like that car ride – it seems it will never end. Just when you think you are almost there and that your destination is right around the bend, you find there are *still* more miles to go. Having no sense of time or mileage, children do not know how to gauge the distance covered. They cannot estimate how much longer the trip will take. They become impatient and cranky. For adults, divorce presents that same never-ending road. Having never traveled down this road before (even if this is not the first divorce, each divorce is its own unique journey), we have no sense of how much longer we have to go, or if we are almost there.

"Have patience" we tell our children. In truth, we adults have little patience when it involves having our expectation come to fruition. Somewhere in the midst of your divorce process you will experience feelings of weariness and impatience. You will long for the whole thing to just be over. This increasing impatience – with the system, your soon-to-be-ex, and your lawyers may reduce some of your fight and resistance.

It may feel as if you want to stop the process, either by giving in to the demands or by stopping the divorce entirely. Sometimes reason is born of weariness; other times weariness can diminish our ability to act in our best interests. Before you make any decisions that are irreversible, talk with your lawyer, your therapist, and a trusted friend. Then sleep on it. A decision that will affect the rest of your life is worth at least one night's consideration. Remember, even though it delays our trip, we need to stop to refuel. We may be anxious for this trip to be over, but we don't want to risk a breakdown along the way.

Today I feel weary and impatient right down to my bones. I just want this to be over. I feel like I cannot last through one more day of fighting, courts, lawyers, and that endless stream of paperwork. However, I cannot let my weariness dictate or distort my position. I will compromise if it is appropriate, but I will do myself a disservice if I merely surrender to my exhaustion and frustration.

Notes

Month Five

We strive to be the best woman, friend, wife, mother, daughter, sister, worker, neighbor, we can be. In our commitments to others, we give our best effort. We do that for a number of reasons. One is that we have been taught, through both subtle and explicit messages, that life is fair. That is, if we are good to others, then they will be good to us. Our first introductions to this concept begin early in life with fairytales – the good girl always comes out a winner. Cinderella and Snow White overcame incredible obstacles through their goodness and then they lived happily ever after. As little girls, we listened to these stories over and over again with rapt attention. We learned that goodness, loyalty, virtue, and honesty are rewarded time and time again. Some religions teach us that "What goes around, comes around." Our culture is filled with slogans, lessons, parables, fables, all of which enforce this lesson: If you do good things, then good things will happen to you.

Then we find ourselves in the midst of a crumbling marriage... didn't we do everything we possibly could? Didn't we try hard enough? Weren't we pretty enough, young enough, smart enough, sexy enough? Something must be wrong with us! After all, if we did it *right*, everything would be *right*. Life is NOT fair! This is a difficult idea for many of us. It may feel as if our value system is crumbling. However, this new perspective can be enormously freeing.

Instead of thinking that it must be your fault if something is wrong, you are now freed from the entire responsibility for things going awry. Things do go wrong. Sometimes, they go very, very wrong. However, life is neither fair, nor unfair. Life just *is*. To quote Rabbi Kushner, "Sometimes bad things happen to good people." If you keep thinking life is fair, then every time something bad happens, your belief system will lead you to the conclusion that you deserved it. Look at how many times tragic things happen to innocent people. It happens all the time.

Today I begin to recognize that life is not fair and that helps me see life in a more realistic and mature way. I will do the best I can, but often the outcome is beyond my control. I can take solace in doing my best and being the best person I can be.

One of the things that happen during divorce is that our friendships change. As we evolve from a married person to a single person, needs and interests evolve. Friends are always evolving but during divorce it may be more obvious. The staff in your attorney's office may suddenly have become more important than the friends that you knew as a couple. New friends may seem to offer us greater understanding and support of our new situation, while our old friends seem to fade away.

As you travel this new road, be aware of the people you meet along the way. Remember:

- Every friend started as a stranger.
- Friends do not have to be close intimates to have value.
- We need acquaintances as well as best friends to have a healthy, balanced, supportive social network.
- Friends are constantly moving in and out of our lives.
- We need to be aware of replenishing our friend network.

Every **stranger** is a potential friend. When you say "Hi" to someone walking down the hall at work, or in the supermarket, or at your child's soccer game, you have made an **acquaintance**. When you exchange info – about the weather, the boss, the price of cantaloupes, or the soccer coach and you do this frequently, you are becoming **good acquaintances**. If you find yourself seeking out this person to exchange information not related to the original connection, you are becoming **casual friends**. From casual friends, you may begin to spend some time together. When you ask another mother you met at your son's soccer game to go to a movie, or have dinner, you are taking the relationship up a notch to **friends**. The frequency with which you talk and get together, along with the level of personal information shared, determines how good a friend she becomes. **Close friends** are those people with whom we share very personal information. We trust them and they trust us with private thoughts and feelings. **Intimates** are the "chosen" few. They are the ones who know us "better than we know ourselves." We think of them as sisters or brothers. We can call them at any time, day or night, and they will be there for us. They can do the same. The friendship is unconditional. These relationships are special. They do not occur frequently and they take work and commitment. We do not have many intimates at any one time in our lives. It isn't possible to be that connected and committed to more than a few at a time. It would be a full time job!

Today I will think about my friends. Do I have acquaintances, friends and intimates? Am I doing everything I can to nurture all my relationships?

Sit in a comfortable, quiet place in your home, free from distractions. Leave yourself twenty minutes for this exercise. Read this over a few times, then close your eyes, take a couple of deep, cleansing breaths to clear your mind and relax your body, and then begin.

"See yourself in your mind as you are today: an adult, maybe a mother, a caring nurturing person. Imagine yourself getting in your car and driving to your family home, not your home today, but the home in which you grew up. Imagine yourself outside the house. You do not feel afraid, you are a grown-up, and you feel capable and curious. You begin to climb up the steps to the house. See the house as it was, remembering how it looked, how it smelled, the noises in your home. As you continue up the front walk, you can hear a child crying. You know that child is you. You proceed into the house and find the source of the crying. You are an adult, seeing yourself as a child, crying. Gently, you pick that child up, you hold her on your lap, and you comfort her, as you would like to have been comforted. You and you alone, know what she needs, what she wants to hear. Comfort her, love her. Spend time with your inner child."

Take your time.

"By now, you have begun to quiet and reassure your child. Tell her that you love her and will always be there for her and she will never be alone again. Whenever she needs you, you will be available to comfort her. Say good-by, put her down and as you exit, notice how much smaller everything looks in your house. Smaller than when you were a child. You feel bigger and more in control. You feel like an adult. As you leave, you do not feel sad, only confident and proud that you could take care of that child and of yourself.

Now you leave the house, walk down the stairs toward your car. You get in the car, adjust the seat belt and then take a moment to look in the rear view mirror and see yourself as you are today – competent, strong, full of love. Then start your car. See yourself driving on the road leading to your home today. Still keeping your eyes closed, see yourself in your home. You feel safe, competent and in control. Acknowledge that you have done a good job of comforting the child and that when you need to, or she needs you to, you can go back at any time and comfort her again."

Today I am aware of the little girl inside of me. As I go through my divorce, I will notice when she is crying out for help and reassurance. I will nurture her, attend to her, listen to her, and comfort her. She will never be alone again. I am with her.

Do you still feel great physical attraction for your ex-husband (or soon to be ex), even though you are getting divorced? Well, you are not alone. A woman may find a man unappealing in many ways, but chemistry may still exist. Some women find that men who are emotionally unavailable fuel their chemistry. If you still find your estranged husband attractive, you may feel as if you are sky-diving without a parachute.

It is difficult to disengage from a spouse when the chemistry still feels so intoxicating. Your friends may not understand it, and you may feel uncomfortable and secretive about those feelings. Some estranged couples continue to experience wild, passionate sex. Sometimes the acrimony can fuel the passion and the sparks ignited by arguing can explode into a sexual liaison. In the HBO movie *Good Friends*, the couple played by Greg Kinnear and Toni Colette share this kind of marriage. It is clear from the outset that they have little in common, but their fighting serves to ignite passion between them.

Staying away from him is complicated. You may not be able to stand him, but you can't imagine being without the great sex. Setting those boundaries is difficult but critical if you are to move on and have other healthy relationships. You also cannot grieve and heal from something you refuse to leave.

How do you give it up? Think of it as dieting or quitting smoking. How did you do at those? What techniques worked best for you? In both of those cases, many people set a date they choose to quit smoking or begin a diet. Usually the night before is a huge feast of excess. Maybe you need to quit your physical relationship in the same way. Like food or smoking, indulging brings pleasure for the moment and remorse later on. Remorse and regret lead directly to lowered self-esteem. Is that what you want? Are you willing to trade a few minutes of pleasure for your sense of self? Think of him as you would cigarettes: they are toxic for your body, he is toxic for your soul. Or think of it in the context of food. Highly saturated fat can destroy your physical health; continued liaisons with him will ruin your emotional health. It will hurt at first – deprivation always does. Keep in mind, there is a "greater good" at stake here: your own self worth.

Today when I look at my ex and feel attraction, I will think about how toxic this connection is for me. I will choose to do what is good for me, not what feels good to me. It may feel awful to deprive myself at first, but in time, the benefits will far outweigh the immediate discomfort.

"What if there is no one else for me? What if I end up all alone?" While there are no guarantees that you will fall in love again, a large percentage of women do remarry. Approximately seventy-four percent of divorced women remarried in three years (Orli). So, you stand a pretty good chance of meeting someone else.

Karen shared this parable with me:

> "I was on a train. It pulled into the station and I knew it was time to get off. The conductor told me it was time, as did other passengers and my common sense. But I was worried. What if another train did not come along? Or what if it did and it was the wrong train? I was so fearful of not being able to reach my destination that I refused for a long time to get off the train. The conductor finally said to me, 'Lady, if you don't get off the train and let it go on its way, your train will never get here. This train needs to move off of the track to make room for the next one.'

> 'But what if the next train is not for me?' I cried. 'Then what will I do?' 'You will not know until you let this train pass,' he replied. Then more gently he said, 'Let it go, it is not for you. It will not take you where you want to go. Let a new train have the opportunity to pull into the station. Let it go.'"

Are you staying in a relationship that is wrong for you? Are you merely there because you are afraid that another won't come your way? While there are no guarantees that another relationship will enter your life, if you stay in the relationship you are in, you will never have the chance to find out. You have to get off the train to make room for another. Let it go.

Trust that something else will come your way. Just by getting off the train, something else does come your way, almost immediately. That something else is opportunity. Without opportunity, there is no chance of anything changing. Often, we throw up roadblocks to opportunities by staying stuck in the patterns we are in. This is often due to fear. When we acquiesce to our fear, we deny ourselves the very changes we yearn for. Do not let your fear rob you of opportunity.

Today do I stay stuck in a relationship that is going nowhere? If so, why do I stay? What am I afraid of? Inherent in taking advantage of opportunity is the reality that risk is involved. Will I let my fear rob me of the life I want and deserve?

There are many milestones in the divorce process for the couple. These include filing the divorce papers, receiving the papers, and the day the decree is finalized. For children, these events have no real significance. In fact, children do not even need to know of these events.

For children, the divorce begins the day one parent moves out of the family home. This signifies the end of living in a two-parent family and the beginning of adjusting to having two homes. It is the beginning of a new way of life. Whether the legal divorce is final before or after the move takes place, it is important to remember that for children, this is a day of great significance. Their parents will now live in separate residences and that will require some adjustment for them. To that end, parents must be sensitive to how the move will affect their children. While they may be thrilled to see their spouse leave, children may feel differently. There are a number of things you can do to make it easier for your kids. Adjust the following suggestions to keep them age appropriate:

The moving parent can:
- If possible, have the child see the new apartment/house before he/she moves there.
- If possible, have a separate bedroom for the child or at least an area which will belong to him/her.
- Allow your child to have some input into decorating his/her new area.
- Give the child the new address and telephone number.
- Take the child to see the new apartment as soon as possible after the move.
- Have the child help unpack some things.
- Let the child know exactly when the move is going to occur.
- Avoid "pumping" the child for information about the other parent when they come to visit.
- Let the child help with sorting of things and rearranging the new place.
- Allow the child to bring friends, especially until he/she knows new kids in the area.
- Be upbeat and reassuring.
- Avoid fighting with their spouse about furniture (or anything else) in front of the child.

The parent who is staying with the child can:
- Allow the child to take some of his/her things to the new house.
- Not have the children watch the parent move out. Let them spend the afternoon with friends.
- Allow the child to call the moved parent or visit that same day, if possible.
- Encourage the child to visit the new place.
- Be upbeat and reassuring.
- Rearrange the furniture as soon as possible to "fill in the holes."
- Not complain about the "missing" furniture.

Today I will remember that this day means something different to me than it does to my kids. I will pay attention to their needs and try to make the transition as easy for them as possible. Today signifies the beginning of having two families instead of one and I will try to be sensitive and supportive to them as they face this new chapter in their lives.

If only this, if only that...

No one wants to go through a divorce. It feels overwhelming. We make deals in our head all the time. We try to adjust, mollify, acquiesce, compromise. We have a million scenarios. Most of them begin with "if only." And then we make a commitment to ourselves to make the "if only" a reality. Often we take these scenarios to our husbands. We plead, scream, beg, bargain, threaten, explain, rationalize, theorize. We suggest counseling, marital therapy, talking with our pastor, our priest, our rabbi, our parents, his parents, his best friend, your best friend, your doctor, a psychiatrist, a support group, a twelve step program. We suggest, we urge, we make ourselves crazy. We make them crazy.

And we are exhausted. And still nothing happens.

Do we ever really sit and think, "Let's say he did see the counselor, or talked with his best friend, or went to a twelve step program, or whatever. Would it really, *really* be enough?" Think about this realistically. Think about what changes are realistically possible. There is no magic cure for everything. The question "would it be enough?" is based on what is real. Let's say he did follow through with one of your suggestions – would it really be enough for you? When we allow ourselves to be honest with ourselves, often the answer is no. It may simply be too late. Sometimes nothing would be enough.

Hanging onto hope and "what ifs" give you more ammunition to blame him. You can say, "Well, if he only did such and such, this marriage could have worked." Deep down inside you know better. You probably know you are through, too. But sometimes our anger wants to create more things to be angry with so we can go around thinking and saying HE didn't try hard enough. Blaming him gives us something to do with our pain.

Let it go. There are so many real things to do, and to feel sad and angry and hurt about. Don't compound and complicate things anymore. That ammunition you are using to "get" him will just ricochet off of him and hurt you.

Today I will begin to say there is nothing that would have been enough. I will accept that as the truth. What I want is a miracle and that isn't going to happen. I will stop fueling my anger by finding additional ways to make this his fault. It is done. I have to let it go.

Over 60% of men in marriages say they have had extra-marital affairs. Below are listed some of the reasons I have heard to explain the behavior:

- Sex. Some men say they were "driven" to cheat because their wife was not keeping them sexually fulfilled.

- They're dissatisfied with their relationship but are not sure how to do anything about it.

- Their wives are totally involved with the children (careers, school, parents) and they feel ignored and neglected.

- They are unhappy in the relationship but afraid to address it due to familial, emotional, or practical concerns.

- They hope their wife will find out and divorce them.

- They aren't stimulated anymore… either physically or intellectually.

- They don't share their interests with their wife because she doesn't have the inclination to join in.

- Their wife isn't there when they need her most and somebody else offers their shoulder for support.

- Something is missing and they don't know what it is.

- Boredom.

- They feel older, unattractive and under-appreciated.

Regardless of the reason for infidelity, the result is devastating for the woman. There is a sense of betrayal, deceit, and disrespect. Many women who, in truth, are no longer in love with their husbands and even want the marriage to end, can find themselves reeling from the news of infidelity.

The breaking of the vows hits women the hardest. Some women even say that physical abuse is not as horrible as infidelity! Why is infidelity the final straw for so many women? Perhaps it has to do with our connection between love and sex; that is, we place a greater value on the emotional intimacy of sex than men do. Or perhaps bringing another woman into the picture evokes feelings of inferiority and competition. Often when an affair takes place, women are distracted from looking at all the other issues in the marriage. Infidelity blinds them from looking at other problems that may have existed. The pain and sense of betrayal are enormous.

Today if my husband cheated on me, I will not take blame for his behavior. True, he may have been unhappy in the marriage, but it was his choice to act out that unhappiness by having an affair. I will try to stay focused on the marital issues even though it is harder now that this betrayal has occurred. I need to know that I am not responsible for another person's behavior.

The importance of soothing ourselves and creating a sense of calm when going through crisis cannot be overstated. This is true for our children as well as it is for us. Angela J. Mazur, LCSW, of Farmington, Connecticut is a therapist who specializes in child and adolescent issues. She shared the following strategies for helping our children learn self-nurturing rituals:

- Cuddling/touch – Helps the child feel safe, secure and loved. It is as relaxing as a massage is for adults.
- Music – Different kinds of music encourages your child to move freely and express what he feels.
- Exercise – Movement of any kind.
- Simple meditation – Teach a child to breathe deeply to help with anxiety or impulse control.
- Create an imagery tape with your child using your voice – For example, imagine you are at the beach or in a field and that the two of you take all of the things that are upsetting you and gather them in a basket. Then you release them, leave them or throw them all away.
- Create a bedtime ritual – Each of you share what made you sad, mad, scared or happy during the day.
- Use transitional objects – If the child is afraid to go to bed or to leave you for visitation, giving him/her a piece of your clothing (such as an old tee shirt to sleep in) can comfort the child.
- Journal – Children enjoy writing down their thoughts and feelings.
- Draw – Children can create visual expressions of their feelings.
- Find a support group for children experiencing divorce – The school social worker or psychologist is a good resource. If your school doesn't offer one, encourage them to start such a program. Peer support is invaluable in diminishing shame and isolation, and creating validation and acceptance.
- Make a cassette tape reading your child's favorite bedtime stories and let him/her take it with him/her on visitation – Listening to the tape at bedtime can help the child feel more connected and secure.
- Use the soothing power of water – Swim together or prepare a relaxing bubble bath for your child.
- Enroll him/her in karate – It builds confidence and self-esteem, develops impulse control, and provides a healthy venue to express anger.
- Have puppets in the house – Encourage your children to create stories using them.
- Free-play – Let your child take the lead and play whatever he/she wants. This encourages self-expression. Don't correct, criticize or offer solutions. Let him/her create the script and express whatever he/she feels.
- Get a punching bag or an "angry pillow" – Let the child express anger in a non- destructive manner.

Trial and error is the best way to figure out what is most effective for your child. All are adaptable for all children, if you are mindful of creating an age-appropriate experience.

Today I know the importance of providing my child with outlets to express his feelings and nurture himself. I will take just one of the suggestions above and incorporate it today into our daily routine. Soon my child will come to me and express his need to nurture himself.

A huge movement in assertiveness training began in the early 1970's, coinciding with the height of the women's movement. Invariably, assertiveness is confused with aggression. **Assertiveness** still has some negative connotations despite the fact that assertiveness training is not a new concept. Aggression is an underpinning of violence and most women's reaction to violence ranges from uncomfortable to downright abhorrent. Let's clear the air on assertiveness communication, which has been badly maligned. The three types of communication are:

- **Passive communication** – The message is that you are everything and I am nothing. In passive interchanges, one person acquiesces to the other one's needs, whether or not they want to. Many passive communicators say they do this to avoid confrontation.

- **Aggressive communication** –The message is that my opinion is everything and yours is nothing. When engaged in aggressive communication, the sender's concern is to win. How the other person feels is not important. Aggressive communication includes manipulation, threats, insults, put-downs, or guilt.

- **Assertive communication** – Based on the premise of mutual respect, the sender does not demean or diminish either herself or the receiver. In assertive communication, we "agree to disagree." There are no "strong-arming" tactics and no undermining and silencing of one's own beliefs.

The notion that we can stand up for ourselves and not be aggressive may be a new concept to you. There are many techniques that we can utilize to improve our assertiveness and our style of communication. One book, *Your Perfect Right* by Alberti and Emmons (1995) is an excellent resource.

Before you can utilize any techniques, there must be an internal change: you must embrace the notion that you have a right to your thoughts and feelings and that you have a right to express them. Building confidence and self-esteem in all areas of your life can help create the shift into assertive communication. If we remain passive, we will go through our lives frustrated, undervalued, and even ignored. If we have a more aggressive approach, we will lose friends, family, and co-workers, as they will gradually distance themselves from our unpleasant way of relating to them.

Today I ask myself, am I assertive in some areas and passive or aggressive in others? Does my style of communication change depending upon who I am with? Is there someone whose communication style I admire? I can imagine how good I will feel when I honor my own opinions and give them voice in a way that does not demean or undermine another human being.

By now you may be asking "How long is this going to take?" The length of the marriage, your assets, and whether or not you have dependents are variables that contribute to the duration of the divorce process. How cooperative you and your partner are is another variable that impacts the length of the process. Where you live will also have an effect, as the divorce laws differ from state to state.

Between you and your husband, there are FOUR divorces going on. First, the two legal ones, comprised of your separate visions of what the result of the divorce should be. The further apart you are in your vision, the more acrimony there will be and conversely the closer you are in your vision, the less acrimony there will be. Ultimately, there will be one divorce, which represents a compromise of both your goals.

Emotionally, there are also two divorces going on. If you think of divorce as a process, chances are that the one who filed for divorce is further along in that process. Prior to filing for the divorce, the petitioner had lost all hope. That person has usually gone through much of the anger, sadness, bargaining, and denial and has begun to move on to acceptance. On the other hand, the person who receives the papers is often just beginning the emotional process. They may feel blindsided and unaware. Often, they feel that the problems were not so insurmountable and they may see the petitioner as uncaring. The petitioner of the divorce is not really cold and uncaring; he/she has gone through the same process, just at different times. This dichotomy in the couple's process creates the two different emotional divorces. Each person has difficulty understanding the other person's behavior and emotions, thus fueling the emotional conflict. The legal and emotional divorces exist on different continuums. You may be emotionally divorced before your legal divorce is final, or vice versa. There is a good chance that your emotional continuum will differ greatly from that of your spouse. It helps to remember that he experiences many of the same feelings but at different times. The presence of multiple divorces compounds the conflict during the divorce process.

Today it helps to understand that everyone is at a different stage of the divorce. This can help me be less judgmental and feel less personally wounded when my spouse's emotions and behavior are different than my own. There is no "right way" to do this and no "correct" time line. I will respect my own process. I will try to be patient with both of us.

Day 12   Separation, Legal Separation, and Divorce

The differences between separation, legal separation, and divorce are not very clear. Furthermore, the definitions vary from state to state. Attorney Laurie G. DeNigris, New Britain, Connecticut, helps clarify how each is different, and she cautions that these distinctions are based on Connecticut law and may vary from state to state. As with any legal advice, it is imperative that you seek counsel in your own state.

According to Attorney DeNigris, many people are not aware that just moving out of the family residence does not constitute a legal separation. You must see an attorney and file the appropriate paperwork with the court. In Connecticut, a legal separation is like a divorce, with the following exceptions:

- It doesn't invalidate your will as getting a divorce does.

- It may entitle you to continue to be eligible for health insurance benefits under your husband's policy.

- You cannot remarry.

- The division of assets may not be final.

- It may make you immune from further financial obligation; that is, any debts he may incur after the legal separation.

- It is not final. If circumstances change, your settlement may also change.

When is it advisable to seek a legal separation instead of a divorce?

- If there are religious reasons that you do not want to seek a divorce.

- When medical benefits are a consideration.

- When you do not intend to remarry.

Today I am always learning new things about life, myself and this process called divorce. One of the things I am learning is that it is okay not to know everything and to ask for help from my attorney. That is his/her role. I must remember that I have a right to ask questions and that I will not feel ashamed for not knowing the answers. The harm lies with not asking. The more I ask, the more I will know and the better the decisions I will make.

How we hate change! Is it our fear of the unknown? Is it the loss of what we have? Is it the fear that we made a bad decision? Does transition makes us feel unsteady? For each of us, change represents different things and can cause great anxiety. When we consider divorce, we know that all the elements of our lives will be thrown into a state of chaos. Even if we are unhappy with our present situation, there can be comfort in what is familiar. Consider this: You are seated in a rowboat, at the back. You want to move to the front of the boat. Is there any way that you can do this without rocking the boat? Of course not. However, if you are afraid of the water, or cannot swim, or the water is filled with alligators and snakes, then rocking that boat, even slightly, may feel perilous. Divorce can feel like that.

In divorce, the stakes are certainly high. There is much you can lose, but there is also much to be gained. Right now, you can only see what you are giving up and not what you might receive. The idea of change can be terrifying. Rocking the boat and stirring things up is the cost of change. Change cannot happen without some upset of the equilibrium. You need to decide how important the change is, and how much of the unknown you can handle. Clearly, the more you research divorce laws, work with your attorney and with your therapist, the less frightening the unknowns will be. But they will always exist. We can only imagine what it will be. We can work to create the life we want, but there are, of course, no guarantees.

All of us are scared of change and what it may bring. Is your fear greater than your need to change your life? If so, then maybe you need to sit in the back of the rowboat a little bit longer. And that's okay. Meanwhile, you can continue to imagine how it would feel to sit in the front of the boat. If that is your dream, meditate on it, believe in it, and work at it. One day you will get up and change your seat!

Today I will think about other times in my life when I needed to rock the boat. Did I do it or did I merely sit there? Did it feel scary? How did my family handle change when I was a child? What did that teach me about change? I will work to come to terms with my anxiety so I can build confidence to move forward with my life in a healthier way.

Some women have viewed finances as their husband's responsibility and have no idea of how the money is allocated, saved, invested, and spent. Before you begin the process of dividing the assets, it is imperative you have a thorough understanding of what they are and what their value is. You will do yourself a grave disservice if you say, "I will trust my husband to be fair" or "He always took care of the money, why should I learn about it now?" The most generous husband can become the most penny-pinching ex-husband. Knowing your rights and knowing about the marital finances is part of advocating for yourself. It gives you a realistic picture of what you have accumulated and, therefore, what there is to be shared. The following contribute to your list of assets:

- Family home
- Checking accounts
- Retirement accounts
- Stocks and bonds
- Pending tax refunds
- Contents of the home

- Vehicles
- Brokerage accounts
- Business interests
- Inheritances
- Life insurance policies
- Jewelry
- Contents of safety deposit boxes

- Savings accounts
- Pension plans
- Rental property
- Boats, trailers, campers
- Certificates of deposit

Prepare a detailed list of each of these items and their value. Include assets which are owned jointly and those which are held in only one spouse's name. Assets that you had prior to the marriage are usually not included in the division of marital property. If you liquidated assets to contribute to joint property, make a note of that, including how much the asset was worth. For example, if you owned property prior to the marriage and sold it to use the proceeds to go into the marital home, you may be entitled to reimbursement for that contribution. Having documentation and proof of all assets is extremely important. Taking the time to do this research will assist your attorney in being able to do the best job he/she can. You want to get all that you are entitled to. While this may feel extremely cold and calculating, this is the business aspect of divorce. Separate the emotional pieces from the legal and financial entanglements. Being clear about what assets exist in the marriage helps you understand and obtain what is rightfully yours. Years from now, you won't have regrets that you didn't do all your homework!

Today I will start accumulating the necessary information. I will do a little each day and it will be done before I know it! I need to learn about finances. This is critical so I can be in charge of my own financial destiny. I no longer need someone else to make monetary decisions for me.

We learn at a very early age that different relationships and venues call for different behavior. A small child knows that how she behaves in church is different from how she behaves in the backyard. She also has learned that how she behaves with adults is different from how she behaves with other children. We develop a knack, in early life, for discerning which relationships call for what behaviors. As young girls, we are taught to please and to read people's moods. Sometimes, this ability is an asset, as it helps us establish rapport and connection. Other times, it can be a detriment. We may read people so often that we do it without thought or regard to our own needs. When we do that, we diminish ourselves.

Occasionally, we have relationships where we can really be ourselves. Those folks consider us good enough just as we are and cherish and support us. This kind of unconditional positive regard does not come into our lives frequently. It is the cornerstone of all our important relationships. Acceptance must exist in a relationship for it to be nurturing. A good relationship also offers us patience, kindness, and respect.

When we have this kind of acceptance, we can be our authentic selves. We are free to be silly or grumpy, foolish, frightened, or vulnerable. Whatever negative traits we imagine we possess are met with patience and caring. When we are cared for in that unconditional way and accepted for who we are, we simply flourish. When we flourish, we become the best person we can be. In an environment without criticism, sarcasm, hostility or insults, we find that we can grow and evolve into our best selves.

- Did your husband provide you with that kind of environment?
- Did you provide him with that kind of environment?

If the answer to either of those is no, then the marriage was not living up to its potential. A good marriage is a partnership that enhances each person, encourages and applauds goals, dreams and hopes. This does not mean there are no hard times, no compromises, and no fights. It simply means that in this relationship, you feel good about yourself. What you see reflected in your partner's eyes are your positive qualities and attributes. That kind of support and caring buoys our sense of self and feeds our confidence and strengths. Did you have that?

Today I see that I may not even be aware of what my best is, but I know when I feel good about myself. Did I feel that way in my relationship? Did I feel valued and cherished, or was I demeaned and criticized? I will look honestly at what I got from the relationship.

Throughout this process, it is not uncommon to have doubts about whether divorce is the right route to take. Many women, especially those with children, find themselves frequently questioning their decision. One of the questions they ask themselves is "what about the kids?"

Children do best in a consistent stable environment. If your marriage is in trouble and your children are living with yelling, fighting, verbal abuse, domestic violence, substance abuse or alcoholism, or even stony silence, then divorce is really better for them. Your situation may be less drastic and the choice may feel less clear. You may have a loveless marriage, or one that is cold and unaffectionate. Or it may simply be two people who have gone their separate ways. Is it still better to divorce? A loveless environment robs children of the warmth and affection that make a house into a home. It also provides children with a role model of marriage which is certainly less then stellar.

Many children grow up in single parent homes. Adoption is now open to single people, which is testimony to one's ability to raise a child independently. More frequently, single women are opting to become mothers, either through adoption or sperm donors. While most would agree that they wish they had a partner, they also are clear that they do not want to marry just to provide their child with a father. The most important elements for children are love, stability, and harmony in the home. If the parent(s) are happy and content, then the children will be able to reap all the joys of being raised in a safe and stable home, regardless of whether it is composed of two parents, one parent, or two parents living separately.

Divorce is a complicated matter. There are doubts and unanswered questions. Each woman must make the determination of what is best for herself and her children. Sacrificing your happiness may not be in the best interests of your child. If doubt persists, speak with a therapist or clergy member or other women who have faced the same challenges. As always, educate yourself and seek assistance and guidance. But, ultimately, make your own decision, as your situation is uniquely yours. Be cautious, however, not to use the idea of your "children's best interests" as a way to avoid making hard, sometimes scary decisions.

Today I will consider all aspects of this difficult decision as it relates to my children. I will seek counsel and information. Ultimately, I will make my own decision. I am learning to trust myself as a person, a woman, and a mother.

It is difficult to move forward when you don't have a vision of your destination. You may have some idea of what you want, however the details may be hazy. If you stay where you are, you know exactly the kind of life you will have. It is right before you; what you see is what you get.

Too often, women attempt to stay in their marriage by creating a fantasy of what the relationship *could become*. This involves a lot of "If only" or "I wish." Making a decision about whether or not to stay in your marriage is difficult enough without distorting your reality. One of the ways to explore your options is to consider *what will not be*. For example, if you leave your marriage you also leave:

- Yelling
- Emotional abuse
- Walking on eggshells
- Drugging
- Tension
- Disrespect
- Lying
- His awful friends
- Anxiety about what will happen each day
- Physical abuse
- Sexual abuse
- Drinking
- Fear

Will you miss those things? Can you imagine a life free from those behaviors? Most of us long to be rid of that lifestyle. What you can imagine as you move forward into your new life is:

- Independence
- Being yourself
- Safety
- Calm
- Less tension
- Choosing your own friends
- Peace
- No fear

These are basic elements of a healthy life. If you stay where you are and he isn't willing to change, then nothing will change. It might even get worse.

When you find yourself getting scared of how you will "make it," remember you have been making it for years. You have been taking care of everything that needs attention. Without the added tension and anxiety of living in a destructive relationship, life becomes peaceful and far less complicated. The rest is easy.

Today When I have trouble thinking of how my life will look when I am on my own, I will simply list what negative things I will leave behind and then imagine my life without that stress eroding my self esteem and tiring me out. I will allow myself to really imagine how good that can feel. Then, even with doubts, I know I can move forward.

Women talk about how they have their 'buttons pushed" by their ex-spouses. They lament at how they "can't help their responses" and if he would "only stop," then they wouldn't have to respond like raving lunatics. It would be great if everyone would behave as we wished they would! Unfortunately, they won't. So we are left with our own feelings and responsibility for our responses. You can choose to feel and behave another way. This will empower you. When you are in charge of your behavior, you will feel more confident, competent, calm and in control.

Here are some ways to avoid getting your buttons pushed:

- Know that he pushes your buttons and WILL yourself not to give him the satisfaction of seeing you go ballistic.
- Before you have to see/talk with him, imagine a big plexi-glass tube enclosing you and protecting you. When you hear his words, this magic plexi-glass filters out the feelings.
- Visualize a television screen around him. In your hand is the imaginary remote; use it to silence him by pushing the mute button.
- Imagine he is a character in a soap opera. How would the leading lady respond?
- Imagine you are a therapist/journalist observing his behavior in order to write an article on it. Since you need to listen to his words objectively, there is no room for you to experience them personally.
- Imagine you are Wonder Woman and that your magic bracelets can ward off evil words.
- Imagine his words bouncing off you and landing right on him (I'm rubber, you're glue... Remember that from childhood? Whatever you say, bounces off me and sticks to you!)
- Imagine his words are handfuls of mud being thrown at you. All you need to do is DUCK!

The above techniques have one thing in common – they are designed to help you detach emotionally and not take whatever is said personally. They may seem light-hearted and not "serious" enough to deal with the problem. It is the lightheartedness, the ability to keep your sense of humor that helps you detach! Even if these seem silly to you, try them. You may find you are so busy imagining those bracelets or playing with the mute button, that your buttons don't get pushed at all!

These techniques are useful in all relationships. The ability to detach can go a long way to diminish your stress and create a sense of calm in your life. Good luck and have fun!

Today since I accept I cannot change another person's behavior, I will look to change how I respond. Instead of feeling out of control, I will take control of my own feeling by detaching from that person's words. Another person's words hurt me only if I believe them. Today, I will not believe them... I won't even consider them!

"Stinkin' Thinkin'" is a term that is used in Alcoholics Anonymous. You do not have to be an alcoholic to understand the phrase or to find it useful in dealing with your own thought process. Stinkin' Thinkin' refers to thoughts that make you think or feel badly about yourself or others. Negative thinking can spur on unhealthy behaviors and create many unhappy situations for you. Negative thinking includes:

- Assuming you know how things will turn out
- Expecting the worst
- Self-criticism
- Assuming you know what others are thinking, feeling, doing
- Worrying
- Interpreting someone's behavior
- Self diagnosing
- Taking things personally
- Self-blame
- Blaming others
- Shame
- Revenge
- Seeing yourself as a victim
- Making assumptions

If you think negative thoughts, you begin to believe negative things. Before you know it, you have a negative life. You might be so adept at Stinkin' Thinkin' that you aren't even aware that you are doing it. Here are some examples of Stinkin' Thinkin':

- When someone is late for a dinner date, do you immediately assume they stood you up, or got in a traffic accident?
- When the boss calls you into the office, do you feel like you will get in trouble or be fired?

These are examples of situations when we use Stinkin' Thinkin' as a matter of habit. You may find you do it more than you think! Negative thinking sets you up to be unhappy and creates anxiety and paranoia. Then, you act in response to those feelings, as opposed to responding to the reality of the situation. If we interpret every headache as a brain tumor, we live our lives in fear and anxiety. It's not a very happy or productive way to experience life!

Today I ask myself, am I guilty of Stinkin' Thinkin'? Do I always assume the worst? Am I waiting for the other shoe to fall? Do I react without hearing the whole story? Do my responses sometimes get me into trouble? Do I have to apologize frequently for overreacting? If so, I now have an opportunity for growth. I will become aware of my behaviors and my thought patterns. I can use meditation, prayer, mindfulness, therapy, or even medication to reach my goal. I will imagine how much more enjoyable life would be without the anxiety, anger and shame that accompanies Stinkin' Thinkin'.

Transition always involves some sense of the unknown and this creates stress. Experts say it is not the stress that is so damaging to our well being, but the fact that we don't have a break from it. Going through a divorce is one of the most stressful experiences you will endure in your life. The good news is that it does not last forever (although it can feel that way). Here are several tips for creating a break from stress to give your mind and body a chance to rejuvenate.

- Breathe. The most simple and fundamental relaxation technique in the world. Close your eyes and imagine exhaling all the stress in your body and breathing in calming fresh oxygen.
- Occasionally try eating in silence and by yourself. Do not watch television or read. Pay attention to the taste, texture, and smell of your food. Notice how your body reacts to being satiated.
- In the morning before jumping out of bed, allow yourself a full body stretch before arising to face your day.
- Try arriving at appointments a few minutes early. Use those moments to simply relax or read a magazine.
- On your drive home from work, make a conscious effort to transition your thoughts from work to home. By the time you arrive at your home, your thoughts should be clear of work issues and ready to focus on family.
- When you get home, change out of your work clothes into your "play clothes."
- Try driving in the slow lane to work.
- Pet your dog or cat, allowing yourself to really feel the softness of their fur and their loving response to you.
- Notice if you are rushing. Make a conscious effort to slow down and make sure you breathe deeply.
- Laugh. A good belly laugh is a wonderful tension releaser!
- Keep a favorite saying or proverb on your desk or use it as your screen saver on your computer. Let it anchor you when you feel stressed.
- Count ten blessings, while slowly breathing them in.
- Shrug your shoulders a few times a day, slowly and deeply, feeling the neck and back muscles release.
- Keep a photo of your children, family, friends, or pet on your desk. Allow yourself to feel affection and gratitude for those you love..
- Listen to your favorite songs in the car and sing along. Allow yourself to get caught up in the moment.
- Take at least one moment every day to stop and notice some miracle of nature: the blue sky, the smell of the rain, the feel of the wind.
- Visualize yourself in your home, then your town, and then your state. Then broaden your focus to the country, the world, the universe. When we see ourselves as part of the big picture, our perspective shifts and our problems and stresses shrink in importance.
- Ask yourself "Will this matter a year from now?" Most things we worry about won't even matter the next day. Make conscious choices about what to worry about.
- Smile, even if you don't feel like it. It can help shift your mood and give you a break from the stress.

Today I could try just one of these changes and not feel overwhelmed. They each take little effort and I may find that they have big effects. Some will work for me better than others. I will adopt those that work and make them part of my daily routine. Any reduction in my stress is a very good thing!

A divorcing woman gives a lot of thought into deciding whether it is better to leave the marital home or to stay. If children are involved, staying in the home they were accustomed to reduces the number of changes and gives them time to adjust to the divorce while minimizing confusion and loss. On the other hand, staying in the marital home may be painful for you. It can provide a constant reminder of the loss you have experienced. If you are the one who stays in the marital home (often the case for women), it is critical to make it your own space. Memories of life as a couple are everywhere. After he leaves, there is an undeniable absence. It resonates through the home, leaving it feeling unfinished. Re-creating the space to reflect your personality minimizes those feelings of loss. In death, we often want to keep our loved one's things around us, as they offer comfort and solace. In a divorce, these same mementos may not feel comforting, but rather intrusive and hurtful.

Colors, smells, textures, and sounds all impact our brain. Each of us finds comfort in different ways through different sensorial experiences. We must use those preferences to create a space that expresses who we are, what we like, what soothes us. These changes can be as simple as buying a new set of sheets or arranging the furniture. Certainly, removing his photographs from the common space and putting them in your children's room is one quick easy way to claim the space as your own.

If you are the one who moved out, the same is true for you. Create a pleasing, nurturing environment, which is your safe haven – a kind of harbor in the storm.

Create a place to return to at the end of the day that envelops you with warmth and caring. Rather than reinvent your space, you will create and build your own environment.

Today I will begin to think about removing things that are symbols of the marriage. I will imagine how I want the space to look, feel, and smell. I will imagine a space that reflects me. I will create space that expresses who I am and who I am becoming. Today, I will make one change in my space, no matter how small it is, to reflect who I am.

Sometimes in divorce, a parent not only leaves his spouse, he also leaves his children. The reasons for this are varied and complex. Some of the reasons include acrimony between the adults, alcohol and substance abuse, or moving to another part of the country. Often, it has to do with the psychology and the maturity of that individual.

Children have a tendency to blame themselves for their parent's behavior. Their thinking is somewhat linear and concrete, "If I were loveable enough, Daddy would still be here and wouldn't have chosen work (drugs, alcohol, girlfriend) over me." To rail against their father, to call him names and condemn his actions, may only make the child feel worse. On the other hand, making excuses for the absent father teaches the child to mask and deny unacceptable behavior. To minimize the impact of abandonment to the child only denies the child freedom to express his pain and loss. So, how do you handle it?

- Let the child express his feelings without you judging them.
- Offer comfort, not explanations.
- Encourage the child to share his feelings with a best friend or a counselor. You are NOT the most objective listener here. The child needs that objectivity.
- Let the child know, frequently and emphatically, that the parent's abandonment is NOT her fault.
- Offer the child simple age-appropriate information, regarding the father's whereabouts.
- Encourage the child to write or draw pictures about how he/she feels.
- Provide other positive male role models such as coaches, teachers, and uncles.
- Remember that no matter how bad a father he is, the child will long for the relationship. It is natural for children to want to be loved.
- Help the child deal with feelings of rejection and anger without letting your feelings get in the way.
- If the father does resume communication, do not discourage it. While you may think he may not deserve a relationship with your child, your child needs the relationship with his/her father.

Finally, put your child's needs first. Remember that the child's relationship with the father and your relationship with your ex-spouse are two different relationships. Think about your own relationship with your father; that can help you empathize with your child's feelings. Stay focused on your child's experience without getting it muddled with your spousal issues.

Today while I may not have much use for my ex-spouse, I empathize with my child and his/her loss of a father. I will not use my child's pain as a vehicle to express my own anger and disappointment. I will use different resources to process my feelings. When I talk with my child about his/her father, I will stay focused on their relationship, providing my child, to the best of my ability, a safe place to grieve.

"*The weekends are the worst.*"

This is a frequent complaint of many women in the beginning stages of separation. They adjust to living by themselves during the week as the weekdays are jammed packed with things to do. Often these responsibilities keep women from really doing much introspection. It is on the weekends, especially the evenings, when women report they have the most difficult time. That is when they feel the loneliest. This loneliness is often accompanied by sadness, much of which is brought on by reminiscing about the good times.

Why do we do that to ourselves? Much of our lives are spent caring and doing for others. When we finally have time to ourselves – time we always complain that we don't have enough of – we tend to be immobilized and lost. Perhaps most of our loneliness is boredom. Suddenly, we have "down time," and we don't know what to do with it. We may be in a quandary as to how to make ourselves feel better. So consider the possibility that maybe you aren't really lonely; maybe you just have nothing to do! Try the following to help ward off those lonely feelings:

- Try to plan a special time with a friend and a special time for yourself, EACH weekend. It will give you something to look forward to instead of mooning over the past.
- Schedule special time for yourself on the calendar just as you would Bobby's dentist appointment or Susie's soccer game. Make this time *non-negotiable.*
- Keep a list of things around the house that need to be done that HE would do. When you have those lonely or bored minutes, use the time to tackle some project you usually wouldn't do. Get a book from the library or use the Internet and learn new skills to do these projects. Start with a simple project and slowly advance. You didn't always know how to cook (or sew, knit, drive) but you learned. Learning something new and finishing a project will enhance your self-confidence.
- Make a list of unwatched movies or unread books. Take time to catch up on both.
- Practice going out by yourself. If dinner alone intimidates you, try lunch at a nice restaurant. If going to the movies in the evening by yourself feels a little scary, start with a matinee.
- Use the time to pamper yourself – a massage, a pedicure, or even a bubble bath by candlelight.
- Learn something new – yoga, sailing, jazz, it doesn't matter. Use the time for self-growth.

It may feel strange at first – this notion of being *with* yourself instead of *by* yourself is the goal. After years of taking care of others, you probably don't know what you like and dislike anymore. This is your time to learn. There are many payoffs – emotionally, spiritually and physically, to self-awareness. Whatever happens in your future, you will learn to enjoy yourself and your own company.

Today I will begin to think of loneliness as boredom and boredom as an opportunity to grow and enrich my life!

- In 1996, among all female murder victims in the United States, 30 percent were slain by their husbands or boyfriends. – *Uniform Crime Reports of the U.S. 1996, Federal Bureau of Investigation, 1996.*
- Nearly one-third of American women (31 percent) report being physically or sexually abused by a husband or boyfriend at some point in their lives. –*Commonwealth Fund survey, 1998.*
- It is estimated that 503,485 women are stalked by an intimate partner each year in the United States. – National Institute of Justice, July 2000.
- There are estimates that range from 960,000 incidents of violence against a current or former spouse, boyfriend, or girlfriend each year to 4 million women who are physically abused by their husbands or live-in partners each year. – *Violence by Intimates: Analysis of Data on Crimes by Current or Former Spouses, Boyfriends, and Girlfriends, U.S. Department of Justice, March, 1998.*
- While women are less likely than men to be victims of violent crimes overall, women are five to eight times more likely than men to be victimized by an intimate partner. – *Violence by Intimates: Analysis of Data on Crimes by Current or Former Spouses, Boyfriends, and Girlfriends, U.S. Department of Justice, March, 1998.*
- Violence by an intimate partner accounts for about twenty-one percent of violent crime experienced by women and about two percent of the violence experienced by men. – *Violence by Intimates: Analysis of Data on Crimes by Current or Former Spouses, Boyfriends, and Girlfriends, U.S. Department of Justice, March, 1998.*
- Of women who reported being raped and/or physically assaulted over the age of eighteen, three quarters (76 percent) were victimized by a current or former husband, cohabitating partner, date or boyfriend. – *Prevalence Incidence, and Consequences of Violence Against Women: Findings from the National Violence Against Women Survey, U.S. Department of Justice, November, 1998.*
- In 1994, women separated from their spouses had a victimization rate 1 1/2 times higher than separated men, divorced men, or divorced women. – *Sex Differences in Violent Victimization, 1994, U.S. Department of Justice, September, 1997.*
- Forty percent of teenage girls age fourteen to seventeen report knowing someone their age who has been hit or beaten by a boyfriend. – *Children Now/Kaiser Permanente poll, December, 1995.*
- Females accounted for thirty nine percent of the hospital emergency department visits for violence-related injuries in 1994 but eighty four percent of the persons treated for injuries inflicted by intimates. – *Violence by Intimates: Analysis of Data on Crimes by Current or Former Spouses, Boyfriends, and Girlfriends, U.S. Department of Justice, March, 1998.*
- One in five female high school students reports being physically or sexually abused by a dating partner. – *Massachusetts Youth Risk Behavior Survey (YRBS), August 2001.*

Today If I fit into any of the above risk groups, I will seek help immediately from a friend, an area shelter, or the police. I will not minimize the risk to my children or myself. There is no shame in asking for help. I would rather be safe than sorry.

Who gives you a lift?

In whose company do you feel better?

Who is the best listener you know?

Who is the best teacher you know? Who continues to provide you with knowledge?

Who, in the last six months, has done something really nice for you?

If the phone rang right now, who would you like to hear from?

When did you have your last really good belly laugh? What happened to cause it?

Who cooked you the last great meal you had away from home?

If you were really upset, who would you call?

Who is the most caring person you know?

Who is the most humorous person you know?

Who gives you the best counsel with regard to work issues?

    … child issues?

    … divorce issues?

    … emotional issues?

Who would you call if you had an emergency in the middle of the night?

Is there anyone you over-utilize?

Today I will answer as many of these questions as I can. Then, I will rejoice for the people I have in my life. I will be grateful for those who care for, love, and nurture me. Today I will allow myself to experience the joy and comfort of someone caring for me. That is all I will do today. That is enough!

Did you know that infants can get depressed? Angela Mazur, LCSW, is a children's therapist in Farmington, Connecticut. She explains that there can be signs of depression in a child under two years of age. These include lack of facial expression, slowed growth and slowed cognitive development. While other factors can also contribute to these symptoms, depression should not be ruled out, especially if there have been recent changes in the infant's life. Babies may become fussy and irritable and demonstrate apathy, sadness, and clinginess. When parents divorce, they need to watch for these symptoms in their baby. Some of these behaviors can be part of normal development. What separates the normal developmental stages from problematic issues is the severity of symptoms, the number of symptoms and their duration over time. If these behaviors continue for four weeks and interfere with the child's functioning, then they are not part of normal, healthy development. Depending upon the attachment to the caregivers, the child's depression may manifest over the loss of contact with a caregiver. If Dad was very involved in the care with this child and now is less available, the child will grieve that loss. Young children also experience loss when a primary caregiver, although still present in the child's life, is not emotionally available because of her own response to the divorce. If she is distraught and distracted as she experiences her own grief and sadness, the infant may react to her emotional unavailability by displaying some of the above symptoms.

There are ways to remedy this situation. Re-establish a routine for the child that includes more time for cuddling, holding, and rocking. When possible, more frequent contact with Dad would be positive. For young children, the frequency of visitation is more important than the length. If it is feasible, daily contact for an hour or so can greatly improve the situation. If the father is not available, family members and friends can be helpful in supplying extra emotional and physical contact to the child. If your child is displaying symptoms of depression, then get input from a child therapist. A consultation with an expert can provide insight and ideas that can help remedy the situation and put the mother's fear to rest.

Today I will be mindful of my young child's needs. When I am interacting with my child, I will concentrate on being present and involved. For that time, I will push aside all of my own issues and give my complete attention to my child. Not only will that be a positive experience for my child, but I will find that in my reconnection, it will be a positive experience for me as well.

Have you ever had a dialogue with your husband that took place completely in your mind? These conversations can be ongoing, free-running diatribes in which you try to explain your anger, defend your position, elicit pity, or create clever comebacks at his unjust behavior toward you. Soon, you begin to feel as if a tape is playing – the thoughts seem to take on a life of their own as they whirl around in your head, like a song you can't get off your mind. It is helpful to write these thoughts down, for a number of reasons:

- Just getting them out of your head can alleviate those intrusive and hurtful thoughts. It can help you let go of your anger and stop using it to hurt yourself. It can free your mind up to deal with other more important, relevant things.

- When you see your thoughts on paper, you can begin to see your own patterns and deal with your own responsibility. This is not about blame but about taking responsibility.

- Writing down your thoughts and keeping them in a journal gives you a record of this difficult time. Later you can look back on what you wrote and see your growth.

- When you write it down, it can validate your experience and make it real. It affirms your response to the situation.

However, some women feel that writing down their inner thoughts and feelings is not effective unless someone else reads it. Usually, they want that other person to be their husband. The idea is that somehow he will "get it" and therefore reform, repent, apologize, and transform. Their hope is that there is something he can say that will make them feel better. Since he is the cause of their pain, shouldn't he be the cure as well?

Sending your letters to your husband is usually a bad idea. The truth is, if he hasn't gotten it by now, he probably isn't going to get it. Furthermore, he now has written documentation of your inner thoughts and you have no control over how he uses it. How would you feel if he sent it to his lawyer? Showed it to his/your parents? Your children? His new girlfriend? Once you write it and send it, it is OUT OF YOUR CONTROL. Think before you act.

Divorce is an extremely emotional time for both people. Often, we act impulsively and then regret our actions. One of the best ways to protect yourself from his wrath and your own regret is to slow down that impulse to act.

Today I will try writing down my thoughts and feelings and see if it helps me feel less burdened and overwhelmed. I will not give in to the temptation to share those pages with my ex-husband. My writing is to free ME and when I share it with my husband, I run the risk of losing that newly-attained freedom.

"Respect: high or special regard, esteem, to consider deserving of high regard" – Merriam-Webster Dictionary.

Is there respect in your life? Did your husband treat you with respect? Did you treat him with respect? What about your relationships with family, friends, co-workers, and children? Most importantly, do you treat yourself with respect? Learning to respect yourself means treating yourself with special regard and choosing people who treat you by the same standards. When we pick people to be part of our lives who do not treat us with respect, we are demeaning and insulting ourselves. We are basically saying to others and to ourselves, "I am not worthy of being treated with respect. I accept this treatment because I do not think I deserve anything else."

Treating yourself with respect means to take care of yourself, physically, emotionally, spiritually, psychologically, professionally, practically and relationally. It includes everything from getting enough sleep to reporting sexual harassment. It may sound like a daunting task, but in truth, it is the simplest thing you can do. When you live a life filled with respect, you will experience less chaos and crisis. You will be healthier, your relationships will be more stable, your jobs more secure. You are less likely to suffer from depression, eating disorders, alcohol and drug abuse.

We cannot demand respect from others. We cannot order people to behave the way we wish. We cannot change another person's behavior. Screaming, yelling, pleading, explaining, or threatening him simply will not change him. Rather than putting all of that effort into trying to re-do him, use that energy to respect yourself. If you are leaving a marriage where respect didn't exist or has dwindled to almost nothing, respect may feel foreign to you. Bring respect into your life in simple ways: eat better, work out, stop smoking, pay your bills on time. Put your best into everything you do. Stop accepting abusive people in your life. Which of your relationships are filled with disrespect, abuse, or aggravation? Begin to set boundaries with people who treat you poorly. Stick to those boundaries. This will not change the way other people act. Setting boundaries changes the way YOU act. This begins to build self-confidence. This puts you in charge of your life and empowers you. This is self-respect. When you respect yourself, others will respect you too.

Today I want respect in my life, but I can't demand that others change their behavior. If I want respect, I need to respect myself by engaging in healthy behaviors. I will begin to set boundaries. When I choose to set boundaries, I am choosing not to be treated with disrespect.

Divorce signifies the end of a marriage. There are peripheral losses that accompany divorce, such as loss of relationships with in-laws and some friends, perhaps the family home, financial security and so on. Even when a woman is the petitioner, she often finds herself grieving losses – some expected and some unexpected. Every culture has rituals to mark important events in our lives such as baptisms, weddings, funerals, bar mitzvahs, and birthdays. We also have rituals to celebrate holidays, Christmas, Easter, Valentine's Day, and so on. By participating in ritual, we honor the importance of these events in our lives, standing with friends and family to celebrate or mourn significant events.

With divorce, no ritual exists. The court experience is often cold and anti-climactic. It lacks empathy and ceremony. Many women leave the courthouse on the day of their divorce feeling empty because of this lack of ceremony. The detachment and minimization of the legal process can diminish the importance and impact of the event. The creation of divorce ritual helps us reach closure with our marriage. As with a funeral and burial, we come together to mourn, to share, and to support each other. Divorce is the death of a marriage. We need the same kind of validation and support to "officially" mark the finality and experience closure. When we experience closure, we also acknowledge new beginning and hope.

So what does a divorce ritual look like? Each woman's ritual is as unique and special as she is. Some women have "divorce showers," while others enjoy a dinner out with close friends. Other women have spent the night of their divorce going through old love letters and burning them, or putting the wedding album away in storage. Others have planted trees. Some have buried mementos of the marriage and planted flowers. For some, the ritual involved simply taking off their wedding ring.

Think about a gesture or ritual that has meaning for you. Take your time planning what you want. Do not minimize your need to grieve. Use ceremony to acknowledge and support that need. Honoring your loss honors you, your marriage, your grief, and also your hope for the future.

Today I will begin to consider and plan for my divorce ritual. I will look to my marriage experience to identify the things I truly grieve for. When I have identified those losses, I will plan to honor them. I may look at some books on rituals, or I may consult with friends for ideas, but I will ultimately do what feels right for me. When I honor my loss, I honor myself.

A curious phenomenon about this whole divorce experience is how many women see their marriages as failures. When I ask what criteria they use to reach that conclusion, they say, "Well, it ended in divorce, how you could call that anything but a failure?" Considering how much work a marriage is and how complex the issues are, I find it startling that the only criteria for failure is that is did not last forever.

When I see long-term marriages that end in divorce but launched healthy successful children, or marriages where each supported the other professionally, I have a hard time referring to them as failures. The problem with labeling these marriages failures is that it negates all the positive aspects of the couples' lives together. It indirectly diminishes the children. When we say our marriage is a failure, we imply that our relationship, and all relationships inherent in that relationship, were unsuccessful. Why is it that something that does not last forever is a failure? True, we do vow to love, honor, cherish, "'til death do us part." However, I see many marriages that do not end in divorce that I would label failures. Here are examples of failed marriages where the couple stayed together.

- Marriages where there is violence or abuse of any kind.

- Marriages where one person sacrifices everything for the sake of keeping the marriage together.

- Marriages where the people don't love each other.

- Marriages where there is untreated alcoholism or drug abuse.

- Marriages where people stay together for fear they can't make it on their own.

These relationships are failures because the marriage does not provide an environment in which growth, trust and love are present. We can expect to live well into our 70's. When a person dies before the national average, we do not call it a failure. We say "what a loss," or "how sad," We never say what a "failure" his life was. It would be insensitive! When a marriage ends, it signifies the death of a relationship. Can't we say "what a loss" or "how sad" as an expression of our grief and reserve the value judgments?

Today I will stop thinking about my marriage as a failure. I will honor all the positive and wonderful things that came to be as a result of that union. I will think of its end as a loss and with sadness, but I also will honor the joys and successes. I will feel grief, but I refuse to feel failure, shame, or blame.

Notes

Month Six

"It is the deep waves of life that make us better swimmers."

All of us long for peaceful times in our lives. However, it is inevitable that there will be turbulent times. As difficult as they may be, hard times provide the challenges that make us wiser and stronger. Difficult times also help us appreciate when things are peaceful and calm.

Sometimes we are terrified of life's challenges. We wonder if we can handle them when we feel so weak and vulnerable. Getting through these times reinforces our abilities and skills. Asking for help does not diminish that experience, as long as we don't accept or rely on someone else to make the decisions for us. Occasionally, we all need a life preserver to assist in conquering those deep waves, but that is not the same as letting someone do the swimming for us. As girls, we may not have seen ourselves as strong. We may have been raised to think of ourselves as "the weaker sex" and that we need a man to rely on and take care of us. Navigating our way through those deep waves gives us strength.
Some women may think of the peaceful times as boring, particularly if they grew up in a family where there was lots of fighting, abuse, or alcoholism. In that family, they may have learned to adapt to chaos, and it may feel so familiar, that they perceive it as normal. Some women who grew up with chaos thrive in chaos in their adult lives. They may pick relationships that recreate the chaos they knew as children. They may find themselves struggling to keep afloat in deep waves, over and over again.

Regardless of how you perceive the deep waves and the still waters, every one of us will experience both in our lives. It is the natural cycle of things – good and bad, calm and turbulent, high and low. This is a part of life. The lessons we learn in the deep waves help us appreciate the times when the waters are still.

Today I will recognize that I am becoming stronger from the challenges I am facing as I go through my divorce. I will try to meet each challenge with curiosity, courage, and enthusiasm, knowing that an important life lesson is to be gained with each new wave that comes my way. While I acknowledge this is a difficult time, I also acknowledge and celebrate my growth.

In Connecticut, attorneys for the minor child are appointed when:

- The parents are having difficulty agreeing on what is best for the child.
- They cannot agree on a parenting plan.
- When one parent questions the parenting skills of the other.
- When the child wants a change in visitation.

The child's attorney advocates for the child's wishes. The attorney is not a witness. If the attorney feels that the child is not asking for what is in his/her best interests, then a Guardian Ad Litum is appointed. The Guardian Ad Litum (GAL) does serve as a witness. He reports on what is in the child's best interests. If the child is under the age of five, the Attorney for the child always appoints a Guardian Ad Litum. The attorney will argue on behalf of the Guardian Ad Litum. The appointed adult's role is to make sure the child gets his/her say in issues of custody and visitation, but ultimately the adults make the decision.

Psychologically, it is critical for the child not to be given too much power. When a child is appointed counsel, some parents try to sway the child to "their side." Putting a child in the middle and giving him/her responsibility of this magnitude is damaging to the child. Adult children who remember having to choose between their parents, and in some horrific instances actually having to testify in open court, report that years later they experience grief, guilt, confusion and regret about the role they played in the divorce. Divorce is a grown-up issue. When possible, adults should leave the children out of all legal proceedings.

How can a child feel safe with a parent who cannot constructively deal with the other parent? How does a child trust the parents when a stranger has to be appointed to protect the child? Of course, when there are serious problems endangering a child's welfare, court appointees for the child serve a vital role in protecting the child against harm. It is always best for all involved when the parents are able to put aside their differences and resentments and put their children's needs first. Check with your individual state with regard to its rules governing court appointees, or ask your own attorney to educate you on whether this is an option you should pursue.

Today I ask myself, how far apart are my child's father and I regarding my child's welfare? Does my child need an attorney to protect his/her rights and a Guardian to decide what is best? Is my child really in danger without this additional protection? If I have doubts, I will discuss it with my own attorney.

Day 3 Divorce is the First Decision You Make as a Single

Many women who want to leave their marriage find themselves almost paralyzed just before filing the papers. It is not that they have doubts about the decision. They find themselves in a strange predicament; they are so accustomed to making major life decisions as a couple that they continue to look toward their husbands for agreement/approval with regard to the divorce.

Women in this situation often do not realize that this is holding them back. Major life decisions, such as buying a house, having a baby, or purchasing a car, are made as a couple. The decision to get married is the first major life decision that is made as a couple. The decision to get divorced is often the first major decision you will make as a single. Rarely does a couple agree on getting a divorce. Usually one party has reached the conclusion that the marriage is over before the other one has begun to even deal with that reality. Women who want a divorce often find themselves in a quandary. They struggle with the need to move ahead and yet they want their husband's approval. They bring their husbands to couples therapy, buy self-help books, cite experts, and present their husbands with a list of attorneys. Ultimately, they find that their spouse is not going to agree. Unlike all the other marital decisions that have been made, this is not one that will be made with the agreement and support of both parties.

When men file for divorce, it stings women that they had no say in the matter. It feels like the ultimate betrayal of the marriage. It marks a significant change in the decision-making process and one which clearly says, "I no longer have to consult you. We are separate entities. I can do what I want."

It is critical to remember that you can't control the fact that your spouse is not on the same time line as you. Whether you are the one who wants the divorce, or wants to stay married, you cannot make another person feel as you want them to feel. Frequently after the divorce is over, the resistant party often agrees that divorce was the best thing and they are grateful it happened. But to try to convince another person that your way is "right" can ultimately lead to more conflict and hurt feelings.

Today I respect my partner's feelings about my decision, but I also respect my own. I will move ahead as I need to, recognizing I will not get their support for my decision. I will think of this decision as the first decision I make as a single person. It is part of my emotional divorce. I will honor the fact that each of us will go through this in our own way and on our own time line.

From Ex-Wife to Exceptional Life

Day 4 When Your Children Turn Away From You

In some divorces, children choose to distance themselves from one parent. If that parent is you, it can be frightening and hurtful. We cannot imagine how a child could divorce a parent, anymore than we can imagine a parent could divorce a child. Why does this happen? The answers are as varied as the children themselves. Adolescents and teenagers often see the world in black and white. They often elect a good guy and a bad guy. Sometimes girls take their father's side as a way to gain approval. Sometimes they gravitate toward mother as part of gender identity. Boys may gravitate toward Dad or move toward Mom if they feel it is their responsibility to "take care of her" now that Dad has left. Often the relationship you had with your child before the divorce gets magnified during the divorce. If a child's relationship with both parents is solid, then chances are the relationship will remain intact after the divorce. If the relationship with one parent was strained, then chances are the strain will grow as the couple goes their separate ways. On the other hand, if a child's relationship with his Father was strained, he may use the crisis of divorce to move toward his father, feeling that he could have a stronger relationship without the conflict. He may feel that his father is now freer to concentrate on parent/child time. Feeling secure that the relationship with Mom is intact, he then feels free to work toward building the relationship with father. It's important to be patient. "Nothing is constant but change," and children can change their allegiance and feelings at the drop of a hat. Developmental changes and maturity also work to change a child's perspective. If your child has turned away from you, here are some do's and don'ts:

- Don't whine to them.
- Don't "hound" them.
- Don't try to buy them.
- Don't bad mouth the other parent.
- Don't try guilt or manipulation.
- Don't try to force them.
- Don't confide in your child.
- Don't use physical or verbal abuse.
- Don't stop parenting in a desire to "win them over."

- Do set your own boundaries and stick to them.
- Do let your child know that the door is always open for him/her.
- Do remain upbeat and positive when you do see or speak to your child.
- Do be patient.
- Do stay in touch.
- Do accept whatever overtures are made, without complaining.

Today I will remember that relationships are forever evolving and changing. Just because my relationship with my child is strained today, doesn't mean it will always be that way.

Needing validation is a part of the human experience. We find pleasure in compliments and approval. However, the need for approval can drive us to think and behave in ways that are not in our best interest. This happens when we give so much credence to other people's opinions that we stop trusting ourselves. If your self-esteem is low, you will doubt yourself, your opinions and your decisions. This makes you vulnerable to accepting other people's opinions over your own, which disempowers you and creates anxiety and depression. Lack of confidence in ourselves makes us prey to everyone else's needs or desires. Sometimes we look for approval from the wrong people. It is not uncommon to hear a woman who is making the decision about divorce say she wants her estranged spouse's approval. She may not even be aware that this is what she wants. She may say, "I need him to understand" or "I want him to apologize" or "I want him to know how he hurt me."

When we decide a course of action based on what we think we "need" from someone else, then we are, in fact, giving up our personal power. We are giving their opinion more credit than our own. We are asking for permission. Making the decision to divorce might be the first decision you will make without your partner's approval. It is the beginning of thinking about yourself as an independent person capable of making decisions on your own. Sometimes, though, to act without advice/counsel can have drastic consequences. Some women forge ahead, without thought to what their actions will mean to others and to themselves. This can create chaos in your life. It is critical to look toward positive sources of approval and support, such as objective professionals, or friends and family who have your best interests at heart. Remember, your spouse is not objective and surely his own agenda will cloud whatever advice he offers.

Today I will consider my sources of approval. Do I need everyone's approval? Whose opinion is most important to me? Do I value my own opinion? Do I feel that ultimately I can make good decisions about my life? How do I deal with opposition? Ultimately I will work at trusting myself and putting my own voice above all others.

The Two to Five Year Old

When looking at how divorce affects children, it is important to consider the age of the child. Developmental stages account for much of the behavior changes we see in children. According to Angela Mazur, LCSW, Farmington, Connecticut, at different stages of development, the response to divorce will be different. At all ages, children experience the stages of grief: shock, denial, anger, sadness, and acceptance. These are normal responses to loss. Sometimes these emotions are expressed in what is referred to as regressive behaviors. In the two-to-five year-old child, these include a return to thumb-sucking, bedwetting, baby talk, and tantrums. Sometimes a child this age will complain of stomach aches and headaches. Disruptions in sleep may occur, including difficulty falling asleep, staying asleep and having nightmares. You may observe your child having a lower frustration level, being easily angered or suddenly having a fear of abandonment. This age group also may blame themselves, feeling that if they were a "good boy or girl," that the divorce would not have occurred. They may also express anxiety about not wanting to grow up because adulthood looks too difficult. What they are saying to you is that they really need you to take care of them.

The acute stages of these symptoms should last one to two months, depending upon a variety of circumstances which include the level of acrimony, amount of contact with both parents, and the on-going relationship between the parents. Providing the child with more attention, structured routine, and increased contact with both parents should help the symptoms abate. If, after two months, these symptoms get worse or show no improvement, then it is time to talk with a child therapist for some guidance and insight. As with any age group, any references to suicide – not wanting to live anymore, not wishing to be here – should be addressed with a professional immediately. Suicidal thoughts are not part of the grieving process and are a clear indication of something more severe.

Today I will be aware that some of my child's regressive behavior is his way of grieving his loss. I will maintain a routine for him and spend extra time with him. I will not blame myself for his experience, but will do everything I can to minimize his fears and anxieties.

Women characteristically like to see conflict resolved. Whether this is a product of nature or nurture could be debated. We are caregivers, peacemakers, mediators, problem solvers. We are arbitrators, healers, chauffeurs, cooks, cleaners, psychologists, and cheerleaders. We play all these roles in our families. One of the reasons we do is that it, "makes us feels good about ourselves." Another reason is, if we are completely honest, that we want everyone to like us. We hate it most when someone is angry at us.

It is not surprising, therefore, when women are concerned about having a friendship with their ex. What is surprising is that many of the women who ask this question have been either emotionally or physically abused by their husbands! "Can we be friends when this is over?" they ask almost pleadingly. If you were friends during your marriage, you probably wouldn't be divorcing. Friendship is reciprocal. It is a two-way street, based on respect and trust. What you perceived as friendship may have been a one-way street, with you behaving in a certain way to win his approval. Perhaps, now, what you really hope for, is a way to get through the divorce without your spouse getting angry.

If you were the one who finally said, "I have had enough," then chances are that your spouse is angry. Do you really want his friendship, or do you want absolution from your guilt? Do you want his approval?

One of the hardest and most important lessons we learn from divorce is that we simply cannot make everyone happy. Finding our voice, paying attention to our needs, and not being afraid to advocate for ourselves is pivotal in being a happy, healthy individual.

Today I will examine my desire to be friends with my ex. Is it friendship that I want, or absolution? Is it a guarantee that he won't say bad things about me? Am I afraid I will be hurt? Do I want a cordial relationship for the sake of our kids? If we were really friends, we would probably not be going our separate ways. I will pay close attention to how I use the word "friendship" and what it means to me. This will help me to see my relationship with my ex for what it really was.

Until recently, divorce was a pretty standard process. Each person hired an attorney, then they slugged it out in court. Attorneys and family therapists recognize that these free-for-alls frequently result in long-term damage to the couple and their children in emotional, legal, and financial terms. As divorce becomes more prevalent in our culture, ways to minimize the acrimony and damage have evolved. Your choice of legal counsel can set the tone for your post-divorce relationship with your ex-husband and your kids. Here are some examples of your options. (Each state has different rules and procedures regarding divorce. Check out the legal requirements of your specific state.)

The Divorce/Family/Matrimonial Attorney – These are attorneys who specialize in legal matters pertaining to the family. Often they have taken special training and have vast experience in the field. Hiring a specialist is preferable to a general attorney who does divorce "on the side." In the long run, their expertise will save you time and money and ultimately get you the best settlement possible.

The Collaborative Divorce – In Collaborative Divorce, each person has their own lawyer to advocate for them. Rather then fanning the flames, these attorneys are interested in what is fair for their client, not in seeking revenge. If the couple cannot agree and decides to go to trial, collaborative lawyers will withdraw from the case. This is agreed upon at the beginning and all parties have to agree to this method in order for it to work.

The Mediated Divorce – A mediator can be either an attorney, or a therapist who receives special training to help you mediate your divorce. You both use one mediator and do not have representation from lawyers. You represent yourself. This can be very cost-effective but only works when the couple can be civil to each other, and when both parties can advocate for themselves and not feel intimated by their mate. Obviously, if this marriage involved violence or abuse, or if there are large amounts of money and property involved, it is more appropriate to consult with individual attorneys. Even in a mediated divorce, it is recommended that you consult with counsel before signing any final agreements.

The Pro-Se Divorce – This is when one or both partners represent themselves, file all the papers and draw up their own agreement. Again, if there is any kind of inequity in power – emotionally, physically or financially, this is not recommended. This is also not recommended when there is child support involved.

Today I am learning that I have choices in everything I do. I may not like the choices presented, but I am in control of the path I choose to take. In order to choose wisely, I will take the time to learn about my options and consider what is best for me. I will do this as I move forward with my divorce and I will practice doing this in all areas of my life.

As a therapist, my job is often to help people explore what they are feeling and to help then achieve a sense of peace in their lives. The Dalai Lama states, "The goal of each person is to be happy". (Cutler, 1999) Usually people come to therapy because they are looking for happiness in their lives.

When we are happy, we smile. It is part of the mind-body connection. The mind-body connection works both ways. That is, there is a body-mind connection as well. Eastern religions, which emphasize Yoga, Reiki, Tai Chi and other forms of mind-body work, have known this for years. Doesn't it follow that if we smile, we can perhaps stimulate our own feelings of happiness?

As you read this, take a deep breath, think of something pleasurable, and allow your body to experience the pleasure of that thought. Now smile: not one of those big dopey camera "cheese" smiles, but a true, sincere smile. Notice how your face feels when it smiles. Notice the muscles in your face and neck. Now go stand in front of a mirror. Relax your face and let your face become expressionless. Notice how you feel when you see your face without expression. Again, think of something pleasurable, let your body feel it and let your face express it. Now smile again, watching your face the whole time. How do you feel when you see yourself smiling? Does it feel uncomfortable because it has been so long since you have smiled? Have you forgotten how it feels?

You do not want to forget how to smile. Smiling can help you feel happy and happiness can breed more happiness. When we are happy with ourselves, we are more loving and forgiving of others, which in turn only helps us feel even better. Being happy with ourselves doesn't mean "when I have lost ten pounds." or "when I get this promotion." It means for right now you are content to be exactly who you are. This moment's smile is about acceptance of yourself and others. It doesn't mean accepting things will remain the same; it simply means that for this moment you can choose to be happy with yourself. If you can't feel it, smile anyway. If you do it often enough, smiling will impact your sense of self and your relationships.

Today I will try to be conscious of smiling. I will smile at the day, at my children, at my co-workers, at strangers, at my cat. I will greet this day with a smile rather than a frown. I will assume good things will happen rather than assume bad things. I will smile, smile, smile. I will rejoice that even for just a second, a smile can lift my spirits.

Carol Miller Pekrul, ChFC, of Newington, Connecticut is a chartered financial consultant whose clients include many divorced women. I asked Carol what were the most common pitfalls that result in women getting less than their fair share of the assets accumulated in the marriage. Below are listed considerations that women often omit when negotiating their divorce. By including them in your agenda of goals for yourself, you can avoid financial problems later on.

- **Think long term** – We tend to be overwhelmed when going through a divorce. It feels difficult to think about tomorrow, impossible to think about the future. Keep a clear head. The financial decisions you make now will affect you for the rest of your life.

- **Think about the tax consequences** – For example, lump sum settlements are tax-exempt, while alimony is considered taxable income.

- **Everything is on the table** – Simply because your husband says you are not eligible for his retirement (or pension, or business, or boat), doesn't make it so. Everything is negotiable. Everything is on the table.

- **Alimony can always be modified** – Women are often relieved to hear this, assuming that it means if their financial needs change, they can go back for more money. What they forget is that it goes both ways. Since husbands are usually a few years older than their wives, they may retire earlier. Once they do so, their income changes and *they* can go back to court to change the settlements in their favor. The court cannot make someone keep working when they are ready to retire. So, keep in mind that your circumstances may change and your alimony can be decreased as well as increased.

- **Make a list of everything you want** – Make sure you include everything, such as educational costs, retirement, vacation home. Be very thorough, because if you leave it out, then it is out of the negotiation. It is not the job of the lawyers, your ex-husband, or the judge to ask for what you want. Make sure you list everything, even if you are not sure you "can get it." Have everything itemized in writing.

Today I acknowledge that I need to spend some time considering the ramifications of my settlement. It may be helpful to speak with an attorney, accountant, or financial planner. I may be able to find information from my local adult education program or on the Internet. I will not let finances intimidate me into ignoring my financial health. I will take good care of myself. Like everything else, if I am patient and diligent, I can access the information and learn what is necessary to help insure an economically secure future.

"It is over and done. I know I can no longer be with this man. I don't even love him anymore. Why do I feel a twinge when I hear he is going on vacation? When I see him, and he looks good, why do I feel this pull towards him? I know I don't want him, but when I think of him with another woman, I get upset. I tell him not to call and then he doesn't and I get upset. I think I am going crazy." Sound familiar?

The transition from spouse to ex-spouse is gradual and does not occur in a linear fashion. As with other elements of divorce, this is a huge roller-coaster ride. Your feelings are not predictable and you feel out of control. During this process, your feelings change faster than you change your outfits. Remember this is a "process." Divorce involves transition and gradual changes. It takes time and a lot of emotional energy and patience.

Patience with yourself is the major key to getting through these difficult emotional times. Allow yourself to feel whatever you are feeling, but recognize you don't have to do anything about it. For example, if you feel sad or anxious because he hasn't called you (especially at your request), don't run to the telephone and call him. Feel the feelings but don't "act out." Acting out is done without thought and is spurred on only by pain or anger. Frequently, when you do act out, you will not get the response from him that you desire.

Then, you may feel even worse than before you acted on that specific feeling.

If you have asked him not to call and he has respected your wishes, you may find yourself feeling upset. Ask yourself, "Why am I so hurt (angry, disappointed)? He is doing what I wanted. He is respecting my wishes." You may be feeling loneliness or fear or self-doubt about your decision. Whatever it is, it is not about him but about your own growth. Acting out merely renews the roller-coaster ride and doesn't allow you to learn how to deal with your feelings.

Acting out is like fanning the flames of a dying fire – you will rekindle it and it will burn even hotter. You will have feelings and thoughts about your ex for a long time. Allow them to pass without taking action. Eventually they will wane and even disappear.

Today *when I feel a yearning to call him because I think it will ease my uncomfortable feelings, I will resist that impulse, knowing that when I act out my feelings, I hurt myself. I can discuss these feelings with a trusted friend or my therapist. I can write about them or I can scream if I need to. But I won't hang on to the fantasy that he can take away my pain.*

One of the biggest challenges a divorcing woman faces is managing her finances with less income. There are creative ways to cut back which can save considerable money and not compromise your life-style. By making some adjustments, we can trim our budget. Here's an example:

Ellen was an avid reader and she enjoyed buying bestsellers as soon as they were published. These books cost between $25.00 and $35.00 each. Since she bought about two novels a month, she spent more than $600.00 a year on novels. Going to the library gave her the opportunity to read the novels when they were newly-published and in hardcover, which was her preference. She saved considerable money with this one alteration to her buying habits. Below are some other examples.

	SAVINGS	
	Daily	Annual
Quitting smoking (a pack a week)	$5.00	$ 260.00
Bringing your lunch to work instead of buying it	7.00	1820.00
Renting a movie instead of going to the movies (for four, six times)		180.00
Washing sweaters v. dry cleaning them (12 washes a year @ $7.00)		84.00
Decreasing haircuts by two per year		80.00
Basic cable instead of deluxe		360.00
Borrowing library books inside of buying		500.00
Paying bills on computer (using less postage) 10 bills per month @$.37		44.40
Omitting that morning coffee at Starbucks or Dunkin' Donuts		625.00
Total saved		**$3953.40**

Write down EVERYTHING you spend for one month. You will be amazed at how the "little things" add up! Another suggestion for budgeting is swapping services. Here are some examples.

Janet had expertise in bookkeeping and medical insurance. She proposed to her dentist that she would straighten out his books, if he would straighten out her teeth. She spent a few hours a week working on his accounts and was tenacious with insurance companies and collection. She recovered fees that more than covered the cost of her braces. Last time I saw her, she looked radiant, grinning proudly to reveal her new teeth. When I complimented her, she proudly told me that she was still working with the dentist, paying off her children's dental bills.

Linda got a job at the cosmetics counter in a big department store for the holidays. That environment was very different from her day job as a paralegal in a small law firm. This position energized her. She used the additional money to pay bills and used the store discount to buy Christmas presents!

Try cutting back, swapping, or getting a part-time job. The possibilities are unlimited. Be creative. Post a flyer at your local coffee shop, ask friends, run an ad in a local newspaper. You will be surprised at your options! You will save money, meet new people, and acquire new skills at the same time.

Today I acknowledge that although living on one income is scary, I can be creative, expand my interests, and tap into my unexplored talents. I will see this challenge as an opportunity to build my self-esteem and boost my self-confidence.

When a husband leaves a wife, there is grief, loss, and anger. Feelings of abandonment, bewilderment and betrayal may be the hardest to deal with. Women tend to blame themselves. We think of things we didn't do, things we did do, things we said, and things we didn't say. Every behavior, every utterance and nuance is analyzed and dissected for hints as to the catalyst of his actions. We struggle for answers, and may create scenarios to try to make sense of what has happened in our lives. Often when we do this, we end up judging ourselves harshly and avoid distributing the responsibility evenly. Why do we do this? One of the reasons may be because we want to avoid getting angry at him. We may do this for a couple of reasons:

- We hope he will change his mind about splitting up.
- We never get angry with anyone.
- It feels so "unladylike."
- It keeps us attached.

There are a number of problems with this approach:
- Whether you get angry or you don't will have no effect on whether he will come back.
- Not getting angry puts us in a place where we accept unacceptable behavior.
- Not acknowledging our anger doesn't mean we don't feel it. Suppressed anger can make us sick.
- Staying attached makes it impossible for us to move on with our lives.
- Not getting angry makes us the perpetual victim.
- Not getting angry doesn't allow us to create distance.
- Not getting angry lets fantasies thrive.
- Not getting angry allows us to continue to blame ourselves.

Cheryl kept saying, "I don't want to be angry with him, I still love him." She resisted the reality that her husband had cheated on her and lied to her for years. She also has had several heart attacks. One day, she reported she had an epiphany.

"I got it!!!!!" she enthusiastically announced. "I am not responsible for his behavior. It wasn't my fault. I am angry with him and wouldn't want someone back that treated me so badly. I am also angry with myself for accepting so little in our marriage. But you know, I feel better now. It is such a relief to not have to feel responsible anymore. I feel good letting him go. I realize I was just trying to hold on because I was scared of the unknown."

Her healing and growth began that day. Recognizing that she was angry was her first step in becoming an independent and self-confident woman. She did not have to accept inappropriate behavior! This freed her from him and validated her own worth. She can now move forward with hope and optimism in her life.

Today I will look at why I protect my spouse from accountability in the relationship. Why do I have to shoulder all the blame? Why am I afraid of my anger? I will begin to consider how it would feel if I did get angry. What could I gain? What am I afraid I would lose?

A child's exposure to the father abusing the mother is the strongest risk factor for transmitting violent behavior from one generation to the next. – *Report of the American Psychological Association Presidential Task Force on Violence and the Family, (APA, 1996)*

Domestic violence can affect children in many ways. Individual children may respond differently even within the same family. Some children may become violent themselves, while others may withdraw. Some may "act out" at home or at school, some try to be the perfect child and some try to be invisible. Young people may sometimes witness terrible acts of violence against their parents or caregivers. Some children may never see the violence firsthand, but they may feel the tension, hear the fighting, and see the resulting injuries. Young people may be physically injured themselves if they try to intervene to stop the violence. Children may be asked to call the police or to keep a family secret. No matter the details of a family's situation, children and young people bear the burden of domestic violence, too.

Although the impact of domestic violence on the child is tremendous, it is only recently that domestic violence has been taken into account when determining child custody in families where domestic violence has occurred. The laws regarding child custody in families with domestic violence histories still differs from state to state. Even when a violent relationship has ended, the abuser may continue to have contact with the children. It is important to plan for the safety of the children and adults in the family at all times.

If there is violence in your home, do not minimize its impact on you and your children. It is imperative that you tell your attorney or therapist and allow them to advocate for you. While there is often fear that the abuse will escalate if you ask for help, fear of "telling" will only make matters worse. In the shrouds of secrecy, the abuse will almost always increase.

Today I know that even if I tell my children that the violence is wrong, that does not mean they will not behave violently in their own relationships. If I do not make a stand, my children will get a mixed message from my behavior. My children will do what I do, not what I say. They will learn how to behave through my example. Am I setting a good example for my children?

...I Only Want to Be With You

The above lyric, from a Dusty Springfield song, pretty much sums up our idea of *unconditional love*. This song is from the sixties, but every generation has their own set of "abuse me" love songs. We also learn about love from the movies. From *Gone with the Wind* to *Pretty Woman*, women are repeatedly presented with a skewed role of romance. Some of us did not outgrow the influence of these messages. We make our men the center of our lives. Our relationships are always paramount in our minds, discussions, and lives. What we wear, how we look, how we smell, how we cook, how we are in bed, how smart, how much money we make, are all focused on getting/pleasing/keeping the man.

Sublimating our needs starts when we are even younger. "Good girls are seen and not heard," "Boys don't like girls who are smarter than them," "Don't be conceited" are messages you may have heard growing up. You internalized clear messages about what girls were and weren't supposed to be and how to *catch a man*. Our families, our culture, our generation, and the media all gave us a clear message of our role as women and our place in our relationships with men.

The price a woman pays in focusing all of her time, thought and energy on a man is very high. She pays with her sense of self. In fact, your divorce may be so frightening and painful because when he became your entire focus, you lost YOU.

Think about the messages you learned about relationships. Write them down – the good, the bad and the in-between. You may subscribe to some and others you may choose to reject. The first step is to be aware of them. Only when we have knowledge can we choose to reject or accept the messages with which we have been bombarded. Knowledge is power.

Today I will focus on what I learned about what it means to be a woman. Are those lessons helpful to me or do they keep me in a passive, unhappy situation? I will think about what I feel, think, and want. Only I know what is right and healthy for me. I will know it is okay to be the woman I am and I will rejoice in the woman I am becoming.

Couple's therapy gets a bad rap. Many women report that they attended couples therapy for only a few sessions before giving up. They felt so uncomfortable, that they didn't really talk about their true feelings. Some couples only pursued therapy after a huge crisis such as an affair, or when one party has filed for divorce. Many say it was a last stop before divorce court.

Couple's therapy is hard stuff. Your marriage didn't get to this state in a few hours and it isn't going to get better in a few hours. Couple's therapy takes commitment and a willingness to see things through your partner's eyes. Both need to admit to mistakes and have the fortitude to stay with it and support each other through the rough spots. It is not about assigning blame, nor is it about assuaging guilt for wanting to leave your marriage. It is about gaining insight and learning new skills. And like any treatment, the more advanced the condition, the longer it will take. It is important to utilize couple's therapy before any irreversible damage has been done. Resentment, affairs, abuse, damaged self-esteem, loss of trust, and disrespect are often irreversible. Even a saved marriage may carry some battle scars.

I am not suggesting you run off to therapy with every little problem or skirmish that occurs. But if there appears to be a pattern of disagreements that are escalating without resolution, it may be a sign that something is wrong. Furthermore, if you find it increasingly difficult to recover from these disagreements, and that you stay angry longer and that the anger is growing in intensity, then it is time to get some professional help.

Think of your marital health the way you think of your physical health. Sometimes you go for a check-up, just to make sure things are in good working order. Sometimes you see a physician when something is ailing you. If you ignore the symptoms too long, the condition may be so advanced that there is nothing left that the doctor can do. Don't wait until your marriage is a corpse to drag it in for couple's counseling. An occasional check-up can't hurt. Seeking help when something is awry is the healthy and responsible thing to do.

Today I know it may be too late for this marriage to be saved, yet this is a valuable lesson for me to learn. Waiting to seek professional help often only makes things worse. It is better to be proactive than to end up dealing with a situation that is out of control.

Diane shared a scene from a movie she saw many years ago that had a profound effect on her. "A small group of fighters are surrounded and outnumbered by the enemy. They know they will lose the battle and that there is no hope. Rather than suffer and give victory to the enemy, they choose to take the poison their leader gives them and die with dignity."

Was Diane suggesting that she just lay down and die? "Oh no," she hastily replied. "That is not an option in divorce or in life. Dying would not be taking the victory from him as much as giving it to him." She laughed, "And that is the last thing I want to do. I have been considering what it is I am fighting for and how much ammunition I want to give him to use on me. That is the way I take the victory from him."

Other women found this metaphor useful as a way to facilitate their healing and emerge victorious.

- "When my children are with him, I will make plans to be with friends. When I sit around and obsess, I only add to his victory."

- "When I follow him or pass his house looking for signs he is seeing someone else, I am surrendering my time and dignity to him. I will stop doing that."

- "When I call him up with expectations and then get shot down, I am giving him victory over me."

- "When I consider using my inheritance to fight him in court over some assets, which I may or may not be entitled to, I am giving him the victory. I could really end up a loser."

Taking back your victory does not mean giving up. Quite the contrary, it is about making choices based on what is good for you, rather than on winning or on revenge. When our behavior is filled with negative emotions and motives, we might as well just wave the white flag. When it is filled with expectations and hopes that cannot and will not be met, we are setting ourselves up for disappointment and despair.

Victory is about getting on with your life. It is about learning all the lessons that divorce teaches and about incorporating all of that new information into our future choices. Victory is about courage and rebirth. It is about rebuilding and rejoicing in future opportunities. It is not about ruminating over the past. It is not about regrets, guilt, depression or hostility. Victory is coming through the battle a better human being for having fought it.

Today I will think about what strategies I can implement to be victorious in my life. Are there behaviors that I engage in that sabotage my recovery? If so, what kinds of things do I need to do to change? Do I feel myself growing and changing as I meet the challenges and hurdles of divorce? Victory is becoming the woman that I want to be.

In her 1979 book *Love and Limerence*, Dorothy Tennov, Ph.D discusses limerence. Words that are synonymous with limerence include madly in love, head over heels, lovesick, crazy in love. However, limerence is different than "falling in love" because it demands reciprocity. It is different than loving someone when we care about their well-being regardless of how they feel about us.

Limerence affects us physically. Our body produces hormones and chemicals which result in a heightened state of passion. During limerence, we feel more sexual and attractive and experience a heightened sense of well-being and confidence.

Limerence feels as if we have been touched by magic. We feel as if we have found our soulmate and he feels the same way! We cannot imagine we will ever feel annoyed, argue, or fight with this person. We believe we will feel this ecstatic forever! However, limerence is a passing stage. Unfortunately, many couples marry during the limerent phase. As limerence wanes, usually within a few months to 18 months, they may feel disillusioned. They may feel irritated, annoyed, completely shut off sexually and generally discontent. It stands to reason that many relationships end during this phase.

Some people are addicted to the "high" of a new relationship. They crave those feelings of arousal, heightened sensitivity, and passion. These folks often go from one relationship to another and end up with a string of short term, yet wildly passionate relationships which suddenly "just fizzle." If your partner's feelings suddenly abated, just understanding the role chemistry plays can help you take his change of heart less personally. In a long-term relationship, wild lust does not exist all the time. A caring, committed, loving relationship offers other joys: security, trust, and the commitment to build a life together. If this was a limitation of your partner, use the information to help you detach from feelings of blame or hurt.

If you are the limerent partner, you may want to consider whether you really want to throw away this relationship. Maybe the marriage should end, but you owe it to yourself to check it out. A good therapist can help you sort out your feelings about your spouse, your marriage, and mostly yourself. Learning about "what makes you tick" may save your relationship or make you healthier for the next one. If you are intoxicated by a limerent connection and it runs wild, it can ultimately cause you many disappointments and heartbreak.

Today I see that this whole process of divorce affords me new ways to look at myself. Learning about myself is what is most important in my life. The more I know about who I am and what I need, the more likely I am to achieve my heart's desire.

"Two very rich people get divorced, and their lawyers live happily ever after."

This may be a funny joke to someone not experiencing a divorce. But if you are embroiled in the process of divorce, it probably does not seem at all funny. Maybe that is because there is a great deal of truth in the statement. We can get lost in the battle, seeking revenge as a way to even the score for the wrongs done to us in the marriage. We can get caught up in winning, fighting for principle, or the need to hurt the other party. But what is the cost to keep the battle going?

There is truth in the statement, "Living well is the best revenge." Think about what you are fighting for – is the time, money, and effort really worth it? Are you using your savings or vacation fund to fight over something of far less value in the name of justice? How has the strain affected your health? Your sleep? Your work? Are friends and family beginning to make excuses not to spend time with you? Are your thoughts constantly on the legal battle? Do your moods swing widely, based on the current status of the battle? Are you so caught up in the conflict that the rest of your life is suffering?

Somewhere in the process, you may finally decide that the desire to see "justice done" is really harming you. Your children are also being affected. You might think you are keeping them insulated from the battle, but your level of stress is bound to overflow into your dealings with your kids. You may not even be aware of how the divorce battle impacts them until years later. Is this battle really worth the cost to you? Discuss it with a close friend or a therapist. Ask your attorney for his/her opinion of the case. Has it gotten out of hand? Are you being unrealistic? What would they do in your place? Ask yourself if this is really how you want to continue spending your days, or is it simply time to get on with your life?

Today I am aware that others have used litigation as a way to seek revenge on their ex. While this may work for other people, I really need to think about what is best for my children and me. Am I fighting for what is justly mine and my children's, or am I merely trying to hurt him the way he hurt me? Is this really how I want to spend my time? Do I like the person I am becoming? Ultimately, the decision on how to proceed is mine, and so are the consequences for my behavior. I will think carefully about my choices so far and consider carefully before I proceed with further litigation.

"Comfort foods" are those foods we desire when we are stressed, hurt, sick, upset, or feeling child-like and in need of nurturing. These foods differ for each of us. Often, they are foods we were given as children and we eat them for emotional rather than nutritional reasons. After September 11, restaurants in New York adjusted their menus to accommodate the requests of their patrons. These included meat loaf, fried chicken, mashed potatoes with gravy and even Jell-O! During this time of national crisis, we yearned for times that felt simpler and longed to feel safe.

Comfort foods vary widely. Usually they are rich in carbohydrates. Ethnicity, culture, and region play a part in what each of us defines as a comfort food. Kathy craves grits as her comfort food. She grew up in Connecticut but her mother was from South Carolina. Margo craves red Jell-O. She associates it with her elementary school cafeteria – a place where she felt safe. Leslie comforts herself with orange juice and brandy. Her mother used to give it to her as a child. Then she realized that it had contributed to her own early taste for and use of alcohol to comfort herself. Other comfort foods that people have told me about include chicken soup, tapioca, mashed potatoes, applesauce, ice cream, cookies and macaroni and cheese. The foods we crave in times of stress or sickness are one way we take care of ourselves emotionally. They make us feel safe.

Pat Froberg, RD, Avon, Connecticut, notes that using comfort foods is not an unhealthy thing as long as we are aware of their power and use them in moderation. When we eat these foods to the exclusion of others, we get ourselves into trouble. Relying on any one food or food group throws our body out of balance and denies us our nutritional needs.

Today I will think about my "comfort foods." Have I been over indulging in these foods to the exclusion of others? Am I eating to fill an emotional hole in me or am I using comfort foods occasionally and mindfully, knowing that while they may soothe for the moment, they are not the answer, either emotionally or nutritionally? I will make a list of my comfort foods and notice how often and how much of them I eat. I will do this not to "beat myself up" or even to deny myself, but just to increase awareness of my choices. Without awareness, I lose my power to make choices.

Do you set yourself up to be disappointed by your husband's behavior? Does it seem to happen over and over again? Do you feel betrayed, let down, disrespected? Consider how these expectations were created. Do you base them on history or on hope? Hope is a human strength, without it, we become cynical, suspicious, and negative. Hope helps us maintain optimism. It is a part of having a happy, healthy life. However, it can be a two-edged sword; when hope lingers in the face of all evidence to the contrary, then it becomes denial. Denial is not about optimism, but rather a way to hide from reality. Denial sets us up for disappointment. In divorce, denial can set you up for legal turmoil and emotional pain.

Let your history with this man be the yardstick for your hope. Look at his past behaviors, at his ability to change, and his ability to accept responsibility for his mistakes. Consider his desire and willingness to grow. Look at how he has treated you throughout the marriage. How did he behave when he felt angry, cornered, misjudged, or disrespected? Look at his ability to resolve conflict. Many women think their husband will "step up" or "take the high road" during the divorce process. If he didn't behave this way before, why would he change now? It is not that people don't change. But in order for change to take place, someone must *want* to change. They must be ready and willing. It takes time and effort and motivation.

People leaving marriages often feel as if they couldn't or wouldn't make the changes needed to create a healthy relationship. If the motivation to change in order to save the marriage isn't there, there certainly will be no motivation to change through the divorce. Most people simply dig their heels in, push their spouse's buttons, and hope the divorce process will proceed swiftly and in their favor. Our relationships tend to deteriorate during conflict. Of course, there are exceptions; if you happen to be one of those couples who gets along better in divorce than marriage, you are among the lucky few. But don't count on it. Don't set yourself up to have your heart broken again.

Today if I find myself saying, "Oh, no. He would never do that to me," I will consider the possibility that my hope is clouding my good judgement. And when I allow that to happen, then I am sinking into denial, and that distorts my ability to make good decisions.

Now that you are getting a divorce, maybe you are wondering what you should do with the wedding photos. While this visual testimony may be painful for you, the wedding photos are critical in your child's personal history.

Fran asked her divorced father if she could make a video tape of all of the old 8mm movies from her childhood. He deliberately held back the movies of his marriage to her mother. When she pressed him for those reels, he replied they are not part of her history, but of his, and that he preferred not to have those pictures preserved for future generations. She was understandably distressed at his self-centeredness. Fran's father was unable to see that his feelings about his marriage to his ex-wife and Fran's feelings about her parents' marriage are very different. The wedding and marriage were a critical part of her history, for without it, she would not exist!

Wedding pictures, albums, and videos, not only of your wedding but of your years together with this man, may be too painful for you to look at right now, but don't disregard their relevance in your children's history. Trying to make believe the marriage didn't exist can confuse and invalidate the children's experience of themselves and their role in the family. You may not want to look at those photos now, but put them away for your children. It is their history and they have a right to it.

Today I would like to throw out all of the photos and memorabilia connected to my ex-husband and our marriage, but I know they mean something else to my children and to my children's children. They are part of their history. With respect and foresight for future generations, I will safeguard these photos, recognizing that they represent part of my children's legacy.

Today I will give myself a "grown up time out." My life has been filled with so many activities, appointments and tasks that I simply must allow myself to stop for a day to reflect, to digest, and to simply rest.

Today nothing will clutter my mind. I will put aside my "to do" list as much as I can and simply focus on living in the present. I will not do laundry, grocery shopping, cleaning or anything else that can be put off. I will take full advantage of this break, as I have earned it. I will approach the tasks I must do such as showering, dressing, taking care of the children, feeding the dog, and going to work, with a new attitude. I will experience them as if I were doing these things for the first time. I will concentrate totally and fully on what I am doing at the moment. If my mind starts to drift, I will gently call it back to the task at hand. Varying my routine, even slightly, can help me stay in the moment. I will start in the morning. In the shower, if my mind starts to drift, I will bring it back to what I am doing, feeling the water and soap on my skin and allowing myself to feel the pleasure of the touch. Perhaps I will take a different route to work. On my drive, I will stay aware of all the new sights and sounds that accompany me on my trip. When I feed the dog (or cat or bird), I will take a moment to play with him. I will appreciate his presence in my life. I will look at my children as if seeing them for the first time. I will notice the small endearing things about them. I will allow myself to fill with loving feelings and gratitude about having them in my life.

Just for today, I will not worry, obsess, plan, and strategize. I will not engage in any behavior, thoughts or deeds that pertain to my divorce. By doing this, I will give my mind and body a vacation from the stress that is in my life. Nothing is so urgent that it cannot wait for twenty-four hours. Not worrying will not make things worse!

All of the things I need to do will be waiting for me tomorrow, but just for today I will allow myself a well-earned rest. I will experience the things in my life that bring me joy and I will feel gratitude and peace.

Today I will exhale.

Much has been written about how to act assertively. There are books and articles that teach the "I" statement and give you other verbal techniques to help you act with confidence. These techniques can assist you in asking for what you need.

However, before we even open our mouth to utter our assertive statement, our body language and style of dress speak volumes about our confidence and assertiveness. You can learn to set the stage for being assertive before you speak. This attitude will support your assertiveness and offer reinforcement for your message.

Try this the next time you are meeting with a difficult or intimidating person:

- Walk into a room with your hands at your side. No hair twiddling, no hand wringing.
- Look the person in the eye. If you have trouble with that, try looking at their nose, forehead or alternating one eye, then the next. They will never notice.
- Don't slouch. If you can, wear heeled shoes to look taller (even if you are tall) and to feel taller. It will empower you.
- Wear something "grown up." Don't go for confrontation in sweatpants and a tee-shirt. You will feel too relaxed and you won't be taken seriously.
- Don't shift your weight from hip to hip. It can make you look aggressive and hostile. Along with that, don't cross your arms or chew gum.
- Feel "grown up." Keep something in your pocket that reminds you of your success and ability to achieve: keys to your car, checkbook, identification card. These are all touchstones to our adult life. Keeping one in your pocket can help you stay anchored in the role of adult, rather than child.
- Don't use your hands too much when you speak. Waving them around is distracting. Never, never point at the person. It is hostile and combative and will only serve to increase the hostile atmosphere.
- Don't take baby steps; try to use a long stride.
- Think of someone you admire. Imagine how they would handle the situation.
- Let the other person talk and don't interrupt. Nod your head politely to let them know you are listening. Most people are afraid they won't be heard.
- Offer a strong, firm handshake (if appropriate) without breaking eye contact.
- Wear vibrant colors. Stay away from pastels and florals. When the president wants to look "in charge," he wears a red tie. When he wants to come across as compassionate, he wears a blue one. Colors help set the tone and say something about who we are.

Paying attention to how you look sets the stage. It lets the other person know you are capable, calm, and confident. It sets the tone for the discussion. Without being conscious of it, we all make assumptions about people by their presence and body language. You can use that knowledge to your benefit and create an environment that will support you.

Today I will be more aware of how I express myself. I will even "experiment" in safe relationships. I will notice if the atmosphere changes when I change my body language and presentation.

In the beginning of our relationship, things felt wonderful. It was a time when we felt wanted, loved, and respected. Women who have been married to controlling or abusive men examine the early days of the relationship to find clues as to how the relationship evolved from dream to a nightmare. Here is Sue's story:

> "He was never abusive (controlling) at the beginning. If he had been, I would have never married him. I didn't see it coming. He was always so loving, always so attentive and concerned. He was willing to do anything for me. He wanted me to be his whole world. He said we didn't need anyone else, as long as we had each other. He would meet me daily for lunch and be sad when I wanted to go out with my friends. Sometimes, when I did go out with my friends, he would show up unexpectedly and surprise me. He always wanted to know where I was and who I was with. He was more attentive than any guy I had ever known. I never felt more loved."

Does Sue's story sound familiar? Sue's husband was attentive, but he was also insecure and jealous and distrustful. Wanting to isolate her and "have her all to himself" is not a loving behavior; it is a controlling one. Following her with her friends and wanting to know her every move are signs of an insecure and immature person. It is unrealistic to believe that one person can be our whole world. It is unhealthy to impose that belief system on your partner. Possessiveness is the behavior of a controlling and suspicious person. Control is often born of insecurity, anger, and fear. Sometimes these men are afraid of abandonment or rejection, or they see women as their property. Sometimes they are simply mirroring how they were raised. Regardless of the reason, possessiveness is not a part of healthy love.

In our example, Sue's husband wants to spend time with Sue, but he also needs to recognize that she is a separate person, with separate needs from his. Not letting someone spend time with friends or have lunch with a co-worker is not love. It is tantamount to putting your spouse in a prison. Giving in to someone's need to control does not diminish their fears. In fact, just the opposite seems to happen; the more they control, they more they seem to need to. The more a woman works to dissuade and cajole, the more controlling some men become. It is critical to see that the seeds of control existed in your relationship even at its inception. This is not so you can blame yourself and feel guilty. The insight is important because once you learn how to recognize the behavior; you won't be taken in again.

Today I will study the nuances of my relationship. Was his behavior loving or controlling? Insight teaches me many lessons about myself. It also gives me confidence and information to make better choices in the future. Divorce is difficult, but the pain can be diminished when I search fervently for the lessons.

Day 26 Say What You Mean, Mean What You Say...

...and Don't Say It Mean.

As women, we often struggle with what to say, when to say it, how to say it. We may have difficulty expressing what we need. Through our experience, we have learned that expressing what we need may result in the displeasure of others.

We may be concerned that self-expression or assertiveness will be seen as aggression. If you have experienced physical, emotional, or verbal abuse either in your family of origin or in your marriage, you may think you will "get into trouble" for expressing your thoughts, needs, and desires. The ability to express one's feelings without fear or shame is the cornerstone of all good relationships. When we need to "walk on eggshells," then power is being used inappropriately and the partners are not equal. Even when there is no threat of violence, women sometimes silence their own thoughts and feelings to accommodate others or for fear of "hurting someone's feelings." We worry that we will not be liked if we say what is on our mind. There is a price we pay for holding in our feelings. Stuffing our feelings is a major cause of depression in women. Subjugating our needs to "keep peace" can wreak havoc within our bodies. Stomach ailments, back and neck pain, headaches, high blood pressure, and eating disorders can all result from suppressing our voice.

I am not suggesting that we scream and yell and say horribly abusive things. That is NOT being assertive and that certainly does not build healthy relationships. Assertiveness is not aggressive and it is not submissive or passive. It is self-advocacy. It is clear, direct communication with another person and it needs to be practiced in every area of our lives.

What exactly does it mean to be assertive? It means we can make our needs heard in a way that does not damage another person. The expression, "Say what you mean, mean what you say, and don't say it mean," is assertiveness in a nutshell. If you adhere to this principle in all your relationships, they will grow healthier and you will feel better about yourself.

Today I will try to have at least one assertive communication. I will start with an easy relationship, maybe my dry cleaner, a clerk in a store, or a waitperson in a restaurant. I will see how good it feels to be heard and to get my needs met. Then I will begin to practice assertiveness in all aspects of my life.

Most women, no matter how much they want the divorce, have some kind of reaction to finding out their husband is dating again. Reactions range from a feeling like a punch in the stomach to mere annoyance. The more time that has elapsed between your marriage and his next relationship, the easier it is to come to terms with.

There is curiosity about this NEXT woman, not so much in relationship to your ex, but more in relationship to yourself. You may find yourself reacting to her age, height, weight, education, looks, financial security. You may compare yourself to this new woman, and revel if she is older and less attractive and crumble if she is younger, prettier, or thinner. Why do we look at the next woman and compare ourselves to her? When we don't feel good about ourselves, we tend to be more vulnerable to seeing the other woman as competition, vying for the same prize – THE MAN. Reality television has introduced us to *The Bachelor*, where putting twenty women in one house, competing for the love of one man, reinforces the message that other women are a threat and men are the prize.

The new woman in your husband's life is no threat to you. She has what you didn't want or what no longer works for you. It doesn't automatically follow that if his relationship with her works out, then the divorce was your fault. It merely means a man who is bad for you may not be bad for someone else.

Today before I go crazy about this next woman, I will try to relax. What am I so afraid of? How can she hurt me? Why is it that we couldn't be friends? Why does it always have to be competitive? I really do need to relax. Whoever she is and whatever reasons they chose each other, it has nothing to do with me.

Divorce throws our lives into absolute chaos.

Schedules, rituals, and patterns are suddenly in an uproar. Laundry doesn't get done for days, there is no food in the fridge, your phone bill is overdue. You can't find your keys. You forget to pick your child up from soccer practice, and you go to the hairdresser when you were supposed to be at the gynecologist. Work deadlines are missed, the lawn is four feet high and you can't remember when you last slept for more than three hours at a time. In the middle of all this, you are single parenting (or gearing up for it), preparing to live as a single person, and struggling to get together the reams of documents your lawyer has requested. There are school conferences, therapist appointments, orthodontics, family commitments, and on and on. Not to mention all the emotions you are trying to deal with.

The first strategy to gain some control is to implement a routine. Routine will provide a sense of control and order as it helps organize your life in a mindful way. You may already have some routine to your day. Most of us have certain rituals we perform every morning: showering, brushing our teeth, getting dressed, making the coffee. But for a lot of us, the routine ends there. From that point on, we are thrown into a frenzy of rushing from project to task to commitment without any plan.

Try this: think about the mundane things you do daily, weekly, and monthly to manage your life. Do you schedule those things that must be done, or do you just "get to it when you can?" By setting aside specific time to accomplish these tasks, you no longer have to obsess or feel anxious about when you will get them done. Designating Friday as "laundry day," Monday as "grocery day" and so on, organizes those tasks so that they are far less overwhelming. You will be less concerned about things, "falling through the cracks" if they are scheduled into your life. When you follow a schedule, it becomes a routine. It will take less emotional energy and time to accomplish those things that keep your life running smoothly. That will open up more "down time" to do things that are healthy and enjoyable. Life will become less stressful.

Today I will bring routine into my life as a way to free up some time, both emotionally and practically. This does not mean I need to be rigid about how and when I do things. My routine will be a guideline to establishing a rhythm to my life. The payoff will be less anxiety, confusion, and chaos.

Spring is the season of hope. Easter and Passover are two of the most sacred holidays for Christians and Jews. Both celebrate renewal, rebirth, and new beginnings. Like Christmas and Rosh Hashanah, both holidays are steeped in family tradition and ritual. If this is your first Easter since becoming separated/divorced, it may be a difficult time. It is likely that, at some time, your spouse will have your children for Easter. Many of the family rituals might have been child focused such as painting eggs, Easter egg hunts and so on. Without your children on Easter, you may feel adrift and displaced.

Passover is also a family-centered holiday and steeped in tradition. Families gather for the ritual Passover meal, the Seder. If your tradition included spending Passover with your husband's family, you may also find yourself adrift, and alone. Furthermore, if your husband has the children for Passover, then you may feel rejected and isolated.

Both of these holidays teach us about loss, transition, strength, hope and rebirth. Even if you celebrate neither holiday, you only have to look around you to experience the wonder of spring and the magic of renewal. The year of divorce and separation is a difficult one but it can also be the year of your rebirth.

Try this: Find a sunny room, or if it is warm enough, go outside and find a sunny location where you will not be bothered. Stand very still with your eyes closed and your arms at your side. Take a deep breath and as you exhale, imagine you are your favorite tree or flower and that you are sending your roots down into the soil. See yourself as growing stronger as that root system strengthens and extends. On the next inhale, see yourself emerging from the soil growing strong, straight, and erect. Feel your sturdiness. Then, on the next inhale, visualize your tree or flower as it begins to turn green, then bud, then flower. Take your time breathing deeply as you so this. Turn your face, with closed eyes, toward the sun and feel its warmth permeate and nourish every cell of your being. Use your arms if you like, extend them over your head or to the side, visualizing them as branches or flowers. Feel renewal in your body. Feel the groundedness of your roots in the earth. Feel the sun bring life and renewal into your body. Stay like this for as long as you want, breathing slowly and deeply, relishing the feeling of rebirth. When you are done, gently lower your arms and take a few minutes to affirm your strength and the wonder of life cycles and renewals. When you open you eyes, take the feeling of strength, hope and new life with you throughout your day.

Today although I feel strange thinking of myself as a tree or a flower, if no one is watching, maybe I can do it. It doesn't have to feel scary, just because it is new for me. My life is filled with new things now, and just because something is unfamiliar to me, doesn't necessarily mean those are things I should avoid. Part of my rebirth is trying new things, and knowing I can take risks to find out what works for me and what doesn't. Trying new things can be fun, if I allow myself the spirit of adventure.

The role of in-laws varies in every marriage. In the television comedy, *Everybody Loves Raymond*, the in-laws are an integral part of the family. They offer support, insight, and love. They are also interfering, critical, and annoying. Depending upon geography, ethnicity, prior relationship, and family dynamics, the role of the in-laws can vary greatly. Each marriage has its own story about how in-laws support or detract from the marriage. When divorce occurs, we assume parents will side with their adult children. However, sometimes your parents side with your ex. Or your ex-husband's parents may take your side. This can add to the level of betrayal and confusion.

Paternal in-laws may side with the wife if there is domestic violence, substance abuse, an affair, or if they have no daughters of their own. Paternal grandparents may worry about losing touch with their grandchildren. They may align with you, to ensure this does not happen. This can feel like a victory and validation. Having your in-laws' support can be enormously helpful in a practical and emotional sense, but they are still his parents. If they have turned on him, then I would be particularly suspect of them. Their lack of loyalty and commitment may be no different than his. Resist the temptation to throw this loss in your ex's face. Whether he shows it or not, he cares what his parents think. To flaunt your closeness with them will fuel acrimony and have a negative impact on your post divorce relationship. You may feel as if he deserves to lose his children and his parents, but that is your anger speaking. Use your common sense. It will only come back to hurt you if you encourage that chasm.

On the other hand, if your parents have sided with your ex, the sense of betrayal and loss is hard to describe. This usually occurs when there is a history of dissension between you and your parents. Their behavior is inappropriate, regardless of what perceived or real transgressions you may have committed. Choose to surround yourself with a "Family of Choice", comprised of a loving supportive network of friends who do not judge you, but care about you and honor your decisions. If your husband is flaunting this relationship divide, ignore it as much as possible. A parent disowning a child because of a divorce is a sad and a terrible loss for all involved. But do not let their behavior define your life.

Today I am aware that the impact of my divorce is resonating through three generations. I feel caught in the middle. But I must be clear that divorce is not about popularity. I need to act in a way that results in my feeling good about myself. I cannot let others govern my choices, my thoughts, or my feelings.

Start your morning with this small exercise: before you open your eyes, notice your body and how relaxed it feels as it awakens from sleep. Take a big stretch and feel your body, its warmth, relaxed muscles, and the overall absence of tension. If you wake up tense, then stretch and focus your mind on relaxing your body. Let your mind receive the message *I am calm, confident, and competent.* Say this to yourself every morning as you greet a new day, even before you open your eyes. Make it mandatory, like brushing your teeth. It only takes a few seconds to affirm yourself and your life. The positive results of starting your day with this focus will reveal themselves through the day and throughout your entire life.

At night, right before you go to sleep, instead of letting your mind run through worries and problems, identify one good thing that happened to you today and fall asleep thinking about *that.* If you can't find ONE good thing, it is not that nothing positive happened, but rather that you aren't looking hard enough! During times of crisis, we tend to become so anxious that we stop appreciating the good things in our life. Keeping your last thought of the day a positive one helps you drift into a calmer, deeper sleep. This results in waking to the new day more refreshed, with that feeling of calm, confidence, and competence.

Today I will greet the day relaxed and calm. I will take a moment to recognize my strength and affirm my courage. I will reward myself with a luxurious stretch and take a moment to open my eyes. I will greet each new day with anticipation rather than anxiety. I will end each day with thoughts of gratitude rather than worry.

Month Seven

There are times when it feels as if the pain will never lift and you will remain in this bleak, bottomless cavern forever. Then one day you wake up and notice that you feel a bit differently than you have in a long time. The world around you seems brighter and more hopeful. Inside, you might feel lighter. Suddenly, you feel your spirit soar and your mood is more optimistic and perhaps even joyful. The feelings may be so strong that they take your breath away. Or they may be so imperceptibly different that you can't even put your finger on what has changed.

Today the unthinkable happened! You did feel joy and hope! Take note of what is happening. Rather than trying to figure it out, simply embrace the feeling and revel in it. Feel the lightness of spirit. Even if you are just having tiny glimpses of that feeling, celebrate its return. The feelings weren't dead within you, just dormant! Like a fire which seems completely cold, underneath is a tiny ember that, when fanned, resurrects into a roaring fire! The flame of joy was not extinguished in you but merely hidden. It is there and you can feel it. And with time it can come back with a roar!

Of course, in the next minute comes the crash. "Two steps forward and one step back" is the rhythm of this process. Don't forget there will be good days and bad days. In time, the good feelings will stay longer and the bad feelings will diminish. This is gradual and there will be disappointments. Keep yourself focused on the progress you have made. Celebrate the victories and minimize the defeats.

Don't compare your progress to anyone else's. This is your own personal journey and how often you stop to rest or take a detour, or how fast you drive, are all expressions of your own unique style. Every marriage is unique, every divorce is different, and every recovery is exclusively your own. Don't let anyone, including you, rush you through it. Think of the person who drives very fast; she may get to her destination more quickly, but she will certainly have missed points of interest along the way. Take your time and be gentle with yourself. Then on days like today when you take that step forward, allow yourself to feel it, really feel it. Celebrate it with a giggle, an ice cream cone, or a little dance!

Today how nice it is to begin to feel joy! I will celebrate myself with complete acceptance and gratitude. I will avoid minimizing or undermining my process. I will revel in this glimmer of happiness and accept that it is a prelude to the rest of my life.

Three Tall Women is a play written by Edward Albee. The three women are really all the same woman at different points in her life: late teens, mid-life and senior. The midlife woman spoke poignantly of her lessons in life. To paraphrase, she said, "As a young girl, I had my whole life in front of me. Like a mountain, it rose steadily in front of me, to be climbed and conquered. But it also blocked my view and I could not see what was on the other side. In my senior years, I climbed that mountain and descended down the other side; my journey was behind me. In middle life, I am at the top of the mountain, able to see so clearly where I have been and able to see the many options that lie ahead."

Divorce affords you the vantage point at the top of the mountain; you can see where you have been, what you have done, and what you might have done differently. You can also look ahead and plan your journey. The view from this point in your life offers you the advantages of insight, wisdom, and experience. It also offers an opportunity of *choice*. We tend to want to rush through this period in our lives.

Eager for the next stage, we often see it as an interim point. We ask, "When will it stop hurting, when will the divorce be final, when can I date, when, when, when?" We are in a big rush. Some women say they feel as if time is running out. If they feel that way, it is even more imperative that they remain patient and make the right choices.

Do not rush into new things blindly. This includes moving, jobs, and relationships. Do not react, *pro-act*. Consider your options and apply the one-year rule: I will wait one year before I make any permanent, life-altering decisions.

Today I can see myself at the top of the mountain. I will look at where I have been and honor how I struggled to get to this point. Then I will turn my vision forward and consider new paths and options. I will think about choices I have made and whether I want to make them again. I will consider paths I have not explored even if they feel foreign and uncomfortable. I will not act until I have surveyed the landscape before me. I will design the best path for me to reach my goals. I will not rush headlong into anything. Today I will be the observer and planner of my own life.

How are you doing today? Let's just take a moment to check in and see how you are getting along. Below is a list of questions regarding your process. Answer them simply with More, Less, Same. This is not a test, but a chance to take a break and reward your progress!

Mood
- Are you crying a lot?
- What is your anxiety level?
- Do you have moments of calm?
- Do you feel angry?
- Do you laugh?
- Do you feel in control?

Legal
- Are you up to date with paperwork?
- Are you more knowledgeable about the court/legal process?

Thought Process
- Do you think about him as much?
- Do you worry about your children?
- Do you worry about the future?
- Do you look forward to the future?

Parenting
- Do you feel more patient?
- Do you spend quality time with your kids?
- Do you feel emotionally available for them?

Self Care
- Are you beginning to eat healthier food?
- Have you quit smoking?
- Are you drinking too much?
- Are you exercising?
- Are you sleeping?
- Do you take time for yourself each day?

Support System
- Are you utilizing your support system?
- Have you brought new people into your life?
- Have you dealt with the social changes resulting from the divorce?
- Do you make time to spend with these supports?
- Are you being a good support in return?

Practical Life
- Are you managing financially?
- Are you living within a budget?
- Is your house in order?
- Are you eating a lot of fast food?
- Are you taking care of the car?
- Have you established a daily routine?
- Are you paying bills on time?
- Are you sleeping?
- Is there food in the kitchen?
- Is the laundry getting done?

Today I will use my answers to help me evaluate my process and progress. I will not beat myself up for areas that have not improved. Wherever there is improvement, I will congratulate myself for the hard work it took to get there. I will affirm that just maintaining the status quo in some areas was challenging enough during the hard times.

We may think: the longer the marriage, the greater the divorce grief. Long-term marriages usually result in more complicated divorces (because of children, accumulation of assets, property, retirement funds), but the short-term marriage is often equally, if not more, painful. Long-term marriages carry the pain of grieving for what was lost. Short-term marriages carry the grief for what could have been. Don't assume the feeling of loss is commensurate with the length of the marriage.

In short-term marriages, there is usually a feeling of failure and disappointment, as well as a loss of confidence in one's ability to make good decisions. The dream is shattered. One grieves for what could have been. Since fantasy is only limited by our imagination, the grief can feel endless. This marriage is like a miscarriage—never having a chance to grow and thrive, the couple feels robbed of the opportunity to experience the relationship. And, like a miscarriage, we must be mindful not to say "Don't worry, you are young, you can try again." Another marriage, like another birth, does not erase this primary loss.

Divorcing women of short-term marriages are sometimes tempted to minimize their own pain, especially when they hear the pain of women who have divorced after many years. They may feel that they are not "entitled" to feel as much sadness as they do. After all, it was a short marriage, with no children, so no one got hurt, right? Sometimes not having children makes many women feel extremely sad. This marriage is without alimony, child support, visitation, and thus there is no need for post-divorce contact. Not only is the marriage final, but there is no longer any need for an ongoing relationship. The finality can feel overwhelming.

If you are a woman who is divorcing after a short-term marriage, do not allow yourself or anyone else to minimize your experience. Your grief will not wash away with platitudes. Do not feel guilty or weak for the depth of your feelings. You are entitled to them. Pay attention to what you grieve for the most. Is it a well-constructed fantasy of what it could have been or is it a well-documented picture of what really was? Being clear about what you grieve will help you grieve it in a way that supports healing.

Today I will allow myself to feel the depth of my feelings. They honor my loss and when I pay attention to them, I honor me. Regardless of the length of my marriage, my feelings will get my attention and validation; I will not measure myself and my loss with anyone else's feelings. To do so demeans me. I am entitled to feel as I feel and today I will respect myself by honoring that loss.

Ah, chemistry. It sets our hearts aflutter, brings color to our cheeks, and makes our palms sweaty. Suddenly, we feel silly and light and pretty and flirty and absolutely great! Chemistry is the first indicator we have that we may have met Mr. Right. But problems exist with chemistry. First, sometimes we mistake chemistry for love. We feel so good that we don't take the time to learn about who he is. That feeling of euphoria is so strong it carries us away. What we don't know about him, we just assume. We fill in the blanks with our own desires and expectations. If we marry during this phase, the result is often regret when we learn the man we married was only a creation of our own desire.

The other problem with chemistry is that it can be an "unhealthy" attraction. With unhealthy chemistry, you see what is missing, but you fall for his "potential." And you make yourself responsible for his actualizing that potential. Some examples of when chemistry is unhealthy include:

- He is unemployed. You check the internet and newspaper for jobs, you write his resume, you buy him clothes to wear to the interview.
- You give him money.
- You pay his bills.
- You spend hours thinking about how to solve his problems.
- He has a drug or alcohol problem that he refuses to address.
- You try to improve his relationship with his parents or children.
- He is married.
- You lose sleep over him.
- You are unhappy, angry, anxious most of the time.
- You lie for him.
- You don't trust him .
- You find yourself going through his wallet, following him, or checking up on him.
- You hear yourself make excuses for him.
- You lend him your car and you take the bus.
- Your bills are late or unpaid.
- People have begun to comment on how out of control your life is.
- He is verbally or physically abusive.
- You find yourself thinking "if only" a lot of the time.
- Your friendships, schoolwork, health or work are suffering.
- You feel like you couldn't live without him.

If you are experiencing this kind of chemistry, seek counseling, either in a support group or with an individual counselor. You need to learn how to concentrate on yourself and to figure out why you would settle for a relationship that causes you so much pain.

Today I am trying to learn that I can't "fix" everyone, but it is difficult. I will try to change my perspective and use my energy to figure out how to fix me, because life as it is has gotten quite unmanageable. The good news is that today I can admit this to myself and that is the first step in changing my life.

Is this person loveable? That is a very different question from *Do you love him?* Sometimes we mistake love for fear of being alone. Sometimes we say we love, but we say it out of habit. Sometimes we love a person's potential. Sometimes we love what we wish they could be.

Imagine you are watching your marriage on a television show. Focus on the husband's behavior. Observe him without attachment; see him only as a character in a movie. Make the movie a contemporary one, taking place today, not years ago when your relationship began. Watch this character carefully as if you were seeing him for the first time. Watch his interaction with his wife, his children, his family, and his co-workers. Ask yourself if you like this character. If so, what things about his behavior do you like? Does he have integrity? Is he ethical and kind? Is he honest? Do you respect the way he conducts his life?

You may actually find that this man does behave with honesty and integrity toward other people. The more relevant question here is, does he behave that way toward his wife? Is he nice to everyone else, but not to her? Does he treat her with respect and dignity? Is he ethical in their relationship? Does he cherish her? Adore her? Care for her? Respect her?

Let's turn our attention to *her*. What do you think of her behavior toward him? Are you angry at her character for behaving in a passive way? Does she seem to put up with a lot of unacceptable behavior to keep her family together? Does she try to keep peace at all costs? Or is she blowing up and picking fights? Is she clearly unhappy? Does she feel good about herself? What would you like to see her do?

Sometimes stepping back can help us see our relationships more clearly. Often we are convinced we love someone, when in truth, it is just dependence or fear or habit.

Today I will really look at what is loveable about this man. I will be honest with myself about the way he treats me and how it makes me feel. I will not delude myself by wishing for it to be as it was, or hoping it will change. I will see him clearly as he is and I will allow myself to explore my feelings about him as honestly as I can, even if it scares me, even if I am not ready to let go.

Maureen, forty-eight, has been involved for more than a year in horrendous litigation with her husband of twenty-two years. Just when it looked as if they would proceed to a long and expensive trial, the couple finally struck an agreement. Maureen reports she was able to hold her own in the arduous four-way negotiations, never once losing her cool.

> "Somehow, the spell has been broken. I used to look at him and fall in love with his physical being all over again. Even though he has done terrible things, when I saw him, I would only remember the good things. I could never stand up to him. It was as if I was in a trance. Now I look at him and I see he is not the person I want him to be. I don't feel threatened by him or what he thinks of me."

Maureen has experienced an emotional divorce from her husband. The ability to be true to herself and not be intimidated by his presence indicates her detachment. Her indifference to what he thinks of her is testimony to how removed from him she really is.

Marriage is a kind of spell. When it is good, it can be intoxicating, like one has drunk a magic potion. When two people commit to spend the rest of their lives together, this vow creates a synergy that can be a powerful elixir when used for positive purposes. Each feels enhanced by and enchanted with the other. We hold our partner in high esteem and feel the power of their loving us. We trust they will use that power for our common good.

No one has more power to influence how we feel about ourselves than our partner. However, when there is dissension and the marriage goes awry, that power becomes black magic. When that power is used against us, then the spell we are under enslaves rather than saves us. It wreaks havoc on our lives and throws us out of kilter.

Emotional divorce occurs when the spell is broken. It is when you see who he is and you aren't sad or angry or hurt or disillusioned. You are free to live without the influences of black magic.

You just don't care anymore.

Today I realize that I may have a long way to go before that spell is broken, but I look forward to knowing that it can happen. It helps me move forward when I focus on who he really is and not on who I want him to be.

If you are holding onto the notion that this is either all his fault or all your fault, then you are stuck in a place that will make it difficult for you to heal and grow. Taking all the blame is a lot of weight to carry around. The guilt can be overwhelming. If you are still furious at him and blaming him for "ruining your life", then your anger will weigh you down and create an unbearable burden for you.

Women who are stuck in blaming their husbands often feel rage and a need for revenge. They may feel like the wounded party or a victim to his "evil" ways. Linda felt that her total sense of happiness came from seeing her husband suffer with his guilt and remorse.

> Therapist: If your happiness comes from seeing him in pain, what will happen if he begins to feel better and achieve a sense of serenity and peace in his life?
>
> Linda: Well, then I will just have to figure out how to make him miserable again!

Linda bases her well-being on his misery. In doing so, she is surrendering her power. She is as emotionally intertwined with him as when she was married, perhaps even more so. Linda knows this, but feels that if she lets go of her anger, she will be giving her approval. If she can detach from the need to see him suffer, she can begin to take control of her destiny and her choices. Then, she can truly divorce him. She admits she has not yet done that. Underneath all of this bravado and rage is her grief. Staying angry keeps her connected to him and disconnected from her own need to grieve.

Are you holding onto all the blame? Why? Single-handedly, you are taking the responsibility for the entire relationship. Think about it. How does that make sense? By blaming yourself, you insulate him from taking any responsibility and you hold him harmless. That is still a way of maintaining connection. You are doing what Linda did – just holding on! In either scenario, disconnection and emotional divorce cannot be completely reached until you accept that the responsibility for the marriage's demise is shared.

Today am I stuck in blaming one of us for the entire breakdown of the relationship? If so, how does that serve me? Do I need to stay emotionally connected? Why? Am I afraid to move on? What is it that scares me? I will consider that beneath my anger or guilt may be some fear that I am not in touch with. I will explore that fear, so I can face it and conquer it.

Day 9   Does Your Husband Have a Gambling Problem?

Gambling (like all other addictions) is hard to diagnose because the gambler is usually the last one to see the problem. If you suspect your husband has a problem with gambling, you need to protect your assets. Check with your state to find out how to freeze the assets. However, someone with a serious gambling problem may not be deterred, even if they know they can face strict legal penalties. You are responsible for debts incurred during the marriage, but filing for divorce or separation can end your liability. Gambling debt can wipe you out and have severe consequences for your future financial stability and credit.

When confronted with unaccounted time, secrets and lies, many women assume their husbands are having affairs. Rarely does it occur to the wife that the husband's obsession with gambling is the explanation for his erratic, unaccounted-for behavior. When the creditors begin to call, the credit card bills roll in, and the savings accounts are seriously depleted, then women begin to recognize the mistress is gambling. Mary Lou Costanza, LCSW, at the Problem Gamblers Service at the State of Connecticut, says women should "trust their reality."

A gambling addiction will not look the same in each individual, but the following criteria can help you assess if there is a problem. If his behavior meets four or more of these criteria, then his gambling has gone beyond entertainment.

* Does he ever try to win back what he has lost?

* Has he gone into debt, including using ATM or credit cards? Is the debt mounting?

* Are the family members concerned?

* Has he missed time from work, family and other obligations due to gambling?

* Is there secrecy? Have you discovered he is lying?

* Does he gamble alone?

Resources for help include state hotlines, the National Council on Problem Gambling or Gamblers Anonymous. You can also contact your Employee Assistance Program (EAP) or an addiction therapist. The financial implications, the emotional impact, and the psychological damage can be substantial. Even if your husband is unwilling to help himself, you need to access help for yourself. You are not doing either of you any favors by entering into denial with him. Without help, gambling will escalate along with the debt. Takes steps as soon as possible to minimize and contain the damage that has already occurred.

Today I will trust my judgment. If I think something is wrong, it probably is.

From Ex-Wife to Exceptional Life

As certain components of the divorce reach resolution, you will find an opening up of both emotional and real time. The space that was occupied by the marriage and then by the divorce is left vacant. You might feel a vague sense of emptiness.

How do you figure out what you want now and how to achieve it? You have learned how to create intention for yourself on a daily basis. Now is the time to create an intention for your life. You can do this in the form of a treasure map. Allow yourself to dream. What would you like to have in your life?

Elsie always wanted a house by the ocean. It had been a life-long dream. On her treasure map, she included pictures of the ocean, beach houses, shells, boats, and sayings that created a visual picture of her dream. Next, she hung it where she could see it daily. One day, when she was driving in a beach community, she drove past a property that was for sale. Even though she knew it was out of her price range, she called the realtor, who confirmed the house was above her means. But the realtor suggested she consider options – such as land or a condo. He put her in touch with a mortgage broker, who put her in touch with a financial planner, who designed a financial plan that could help her realize her dream. She now has a plan and is working to make her dream a reality.

Making a treasure map honors your dream. It is the beginning of transforming a dream into a reality. It doesn't matter what your intention is – to lose weight, meet a nice guy or finish your college degree. A treasure map can contain one dream or many dreams at once. One evening, instead of watching television, take out your old magazines, some tape, and a large piece of paper. Start cutting out things that appeal to you, that will help bring you closer to your dream. Remember that you can always add to or redo your treasure map.

This is about honoring today's dreams. When you are finished, hang it in a place where you see it daily. If you are trying to lose weight and the problem is eating at work, then put your treasure map in the office. You can even make a tiny one and put it in your desk drawer. The point is that wonderful things start with a dream. Dreams provide the fertile soil for harvesting our heart's desires. Tend to them and watch them grow!

Today I will turn my thoughts inward and think about what I want for my life. I will not negate my dreams with negative thoughts, or dismiss them as frivolous. I will respect each dream as I respect myself. When I have finished my treasure map, I will hang it where I can see it daily. I will plan for my life and I will create the life that I want.

Day 11   Starting Your Own Divorce Support Group

The need for women's divorce support groups continues to outweigh their existence. Frequently, I receive letters from women across the country asking how to find a group and if one does not exist in their area, how they can start one.

Groups break down into two kinds: self-help or those facilitated by a professional. In a self-help group, there is no therapist and it is self-governing. In a facilitator-run group, the therapist takes responsibility for both organizing and leading the group. A self-run group can be free and a therapist-run group usually requires a fee. If you decide to start one yourself, you need four things:

- **Participants** – Run ads in local papers, ask friends, divorce attorneys, put notices up at coffee shops, houses of worship, hospitals, doctors' offices, women's clubs. Define your participants. Will the group be limited to women going through divorce? What about women who are thinking about it? What about women leaving long-term relationships? What about women in same sex relationships?

- **Format** – How many participants? How long will your group last? How many sessions? How often will it meet? Will there be a topic each session? Will everyone get to speak in every meeting? Who will be in charge? Will the group be "time limited", or will it continue for an infinite number of sessions? Will it be a closed group (no new members when it starts) or an open group (anyone can drop in whenever they want)? Managing time and making sure everyone has a chance to participate and contribute is also part of the challenge of any good group.

- **Agenda** – What kinds of topics will you cover? How will they be decided? For a beginning group, reading a book and then using that book in your discussions can be helpful. You can pick a different page/topic from this book to discuss at each session. You can also invite professionals to speak: lawyers, therapists and financial planners. All will be happy to donate their time and information with the hope of getting new clients.

- **Location** – Where will you meet? Meeting in participants' homes is one option, but many women may not want to do this as their spouse may still be living there or have access to the home. A more neutral place would be a church or synagogue, a library meeting room, or a senior center. Most organizations involved with community service have facilities to accommodate these kinds of meetings for little or no cost. *Call and ask.*

Although there are many different formats that work, here are some guidelines that may be useful: meet twice a month for one and one half hours, six to eight participants. Rotate facilitators. That person sets the agenda and leads the group, using a predetermined book as a guide. Each group will find its own way and will develop its own personality based on the participants. Good luck!

Today *even if I have never started anything, I will consider starting a group. This is part of my growth, because I am identifying what I need and I will make it happen. I am trying not to be afraid of new things. If it doesn't work out, I will still learn from the experience. If it does work out, I will have the knowledge that I was able to help myself and other women like me!*

September heralds lots of changes. It is the beginning of the school year and the beginning of fall. It marks the end of summer. The days are shorter and the weather grows cooler. Winter is on its way. We begin gearing up for the holiday season. Many people dread this time of year because they experience a shift in mood, a malaise and a general feeling that all is not right. They may have Seasonal Affective Disorder or SAD. It affects approximately 10 million Americans each year and 70-80% of those are women.

Symptoms include tiredness, lethargy, craving for sweets, increased need for sleep, weight gain, and difficulty getting out of bed in the morning. The disorder, which is a sub-type of depression, differs from other depressions in intensity and duration. It begins in the fall, escalates in the winter, and diminishes in the spring. It has been described as a bad case of the "blues," but SAD can be debilitating, causing relationships and work to suffer. If you are going through a divorce, the autumn season can be a difficult one, whether or not you suffer from SAD, because it marks the beginning of the holiday season.

If you suffer from SAD, you can feel pretty crummy. SAD can be treated effectively with anti-depressant medication and there has also been some treatment success with light therapy or melatonin. Knowing that come spring, it will pass, can make SAD more tolerable. The feelings of loss that accompany divorce during the holidays cannot be easily eradicated. During the holidays we tend to eat too much, spend too much, drink too much, sleep too little, and generally feel inadequate and overwhelmed. We have enormous expectations of the holiday season. The media presents a vision of the perfect family having the perfect Christmas. Few families— divorced or not— can measure up to the ideal.

If you think you have SAD, speak with your physician or therapist. Together you can decide the best course of treatment for you. Remember that you are going through a difficult process at an extremely difficult and stress-filled time of the year.

Today am I SAD or sad? Or am I both? I will get the help I need. The holidays are *stressful for everyone, whether they are going through a divorce or not. I will also remember that the holidays, like the seasons, will pass in time, as will this divorce. I will get to the other side of this. Next year at this time, I will rejoice for how far I have come.*

Another Fairy Tale!

Once upon a time in a land far away, a beautiful, independent, self-assured princess spied a frog as she sat, contemplating ecological issues on the shores of an unpolluted pond in a verdant meadow near her castle.

The frog hopped into the princess' lap and said, "Elegant lady, I was once a handsome prince, until an evil witch cast a spell upon me. One kiss from you, however, and I will turn back into the dapper young prince that I was. Then, my sweet, we can marry and set up housekeeping in your castle with my mother, where you can prepare my meals, clean my clothes, bear my children and forever feel grateful and happy doing so."

That night, as the princess dined sumptuously on a repast of lightly sautéed frog legs, seasoned in a white wine and onion cream sauce, she chuckled and thought to herself, "I don't freakin' think so!"

Today I just need to be silly and lighthearted and even a tiny bit catty. Laughing provides a respite from stress and a long overdue mini-vacation. Tomorrow I will be serious again. Today, I am just gonna have fun!

We live in a culture that has very rigid ideas about what makes a "good woman." We are inundated with messages about how we are supposed to look, behave, think, and feel. While we may simply shake our heads in amazement when fathers leave their children, our culture condemns women who do the same. We cannot understand what dire circumstances would lead a woman to make such a decision.

If you are a woman who is leaving or has left your children, you know the pain, guilt, and isolation that arise from making such a decision. In a divorce, when you choose to leave your children with their father, it is an agonizing decision. The reasons for such a decision vary and many women do so for the most honorable of reasons. They may feel that the father of the children is, at that moment in time, better equipped to raise the children, or that she is emotionally unable to care for her children. Reasons for this might include economic and psychological considerations. Sometimes a woman is dealing with addiction and recognizes that until she is clean and sober, she cannot parent. Other times, a woman cites the economic chasm between herself and her spouse. The disparity in incomes can result in a huge difference in lifestyle. These women make the supreme sacrifice of letting the children continue to stay in their home and in the lifestyle they were accustomed to.

Regardless of your reasons, you face a difficult response from the culture. Having the courage to follow what is in your heart and do what you know is right for your children, is the ultimate act of being a good mother. It is an act that involves selflessness and strength. Finding support for your decision is critical for your own healing and self-growth. A therapist, support group, or women's shelter can be of great support and also work as a resource to connect you to other women who have chosen as you have.

Many parents going through divorce let their emotional battle with their spouse impact their ability to make good choices for their children.

There is a Bible story of two women who both claimed to be the mother of the same child. The two women went to King Solomon to settle a dispute. Like the real mother in the story, you may have chosen to let your child go rather than do him/her harm. And like that woman in the Bible, you are a true and good mother.

Today I will allow my convictions to be my guide. I will let them support me against gossip and naysayers. No one else walks in my shoes. I alone know the pain of my decision. I am at peace with the knowledge that I did the best I could.

Do you ever notice how in one venue, you can be calm and collected, the ultimate "grown-up," and then switch the scenario and you feel like you belong in the crib? This lack of confidence shows up in the way we sound. The most assertive "I" statement will carry no weight or credibility if it is uttered in the voice of a little girl. Before we can be taken seriously, we need to sound as if we *should* be taken seriously. Sure, what we say is important, but our tone, pitch, inflection, pace, and volume matter, also. It is like wearing sneakers with a designer gown; the whole ensemble just falls apart.

How do you change the way you sound? Use your answering machine to work on your voice. Listen to your message. Are you happy with the way you sound? Do you sound confident? Do you sound mature and in control? Are you easy to understand or do you slur and speed talk? Are you mouse-like? Are you so quiet that you can hardly be heard? Work on one aspect of your voice at a time. Record your message over and over until your voice sounds just the way you want it. Then practice it. Use your new voice in the world. Try it with friends; see if they notice a difference. They probably won't, but you might. They may listen to you more. You may feel the feedback is different, more respectful. You may feel more credible. Try your new voice on strangers: clerks, waitresses, garage mechanics. See how they respond. Do you notice a shift in how people respond to you? Are you taken more seriously? Good. Keep practicing, because you want that new voice to be a reliable tool when you need it in those "big" situations.

Don't forget to use silence. Silence is one of the great tools, often overlooked or discarded because we don't know how to use it. Try counting to yourself 1-2-3 after someone is through making his or her point. Then respond. This slows down that rapid-fire repartee that escalates arguments. It also gives the other person a sense of really being heard. And lastly, it gives you a chance to think about what you want to say and how best to say it.

Today I wonder… what do I sound like? Am I someone I would take seriously? Am I so quiet that no one is listening to me? Am I so boisterous that I am intimidating and turn people off? Today I will listen to my voice on the answering machine and then re-record my message, thinking about my pace, tone, pitch, and inflection. All of these will assist me in communicating my words more effectively.

"As I go through this process, there is so much that needs attending to, so many decisions to make, and so many things I can't forget. How will I ever manage to get everything done?"

Try this: Write everything down that needs attending to with regard to your divorce. We will call that THE MASTER LIST.

Next, drawing from the Master List, determine what things need attending to first and then schedule them into your life. If you use a planner for scheduling, it will make this easier. During divorce, you will be more forgetful due to the combination of stress and additional tasks that need to be done. Write *everything* down – You will be surprised at the things you can forget, such as picking up your kids from school! If you don't have a planner – GET ONE and USE IT!

At the end of the day, cross out those items you have completed and allow yourself to experience a feeling of success. Put checkmarks next to the items that you plan to accomplish tomorrow. Focus only on what you plan to do on any given day. Celebrate everything you have accomplished. Unfinished projects just get added to next week's list, with no self-criticism. You will be amazed at how competent and efficient you are.

The planner has another important use – it makes it easier to pay attention to what you are doing. Having a zillion thoughts racing around in your head makes you a prime candidate for mistakes and accidents. Writing down your thoughts and tasks will diminish the possibility of you becoming distracted by your "to do" list when driving or involved in other activities that require your concentration. By staying focused, you decrease the chances of having an accident.

Today I will get a planner and I will write down everything that has to be done. I will only focus on the matters at hand. If I do this day-by-day, everything will get done in an efficient, calm manner.

"Volunteer, you say? Are you kidding? When do I have the time to do more? I hardly have any downtime and now you want me to use whatever extra time I may carve out and use it to take care of other people?"

When we volunteer, others benefit from our helping hand. But in truth, we do it because volunteering makes us feel good about ourselves. We can, for a period of time, get outside of our own problems, concerns, and stresses. We can see the big picture.

Often when we are dealing with a crisis, our emotional vision becomes narrow. When that happens, our impression of our issues can become distorted or magnified. We ruminate over our own difficulties, which causes us to re-experience our stress over and over again. In those moments, we feel like our issues are calamitous and insurmountable.

Volunteering at a soup kitchen, a hospital, or a nursing home gives us a new perspective. There is an old Native American expression, "I cried because I had no shoes, until I met a man who had no feet." When we experience first-hand the suffering of others, it changes our perspective from fear to gratitude, which creates a sense of calm and well-being that can stay with us for days.

Volunteering also builds self-confidence. Realizing how much you have to contribute and how valuable you are to others can foster your self-esteem and give you a sense of purpose. Sometimes we begin to think we are powerless in the world. One person helping another creates a chain reaction, the power of which cannot be overestimated. This is our contribution. We are part of a whole and our participation is critical. Experiencing this helps us see our own troubles through a different perspective. It helps empower us and move us from "victim" thinking to "survivor" thinking.

Lastly, volunteering is what WILL change the world. When we share our time, our talents, and ourselves with those in need, we are creating a better world for others. This work is part of the legacy we leave to our children and future generations.

Today I will reach out and volunteer. I don't have to make a big commitment; I can offer my time and services for just one day. In doing so, I will allow myself to feel the power of community and experience myself as part of something larger. It will also give my self-confidence a well-deserved boost. Sometimes I lose touch with how important I am in the world. It will be nice to rekindle those feelings.

Do you accept compliments? If you are like most women, you have a difficult time with compliments. Many of us were raised to believe that it was unattractive to be "conceited" and that accepting a compliment was a way of expressing that conceit. However, rejecting compliments sends two negative messages. First, that the receiver is not worth the kind words and second, that the sender doesn't know what he/she is talking about. You invalidate the sender's reality when you disagree with the compliment. For example, when someone says "I like your hair" (skirt, house, lipstick, whatever!), most women will immediately rebut, "Oh, I hate it. It is too short" (ugly, old faded, cheap, whatever!).

Basically, we are telling the sender that his/her taste is terrible.

Practice giving and receiving compliments. Become aware of the messages you send people when you refuse their well-intended comments. Notice how you feel when someone rejects your comments. Most importantly, when someone compliments you, say "Thank you." Notice how it affirms both the sender and the receiver. After a while you will find that it becomes part of how you operate in the world. You will give more compliments and you will get more, too! You will find both feel really, really nice!

Today I will be open to the positive statements that others say to me. I will give two compliments today. One will be to another person and then, as I stand in front of the mirror at the end of my day, I will compliment myself. I will do this out loud and I will watch how my face breaks into a smile!

...But didn't know it was so bad that he wanted to leave."

How can it be? Are men so unable to express themselves or do we not hear them?

I suspect the truth lies somewhere in the middle. Men may express their frustration in ways we have trouble hearing. Women tend to verbalize more; we process out loud, which means we figure it out by talking it out. Men, on the other hand, go off on their own and figure it out internally. When they think they have a solution, they venture forth with it.

We mistakenly conclude that if he hasn't talked about what is wrong for him in the marriage at length and frequently, *then nothing is really a problem*. We interpret men's sparseness of words as sparseness of feeling. If you consider how your husband solved problems throughout the relationship, you will probably find that he dealt with most issues in a similar way; that is, he took time, went into his cave (John Gray, 1992), and then emerged with a solution or conclusion.

Another reason you may not have heard what he is saying is that you either stopped listening or you simply didn't want to hear it. While that may be difficult to admit, frequently women do stop listening. Life's demands, including children, work, and home responsibilities often exhaust us beyond our capacity. We simply shut off. We assume that since he isn't crying, whining, or demanding that he is, like you, overwhelmed and exhausted, but *okay*. Again, using our way of processing, we figure if he isn't talking about it, *really* talking about it, then there is no problem.

Then there are those times when we know there is a problem but we don't want to look at it. We simply hope that if we don't talk about it, it will simply vanish on its own. Unfortunately, this doesn't happen. When we don't pay attention to marital discord, it reacts like an untreated wound. It festers and then the healing process is far more difficult, if even possible.

Today I will ask myself, did I simply deny the problems because they felt too scary? Did he try to tell me, but I didn't hear him? Did I assume he would express it differently if there was a problem? Figuring out how I missed the cues of someone else's discontent will help me expand my capacity for listening and understanding another's unique style of self-expression.

Just as marriages are unique and varied, so are divorces. Your reaction to the final legal decree will be unique to your own situation and will depend upon a number of factors:

- How reconciled you are to the divorce.
- How much time has passed between the filing of the original papers and the final day.
- How much acrimony still exists with your spouse.
- How much rebuilding of your own life you have already done.

Divorce Day can bring about a myriad of feelings, ranging from extreme sadness to exuberant joy to calm indifference. By knowing yourself and your own feelings about your situation, you can predict how you will feel.

Here are some tips for preparing for your day in court:

- Make a trial run the day before so you know how to get there and where to park. This can help with any anxiety you may have about getting lost or finding parking.

- Ask your lawyer to explain exactly what will happen on the final day. Will she be there? Will you have to testify? Will your husband? Ask any questions you may have. Don't worry if you sound silly. You are not supposed to know all the answers. That's why you hired a lawyer in the first place!

- Bring someone – a close friend, a sister, your mother – someone who is supportive and knows the situation.

- Wear something you don't particularly like. Many women are surprised to discover they never again want to wear the outfit they wore to court. They think of it as their "divorce outfit" and simply want to throw it out.

- Plan to do something after court such as going to lunch with some friends. You can always cancel it, but it offers a "cushion" or "safety net."

- Plan something social for your first weekend as a single person.

- Plan a divorce ritual. Anything goes, but do something!

A word about your kids – They need not be aware of the actual day. It will only fill them with anxiety and trepidation. For children, the divorce begins the day one parent moves out. The rest of the stuff is legal, grown-up stuff. Let your children have an ordinary day and go about their plans as scheduled.

Today I will prepare for my day in court with courage and dignity. I will make this transition as easy as I can for myself. However, I will not minimize or deny my pain. To do so would invalidate my marriage and my experience.

Is your husband well-liked, or successful, or talented, or funny, or popular with other people? Some women shake their heads in disbelief that a man can be so wonderful to others and be so awful to the woman he vowed to love, honor, and cherish for the rest of his life. Do you think, "If he is so good to everyone else and treats me so terribly, maybe something is wrong with me"?

Remember this: A man does not have to be a bad man to everyone else to be a bad man for you.

For some men, it is easier to treat friends and co-workers better than they treat their significant other. Complete strangers speak to each other with courtesy and respect, yet the same people may snarl at their partners, growl at their kids, snap at co-workers, or kick their dogs. Maybe familiarity does breed contempt. However, it is never acceptable to treat anyone in a disrespectful manner. How your husband treats you is the criteria you use for making your decision as to whether or not to stay in the marriage. You are the one who lives with him, and you are the one who knows first-hand what that experience is like.

Asking for advice and validation from friends regarding your experience with your husband may not yield you the support you are looking for. He may be cordial and gentle with your friends and be a complete monster with you. Some men are only abusive to their partner and not with anyone else. It is with their partner that they act out their rage at the world. Many women say their husbands are two people - one for everyone else and one for them!

Honor your own experience. Do not let anyone minimize or deny what you see, think, and feel. Your experience is very real. Find supportive people who validate your feelings. Continuing to allow friends and family to undermine your experience can make you feel abused all over again.

Today I acknowledge that this is my marriage, my life, and MY choice! I am the one living in this relationship and no one else is in a position to judge. Even when I see my husband be respectful and gentle with others, I will remember that I must make my choices based on *my* experience of him and *my* experience only. He is a husband only to me and I alone can choose whether I really want to continue to be his wife.

It is estimated that approximately forty percent of married women are involved in affairs at some time during their marriage. While this is still less than the approximate sixty-five percent of men who have affairs, the numbers for women are growing.

Caught up in the throes of everyday life and providing for everyone else's needs, a woman does not have time to consider whether she is happy in her primary relationship. She takes solace in her children and friends and sometimes her work. By keeping the focus on the needs of others, she ignores what is happening within her. A feeling of discontent can begin to grow and she can become depressed, angry or withdrawn. Because a woman sees herself as the pivotal point in the family, she may feel it is her duty and responsibility to stay in the marriage. While she knows she is unhappy, she feels stuck.

At this point, she may become vulnerable to seeking affection and support from outside of the marriage. Frequently, affairs do not serve to help the woman exit from her marriage. Paradoxically, they often serve to support the woman staying in the marriage. Once her needs are being met through her affair, she feels less urgency to leave the marriage. She can stay in the marriage, maintain the financial security of a two-income home and two parents for her children, and not go through the battle of a divorce. The affair supports the marriage, supplying the needs that were lacking and strengthening the woman's desire not to rock the boat.

The state of a marriage contributes to a woman's vulnerability to having an affair. The fear of discussing attractions can weaken the marital commitment. Secrecy can fan flames of excitement and passion, making the attraction more alluring and seductive. While reasons for affairs vary as much as individuals and their marriages, some of the reasons women seek extra-marital relationships include:

- Physical attraction.
- Falling in love.
- Desire to escape or find relief from an unsatisfying relationship.
- Desire to fill in the gaps of an unfulfilling relationship.
- Desire to punish one's partner.
- Desire for attention, to feel attractive.
- To enhance self-esteem.
- To find relief from boredom.

Often the affair is a distraction from more painful issues. It can serve to mask the underlying difficulties in the marriage. However, there is usually a price to be paid, whether the affair is discovered or not. That price is guilt, resentment, anxiety and exhaustion.

Today I will consider how this affair serves me. What can be the outcome? Am I putting off dealing with the inevitable because it is frightening? If I am to have the life I want, I need to be honest with myself.

Yuck.

Valentine's Day can hurt a great deal if you are going through a divorce. Everyone around you seems to have a doting husband gracing them with red roses and candy. You spend this evening at home with a video and a box of cookies, lamenting how totally unlovable you feel.

Let's get to the reality check. Do most women really feel so loved on Valentine's Day? If so, do they get the same love and respect from their spouse all year? Ask your friends. Most women I have spoken with love Valentine's Day, at least the idea of it. In reality, it isn't what it is stacked up to be. The romantic notion and the fantasy do not often play out in reality. Most of our relationships do not even remotely resemble those television commercials for diamonds.

Actually, lots of men forget the day. Others just use Valentine's Day as a Day of Atonement. They attempt to make up for all the times they were rotten, disrespectful, short-tempered or unsupportive. Usually it is women who celebrate Valentine's Day and really enjoy it. We send each other cards saying how much we appreciate and value each other. We do this not to make up for some transgression, but to affirm how much we care about each other. Kids love Valentine's Day, feeling it is the one time of the year they can be "mushy" toward you without feeling geeky.

How about doing away with all the high-priced flowers and fattening chocolate and declare every day Valentine's Day? We should rejoice in our appreciation of each other all the time, not just on this one day.

So, you are single on Valentine's Day. The Valentine's Days when you were married weren't so hot, nor were the other 364 days of the year. Otherwise, you wouldn't be getting a divorce.

Send your friends and kids Valentine's cards. Show the people in your life that you love and appreciate them. Then do something really nice for yourself. Learn to love yourself in the way you want others to love you.

Today I know how to celebrate my love for the important people in my life, but I am not sure how to do it for myself. What would feel special for me? What do I like? What helps me feel loveable and valuable? Loving myself makes me strong, self-confident and surprisingly more at peace. I will take time on this day to celebrate me. Every day I will affirm my own value and worth.

As the process of divorce unfolds, you will worry about the effects on your child. You may wonder how your child experiences an episode or event. It is not the divorce that hurts the child, but the way the parents act toward each other that is the most damaging. We do the best we can to protect our children from the ravages of divorce. But sometimes our wrath gets in the way and we step out of line by name-calling or reporting to the child some transgression by their father. We may rationalize by saying, "The child has a right to know his father." However, your experience of this man as a husband and your child's experience of him as a father are, and should be, two entirely different experiences. Let the child find out who his/her father is through his/her own interaction. If you repeatedly expose your child to your anger and the details of the divorce, this information and behavior will hurt your child.

Shut your eyes and remember back to when you were the same age your child is now. Did your parents fight? How did it feel? Do you remember what they fought about? Even if you were in a different part of the house, or supposed to be sleeping, you heard the fights. Even if the words escape you, you can remember the feelings you felt. You can feel them even now. How did you feel about each parent? What did you hope would happen?

You can probably still recall those horrible scenes in vivid detail. Is this the legacy you want for your child? Is this the way you want your child to remember you? He/She will remember not only what you said, but the anger and rage with which you said it. He/She will have negative feelings and memories about this time. Don't you wish your parents had protected you from the arguing? Don't you wish you knew less about their personal lives and struggles? If your children are older, you might be tempted to think it is okay for them to be exposed to parental battles. There is no age when children become immune to parental acrimony. There is no age when it is okay to forget that you are a parent. Do not let your own rage rule your behavior in a way that disregards your children's needs.

Today am I behaving in a way that I want my children to remember? Am I creating a good, safe, positive role model? Whenever I begin to lose my perspective, I have only to remember my own experience to know if I am behaving in a way that is harmful or healthy.

The Eleven to Fourteen Year Old

The eleven to fourteen year old child is the one most likely to take on an adult role when his/her parents are experiencing divorce. This is especially true for the oldest child, to whom many additional chores might fall in the absence of the other parent. This may occur not only in the custodial home, but in the non-custodial home, as well. This age group worries about their parents and often feels sorry for the parent who moved out.

They wonder where the parent is living and if he/she has enough to eat. They may try to adopt adult responsibilities in a practical as well as emotional way. They may feel responsible for their parents' happiness and try to "make things better." Some children of this age try to be "perfect" or they may try to take over the absent parent's role. This is a heads-up that the child is not dealing with his/her own feelings, but rather is suppressing them. Consult a child therapist to rule out depression if a child is acting "perfect." Other symptoms of depression and general difficulties dealing with the parents' divorce include:

- Frequent headaches.
- Stomach aches.
- Sleep disturbances.
- Stealing.
- Lying.
- Having sex.
- Sadness.
- Truancy.
- Anger.
- Siding with one parent.
- Eating disorders.
- Social isolation.
- Not paying attention to their appearance.

Any of these symptoms are indications that the child is having a difficult time and should see a therapist. With suicidal gestures or thoughts, intervention needs to be **immediate!** If any of these symptoms are present, do not wait. Expecting them to disappear on their own can have serious consequences.

Today if I notice anything in my child's behavior that concerns me, I will get help from the appropriate professional immediately. My child's well being is my primary concern and cannot be delayed for any reason. It is always better to be safe than sorry!

When you and your child's father create a visitation schedule for your children, it is a good idea to request that you always want the children with you on Mother's Day. In return, swap that day for his having the children with him on Father's Day. While both holidays may have been created to sell more greeting cards, the fact is that Mother's Day and Father's Day for that matter are really the only two days in the calendar that celebrate your roles as parents.

During the marriage, many women feel frustrated when their husbands fail to acknowledge the importance of Mother's Day. Men will argue "You are not MY mother. I have my *own* mother." Disappointment and resentment sometimes surround this day due to that dichotomy of beliefs. As a single mother, that conflict no longer has to be an issue. Children enjoy Mother's Day. They feel good about "taking care" of Mom for a day and showing her how important she is. It is important for children to have this experience. It teaches them compassion and generosity. It teaches them that there is joy in giving. In the past, your ex may have taken the children shopping for cards and gifts for you for Mother's Day. He may not do that anymore. If he does, it is a thoughtful and nice thing to do for his kids. If he doesn't, don't take it personally. Make sure someone else takes your kids shopping or spends time helping them make something to give you. This is as much for the children as for you.

After a divorce, children are often aware of how hard their Mom is working. When you were with their father, they may have taken your role for granted. This is an opportunity for them to express their appreciation. One of the important lessons of Mother's Day is for children to learn to express their affection and caring. Hopefully, this day you get to feel a little pampered. So, let your children make you the priority and make your relationship with them central to the celebration.

Today as my children celebrate the mother I am to them, I celebrate the woman I am becoming. As they express their love and gratitude for me, I allow myself to absorb that positive regard and acceptance and make it part of how I see myself. Sometimes what we see in the eyes of a child can teach us volumes.

An issue that comes up for many women in the process of divorce is whether to change their last name. If you kept your maiden name, hyphenated your name when you married, had a short-term marriage or you did not have children, this probably is not an issue. In these cases, women usually opt to return to their birth name. The situation is more complex when the marriage is longer term, there are children, or a woman uses her married name professionally.

Some divorcing mothers are hesitant to change back to their birth name because they feel it will be confusing for the children to have a different name. They are concerned that a greater alliance will exist with the father because of the shared name. Let's say that you choose not to change your name because you feel it will impact your children negatively. You keep your husband's name and then you decide to remarry (I know, right now you are saying "Never!", but admit this is a possibility!). Your intended is probably not going to be happy if you keep another man's name. So, you change your name. What message does that give your children, about how you value and identify yourself when you change your name for another person but not for yourself? The truth is, most children do not care about the name issue. The divorce rate continues to escalate and women today are more likely to keep their birth name, so children with different names than their parents is not unusual.

How to deal with your professional name: you can use your maiden name as your middle name and then drop your husband's name when the divorce is final. Or you can add your maiden name at the end, using your husband's name as a middle name and then delete it after the divorce. Some women simply send a notice. *"Joan M. Smith announces that effective January 1, 2005, she will use the name Ms. Joan Madison."* Friends will know the change is due to the divorce, acquaintances will probably assume you are getting married and strangers won't ask. It won't be as big a deal to them as it is to you.

The process is really not as involved as it may seem. The final decree can include a clause about officially dropping your husband's name. Many women affirm that changing their name creates a clean slate and that it is a symbol of taking back some power they feel they have lost.

Today I will think about what my name means to me. Does it represent who I want to be? Or does it represent who I used to be? Perhaps I will discuss it with my children, not because I need their permission, but so I can get their input. Does this name clearly reflect the person I am?

It is rare that a woman doesn't tell me, "You know, this would be easier if he died. Does it make me a horrible person to think such a thing?"

This is not a death wish, but a desire to avoid the pain of divorce. The confrontation and acrimony of divorce is so scary that women fantasize about their spouse dying. Most of them would actually feel terrible if such a thing really happened. But the desire to circumvent conflict, worries about money, the stigma, the fear of dealing with lawyers and reluctance to share custody of the children, all make the fantasy of collecting life insurance instead of alimony an attractive one. No matter how angry or betrayed a woman is, she rarely wishes her spouse any real harm. It is the idea of not having to deal with all of this pain that is so attractive.

Just because you have fantasies doesn't mean you are a bad person. Fantasy is one of the coping mechanisms we use to deal with pain. It is important, however, to understand fantasy versus true ill will. Fantasies do not involve any plan of action. We create fantasies in our head to help us through hard times. They are healthy and helpful, as long as we know the difference between reality and fantasy. Thoughts are not actions. If imagining horrible scenarios alleviates some of the pain, then that is positive. It is only when we cross the line and act on our fantasy that there is any danger.

Share your fantasies – both negative and positive – with a friend, a therapist or your support group. You will be surprised to find out that others have had similar thoughts, no matter how bizarre or weird you may think you are. Your fantasies are your creativity at work, helping you cope with immeasurable pain. Laugh at them, find comfort in them, share them. Thoughts won't hurt anybody or anything. Sometimes they can make the pain just a bit more bearable.

Today I will recognize my fantasies for what they are, a desire to avoid all this pain and acrimony. I will share them, laugh about them, and not feel shame for being human. I know the difference between thought and action. Thoughts do not hurt anyone. They merely allow me, in a creative way, to feel a little less stressed and a little less threatened. When I share feelings with others, they create a bridge. Then I will feel a little less alone.

Visitation is often problematic. The custodial parent, while aware of the child's need to see the other parent, may feel conflicted about sending the child for visitation. The child, although needing to have relationships with both parents, may feel conflicted about leaving one parent to be with the other. Finally, the "visiting parent" may question the influence he can have without seeing the child daily. Let's examine some of the issues that each person might be feeling:

• **The Custodial Parent** (usually the mother): May feel anxious letting her child go. Sometimes these fears are legitimate, such as when the father has a substance abuse problem. Other times the desire to withhold the child is more about the mother's own fear of being alone or the fear that the child will "choose" Daddy over her. Sometimes there is concern that the father cannot properly parent the child. Lastly, some mothers withhold visitation as a way of inflicting revenge on their estranged spouses.

• **The Visiting Parent** (usually the father): May feel anxious about the short time they spend with their children and whether they will have a significant role in the child's life. Some fear they will not be able to show the child "a good time" and that the child will not want to see them. Still others simply dread having to face their estranged spouses, sometimes due to guilt or fear of confrontation.

• **The Child:** Children have a myriad of responses to visitation. Many look forward to their special time with their fathers. Many fathers relax the rules (this may be because most visitation occurs on weekends) and the children enjoy the change of pace. Other children may feel anxious leaving their mother. Your child's reaction to visitation can change weekly. Visitation is a transition similar to what we experience when we go on vacation. There is anticipation and anxiety: packing, traveling, unpacking, settling in. Just as vacations are necessary and important, so is visitation.

To really support the child's visitation, you must separate your own needs, whatever they are, from those of the child. Children, even tiny ones, have a kind of "radar system" when it comes to their parents feelings. If you are ambivalent, your child will read that, become confused, and his/her anxiety will escalate. For visitation transition to go smoothly, you need to put your child's right to see his/her father before your own feelings. Divorce is dissolution of the adult relationship, not the parental relationship.

Children need access to, and relationships with, both parents. Unfortunately, there are times when unsupervised visitation is not appropriate, such as when a parent is an active alcoholic or substance abuser, or when the child has been abused. Supervised visits, rather than suspending visitation completely, are usually recommended.

Today I need to consider my issues around visitation. While it may be difficult for me to encourage a relationship between my child and his/her father, I will do it because it is the best thing for my child. To cut the child off from a parent can result in the child feeling loss and anger for many years. They may feel abandoned or build up resentment, blaming me for the absent/unavailable father. Supervised visitation gives my child access to the other parent while ensuring the child's safety.

Many women are unaware that they are usually in two marriages at the same time. One is the marriage of reality - the factual events. The other marriage is a far more difficult marriage to describe - it is the marriage of their dreams. When we walk down the aisle, we are usually committing to the marriage of our dreams. This is especially true in a first marriage, where the realties of how difficult marriage and life can be are only stories. Those difficulties feel distant and remote to the new bride, who says, "We will do it differently," or "We know better."

When the marriage has not been able to sustain the weight of the problems and conflicts of real life, a decision to split up is made. Women at this juncture in their life describe their pain and disappointment as palpable. Underneath lies an additional source of their misery, fanning the flames of their pain and causing even more distress. The marriage of their dreams, the one women commit to with their heart, is the biggest loss of all. It is that loss that hides under the surface, threatening to pull them down into an invisible vacuum.

The fantasy marriage, the "Happily Ever After" marriage, is the ideal with which most of us enter marriage. This is not due solely to our naiveté – The culture perpetuates the myth. As little girls, we hear about "Sleeping Beauty" who lies in a glass box, barely breathing until her prince comes, kisses her, and they live happily ever after. Years later, we are subject to television shows from *Leave it to Beaver* to *The Cosby Show* to *Everybody Loves Raymond*. Television introduces us to the 30-minute formula for conflict resolution. Immediate gratification and resolution in a half-hour (minus commercial time) is our strongest model for marriage. Fantasy is all around us. Unless your parents' marriage is steady and strong and secure, these may be your only role models. When our marriage doesn't live up to the fantasy, we are devastated. We grieve not just for the loss of what there was, but also for the loss of what we yearned for since we were little girls.

Do you grieve for the loss of the marriage as it existed, or the loss of what it could or should have been? Knowing which is which can help you in your process of healing. It gives perspective and insight. Later, if you choose to be in another relationship, you are clear about what is possible and what is fantasy.

Today I ask myself: *what do I most mourn for? Is it the loss of the marriage or is it the devastation of my fantasy? Awareness can help me heal.*

Notes

Month Eight

Divorce is like an iceberg. With lawyers and courts and therapists and visitation and property settlements and in-laws and out-laws and real estate and retirement accounts, it is a veritable mountain of ice. It feels huge and impossible to manage.

But like an iceberg, if you try and ram your way through divorce, the strategy will cause damage and destruction. But, what are your options?

Imagine that you could pull up next to this divorce iceberg. You could handle a little bit at a time. Don't try to take more than what is manageable. You break off a small amount of the ice and put it in your hand. The cold stings for a minute, but then… it turns to water and runs through your fingers. You do this over and over until the iceberg has disappeared. Then you can sail on your way smoothly without damage to you or your boat. Maybe this feels like it will take forever and maybe you are in a hurry. But what choices do you have? You are on this course of action and there is no return, and ramming into this behemoth mountain of ice will prove ineffective and possibly dangerous. So, you proceed with caution, dealing with small amounts at a time. That way you have a good chance of emerging safe and unscathed.

By breaking it down, you avoid becoming overwhelmed and you stay in control of your life. Take your time, pace yourself, and you will find calm waters on the other side. You will also have learned that no matter what future icebergs may lie in your path, you have both the patience and fortitude to deal with them safety, effectively, and patiently.

Today I will break the divorce process down into small pieces and not try to do it all at once. I will take my time and ask for help dismantling this wall of ice. I will not rush it. While it may not seem so, with every handful I am working my way through it, making changes, and getting on with the process. Most of all, I am healing and growing in the knowledge that I can conquer this thing and it will not conquer me.

...is, of course, how we live our lives."

—Annie Dillard

Our lives are frenzied as we struggle to accomplish all the things on our "to do" list. We feel like little gerbils running on those colorful plastic wheels, just zipping along and getting nowhere. As our life commitments and obligations pull at us from day to day, we rarely take time to assess whether we are in charge of our own lives. Being in charge of our own lives does not mean trying to control everything that happens. Many of us try to do that and fail, only to feel badly about ourselves. Much of our time is spent maintaining obligations and commitments that are self-imposed. We think our child "should" participate in sports, scouts, piano lessons. We think we "should" prepare an elegant, full sit-down dinner each night for our family. We think we "should" stay late at the office every night in order to be a success at our job. Then, we find that we are overtired, resentful, and overwhelmed. "Should" decisions distort our sense of self. When that happens, we stop living our life and are just going through the motions, like that gerbil.

Divorce gives us, in part, an opportunity to rewrite the script of our life. Through the losses of divorce, we gain space in our lives. Divorce takes a great deal of time, but the process does not last forever. Single parenting and all the additional responsibilities of the home may feel daunting at first. But in time, when the litigation is done and the children have adjusted, you will find that you DO have additional free time. That time is one gift of your divorce. How you choose to use it is up to you. You have the opportunity to create a more mindful life. Being in charge allows you to live mindfully. You can make choices by necessity and desire, rather than by "should."

Consider these questions carefully. They can change your life in a HUGE way.

- Are you making the most of each day?
- If this were your last day on earth, how would you live it differently?
- Without changing what you do, can you change how you do it?
- Can you change how you think about what you do?
- Do you take time to appreciate all that is good in your life?
- Do you still "sweat the small stuff"?
- Do you feel gratitude?
- Is laughter an integral part of your daily practice?

Today I don't have control over everything that happens to me in my life. How I live my life is my choice and how I choose to think and feel about it is also my choice. I will think about how I spend my time. In doing so, I make conscious choices and can minimize future regrets.

Behaviors exhibited by the husband during the divorce are usually in keeping with his behavior during the marriage. For example, if a man is irresponsible during the marriage and doesn't pay bills or taxes on time, why would a woman believe he would show up for court, bring all necessary documentation, remember meetings, and suddenly be financially responsible? Or if he was argumentative, controlling and unreasonable during the marriage, why would a woman be amazed if he refuses to cooperate and negotiate in a fair and equitable manner? Why would she be surprised when he storms out of conferences with the lawyers, calls her names, and in every way tries to block her from getting what she wants? Women often shake their heads in amazement at this kind of behavior, even though it is consistent with what they experienced in the marriage. They thought that given the seriousness of the matter, their husbands would respond differently, that they would step up to the plate and do their best.

The seriousness of the matter? Isn't marriage a serious matter? The truth is, if he didn't act responsibly during the marriage, he isn't going to act responsibly during the divorce. Stress, worry, and acrimony never bring out the best in anyone. Most people resort to their worst behaviors during times of great change and stress. Divorce is one of those times. Instead of being outraged and disappointed by your spouse's behavior, use your observations and experience of his behavior as testimony to the fact that the divorce is absolutely the right thing to pursue. Seeing this kind of behavior at full throttle can help support your decision to leave this marriage even if you were not the one who wanted the divorce. Is this someone you really want to spend your life with? Is this behavior something you admire, respect, or value? Are the traits that he exhibits attractive to you?

Today I will look at my husband's behavior and rather than feel disappointed and surprised, I will allow myself to accept that this is the man he is today. In doing this, I let go of my fantasy. I can use his behavior to support my journey. If I have doubts or regrets, I can use my observations of his behavior to reinforce my decision.

Day 4   What Was Worse, the Divorce or the Marriage?

Sometimes when women are going through divorce, they are surprised at just how acrimonious the process can be. Frequently I hear, "How did this become so complicated? It is not as if we have tons of money or assets. I thought this would be fairly straightforward. I simply can't believe how crazy this is." Some women even lament, "If I knew it would be this difficult, I would never have filed for divorce."

Really? The relationship, like a bad tooth, has usually decayed to a point where you know there is no saving it. You are comparing an old stress (the marriage) to a new, more current one (divorce). You can't be objective when you do that. Every current pain, either emotional or physical, makes the past pain pale by comparison. This is because you are *remembering* the old pain, but *experiencing* the present one. Every present pain feels as if it is the worst ever.

Objectivity is lost when you are in pain. Second-guessing your choices can lead to confusion and even more pain. If you are thinking about stopping the divorce because it feels too painful, you are basing the decision on the pain rather than on good judgment. If you are having doubts about whether your relationship is salvageable, that is another question.

Let's go back to the decayed tooth analogy for a minute. If you let the tooth fester rather than pull it because you are afraid of how painful the extraction will be, is that a good choice? A decayed tooth, like a decayed marriage, is a chronic situation; if left untreated, it will get worse. Then the situation will present you with much graver consequences. Extracting the tooth, like going through a divorce, is painful. However, the pain is not limitless. Both will be healed and the pain will subside.

Decisions need to be made based on what will provide you with the healthiest outcome. Go back and read your journal or the notes that you perhaps made in this book. Ask friends and family or your therapist. They will remind you of why you needed this marriage to end.

Make your decision based on what will ultimately bring you the most peace. Focus on what is right and healthy about your choice. Most doubt and equivocation is about lack of confidence, not the wrong decision. You wouldn't have gotten this far if something inside of you didn't support your need to do this.

Today I know that no one likes to get a tooth pulled, but sometimes it is the best thing to do.

Mary is a quiet young woman in her mid-thirties, with three children. She has been married ten years. Mary was arrested for domestic violence. Her story is not an uncommon one.

Mary went out after work to celebrate the birthday of a female co-worker and had two glasses of wine. She had told her husband she would be a little later than usual. She was home by 7:30. Her husband flew into a jealous rage, demanding that she tell him who she was "really with."

> "I tried to calm him down and then he pinned me against the wall. He had his forearm across my throat and I couldn't breathe. The children were hysterical at this point. To break free, I pushed him away and in doing so, I scratched his face with my nail. I fled to the bedroom and called my mother. I was terrified and sobbing. The kids were screaming. It was a nightmare."

Meanwhile, her husband called the police. They came and saw a hysterical woman who smelled of alcohol. She could barely tell her story. Because he had a scratch and she had no signs of being hurt, she was arrested. Later, she tried to reason with him. His response was to force her to have sex.

This has been the pattern for almost the entire thirteen years of marriage. She cries, pleads, reasons. He smashes doors, goes through her personal things, and follows her. She stays, she says, because she "loves him."

She really stays because she is lovesick. She is in a relationship where <u>he</u> is her whole focus. She admits the children are suffering. She is losing weight and has dark circles under her eyes. Yet, she continues to believe that she must fix him because she loves him.

When you "love" someone so much that you risk being hurt, then you are lovesick. This is not love, except in the way that addicts love their drugs. When we are drawn so strongly to someone or something that is not good for us, this is not love, but pain. It is an illness called addiction. Do not confuse love and illness. It could be fatal.

Today I acknowledge that sick love doesn't get better without help from a professional, any more than a sick body will heal when left on its own. Seeking professional advice is imperative. I will do this today because I care enough about myself to admit that this is bad for me.

...for Another Man

A woman experiences an overwhelming feeling of betrayal when she finds out her husband is having an affair. This is compounded when the object of her husband's affection is another man. When the affair is with a woman, her sense of self is challenged. The overriding feeling may be that she was not a "good enough" woman. However, when her husband has an affair with a man, there is no competition. While the affair may be shocking, the gender issue may stymie her.

If this happens to you, your marriage can feel like a sham. You wonder if your husband ever loved you. Most men in this situation express great love and affection for their wives. However, they have felt something was missing. Frequently, men may have felt attracted to other men in their youth, but either denied the feelings or thought they could ignore them. Marrying and having the "ideal" life is a strong tradition of this culture. Many men desperately want to be fathers and have a "traditional" family. So they may deny or minimize their feelings for other men. Over the years these feelings may grow. Some men engage in a secret life, having sexual liaisons with other men, rationalizing that this behavior has nothing to do with the marriage. If you are a woman who has discovered her husband's secret, it is important that you focus your energies on healing yourself. Wendy Rosen, Ph.D, Cambridge, Massachusetts offers the following suggestions.

- Focus on the gender difference. This is not a competition.
- Marriage therapy will not fix this marriage.
- The marriage cannot be saved.
- Sexuality is a complex issue. Preferences exist on a continuum, not in black and white.

How do children deal with this news? Interestingly, the gender issue is less important to the children than the demise of their parents' marriage. The divorce is the primary issue, the infidelity is the secondary issue and the last important issue is gender. A post-divorce relationship with your children's father may be easier than you think. His having an affair with another man means this really wasn't about you. This insight can help diminish the feeling of rejection, disappointment and betrayal. Consequently, the animosity can be easier to manage and eventually overcome.

Today I will work to accept the reality of my situation and that there was nothing I could have done to save this marriage. In acceptance, I can find peace, begin to recover, and move on to the next phase of my life.

These days no longer hold a special place on your calendar. However, in your child's calendar of special events, these are still days to celebrate.

This is an example of when your children's needs and your desires are widely disparate. Children love celebrations of all kinds. Now, being divorced, especially newly divorced, the last thing you want to celebrate is the day he was born or his role as a father. You do, however, have to support your child celebrating his father. Supporting your child in his/her celebrating is important because:

- It teaches the child the importance of ritual and celebration.
- It teaches the child the joy of giving.
- It is one way we teach children how to express their feelings.
- It assures the child that you can support his ongoing relationship with his father.
- It models positive behavior.
- It says to the child, "I can support you and your needs, even if I don't want to."
- It reinforces for the child that the parents can work together.

If your own father is available, then maybe spending Father's Day with him will be helpful. If that is not possible, honor the day in quiet reflection or just ignore it completely. Many years ago, one group of divorced women I know decided to celebrate Father's Day in a unique way. Their children were all grown and so they were not called upon to help with presents and visitation. Their own fathers had all passed away. These women rented a sailboat complete with a captain, packed lunch and drinks, and headed off for a glorious day on Long Island Sound. They used the day to celebrate themselves and their friendship.

Rituals around birthdays may be more difficult to deal with. Do something for yourself. Whatever you decide to do is totally your choice – there are no rules, no rights and wrongs. Leave yourself open to the options. You may want to acknowledge his birthday and that is fine, also. Sending an e-mail or a card is fine. Check in with yourself, though, to make sure you do not have an ulterior motive. Be sure you don't have expectations of any kind. That could set you up to feel hurt and rejected all over again.

Today I will help my child prepare for his father's birthday or Father's Day. It gives us an opportunity to share our differences in a loving and respectful way, which can lay the groundwork for all the future differences we will experience. I can honor and respect my feelings without needing to impose them on my child or anyone else.

The Fourteen to Eighteen Year Old

Teenagers between fourteen and eighteen years old face the difficult task of developing a separate identity from their family while continuing in a relationship with their family. They struggle between independence and dependence, vacillating between acting grown-up and child-like. Peer relationships are crucial to teenagers as they explore their own values and ideals within that age group. This is a time when life outside the family is full and demanding.

Teenagers' response to divorce is varied. Feelings of abandonment, shame, depression, and anxiety are typical. Younger teens tend to feel rejected and abandoned. They may also be at high risk for acting-out behaviors such as abusing alcohol and drugs, running away, becoming pregnant, or quitting school. The unconscious rationale is that by getting in trouble, they create a reason for their parents to unite. Older, more mature teens worry about practical matter such as housing and finances.

Be clear that the decision to divorce is final, not reversible, and not their fault. There may be temptation to take teenagers into your confidence and share details of both a practical and emotional nature. Sharing this information with your teenage children changes their role as well as yours. When we make our children our friends, we can no longer act effectively as parents, as the roles become multi-layered and cloudy. Teenage children need a clear definition of parents, now more than at any other time in their lives.

Do not expect your children to take over the role of the estranged husband. Often this happens with teenage boys when their mothers call upon them to take over some of the father's responsibilities. While this is not necessarily unhealthy, the degree to which we rely on them to fill that role can be. For example, Martha felt it was the duty of her 19-year-old son to be her "date" for a New Year's Eve party. Expectations of that sort are inappropriate. If we rely too much on our teenagers to "fill the gap" practically or emotionally, we interfere with their development and foster resentment and rebellion.

Teenagers need to work on their individuation from the family. By providing order, consistency, routine, and stability, we foster healthy relationships with our children and provide them a framework for their developing individuality.

Today I understand that my teenagers may look "all grown up." I need to remember that they are still growing, both physically and emotionally. I will include them in the family responsibilities while not burdening them inappropriately with my emotional needs.

Lydia shared this: "Clearly, no one is perfect. When picking a partner, you need to review the parts of a potential spouse that you like and the ones you don't like. Everyone has flaws. The question is not 'Can I change these flaws?' but 'Can I live with these flaws?'"

When we assume we can change flaws in someone else, we presume two things - first, that we have the right to try to change another person and secondly, that what we label a flaw is a flaw to everyone else, especially the potential partner. One person's flaws can be another's assets. It is arrogant and presumptive to think we have the right to enumerate another's flaws and then change them! Early on, many of us saw aspects of our future spouse's personality that we did not like. We may have called them flaws, or imperfections, or quirks. Rarely did we entertain the notion that we would *have to live with those flaws.*

Rather, many of us assumed we could change those annoying little quirks after we were married. Some of us thought maturity or marriage would magically change those things we didn't like. Or we assumed he would *outgrow* them! Maybe we thought we could *learn* to live with them. The truth is, many of us didn't think about those things at all. We simply ignored them.

That is our denial at work. The problem with denial is that nothing changes. We cannot grow when we ignore or minimize a problem. Sometimes we say, "That doesn't really matter." Now we know it does matter and it *matters a lot.*

Look at those things that feel most troublesome in your marriage; you will most likely find that the seeds of today's problems were firmly planted many years ago. The knowledge that we sometimes deny our instincts even when there is hard evidence can help us admit that there were things fundamentally wrong from the beginning. In some cases, the marriage didn't *go* wrong, it *was* wrong. These insights also provide tools to help us avoid the same mistakes in the future.

Today I will think about if I ignored things that were really unacceptable to me. Did I want to be married so much that I overlooked evidence of problems? Did I think I could change things to my way of liking? Denying what is important to me will not bring me serenity. Being honest about my needs and not diminishing them is critical. In the future, I will be more mindful and respectful of what I want and need. I will pay close attention to myself and I will honor those messages.

Close your eyes and imagine how you would like to be. Gently guide yourself inward, to look at how you would *like to feel, think, and behave*. While you may be clear about what you *don't* want, have you spent time looking at what you *do* want? Most of us stay stuck in disliking things about ourselves. Few of us ever think about how to *change* them.

Just entertaining *the idea* of change can be powerful. You may have gotten used to being passive and feeling hopeless. Part of turning a victim into a survivor is to see that you have choices, and that in the choice, lies the power.

Do not let your thoughts shift into past tense and self-criticism. Keep them in the present or future. If you have trouble imagining yourself differently, try this:

You are chosen to be in a movie. You get to play your favorite character. Who is that character? What do you like about her? Can you imagine what it would feel like to be her?

It is okay to fantasize! You have the opportunity to stretch into realms you may not have thought possible. Have you lost the ability to dream or fantasize? Part of low self-esteem is the feeling of hopelessness. Use your imagination to reopen the door of possibilities.

Today I will fantasize about who I want to be, the life I want, and the life I can create for myself. Every change begins with a dream!

Some guilt is useful. Without guilt, we would not feel badly about hurting others or breaking laws. The desire to avoid guilt may make us more mindful of our behavior toward others. If we do hurt another, guilt can motivate us to make amends, consequently improving our relationships. Healthy guilt can actually help us to:

- Take responsibility for our behavior.
- Learn from our mistakes.
- Make amends (when possible).
- Forgive ourselves.

Healthy guilt can help us build self-confidence, assertiveness, and self-respect. We can begin to see mistakes as opportunities for growth. If we fear mistakes less, we may even procrastinate less.

Guilt and shame are sometimes confused. Guilt usually centers on a specific transgression, while shame is more pervasive. I have heard it put this way, "Guilt is when you have *done* something wrong. Shame is when you think you *are* something wrong." Shame often carries with it feelings of worthlessness, wanting to "disappear," and excessive and painful periods of self-scrutiny. Shame is more likely to occur when a woman has a low opinion of herself. She may have difficulty accepting her feelings and trusting her choices. She may question her own values, morés and boundaries. There may have been instability in her childhood, such as violence, illness or alcoholism. The result is that the child did not receive enough nurturing and care. She may think, "If they can't love me, then who can? I must really be bad." Not surprisingly, these women may be in relationships where they accept behavior that is really unacceptable. If you suffer from this kind of unhealthy guilt/shame, you probably recognize some of these characteristics in yourself:

- I feel I am not good enough.
- I always feel like I have done something wrong, even though I don't know what it is.
- I am constantly trying to please others and get their approval.
- I always apologize, even when I didn't do anything wrong.
- I expect to be ridiculed and rejected if I make a mistake.
- I can't say no to anyone, so I am overwhelmed with commitments.
- I have difficulty letting anyone know I need help.

If you identify with some of the above statements, then you might feel the divorce is your fault. You may have been married to a controlling, dominant individual who put you down and minimized your feelings. Divorcing him means you have a chance to rebuild yourself. If you are suffering from unhealthy guilt, talk with a therapist or a minister or join a women's group. Learning to accept yourself is a major part of the healing process.

Today rather than continue to feel shameful, I will think about the positive things I have done in my life. I know there are steps I can take to free myself from these self-imposed demons. I will share my concerns with another person today. It is the beginning of breaking down those myths that keep me trapped in negative self-talk!

Lucy was not advocating for herself and her children in her divorce. Her husband, a controlling and physically abusive man, threatened not to give her any money. His income was considerably higher than hers. He had a career, a pension and job security. She stayed home with their children, now ten and five, had a high school education, and worked cleaning houses. She confessed that although her attorney thought she was entitled to all the equity in her home, she was hesitant to pursue her rights. "I feel like such a bitch," she said. "I am hoping he calms down and cooperates and will give me what I deserve."

Why does she feel that she is a "bitch" for asking for what she needs? She acknowledges that in her family of origin, she was rewarded for maintaining a passive attitude and putting her needs aside. Intellectually, she is aware of this dilemma. However, she still hopes that he will change. In doing so, she avoids looking at her own behavior.

What would be the outcome if she continues not to advocate for herself and her children? She will be unable to make ends meet. She has not thought about her financial future and that of her kids. What will she do when her children want to play sports, or take music lessons? What if they need braces? How will her cost of living increase in five years?

It is important to recognize that you are not just fighting for your own rights, but also for the rights of your children. They can't fight for themselves and are depending on you to do that for them.

> "I didn't think of that," she concedes. "I was so concerned with keeping the peace that I didn't even think about their needs. When I consider their needs, I don't feel bitchy, I feel like a good mother. I need to make sure they are provided for in any way I can. I cannot stop their father from leaving if he chooses to do that, but I can take steps to insure our future is as secure as I can make it."

Today if I feel that I am being bitchy when I advocate for myself and my children, I will reconsider my stance. While confrontation and conflict are scary, seeing my children go without what is rightfully theirs is even more frightening. I will do what I can to advocate for them. I am all they have. When I think of my children being deprived, that injustice fuels my need to speak up!

We long for harmony. So, we acquiesce to keep the peace. We nod our head and comply. We may say to ourselves, "How big a deal is this anyway?" Or we may seethe with anger. Sometimes our partners read our compliance not as acquiescence, but as resolution. Unaware of our internal struggle, their perception is that things are going smoothly. So, they continue on in their daily life thinking that the marriage is strong and viable.

But inside of our being, we are churning. We are acquiescing for the sake of peace - in the bedroom, in the kitchen, with finances. Then one day, we wake up so unhappy that we do not want to get out of bed. All that acquiescing IS a big deal. It hurts our sense of self and, without our even realizing it, it hurts the marriage. Now we are tired, depressed, angry and frustrated.

For the sake of peace, women often go to extraordinary measures. If you grew up in a home where fighting and screaming were fairly routine, you may have developed a real strong dislike for discord. You say to yourself, "My marriage will never be like that. I will never treat my spouse that way." And so you don't. You recoil from conflict, stuffing it into the core of your being. Then one day, you simply overflow with anger, frustration, and pain. At that moment, you may see your only option is a return to your parents' methods of communication. You begin ranting and raving. He is shocked and amazed! Who is this person and where is my wife? You are also amazed and, deep down, you may be ashamed and humiliated about your behavior.

Acquiescence or volatility were the only strategies implemented in many of our homes, therefore they are the only ways we know how to behave. Conflict resolution is a learned behavior that needs to be practiced. In order to have good conflict resolution skills, there must be mutual respect between the parties. Both must be assertive. Most importantly, the couple must have a mutual desire to resolve differences. Resolution can feel uncomfortable because in order for it to be successful, the couple must surrender the quest to be victor. The focus is not about an individual victory; it is about a relationship victory.

Today when I think about my marriage, I will think about my own conflict resolution style. Did I need to win? Or did I use silence with hopes that I could keep the peace? I can work on developing my conflict resolution skills. These skills will serve me and help enhance all the relationships in my life.

Annulment is often seen as a religious determination. Attorney Barry F. Armata of Bristol, Connecticut explains there is also a judicial determination that a marriage is void. Grounds for annulment fall into two categories:

- Marriages that were void from the beginning. These are marriages that should never have taken place. The annulment recognizes there was never a valid marriage.
- A voidable marriage is a marriage that is valid until a decree annulling the marriage is entered.

The difference between divorce and annulment is that in divorce it is presumed there was a valid marriage. Divorce is dissolution of that union and is based on grounds that occurred *during* the marriage. In annulment, the judgment is that a valid marriage never existed and is based on grounds that existed *at the time* of the marriage. The grounds for annulment include:

- Marriage between family members that are prohibited: a man marrying his mother, grandmother, sister or aunt; or a woman marrying her father, grandfather or brother. Even if this marriage took place in another country, it can be considered void in the United States. (Check specific state laws).
- A bigamous marriage is when someone who is already lawfully married attempts marriage to someone else. This can happen when the dissolution of a prior marriage is invalid or not final. This is a marriage that should never have taken place. If the innocent party continues to cohabit even after finding out about the preexisting marriage, it does not affect his or her entitlement to an annulment.
- A marriage involving an incompetent individual may be voidable and subject to annulment. The annulment would be given with proof that the party was incompetent at the time of the marriage ceremony. Incompetence describes someone who is mentally ill or intellectually disabled or otherwise unable to make decisions on his/her own behalf. Onset of incompetence during the marriage would be insufficient grounds to render the annulment.
- A marriage is voidable if a minor marries without consent.
- Defects in the marriage ceremony or license may render a marriage void. Examples include if your marriage was not performed by an appropriate religious or civil official or you failed to obtain proper blood tests. A marriage is NOT voidable if the only defect was failure to return and record the marriage license after the ceremony.
- If you were fraudulently induced to enter into a marital relationship, you may be entitled to an annulment. Mutuality is required to create a valid marriage.
- Misrepresentations of health or of a physical condition may be grounds for annulment in special cases.

Deception regarding chastity prior to marriage is NOT grounds for annulment, nor is misrepresentation regarding the desire to have children, entering the marriage pregnant by another man, or a partner's willingness to adopt the spouse's religion. If you think you may have grounds for annulment, contact your State Bar Association or discuss this possibility with an attorney as rules vary from state to state.

Today I will remember that educating myself about the legal process better equips me to know my rights. Annulment rules vary from state to state. If I think I may have grounds for annulment, I will contact the State Bar Association or discuss this possibility with an attorney.

Eleanor and Marvin divorced after forty years of marriage. Both were in their late 60's and not in the best of health. They had retired to Florida in their early fifties. They were not rich people; they had been self-employed and worked hard their entire lives. They retired early due to health reasons rather than as a result of accumulating a grand nest egg. Having been in the home furnishing business, they acquired a lifetime of accessories, knick-knacks, and photographs. They could agree on nothing – not who got the silver, who got the bedroom set, not even on who got the photos or the frames that housed them. This couple went through numerous lawyers, mediators, counselors, and two years of litigation. No agreement regarding the property could be reached.

Their case reached the judge, who said to the wife, "Make two lists, dividing everything in your home. Include every piece of furniture, every accessory, every photograph." Then he turned to the husband, "When she has made her lists," the judge said, "You pick one."

The saga continued. The wife agonized over how to prepare the lists, knowing she was not going to get everything she wanted. Ultimately, she divided everything exactly down the middle: half the dining room set, half the bedroom, half the silver, half the good dishes and so on.

What did this couple accomplish? Not much, although they could rationalize that the decision was "fair." In truth, half a set of china and half a set of crystal glasses are not worth much. Each partner found that the possessions they fought so stubbornly to "win" were now really worthless.

Today when I think about what I am really fighting for, I will look at the big picture. I will stop and think before I act, recognizing that being spiteful often backfires.

Day 16   Is An "Organized Divorcing Person" an Oxymoron?

Like "jumbo shrimp," an oxymoron is a combination of words that contradict each other. You may look at "organized divorcing woman" as the biggest oxymoron of all. Now, you handle extra chores and jobs once handled by your husband, plus the additional role of plaintiff or defendant in your divorce. That role requires paperwork, telephones calls with attorneys, and court appearances. All are very time consuming. Short of hiring a half dozen people to assist you through the process, you are going to feel overwhelmed! However, it will abate once the divorce is final and all the litigation stops. A huge chunk of time and psychic energy will be restored. Meanwhile, here are some suggestions to help you get organized. You will spend less time hunting for lost stuff, searching for misplaced papers, worrying about paying bills paid on time, and making numerous trips to the grocery store for items you forgot. They will help life run smoother.

Get a big calendar for everyone to use. Give each family member a different color marker to write down his/her events and appointments. Include visitation weekends for the entire year! Everything goes on the calendar. Older children can write down their own commitments. Explain that if it isn't on the calendar, then it isn't going to happen.

Create a filing system, maintain accurate records, set up a budget and a schedule to pay bills. Many women procrastinate in doing this. Feeling overwhelmed by their financial situation, they simply avoid it and, of course, it only gets worse. Schedule a bill-paying day on the calendar.

Cook Less. Write down everything you will need for that week and go to the store once a week. You will save time and money by doing this. When possible, cook double meals and freeze them. It isn't a leftover if they haven't eaten it in a week! Always have a few meals in the freezer for emergencies, such as when you don't want to cook, haven't got the time or are going out that night.

Deal with the mess. The less stuff the better. Get rid of those tie-dye shirts and maxi coats from your youth. If that feels too drastic, then at least store them away. Do the same thing with old toys, mugs with broken handles, yellowed magazines, ripped sheets and towels, old make-up, expired medications. Throw them out! You will be amazed how liberated you will feel!

Deal with the stuff that is left. Make sure everything has a place. Have a place for toys, a bin for boots, a file cabinet for bills. Plastic bins or old milk crates make wonderful storage/organizational tools.

Diminish primping time. Pick out five complete outfits on Sunday night. Then you don't have to think about it for an entire week. Hang them on a hook, rather than just plan your outfits in your head. This eliminates the frantic morning search for the right necklace or pantyhose. Five outfits still gives you a choice in the morning, but much less opportunity for indecision and chaos. Have your kids do the same with their clothes.

Avoid build up. Put things away as you use them. Take a moment to make your bed in the morning or put your dishes in the dishwasher. Wipe the counter after you use it. Take the trash out with you every day. This will eliminate a "build up" of mess greeting you at the end of the day. Keep cleaning supplies in each bathroom and when you have a moment, clean the toilet or scour the sink. It doesn't have to be done all at once. Break it down into tiny chores and it won't get overwhelming.

Today when I have a few minutes to myself, I will think of one small change I can make to streamline my life. I don't have to make all the changes at once. I will begin in small ways. Change takes time.

Going through divorce can be an isolating experience. Many of your friendships may have been with other married couples. Suddenly they may seem somewhat distant. Your husband's family may distance themselves. Even members of your own family may become distant. Suddenly you may feel cast out to sea without an anchor. This can be a lonely and frightening time. While individual therapy can provide valuable support, a divorce group is invaluable. Like-minded women sharing their experience is heartwarming and healing. Some women worry that hearing other people's stories will depress them. Quite the contrary is true. You can find inspiration and hope in the stories of women who are further along than you in their process. You can offer support and assurance to women who are not as far along. This will reinforce and affirm your own growth.

Unfortunately, divorce groups which are exclusively for women aren't very common. Then join another women's group. It doesn't matter if it is a church group or a quilting group, a drumming group or a book group. The point is to find like-minded women with whom you have something in common, so you can become part of a new community where you are understood and valued. That new community can provide enormous support and nurturance, and can be an integral part of rebuilding your self-esteem, self-confidence, and social network.

The good news is that there are groups for everything and they aren't difficult to find. Try the alternative newspaper in your community. Check out bulletin boards in coffee shops, colleges, churches, and bookstores. Ask friends. Ask at the library. If all else fails and you are feeling brave, write your own ad and put up flyers where like-minded people will see them (For example, for a book group, try the library or for knitting, try the yarn shop).

You may be thinking, "Who has time to join anything?" You do, an hour or two a month isn't a lot to spare. Think of the time you are watching television or surfing the net, wishing you had something else to do!

Today I will remember that I am part of a larger community. I will make an effort to find a women's group that has the same interests I do. It might feel scary to venture out and do something like this, but it can't hurt to try. I can act on my own behalf to create the support and a sense of community that I wish for in my life. When I reach out, I am taking control of my life.

It is helpful in the divorce grieving process to be clear about what our losses really are. Are we grieving the loss of what we have, what we had, or what we hoped could be? Sometimes we grieve the loss of the past—when we were dating, or engaged, or newly married. In this case, it is important to be aware that we are grieving for something that is already gone from our lives.

We also grieve for what could have been. This can be the most painful grief. It contains elements of the infinite. Our imaginations are limitless. We can create any scenario for how we wish the marriage could be and then grieve for what we never had. When we do this, we grieve the potential, not the reality. If you find yourself grieving for what could have been, be aware that you are adding to your own grief by writing the script of the idealized relationship and then suffering its loss. We only hurt ourselves when we do that. Let's turn our attention to now. At the time of the divorce, what was the relationship really like? Make a list of all the things you miss. Be sure that you have not included anything from the past or speculations of the future. To do so will only add unnecessarily to your pain and suffering. Next, jot down some ideas that you think might help you through the process of grieving each of the losses.

Here are a few examples of how other women dealt with their individual losses:

- Beth, who had lived in her house for years, grieved for the loss of the garden she had loved and tended. Before the house was sold, she took cuttings of all her perennial plants and planted them in a friend's yard. Her plan was to retrieve them and replant them when she found a new home of her own. This helped her let go of the home, knowing that she had been able to take a part of it with her.

- Julie had a small family with whom she wasn't very close. Her children would continue to go to their father's for Christmas so she decided to book a cruise for the Christmas holidays and start a new tradition of her own.

- Liz, who grieved the loss of her husband's handiness with cars, decided to take an auto-repair class for women.

Today I will remember that each of us experiences losses unique to our own situation. When I separate the losses of what could have been from what really was, I am not overwhelmed by phantom losses. I can deal with my true losses and find ways to let them go. I will see each loss as a challenge to exercise my creativity. In that way, I can use my imagination to heal rather than hurt me.

Women going through divorce often speak of feeling unable to "let it go." This is usually because of some fear or unresolved connection they feel about their ex-spouse or even themselves.

We all struggle with the concept "let it go." The idea that some things are beyond our control is something we intellectually grasp but which we resist emotionally. To "let it go" can feel like giving up control, a surrender of something we are not yet able to part with. In some cases, we may not even be sure that we want to part with it. To "let it go" may feel like walking away or leaving something undone. We may be left feeling that we aren't "doing it right." Women often lament, "Why can't I let him go?" Then they feel badly about themselves. They are filled with self-recrimination because they are unable to perform this self-imposed task.

Amy only uses the word "Let." That's it – plain and simple "Let." *The Merriam-Webster Dictionary* defines "let" as *permit* or *allow*. Perhaps we could all relax a little by just thinking about "let". When we "let" ourselves just be, we take the pressure off of ourselves to respond in a certain way and on a specific timetable. We simply need to let *ourselves* be with whatever it is we are experiencing. We can learn that that is okay for today.

"Let" gives us freedom to accept ourselves without judgment or self-imposed pressure.

Today I will think of the word "let" throughout my day, every time I have a self-criticizing or negative thought. I will just say "let" and allow myself to relax. When I "let" my feelings be, I get to know who I am. When I "let" my thoughts be, I begin to affirm myself. I will be patient, loving and completely present for myself. I will "Let."

Yes, people really can change. But, no, they won't change just because we want them to do so. While that may seem fairly obvious, the truth is many of us try desperately to change our partners. We may think we know what is best for him. We say we are just trying to help, but in reality we may be imposing our value system on another.

Why is it so important to us that someone be/act/say/think the way we want them to? Without realizing it, we may simply be afraid. We may not even have access to the feeling until we spend some time really looking at ourselves. When our partner doesn't behave the way we want, we may fear:

- Loss of control.
- A challenging of our value system.
- What others may think.
- Change.
- The unknown.
- Trusting others.

Some of these fears run very deep. We come to relationships with a collection of different experiences. These differences can support a relationship by introducing new coping skills and multi-dimensional ways of looking at different situations or they can destroy it.

Some changes we ask for aren't optional. If there is substance abuse of any kind, gambling, or domestic violence—including verbal, emotional, sexual, or physical—the changes we ask for are simply not negotiable. A change is necessary but it may not come from him. If your husband isn't willing to change the unacceptable behavior, then you need to be willing to leave. In cases that involve unacceptable behaviors, outside help from a counselor, therapist, or mental health program is imperative.

Whether you stay together or divorce, you will need to make changes, too. You will need to surrender your desire to change another person against his will. You will need to refocus your options and accept what is out of your control. This can be painful and difficult but if you put half the effort into changing yourself as you put into trying to change him, you will be successful in making the changes you need to make for yourself.

Today I will consider how long I have been trying to change him. I am exhausted. I will use my energy to consider this: I need to accept that he doesn't want to change. Then I will have to look at what I need to live a happy, healthy life. When I look at what I can do for myself, I regain control of my life.

In his book *The Art of Happiness*, the Dalai Lama suggests that a flexible mind is a sign of a healthy mind. He notes that flexibility helps us deal with life's ups and downs and, more importantly, enables us to get through our crises and traumas.

My concern is that flexibility might be misread as acquiescence. Some women have learned to "get along" by compromising. While true compromise is a cornerstone of any good relationship, compromise that surrenders your basic values or your sense of self is harmful. Many people who are leaving a marriage feel they have compromised so much that they have lost themselves.

Flexibility is not necessarily compromise. It may be a different way of seeing things, rather than a way of behaving. To adapt to circumstances beyond our control, we are flexible. That does not mean you are not true to yourself and your ideas; but rather you can see there is more than one way to look at things and respond to them. When going through a divorce, a person with a flexible mind:

- Sees her ex-spouse's point of view.
- Knows the definition of "fair" changes with your perspective.
- Knows that rarely are there absolutes.
- Understands that parenting issues are on a continuum, rather than black and white.
- Has tolerance for others' opinions.
- Knows there is more than one way to accomplish something.
- Sees detours as a challenge rather than an obstacle.
- Recognizes she doesn't have control over everything.
- Works to adapt to situations beyond her control.
- Doesn't take everything personally.

Flexibility is the ability to expand your intuitions and thoughts to include alternative ways to do things. It isn't always easy. Even when we know there is a better way to do something, old habits and fears can cause us to return to rigid behaviors and thinking. Fighting that urge can be difficult, but it can have huge payoffs. Rigidity in thought and feeling can result in additional lawyer's fees, acrimony, aggravation, and confusion.

Today when I think about flexibility, I will consider how rigid or flexible I have been during this process. Regardless of HIS behavior, I will focus only on my behavior. I am responsible for what I think and feel. It means I have the power to change and grow into the person I choose to be.

Lenore has been struggling for years in a very unhappy, verbally abusive marriage. She and her husband do not have children. Both are self-sufficient in terms of income. Divorce proceedings would be fairly simple. Why do they stay together? The answer is simply that they are both attached to the family cat. Lenore is terrified of what her husband will do to get "custody" of the kitty. She is convinced he will literally kidnap the cat and, out of revenge, keep her from seeing it.

The family pet often plays a large role in the family dynamics. Frequently, both parties have a huge emotional investment in the family pet and that level of investment continues through the divorce. If the couple is childless, the family pet takes on an even larger emotional role, often substituting for children.

Animals are far more unconditional in their love and devotion for us than we are with each other. If a couple has been emotionally estranged for some time, the family pet may also provide the love that is no longer present in the marriage. In the deterioration and subsequent dissolution of the marriage, the family pet can offer tremendous emotional consolation.

> Eva has children who are grown and on their own. She spoke of her dogs with great affection. "Since my husband left, I have felt that I am not needed anymore. Then I look at my dogs and realize they depend on me for everything. They must be walked, fed, cared for. Their needs create a structure and pattern to my life. They keep me going when I sometimes don't want to do anything but stay in bed."

Given these emotional conditions, it is not surprising how much weight the family pet carries. Visitation schedules are not unusual. Some women feel devastated at what seems to be their estranged husband's loyal connection to the animal. She may feel that her husband cares more about the pet than about her! In truth, it is simply easier to show affection when we aren't harboring negative feelings. Animals do not judge, correct, dismiss or reject us. The attachment is so unconditional that it is no wonder people who have pets are healthier and live longer. Being loved unconditionally is something we all long for. Our animals provide us with that primal need and we are enhanced by the experience.

Today if I feel like my pet is too much to handle on my own, I will hold him even closer to me. I will recognize that the benefits far outweigh the negatives. My animal companion will not judge, dismiss, betray, or abandon me. He/she loves me unconditionally. I will allow myself to accept that gift without reservation.

"It was two years after my marriage ended that I began gambling." Judith continues, "Since I was the one who wanted the divorce, I couldn't see its relationship to the gambling. My life was as I wanted it to be. I was on my own for the first time in years. I enjoyed my work, my friends, and my family obligations. I did tend to feel overwhelmed at times. The casino offered me a respite from my obligations – a chance to get away and not have to think about anything."

Unlike men, most women find gambling escalates during their middle years of forty to sixty. These women may find themselves alone, through their husband's emotional absence, death or divorce. The casino offers a break from the responsibility of everyday life. There are no clocks dictating a rigorous schedule and no demands. They are treated to free drinks or points to buy meals. They feel catered to and important. The slot machines offer a way to "zone out." The repetitive function of the machines is anesthetizing and makes it easy to lose oneself. Judith, now fifty-five and divorced for twelve years, sees how these factors played a part in her slide into problem gambling.

"It was the one place I could go and be totally anonymous and safe. I felt totally accepted. I rationalized that I had plenty of money and that this was just recreational. After all, it was my money. I could do whatever I wanted with it. I kept pushing the line. I would gamble only with the cash that I brought with me. Then I began to hit my savings. My retirement money was not far behind. My dream was to retire at fifty-five to Florida. If I had kept saving as I had before my gambling, I would already be there. By the time I sought help, I had spent everything I had and had maxed out seventeen credit cards. My only recourse was to declare bankruptcy. I stopped gambling for a while and attended Gamblers Anonymous meetings, but gradually I began to gamble again. Then one day, I was driving some members of my family. I had been up at the casino all night gambling. I was disheveled and exhausted from lack of sleep. I was falling asleep behind the wheel. It hit me then that my gambling wasn't hurting just me, but endangering my family as well."

Six years later, Judith still attends GA regularly. She is a peer counselor working with others whose gambling has gotten out of control. She freely tells her story, not only to help other women, but also to keep herself healthy. She advises women to pay attention to the signs -spending too much and borrowing from friends and family. Gambling is a recreational activity that has its risks. Be aware of the warning signs, your family history, and your behavior. If you feel you are behaving in a way that is out of the ordinary for you, then get help immediately. Don't let shame keep you from talking and seeking help.

Today am I buying too many lottery tickets? Am I spending too much time at the casino? Am I spending more than I can afford? Do I borrow from my credit cards or other sources? Am I preoccupied with the "chase" of winning it back? Do I say "Just this once and never again"? If I am in trouble, I will act immediately on my own behalf. It is how I take care of myself and respect myself.

How do you know when you need medication or when you just need a good cry? Grief is a *normal reaction to an abnormal situation*. It is normal to feel sad when someone dies or when you are going through divorce. That sadness is grief. The more important someone is to us, the greater the loss and the deeper the grief. Grief should not be medicated. Grief is testimony to the depth of our caring and consequently, to our loss.

Clinical depression is comprised of a number of symptoms which characterize it as an illness. When trying to decide whether or not medication is needed, the symptoms, the duration, and intensity are all considered. Below is a list of symptoms that are regularly associated with depression. You may have felt some of these symptoms at one time or another in your life. However, it is the duration and severity of these symptoms that are critical in reaching an accurate diagnosis. The difference between grief and depression can be accurately diagnosed by a mental health professional. Depression can be treated successfully with psychotherapy or medication or both. The symptoms of depression are:

- Changes in sleep patterns. Often difficulty in falling asleep and frequent waking during the night. It is not uncommon to wake up very early and not be able to go back to sleep.
- Change in appetite. Usually weight loss is reported. Occasionally, weight gain.
- Lethargy.
- Loss or diminished ability to concentrate. Mind wanders, often going over the same things.
- Loss of interest in activities and hobbies that once interested you.
- Frequent crying.
- Feelings of worthlessness or excessive guilt.

If you have a number of these symptoms lasting for more than two weeks without relief, medication might be indicated. Consult with your family doctor. He/she can either prescribe it or refer you to a psychiatrist. If, on the other hand, you have:

- Thoughts that life is not worth living
- A plan for how you would end your life

Then you should seek help immediately! Feeling suicidal is NOT part of the grieving process, but an indication of severe depression. Do something to ensure your safety immediately! Tell a trusted friend or relative. If you can't reach your doctor, go to the emergency room.

Today as I look over the list of symptoms of depression, I will be honest with myself about my symptoms. If I have concerns, I will act now. I may not be able to imagine being happy again, but I will do the responsible thing and reach out for help! Even if I cannot feel it at this moment, my life has value.

Why do some people recover from divorce faster than others? Why is it that some people use this crisis to better their lives and other people seem devastated by the marital split? Some psychologists credit resilience as the critical component in determining who recovers the fastest. The following is an excerpt from *Harvard Women's Health Watch*, November, 2001.

WHAT IS RESILIENCE?

Psychologists have learned much about resilience from studies of concentration camp survivors, people with severe handicaps, and children from broken or impoverished homes. Experts conclude that such individuals share many of the following characteristics.

- **AUTHENTICITY**, or a sense of self. People who are content within themselves don't need to maintain a facade, nor does their identity depend on externals such as money or position. Thus, they're less likely to be devastated by losing these things.

- **AUTHORSHIP.** Resilient people don't see themselves as passive victims, even in circumstances beyond their control, such as a serious illness or disaster. Instead, they respond actively. Tapping into their own strengths and taking positive action helps them come to "own" such experiences. It also helps them avoid resenting others or assigning blame.

- **FLEXIBILITY.** Although change is intrinsic to life, changes wrought by loss are the hardest to accept. In general, the resilient perceive change as a challenge – even an opportunity. Thus, they are less vulnerable to the fear and anxiety that accompany uncertainty and chaos. An important aspect of flexibility is responsiveness. Resilient people are engaged in the world around them and aware of new ideas. This helps them adapt.

- **BELIEF** in the transcendent. A sense of purpose beyond oneself – whether it comes from religious faith or a love of nature, art, music, or humanity – can produce an unflagging conviction that life is worth living.

Today I will consider if I am a resilient woman. Do I bounce when I am thrown or do I shatter? How many of the above characteristics do I recognize in myself? Which ones can I work on? I will use the above list not to evaluate myself negatively, but to affirm how resilient I already am and to recognize places where I can continue to grow.

So, you thought your dating days were over when you married.

Then you SWORE they were over when you divorced, but here you are struggling with what to wear, where to go, what to talk about. Dating is far more complicated now. For one thing, you need to have a babysitter. Once your parents offered the restrictions to your dating life and now it is your kids. You are a SPAD, a Single Parent Again Dating!

The considerations around dating are many and varied. Allow your children time to adjust to the divorce before bringing a new person into their lives. While you may be thrilled to be rid of your husband, they wish their father could still live with their mother. They may need more time to heal. Do not put your personal life on hold until they are ready, but be sensitive to their needs. Your children do not have to know everything you do or have input into your decisions. Dating is a grown-up decision, as is the decision to divorce. If your child is uncomfortable with your dating, then you can pursue relationships while your child is visiting his father or out with friends. This does not mean you should lie, it merely means you can be discreet.

Forcing children to accept their mother's new suitor can create many problems. They may feel this new person will take you away from them. Or they may worry that you will "like" this person better than you like them. If your date turns into a relationship, bring the children into the relationship very gradually. The child may resist a relationship because he/she feels it is disloyal to his/her father. You can help here, by stressing that they will always have one father, but can enjoy and have friendships with many people.

Young children may want to be included and you can bring them on occasional outings. But remember, this is YOUR friend. You need couple time, alone. Explain to your child that they have their own friends to play with and so do you. Older children have difficulty seeing their parents dating. They need you to be very discreet with regards to sex. This new relationship may feel like the greatest thing that ever happened to you, but chances are your children will feel differently. Both children and parents need to recognize that this discrepancy is not only acceptable, it is usually appropriate. Adults can have more than one spouse, but children have only one set of parents. Validate and respect your child's feelings, but not at the cost of your own. It is one of those times when you can agree to disagree.

Today I am aware that my roles keep changing – wife, mother, single mother, and now girlfriend. Even though I am ready to date, my children may feel differently. I will honor their needs, but not at the cost of my own. I will work at doing what I need to do for myself, yet staying sensitive and open to their issues.

The intensity and focus required to go through a divorce is all consuming. It takes time, emotional energy, stamina, and attention to detail. Our minds are never still: Processing, recalculating, planning, and strategizing long into the night. We rethink and recheck our position. Like a stubborn driver who refuses to stop for an occasional refueling, we put ourselves in danger of breaking down by maintaining the same frenetic pace. Sleep, good food, and exercise refuel our bodies and keep us in top working order. Relaxation is also vital. Without it, we lose our perspective. If we don't give our mind and body time to rest and recover, we run the risk of burning out, lowering our immune system and getting sick.

Relaxation includes meditation and socialization. It also includes fun. When we were children, everything WAS fun. Watch a young child doing a mundane activity and you will see curiosity and pleasure. There is no anxiety, stress or fear. When children are having fun, they are enjoying the process and not thinking about the product. They have no attachment to the outcome and that is FUN! When was the last time you did something purely for the enjoyment of the process without a single thought to the product?

You may feel that fun is a waste of time. Think of fun as fuel. Fun is critical. Isn't that why we work so hard in the first place? Aren't we always saving or planning for the next vacation, the bigger house, the better car, retirement?

You want fun just as much as any child. You are just putting it off. Fun doesn't have to cost a lot of money. Fun doesn't even have to be planned. Having fun is a state of mind. Like the child approaching the most mundane of tasks, it is his attitude that creates the fun. Ever watch a four-year-old clean a bathroom? Fill the sink with water, give him a sponge and he can be happy for hours. To the adult, the same task is a dreaded chore. Have fun cleaning the bathroom? Absolutely! Put on your favorite music, roll up your sleeves and play around with all that water and soap. You may find that in changing your attitude, the whole experience is new!

Today I will try to approach one of the most mundane tasks in my life with the wonder of a four-year-old. If I try, I can find pleasure in the small daily activities in my life. Some day I might go on that vacation or have that big house, but some day is too far away. Like that small child, I will find the fun in my life today. I will make sure that there is some fun in my life every day.

Self-esteem refers to how we feel about ourselves. Once confused with conceit or arrogance, it had a negative connotation. For adults, lack of self-esteem can lead to depression, anxiety disorders, substance abuse, unstable relationships, or eating disorders, to name just a few. Self-esteem comes to us from our parents, our schools, our community, our friends, and our family. It is from our total experience that we determine our self worth. Whether it was a parent telling us "you're stupid" or that boy in eighth grade who made fun of the way we looked, no one escapes hurtful messages and their lingering effects. You could have a Ph.D and still feel stupid, or be a fashion model and believe you are ugly. We attach major significance to our negative experiences and like a cassette tape gone awry, they play over and over in our heads. There goes our self-esteem.

It is important to recognize that your self-esteem didn't plummet because someone gave a negative opinion about you, but because you believed it. As a child, we see our parents as stronger (they were) and smarter (not always) and we believe what they say. We give our power to our parents to love us, feed and clothe us, and protect us. We are born into this world without the ability to care for and protect ourselves from the ravages of the world. We trust our parents for protection and survival. As children, we believe our parents are perfect – all-knowing and good. Therefore, we absolutely believe what they teach us about ourselves.

As adults, we do have choices about how we see ourselves. No longer dependent on our parents to protect us from the ravages of life, we need to take care of ourselves. We can understand our parents did the best they could with what they knew, but they didn't know everything.

Included in the process of self-exploration is separating the wheat from the chaff - keep the good and healthy messages that the world and your parents gave you, and work to eliminate those messages that are unhealthy or hurtful. It is hard work to let go of the useless messages and replace them with stronger, more positive, more accurate messages. It is a journey of inner reflection and self-awareness. It is a journey taken in baby steps.

Today I need to begin to separate the negative messages from the essence of who I am. I can start with daily affirmations. I will read them daily. I will change my belief system. In doing so, I will enhance my self-esteem.

Even if you are the person who wants the divorce, you may be surprised at how difficult it is to move forward with your decision. Often, spouses who initiate the divorce feel as if they are "breaking up the marriage." They have concerns that they will be blamed by their children, family, and friends. They have guilt that their decision will hurt the children.

When a woman wants a divorce, she has usually thought about it very carefully. She has often read lots of self-help books and tried to talk with her husband. She may go to counseling or try to get him to go to counseling. She has often argued, begged, pleaded, and cried. She has made deals with herself – she has tried to minimize the problems, rationalize, deny or ignore them. She has usually been unhappy for a long time.

However, just because she is unhappy doesn't mean it is her fault. Marriage is a partnership – a two-way street where both people need to be accountable and willing to work. One person alone cannot make those changes. Often, a woman tries many different strategies to improve her marriage before she begins to accept that it is not going to change. She tires of trying to change him. So, she tries to change herself. She works to find ways to accept the situation. There comes a day, though, when she is exhausted, having reached her limit, both emotionally and physically. What happens at that moment is that she loses hope. She sees clearly that the changes she needs will not occur.

Like the coroner who announces time of death, she stands over the lifeless marriage, sees it clearly as terminal, with no hope. And she announces it is over. Like the coroner, she *announces* time of death; she is not the *cause* of death.

Couples can live in denial for many, many years – a relationship with no joy, no love, no respect and no trust is merely functioning on life support. It is no longer viable, healthy, and growing. When a woman says she wants a divorce, she has exhausted all possibilities. But saying it doesn't make it her fault. She was just the one with the courage to say it first.

Today when I think about my divorce, I know that I have tried everything to bring this marriage back to life. I know that asking for what I need doesn't make me a "bad" person; it merely makes me an honest one.

Divorce is a clear-cut decision when there is physical or emotional abuse, substance abuse or infidelity. It is something a woman can point to and say "See, this is the reason." Divorce feels justifiable. The Ambivalent Marriage is one when you think about leaving, but really aren't sure what to do. Ambivalent marriages sometimes lack obvious troubles. There isn't the angst of abuse or infidelity. An ambivalent marriage may be described as distant, cordial, uninvolved. There may be separate bedrooms, little passion of any kind, and hardly any communication or connection.

Many couples live like this for years. Some say they stay for the sake of the children, some say it is fear of making change, others admit to inertia.

Living in an ambivalent marriage can have its own comfort level. In some ways, you are single; in other ways, a couple. You may share household chores. You may own the house together, but keep other monies separate. You may share some friends, but most likely your friendships are separate, too. Often, you come together for the holidays and to some outsiders, it can look like a "Norman Rockwell Family." The level of intimacy is minimal but may be bearable.

The positive side is that there are few demands and compromises. There are hardly any fights. Everything is cordial and "big" subjects aren't discussed. However, it doesn't work forever. Eventually, the children grow and leave the home or one partner desires more. A family crisis may occur which forces the couple to interact on a more intimate level. These issues may shake the status quo of the ambivalent marriage.

Because it "isn't so bad," many women struggle with leaving. Since ambivalent marriages can last for decades, there develops a comfort level that takes very little effort to maintain. It is like having a good roommate. Why would you want to kick him out? The relationship is no longer a marriage, but it does serve other purposes - perhaps financial security, help around the house, the facade of a relationship. The emotional intimacy of marriage has already dissolved. It may seem ironic that it is difficult to move ahead – it seems there is so little to lose. However, without the anger at some injustice or betrayal, it may feel unjustified. So you may settle for what you have, rather than taking the risk of the unknown.

Today as I look back at how I lived my life, am I filled with memories of joy and serenity, or am I filled with regret and disappointment? I can use that perspective to make changes so that I can live the life I want and then look back with a sense of satisfaction and pride.

The day after Halloween, the plastic pumpkins, candy corn, and orange candles are swept aside to the fifty percent off table – picked over, broken, and dated. In place of all that orange and black are Christmas chocolates, glass ornaments and tinsel. Aisles of Christmas cards, bows, and wrapping paper take over! If you thought you were going to ignore the Christmas season this year, the magic of merchandising is going to make that difficult! Then come the Christmas commercials that can make you cry and holiday television specials so corny and sweet that your blood sugar runs amok just watching them.

Decorations seem to explode everywhere, along with Christmas music, holiday invitations, and cards. It is bad enough when we think of Christmas as only one day, but when it gets dragged out into two months' worth of consumerism and sentimentality, even the most stalwart feel a little taken advantage of.

If you are going through a divorce, chances are you have been dreading Christmas. Christmas is no longer solely a religious celebration – it is now an event which honors family, friends, consumerism, success, materialism, food, parties, conviviality, and even world peace. At Christmas, we honor all that we hold precious in our lives. When we are going through a transition such as divorce, it can feel as if we haven't anything to celebrate. We feel we are on the outside, looking in at the rest of the world rejoicing and having a ball. Of course, this simply isn't true. But it sure can feel that way.

The good news about all this hype is that it offers us so many options. If you have spent your holiday season controlled by ritual and routine, having other options may feel freeing. In a culture where half of the adults are single, new ideas abound. Instead of looking at what no longer exists, consider all the options you have. Of course, you do always have the option of pulling the blankets over your head and ignoring the whole thing. And that is fine, too.

Today I will think about what I can do differently during this holiday season so I am not constantly confronted with loss. I will look at the rituals I have established and decide which ones I need to let go of. Making these conscious choices allows me to be part of this holiday season in any way I choose. Next year, I may make different choices. These choices are the ones that work for me now; I will worry about next year when it comes!

Month Nine

The "Leaver" is the person who decides the marriage is over. Whether you are the Leaver or your husband is, there are certain characteristics that all Leavers have in common. They often:

- Are emotionally divorced by the time they announce their choice.
- Feel they have spent a lot of time and energy trying to save the marriage.
- Feel guilty.
- Try to be "nice."
- Are seen as the villain.
- Say they "want to be friends."
- Are bad-mouthed to the children.

The "Left" is the person who did not make the decision. They often:

- Feel abandoned.
- Feel blindsided.
- Feel angry.
- Feel victimized.
- Feel revengeful.
- Try to alienate the children from their other parent.

The Left feels "thrown away." The Left feels his/her partner did not try hard enough to make it work. They feel "surprised" and often deny or minimize the problem.

The Leaver feels that he/she has begged, reasoned, yelled, argued, and strategized ways to be heard. The Leaver often feels that his/her partner refused to listen to his/her concerns. Many say that for years they tried to "make the best of it." By the time they leave, they are exhausted, spent, unfulfilled, and emotionally depleted. They feel emotionally divorced from the relationship. The Leaver will tell you that this took years.

The Left feels dumped without consideration or real effort. In their desire to assuage their guilt, the Leaver may act "nice." The Left may see this as an attempt at reconciliation. This can lead to the Left feeling betrayed all over again. If you are the Leaver, it is important to be polite, but firm. Hedging, avoiding, and equivocating can lead to misinterpretation and thus more angry feelings. Be firm and clear, but gentle and kind. Treat the Left with respect. Be clear of your intentions. In the long run, that is the kindest thing you can do. Eventually, everyone usually gets angry. The Left gets angry when he/she realizes that the Leaver is not coming back. The Leaver gets angry at feeling guilty and torn. This anger can serve as the fuel to give them both the energy to uncouple.

Today whether I am the Leaver or the Left, I need to recognize that my partner has a different perspective. I don't need to understand it, but if I can respect it, then it will benefit me in the long run.

Jill filed for divorce. Her husband, Jack, was verbally abuse and quite cruel. The couple had one child, John, age 5. Jill was shy and passive. She had trouble asking for what she wanted in most of her relationships. With Jack, it was impossible. Jack towered over her petite frame. He had a booming voice and confident style. Standing up to him was extremely difficult for Jill. He was affable and joked with both his lawyer and HER lawyer. This made Jill even more awkward and withdrawn.

When it came to negotiating visitation, Jack and his lawyer asked for "reasonable and customary" visitation. Jack felt a specific visitation schedule would limit his contact with his son. He also felt that he wanted to have a more "spontaneous" relationship with John. Jill's lawyer thought that sounded reasonable. Jill knew she had trouble saying "no" to Jack and now found herself with the problem of saying "no" to the lawyers as well. So, she acquiesced and went along with the agreement.

Jack called her every night asking to see John. She had difficulty saying no, and tried to maintain control by avoiding the phone calls. After two weeks, Jack filed a motion with the court contending that Jill was impeding his visitation and was in contempt of court. Jill became weepy and panicky.

Jill learned that in an acrimonious or abusive divorce, "reasonable and customary" is not enough definition. The rules need to be spelled out. Jill worked out a visitation schedule which included not just days, but times, pick up places, and so forth. By setting boundaries, the schedule allowed Jill to have a life free from the daily intimidation and harassment from Jack.

Sometimes in an acrimonious divorce, it is hard to advocate for what you want. Everything takes so much energy. Vagueness in divorce decrees is one of the most frequently-cited reasons that couples return to court. It may feel petty to put everything in detail, but it is better to have too many rules than too few. While it may take more time, effort, and money at the outset, the divorce decree that covers specifics in all areas, not just visitation, is the decree that will be the easiest to live with.

Today I will remember that this document will impact me for many years and in some cases for the rest of my life. I will take my time and ask for things to be specific. This will reduce future court appearances, costs, and angry feelings. I may get frustrated and be tempted to say, "Okay this is good enough," but I will remember that if I want the acrimony in my divorce to eventually end, a clear and cogent divorce decree is the first step.

Day 3 But He Doesn't Think He Has a Problem!

Our intuition often tells us that something is wrong in our marriage and our experience confirms that belief. Then we give voice to our concern and we are told by our spouse, "I don't have a problem. YOU do." Why are we immediately filled with self-doubt?

If you believe your husband has a problem with alcohol, drugs, gambling or emotional or physical abuse, then he probably does. It is that simple. When one of the above issues is a problem for one spouse, then it is a problem for the marriage. He may be thinking, "Well, this isn't a problem for me, so why should it be a problem for her?" He may be unaware of how his behavior is impacting others. Unfortunately, the person with a problem is often the last to see the problem. These diverse perceptions create disharmony and friction in a relationship. How do you make him see your point of view? Ralph Waldo Emerson said, "People only see what they are prepared to see." While that might sound cold and uninvolved, the truth is that it can be very freeing. When you realize that you cannot "make" someone see your point of view, you can focus your energy in a direction that will create change for yourself.

Which brings us to this point - why do you need him to agree with you? Is it that you need the validation? Or is it that without his willingness to change, you can no longer be with him? When we realize that our life has become unmanageable due to someone else's behavior, we begin to desperately hunt for solutions. We might go to a therapist and ask the question that has been haunting us for years - how can I get him to change? Denial, rationalization, and minimization keep your husband in the dark. As Emerson says, he will only see it when he is ready.

If your marriage is deteriorating because your partner refuses to look at his problems, it will help if you speak with a therapist or attend Al Anon or another support group. You can begin to explore what is possible and what is not. When you focus on what is possible, you will see the changes YOU can make to bring peace into your life.

Today I ask that God grant me the serenity to accept the things I cannot change, the strength to change the things I can and the wisdom to know the difference.

From Ex-Wife to Exceptional Life

Your children's father is dating a woman who is beginning to spend time with your children. Do you have the right to meet her?

If you trust your children to spend time with their father without you around, that means you trust him to make good decisions on behalf of the children. You trust that he will not put your children in harm's way, either emotionally or physically. You trust he will use good judgment. Of course, good judgment doesn't always mean he will do things your way.

Frequently, when women want to meet the new woman in their ex-spouse's life, it has more to do with not trusting their own relationship with their children. When a new person enters your ex's life, it is difficult not to feel, on some level, as if you have been replaced as a partner. The fear is that she will also replace you as a mother. Intellectually, you feel safe in the knowledge of your children's love, but emotionally, it can feel very threatening. One fear is that she will be wonderful with them and you will pale by comparison. Another fear is that they will hate her and she will be wicked and mean and horrible to your children.

Think about all the other women in your child's life – day-care providers, teachers, camp counselors, coaches, friends' mothers, scout leaders. Are you threatened when your children like them? No, of course not. In fact, it brings you great comfort knowing that your children are in good hands and feel affection for these other nurturing figures. The same can be said for the woman in their father's life. She may have a great deal to offer your kids but she will never replace you. In the 90's movie *Stepmom*, Susan Sarandon's character deals with the complexity of watching her ex-husband marry a younger woman, and then watching the relationship grow between this new woman and her children. These children can love the new woman in their Dad's life, but they only have one mother and that is YOU! And that will never change.

Today when I feel threatened by my ex's new girlfriend, I will consider my own relationship with my mother. Regardless of what has happened between us, our bond is unbreakable. While I might have experienced other nurturers in my own life, they could not replace my need and love for my own mother, even if she wasn't all I needed her to be. When I am fearful, I will trust in the bond between my children and me. I will trust in the love I share with my children.

If this is your first Christmas since the separation and divorce, the anticipation can fill you with sadness and trepidation. Here are some solid, easy tips to help make the holidays less painful and hopefully maybe even (surprisingly!) enjoyable!

Let go of traditions that no longer work for you. This is an opportunity to re-invent your holidays. Keep the traditions that you enjoy and get rid of the ones that you don't. No one expects you to be on your best behavior during this time, so you can probably pull it off without anyone getting too upset.

Stick to your regular routine as closely as possible. Sleep, exercise, eat well and don't skip those therapy appointments.

Don't use money, alcohol, food, or sex to deal with pain and sadness. These indulgences will leave you poor, hung over, fat, and guilty on December 26th.

Don't be afraid to do something different. Go away or stay home, but take a risk to use the holidays to try something different.

Most people are depressed around the holidays. Expectations are often the fuel that feeds that "let down" feeling. Instead of focusing on what isn't, focus on what is and what can be.

Don't make New Year's resolutions. We hardly ever keep them. Then we feel like failures and have one more thing to beat ourselves up about. Instead, ask yourself, "What have I learned this year about myself and about life?" Then, if you feel really ambitious, focus on how you can use that information to enhance the coming year.

Volunteer. Nothing makes us feel more valuable and grateful than working with those who have less.

Remember that Christmas is only one day. Anyone can get through one day! One year from now, when you will look back on this holiday season, you will be amazed at how far you've come.

How important is this? Sometimes things seem more important than they really are. Ask yourself this: will this matter to me one year from now? Will I even REMEMBER it?

Take the high road. Just because someone else behaves badly doesn't mean you have to behave badly too. "Giving them a dose of their own medicine" only ups the ante and escalates the conflict. Do you really want someone else to dictate how to behave? You may not like what others do, but you can like what you do. Behaving with dignity enhances self-esteem.

Today I ask myself: how do I want to spend this holiday? One of the things about being unmarried is that I have far more control over how I spend my days. This includes holidays. What do I want to do with this day? If my children are old enough, I will discuss new ideas and options with them, keeping in mind that while their input is valuable, I am the parent and ultimately I choose what feels healthy and right for all of us.

As your divorce progresses, you may find that you actually feel better when you have less contact with your ex. If you do not have children together, this is not a difficult objective to obtain. However, if you are a parent, then you are probably thrown together with your ex more often than you would like.

Whether contact with him is sad or adversarial, there are strategies you can implement that will help diminish the repeatedly painful contact with him. Some of these strategies are:

- If your children are of school age and you live in the same school district, visitation can commence with them taking the school bus directly to their father's home.

- If your children are pre-school age, then day care or nursery school may be an excellent place for visitation transition.

- Try a neutral family member's home as a transitional place. Bring your children there and he can pick them up after you leave.

- Utilize one of the big bookstore chains. Bring the children to the children's department and let them look at some books. Then you settle down in view of them with a frothy cappuccino until their father shows up.

- Try not to transfer kids in parking lots. They feel like cargo and there is always the chance for an unhealthy exchange between the two of you.

- Be on time.

- Be reliable. This includes making sure your child has what he/she needs for the time with his/her father.

- Don't use this time for any divorce dialogue. Exchange only pleasantries. If that's not possible, then silence or no contact is advised.

Remember that when you reduce the chance of an adversarial confrontation, you not only help yourself, but you protect your children as well. Research shows us that divorce itself is not responsible for damaging our children, but the fighting, yelling, screaming, threatening, and general acrimony are extremely damaging for children. It can affect them throughout their lives. By being prudent now about your behavior, you help ensure your child's well being as well as your own.

Today I will think of some options for creating a neutral transition for myself and my children. I will discuss them with my therapist or attorney and together we will consider the best ways to involve the children's father in the process.

If this is your first Christmas without your husband, it is going to be different from the Christmases you shared. Do not even try to do things the same way. They won't feel the same and his absence will loom even larger in the empty space. Rather, try to change some traditions. If Christmas was always celebrated at your house, then go to a relative's or friend's. If your major celebration was Christmas Day, switch the celebration to Christmas Eve. Change the sequence: Open presents after church instead of before, or try midnight mass instead of a morning service. You even have the option to skip it all. You can use the money you would have spent on the presents to take your kids on a winter vacation.

The first year is the worst. Believe it or not, by the second year, you will notice that new traditions and rituals have evolved from the year before. By the second year, you will have created new memories of the first one and the sting will be gone.

Acknowledge this year is different; talk to your kids and family about making some changes. Get enough sleep, spend less, eat less, drink less, and sleep more. The good news is a week after Christmas, a New Year begins.

Today I will acknowledge that Christmas will be different this year and there will be some loss. Rather than trying to over compensate by doing too much, I will accept that this year is going to be difficult. I will deal with that reality by making different plans and considering different options. I can take some comfort in knowing that this day will pass and with each day that follows, I will get stronger and more comfortable with myself and my new life.

As a single parent sharing custody, you may feel awkward about discipline. You may feel that your time is limited and you do not want to "waste" it with grounding or time-outs. Consequently you may feel as if your power and control are slowly being eroded.

Parenting is not always about making your children happy. Good parenting includes discipline. One of your roles is to help your child be prepared for life. Children learn as we all do—by making mistakes. If we let those mistakes go uncorrected, then we are doing our children a great disservice. Many single parents worry more about providing a "good time" than about providing good parenting.

Some single parents are hesitant about discipline because they are afraid their child will want to go live with the other parent. A divorced parent dreads hearing, "I want to live with Daddy (or Mommy). You are such a drag." This is blackmail. When we succumb to it, we give the child too much power and diminish the importance of the parent-child relationship. Unfortunately, some parents encourage their children to disobey the other parent. Often, this behavior is due to unresolved marital anger. Undermining your child's father may give you some satisfaction, but you hurt your child in the process.

Chris and Art divorced. They had one son, Seth, who was thirteen. They were able to put aside their differences when it came to parenting. Seth split his time equally between both houses. He had gotten into some difficulty at school for fighting and Chris was notified. Over Seth's disapproval, Chris requested a family meeting where she, Art, and Seth sat down to discuss the transgression and the appropriate action. Together, the parents agreed that Seth would not be allowed to play video games at either house for a month. This kind of cooperation says to the child, "You are important enough for us to put our differences aside and come together to take care of you." It lets the child know that secrets and playing one parent off against the other will not be tolerated. This united front presents the child with a firm foundation. It provides both security and consistency.

Today and everyday, discipline is an integral part of my job. I will put my child's needs over my need for approval. Love without discipline is chaos. One of my most important roles as a parent is to provide a stable environment, not just in my home, but in all areas of his life, including his time with his father. I can help facilitate this by communicating with his father and putting the child's needs before my own.

It is difficult for parents to gauge the impact of their divorce on their children. No parent wants to see his or her child in pain. It is easy to interpret a developmental issue as divorce-related behavior, or minimize the impact by denying problematic behavior. How do you sort out which behaviors are developmental and which result from divorce? Furthermore, when is it time to seek outside help? Here are helpful guidelines and insights.

There are three key elements to distinguishing a problem. Those elements are: the severity of the symptoms, the duration of the symptoms, and how many symptoms are manifested concurrently. When the child displays several of the symptoms from the list below consistently for one month or more, it may indicate a more serious problem. Then it would be an appropriate time to seek help from a child therapist. Signs of childhood depression include:

- Sadness.
- Lethargy.
- Lowered concentration.
- Decreased interest.
- Withdrawal.
- Fear (especially at bedtime).
- Feelings of not wanting to live anymore.
- Hurting themselves.
- Changes in eating habits.
- Sleep difficulties.

Some parents resist getting help for fear they will be judged an unfit parent and blamed for the child's emotional struggle. On the contrary, parents who seek help from professional sources are advocating for their child. They are taking responsibility for their child's emotional welfare.

If a child is talking about not wanting to live, doing something to hurt himself (such as cutting), or shows signs of an eating disorder, those situations require **immediate** intervention. This child is having difficulties that require immediate professional attention! Do not hesitate to act appropriately.

One final word: Some children manage to hold it together through the worst part of the divorce experience, only to manifest symptoms months later, after everything has calmed down. This delayed reaction often has to do with the child feeling that the parent is now emotionally available enough to be able to parent them.

Today I will watch for signs of depression and other emotional difficulties in my child. I will not panic, but be mindful and attentive. If I see anything that concerns me, I will seek immediate advice from a professional. Acting sooner rather than later is always prudent and reassuring.

Once a woman has decided that her marriage is no longer viable, the next decision she faces is when she should move forward with divorce. Usually one major concern is the well being of her children.

There really is no "perfect" age for children to experience divorce. The very young ones will have less trouble adjusting as long as caregivers and nurturing remain constant. Adolescents and teens, who are beginning to experiment with individuation and rebellion, may have difficulty with divorce unless they are provided with consistency and predictability. In truth, children of all ages will have to make some adjustments to the divorce. The key is not finding the right age, but making sure that acrimony is kept to a minimum and that consistency and routine are still implemented. Children need to express their concerns about what is happening to their family. Most important is the parents' ability to minimize the children's exposure to the adult conflict.

The time of year also plays a role. Some women who are affected by the seasonal changes try to avoid initiating divorce proceedings in the winter, as they are less focused and more lethargic during those months. Other women consider the summer a difficult time as they are concerned about the children being home and perhaps privy to more information than they need to be. Other considerations are birthdays, anniversaries and holidays. Of course, there is no time better than the present. I have heard it said, "Death is inconvenient." Divorce is inconvenient, as well. Putting it off and trying to wait for the ideal time only delays the inevitable. The interim can increase anxiety and hard feelings toward your partner. Be considerate of special days, but also of your need to move ahead.

Surprising your spouse with divorce papers is a "sucker punch" and sets the tone for nastiness. It creates ill will, which is not the best way to enter this final phase of the relationship. Give your partner a few days' notice. Never have the children present. Serving papers at work or in an attorney's office helps contain the emotional response.

Today I need to ask myself if I am finding excuses related to dates, celebrations, weather, or seasons, to put off moving ahead? Without self criticism, I will explore my procrastination. What is really holding me back?

Getting tired of all this? No one goes into a divorce adequately prepared to deal with all the changes and stresses. As active, high-functioning women, we want to do the best we can, in the least amount of time. Divorce is a process, not a single event, and it can be a *long* process. Even if the legal divorce takes only a few months, the fall-out, both emotional and financial, can continue for many years.

To prevent your divorce from becoming overwhelming, recognize that you cannot rush it. The legal system works at its own pace. It requires patience and energy. The emotional components also take their natural course. Each person heals in his/her own time. While there are things you can do to minimize the pain, the process will have to run its course.

Think of your divorce as a marathon, not a sprint. In a sprint, we gather all of our energy and push to our very limits right from the beginning of the race. We can exert that much energy for the sprint because it is short in duration. However, the body cannot sustain that exertion for long periods of time without collapsing. In contrast, the marathon runner must pace herself for the longer race. She trains and prepares, sometimes for months, nurturing and preparing her body and mind with proper food, rest, and equipment. She paces herself, knowing if she pushes too much in the first part of the race, she will lose stamina. When she does push, she does so at times that maximize her position. She also knows when it is important to coast. Every mile is not run with the same amount of exertion. She wisely puts more energy into the more challenging parts of the race.

This divorce is your marathon. Make sure you have good equipment (attorneys and therapists), and that you are in peak physical shape (enough rest, exercise, nourishing food). And as with the marathon, remember to strategize how you will use your energy. Some parts of the divorce, require more energy and work, while others require very little exertion. Choose wisely how you will use your energy and resources and at the end of the race, you will feel proud for having accomplished such a challenging, often grueling process. You won't have any regrets for a race well run.

Today I am a marathon runner, running one of the most important races of my life. I will seriously consider how I want to use my energy, making sure I am as prepared as I can be. When it is over, I will be able to congratulate myself for a job well done. Running this race will empower me. It will reveal my strength and fortitude. This experience will change my life and better prepare me for other life challenges.

There will come a time in your divorce process when you cannot wait until it is over. This is even true of women who did not originally want the divorce. The process can be lengthy and arduous. However, the delay gives time for each party to acclimate to their new lives and readjust to being single again. This transition time, when you are addressing legal and financial issues also serves as a time to heal and grow emotionally. Many women who were originally terrified of the idea of being divorced and resuming a single life find themselves really looking forward to it.

Once an agreement between you and your husband is reached about money, property and visitation, much of the tension and acrimony begin to wane. Usually with time, acceptance and insight replace anger and fear. When one person is unhappy in the marriage, eventually the other realizes that he/she was also unhappy, but was denying it on some level.

When you can see the end of the process is in sight, you begin to see there is "light" ahead. Look back at how far you have come. This can be a moment of great empowerment. Many women are astounded at how strong and capable they are. They also find that they are enjoying aspects of their new single life.

Take some time to list all the things you feared at the beginning of the divorce. As you scan the list, what issues are resolved for you? What issues are still not resolved, but are no longer sources of fear and anxiety? Are there still things you fear? What amazes you most about this process so far? What amazes you most about yourself? How have you changed?

Now that you can see the light at the end of the tunnel, do you have plans for the future? Do you still experience divorce with the same amount of fear as before, or is the fear gradually being replaced with anticipation and perhaps excitement? As you look forward, are you able to see dreams and promises and hope for a good life? As you look at your ex-husband now, how have your feelings for him changed?

Today I know I am not "there" yet, but I am getting pretty close. As I approach this last part of the divorce journey, I know it is not the end of my story, but only the closing of a chapter. I can see the new chapter is just beyond my grasp, but getting closer. While I don't know what it holds for me, I will move toward it with grace, excitement and joy.

When the relationship ends, you might feel badly about yourself. Some reasons for this are that your spouse may have been abusive, you may have behaved in ways you are not proud of, or you may feel that the demise of the marriage is your fault. A marriage takes two people, hard work, and a little good luck to sustain and evolve into a strong, healthy, long-term relationship. The demise of a marriage is never one person's fault. Do not take on blame, but take responsibility for your part, so you can grow and learn more about yourself and your future relationships.

One of the most difficult aspects of distinguishing between responsibility and blame is not taking it personally. For example, Lena's husband told her that her being overweight was responsible for the break-up of the marriage. Her husband's opinion about her weight was just that, his opinion. It was about him, not her. When people voice opinions and we take them personally, we do ourselves a great injustice. Why is everything about us? The opinion belongs to the person who voiced it. It is a subjective opinion and not an objective reality. It does not have to be received. We are vulnerable to taking things personally all the time. If someone comments, "Gee, you look tired, maybe you are coming down with something," do you believe them? Does it change the way you feel? The converse is true; when someone says, "Gee, you look great today," do you take that to heart as well?

The critical message here is that the sender's opinion does not automatically need to be true for the receiver. When we allow those opinions to alter the way we feel about ourselves, we become extremely malleable. In *The Four Agreements*, Don Miguel Ruiz speaks at length to this subject. When we stop believing others' opinions about us, we become freer to be ourselves. When we are dependent upon others to fill us up with compliments, we are looking outside of us to raise our self-esteem. That makes us vulnerable to feeling hurt, resentment, inferior, angry, unappreciated, and criticized. Those are feelings that diminish rather than add to our self-esteem.

Today I will think about how dependent I am on others' opinions of me. I will think about how I often feel hurt or angry at a random remark. I will focus on the remark being the opinion of the sender, rather than an accurate picture of who I am. When I take things personally, I surrender my personal power to the sender and I diminish my own strength and self-worth.

Barbara told me how she was resistant to confiding in her friends and asking for help. She felt the same way in her support group. This woman had a large support system but seemed hesitant to utilize it; consequently, she was feeling alone and isolated.

> "I still love him," she began, "and I am not ready to stop loving him. I know he behaved terribly, but when friends get angry with him, I feel the need to defend him."

> She was quiet for a minute and began again. "And when I am defending him, I am dealing with their anger toward him, and that doesn't comfort me."

How true it is! In her support group, the women rallied around Barbara, but it was always about his philandering and how she was better off without him. In getting angry with him, they were absent for her! Their compassion and support were replaced by their anger at what this man had done.

While their anger was understandable, Barbara was absolutely right. In expressing their anger, they were dealing with their own feelings and not with hers. Her need for compassion, comfort and understanding was completely ignored. No wonder she stopped asking for help!

This was an important revelation for Barbara, who felt better just knowing what was happening. Of course, the next step for her was to be able to ask for what she needed from her friends, family, and support group. She needed to tell them that their compassion and understanding were what she longed for and that their anger simply wasn't helpful in any way.

"I can do that," she said simply.

Today I will look at the ways I offer compassion. Am I giving my friend what she needs or expressing what I feel? Am I really listening to her or am I reacting to my own anger and sense of injustice? Are my friends giving me the support I need or are they, unintentionally, focused more on their own feelings and issues? Since I cannot read anyone's mind and they can't read mine, I will have discussions with my friends about what we give and get from each other. This will help deepen our connection with each other and improve my communication skills. These are gifts that will serve me well, not only now but also in my future relationships.

...You Start to Stink"

Inspiration and wisdom come to us from many places. The above words are from Valerie Harper's character Rhoda Morganstern from the 1970's television comedy series *Rhoda*. She was trying to convince her sister Brenda that she could benefit from participating in an assertiveness training class. What a great endorsement for speaking one's mind! Speaking one's mind is vital for mental health and emotional serenity.

People try different strategies to keep the peace. One of the strategies you might have implemented was not to speak about what was truly on your mind or in your heart. Some women do this, because they are fearful of the consequences of speaking up. Others "hold it in" because they are simply too tired to argue anymore. Still others are silent because they do not see options: In their family of origin, they were taught that speaking up was taboo.

If you are a woman who has difficulty speaking your mind, be aware that while you won't literally "stink" from withholding, you will begin to unravel emotionally. Sleeplessness, resentment, nervousness, and lethargy may all be symptoms that you are not being authentic in your relationships. Other symptoms may include back and neck pain, stomach problems, and depression. Do you ever say "This is killing me," or "This is eating me up"? These expressions describe the physical result of withholding thoughts and feelings we should be sharing.

Of course, you should not blurt out everything that comes into your mind. That would be going to the other extreme. People would distance from you. Think of a friend whose assertiveness style you admire. What makes her communication more effective than yours? Use her style as a model for your own. If you worry how others will receive you, look at how people respond to your friend. If she is an effective communicator, her relationships are healthier and so is her self-esteem.

Today I will not ignore my most important thoughts and feelings. I may have some trouble expressing myself as I would like, but I will work hard to be mindful of what I need and take the risk to express myself. With awareness and practice, expressing myself will become a habit. The result will be greater self-confidence, a lightness of spirit, and a healthier me!

Assertiveness techniques are fun to practice. Using these techniques in conjunction with appropriate body language, attitude and voice inflection, will assure an assertive presentation that is bound to be effective! Here is one technique that with a little practice can make a huge difference in your communication style. It can also influence the pace and tenor of the entire interaction.

A relaxed pause in the dialogue can communicate a confident person with confident expectations. Whether making a request or having one made of you, take a moment in silence. Not only does the silence give you time to think over your response, but it also gives the other person a moment to slow down and take a breath. Often dialogue escalates into arguments as the pace and fervor accelerates without our even being aware of it. A pause can slow down that escalation and keep things moving at a more manageable pace.

Be aware that silence also gives the other person time to finish what he/she is saying. We tend to think quick comebacks demonstrate how smart we are. Sometimes we don't wait for the other person to finish their thought. This results in their feeling "not heard." Those feelings invalidate and create defensiveness. The person may raise their voice or speak faster as they become more anxious that they are not being heard. After the person is done speaking, try a moment of silence, with eye contact and a small nodding of the head to indicate that you are engaged and thinking over what the other person said. If he/she asks, "What are you doing?" respond with, "I am thinking about what you said." It can be a disarming technique to let the other person know that you are listening to them.

Today I will try some silence. Maybe I will practice with a friend and then move on to test my skills in increasingly challenging situations. Once I am feeling more confident and comfortable with the technique, I will use it in those relationships that most push my buttons and threaten me. Change can be scary, but change can also be healthy.

Debts and liabilities of the marriage are two important financial issues that will be addressed in your divorce. If you are unsure as to the extent of your debts, you can request a copy of your credit report from one of many sites on the Internet. You want to prepare a complete and accurate picture of your finances for your attorney. Itemize all debts and liabilities. Divide them into three columns: yours, his and joint. Include the following items:

- Mortgage.
- Car loans.
- Personal loans.
- Home equity loans.
- Bank loans and liens.
- College loans.
- Back taxes.
- Credit cards.
- Business loans.

Remember that the divorce decree will divide liability, but a lender may not see it that way. Let's say the house mortgage is in both names and you sign over ownership of the house to your husband. Unless he refinances that mortgage solely in his name, your name is still listed as co-mortgagee. Therefore, if he defaults on his payments to the bank, they can come after you, even though your divorce decree says the house is his. It is best to insist that your husband refinance those debts in his name only.

Transfer all loans for items that are in your possession to your name. Although he may try to convince you to trust him and he may intend to continue making payments, sometimes events occur in lives that are out of everyone's control. With an unexpected layoff or emergency medical bills, he may find he is unable to keep his promise to you.

Today I acknowledge that looking at debt and liability can be depressing, but as I assess what my financial situation is, I know I am taking charge of my own life. Without a clear picture, I have no way of knowing how to proceed. With the help of my lawyer and my accountant, I can begin to make financial decisions that will secure my future. Taking care of my financial health is another way of taking care of myself.

Divorce is certainly a time of loss, but it is also is a time of reflection and hope. It is a time to slough off old behaviors and beliefs, a time to re-examine your goals and expectations for your life. Many women feel confused and overwhelmed. How do you figure out what makes sense to you? How do you want to live your life?

Your goals and dreams are yours. Whether they are large or somewhat mundane, it doesn't matter. What does matter is living your life as you want to. You can enlist help along the way: mentors, therapists, friends, teachers, neighbors, and children are all part of your team. But you are in charge of the plan and the ultimate outcome.

One effective tool is to write your own obituary. That is not as ghoulish as you may think. Writing your obituary gives you another perspective. It is a way to imagine looking back and considering what your life means to you. What do you want to be remembered for? What do you want as your legacy? What would you like your family, children, friends, and colleagues to say about you after you die? What mark do you want to leave on the world?

Sit down at your computer or with a pen and paper and begin to write. Start with your name, the names of the people you love. Write about things you have done, things that you have yet to do, and things you dream of doing. Write about how you want to be remembered. Write about your contributions to the lives of others. Include, if you want, what kind of flowers you like or what charity/fund you would like donations to be sent.

When you are done, date it and tuck it away. Take it out one year from now and review it. What things have you accomplished? What variations do you need to make in the original document? What things do you need to add?

Today one of the ways to celebrate my life, who I am and who I am becoming, is to utilize the gift of distance. By writing my obituary, I get a chance to look back on my life and how it was. This new perspective helps me as I live my life going forward. It will help me realize my goals, diminish my regrets, and appreciate what I have and who I am.

Saturday night seems to be the hardest time of the week for newly-divorced/separated women. Especially difficult are the weekends when children are staying with the other parent. In this culture, Saturday night has always been "date night." When we were young, not having a date on Saturday night was tantamount to being a social pariah. As teenagers and young adults, some women refused to leave the house on a Saturday night unless escorted by a young man.

We frequently allow popular thinking to direct and control our behavior. When we allow social norms such as "date night" to dictate our behavior as well as our sense of ourselves, we are giving up too much power. The notion that we are unpopular, not loveable or attractive, or that we are social flops unwanted by anyone, only has power over us if we allow it to. Clearly, not having a date on a Saturday night is not the most catastrophic thing that can happen in one's life. But when we refuse to go out with a girlfriend or by ourselves because we are concerned with how others will see us, now that is a catastrophe!

When we feel ashamed about not having a date, what does that say about how we feel about ourselves as women? Why do women think that without a man on their arm they are judged as less worthy than others? Why do we assume that having a man in your life means your life is better? As someone leaving a relationship, you know that idea is simply false. Being in a relationship is not a guarantee for happiness and serenity. Yet cultural morés and stereotypes continue to distort our experience.

Changing the way we feel about ourselves includes debunking myths about what it means to be a "successful" woman. A woman who is not in a relationship is no more a failure than a woman who does not have children, or does not work outside of the home. Keeping our focus so narrow traps us into limiting our potential. It also distorts the way we see our relationships with other women. If men are the prizes that complete our sense of self, then do we compete with and distrust other women, anxious that they will "steal our man away"? Any time we allow our actions to be dictated in such a manner, we deny our own potential for growth and freedom. We deny spontaneity, connection, creativity, and joy.

Today I will consider how I limit myself by accepting the unacceptable. When I surrender to cultural stereotypes, I surrender my power and freedom. Do I judge other women and their choices as I judge myself? I will think about ways to honor and accept different lifestyles and not judge them by the standards of others.

In our communication with others, we don't always deliver a clear message. Some women say they try to "soft peddle" their true feelings, so that they do not offend the other person. When we do this, we are often wordy and ambiguous. It follows that the receiver of the message will be unclear as to what we are saying. Then, we find ourselves over-explaining and struggling to be heard, yet not wanting to create ill feelings. The receiver has, by now, caught onto our discomfort and recognizes that they can wear us down by arguing with us. Exhausted and frustrated, we simply surrender.

Jan's insurance company refused payment after she had an expensive medical treatment. She wrote letters, called and still received no response. She finally gathered together all her bills and medical documentation and sent them to the state's insurance commissioner. They were overwhelmed with cases and every time she wrote a letter inquiring as to the status of her claim, she got back a form letter. She switched to calling, once a month, leaving cordial but firm reminders about her case. It took almost two years, but she recovered the money owed her. It took time and patience, but in the long run, her persistence paid off. She stayed focused and stuck to the main issue, which was to recover her money.

This technique also works one on one. Rather than defending, rationalizing or explaining yourself, simply repeat your original request until you are heard. This does not mean being nasty or rude. Maintain your composure and state your desire with confidence and conviction – over and over again, if necessary. If you are polite and stay calm, eventually you will be heard.

Today I will think about times I said too much, or lost my temper, or got frustrated and gave up. I will try to stay focused on my desired outcome by keeping my goal in mind. It will be nice to feel heard!

Whenever a marriage ends, there are losses. Regardless of whether you want the divorce or not, you will feel loss. Divorce is complicated and is never a black or white issue. There are good things as well as bad in the marriage and it is for those good things that we mourn.

One of the things we mourn for is the loss of what could have been. Sometimes we see the potential in something and confuse what really was with what *could have been*. When we focus on the potential and not the reality, our imagination creates the relationship of our dreams. When we create a fantasy and then mourn for its lack of existence, we create our own suffering.

Another way women create their own suffering is through mourning for what used to be. They mourn for the relationship they had when they were dating or when the marriage was new. Most women agree that the marriage that existed in the most recent years was unacceptable. Mourning the loss of a marriage is normal, but there is no need to create more suffering for ourselves by mourning for what could have been.

Denying or minimizing our pain by numbing ourselves with alcohol, drugs, or other romantic relationships will only harm us further. Our grief is a testimony to the reality that something that meant a great deal to us has ended. It is critical that we do not create more pain and suffering by mourning fantasies or memories. Furthermore, when we allow ourselves to focus only on the real losses, we are more likely to experience the lessons they hold for us. Then our grief becomes part of our growth and we become stronger, more self-aware women. When we inflate our pain by fantasy or memory, we only create more angst and often the lessons are lost.

Today I will make a list of the things I miss the most. Then I will divide those items into three columns: memories, "if only's" and true losses. When I have done that, I will keep the last list and throw away the other two. I will not allow myself to experience unnecessary pain. When I mourn for only the real losses, I diminish my pain. I choose not to suffer needlessly.

Pain is a physical sensation. Suffering is the amount of emotional distress we feel about that pain. Often we do not distinguish between suffering and pain – we see them as one and the same. For example, if you have a headache, you experience a physical sensation. This is pain. If you interpret that pain as a brain tumor, then you may become anxious and tense. Wondering what will happen if you will have brain surgery, if it would be unsuccessful, and if you will die, creates anxiety which in turn, creates suffering. Therapists call that catastrophizing.

Catastrophizing is one of the ways we make ourselves suffer. Worrying about the worst thing that could happen is merely self-inflicted suffering. When you go to the doctor and find out it was only a stress headache, then the pain seems to actually lessen. What has changed is your *interpretation* of what the pain meant.

We also create suffering when we think that things will never get better. Most of us can stand almost any kind of pain, if we know it is finite. However, we often give ourselves the message that it will *always feel like this*. Of course, intellectually we know that nothing stays the same forever and that things will change, but in moments of distress, we cannot see that eventually things will feel different.

When you are experiencing divorce, every day is different. Your thoughts, feelings and ideas seem to change daily. In one year, you will look back and see your growth. Even if you can't see it now, just having the belief that things will get better can be very helpful. Lastly, we create suffering when we think of past events. Sometimes thinking of the good times creates suffering for what we lost in the relationship. Sometimes thinking about the bad times creates suffering for what we lost in ourselves. While introspection and analysis of the marriage can be productive, it can be harmful if the primary result is additional suffering.

Today I will notice when I am experiencing pain and I will notice my degree of suffering. Do I create discomfort for myself with catastrophisizing, worrying, interpreting, or spending too much time in the past? I will become aware of which of my thought patterns create suffering and I will consciously work to change them.

How often do you say "should?"

"Should" can be one of the most damaging words in the English language. Louise Hay, author of *You Can Heal Your Life*, writes that she wishes "should" could be abolished from our language completely! Why such a vehement reaction to this one little word? "Should" takes away our personal power. "Should" doesn't address what we *want* to do, what we *could* do, or what we *need* to do. It addresses only the requirements of others! We struggle between what we are programmed to believe in and what our own experience tells us is right for us. As that chasm widens, so does our guilt. Mean, nasty guilt takes root and grows. Soon our guilt entangles our own belief system with the belief system of others. Then we have difficulty discerning which are our desires, hopes, dreams, and thoughts and which are those of others being thrust on us.

When we are aware of the difference between our needs and the "shoulds," we make better choices. A better choice might even result in our doing the same thing as the "should." However, if it is a choice instead of a "should," we feel empowered rather than guilty. Then we do not feel like a victim.

When you exercise your right to choose, you feel empowered and that builds confidence. It also is part of the process of getting to know yourself. It is how you untangle someone else's values from your own. When you act without unnecessary guilt, you are free to do the best you can. You can act with compassion and responsibility, not with regret and anger.

Today I will not "should" upon myself.

Do you find yourself saying, "If I try harder, perhaps this can change," or, "If I show him how I want him to be, maybe he will get it"? Do you stay up nights obsessing about how to change things, make them better, fix him, or get him to understand you?

When women are in unhappy relationships, we spend a lot of time figuring out how to fix it. Often, we look at our partner, see the "problem," and work to come up with the remedy. Then we are so excited about our findings that we can't wait to share/implement them. When we are met with resistance, denial, or anger we can't believe it! If only he would listen and do it OUR way, then things would improve!

This seems to be especially true when we are dealing with big problems such as alcohol, drugs, violence, emotional abuse. It seems the more severe the problem, the harder the partner works to solve it. That is what co-dependence is all about – when one partner takes responsibility for the other partner's behavior and tries to fix it, change it, or modify it. That person is no longer focusing on her own growth, but on her partner's. When this happens to extreme, it is called co-dependence. The co-dependent person thinks, "If you would just get better, then I would be happy."

Women are society's appointed caretakers. We campaign to change the situation. If we can just find the key, the right words, the right way to explain it to him, he would "get it." We keep trying because we think it is our job and because we really believe that we need that person to act a certain way in order to be happy. We are tenacious. We keep trying, but nothing changes.

The definition of insanity? Doing the same thing over and over, expecting different results.

Today am I doing the same thing over and over in my relationships? Am I repeatedly planning and scheming with hopes that I can make the situation more to my liking? Is anything really changing or am I just feeling crazy, unheard, frustrated, angry, and depressed? Maybe, just for today, I can imagine what it would be like to find happiness, peace, fulfillment, and contentment without changing the other person/situation. Then, perhaps, I will find the courage to do something different in order to bring about different results.

"No" is a little word with a big impact.

Many women lament that it feels almost impossible for them to say no to almost anyone. Why do we have so much difficulty with "no"? In truth, saying "no" is a lot healthier and more honest, than saying "yes" and not following through. It is also a lot healthier to say "no" than it is to say "yes" and not mean it. "No" discourages people from trying to take advantage of you and is important in building boundaries. Boundaries are necessary for relationships to be strong and healthy.

Saying "no" can feel selfish and uncomfortable. Do it anyway.

If you really don't want to do something, say it. With enough practice, "no" will stop feeling strange and will begin to empower you.

Healthy people will respect your honesty and value you more. By saying "yes" all the time, we leave ourselves open to being misused and abused. Then, we feel resentment and try to avoid relationships. A relationship that is built on saying "yes" all the time is not a healthy relationship. Eventually the "yes relationship" will complicate your life and can have a negative impact on both your emotional and physical health.

Finally, our children must learn to say "no." They need to say "no" to alcohol, tobacco, drugs, inappropriate behaviors and sexual advances. When you say "no" with comfort, you role model positive, assertive behavior for your children.

Today I will look at how often I say "yes" when I mean "no." I will focus on what changes I can make to be more authentic in my relationships.

Of all the practical things women need to contend with when going through divorce, money is often their greatest worry. When asked by their attorneys about their financial status, women are often surprised to find out how little they know about money management. Some women had no interest in participating in matters of finance during the marriage and others may say their husbands claimed finances as their domain.

When you are on your own, you have to learn about many new things, some of which you may have relinquished in the past. Many women regret having given up their say in the financial arena and are now eager to acquire the knowledge necessary to make informed decisions. Others find that they are reluctant to learn about financial issues. But necessity requires that they do so.

Carol Miller Pekrul, ChFC, of Newington, Connecticut is a financial planner who offers the following tips for the woman who is shopping for a financial planner of her own.

- **Referrals** – Ask friends, especially divorced women friends, about their experiences with financial planners. Find out who they felt comfortable with and get the name of that person.

- **Interview** – After you have a couple of names, set up appointments to interview these people.

- **Pay attention to rapport** – If you feel at all intimidated, then this person is not for you.

- **Take your time** – Don't allow yourself to be pressured. The financial planner works for you, not the other way around.

- **Do not hesitate to ask questions** – Ask LOTS of questions. The financial planner's job is to assist you in making good, informed decisions. No question is irrelevant or stupid.

- **Check credentials** – Investment advisors have regulatory groups; check on the Web to find out more about the planner you are thinking of choosing to work with you.

- **Pick an independent** – Some financial consultants work for specific companies and, therefore, may "push" that company's product. An independent financial planner does not represent any one company and, therefore, has a broader range of products. His/her alliance is to you, not the company.

Today I am learning that I desire and deserve the best. To that end, I am making better choices: taking my time and choosing to have people in my life who will enhance it. This is true both personally and professionally. I will think of myself as the head of my own corporation and I will pick my staff wisely and carefully.

...If He Just Hit Me!

Many women wonder whether their scenario is "bad enough" to warrant breaking up the home. Frequently, when women hear other women's horror stories, they feel gratitude that there is no violence in their own home. But with the gratitude comes guilt and self-doubt. Each woman struggles with "how bad is bad enough?" Many stay for years in marriages where the love and affection and respect dried up long ago. They live in a "cold war," often in separate bedrooms, with separate friends, and separate funds. They hardly speak to each other. They rarely fight. There is no intimacy – physical or emotional. There is no joy. They are roommates. They were emotionally divorced years ago. So, why do they accept a non-relationship as a relationship?

For each person in this situation, the answer is different. Sometimes there are extenuating circumstances, such as the care of a disabled child, economic ties, religious concerns, a joint business. Sometimes the reasons are practical, other times they are emotional and often they are fear-based. Change brings up many issues related to fear.

Women who have lived with this ambivalence for a long time pray for "a sign" that will make the decision easy for them. They have fantasies of being hit by their husband or of his leaving, or even (and some feel shameful about this) fantasies of their husband dying. Their fantasy is really about someone else making the decision for them. The paradox here is when someone makes a decision for us, it does not free us. In truth, we become victims of *their* choices. When our happiness and freedom are dependent on others making our decisions, we are like children asking for permission.

We must learn to become more comfortable with the decision-making process. Decision-making is directly linked to our self-confidence. Before we can feel good about ourselves as women, we must build the confidence it takes to advocate for ourselves. You don't have to be hit to leave your marriage. You can leave because you choose to leave. You can leave because you know this is not the right place for you to be. You can leave because you have tried everything you can to make this relationship work, and it simply won't. You can leave because it is good for you to leave.

Today I wonder why I feel something drastic has to happen before I can act on my own behalf. I will pledge to myself that I will work to find the strength I need to claim the life I want and deserve.

Many women going through divorce admit they don't take time for themselves. Some say they are too stressed out, or that they don't deserve it, or that there is no time. Downtime is like a mini-vacation. Take up activities you enjoyed in the past or try a new activity. Make sure the goals are manageable and accessible, so that you are able to follow through. Be aware of the negative messages you learned in your family of origin about relaxing (was it used as a reward for having worked hard?) and your own negative self-messages (having fun will take away from what my kids need). Gently push those self-sabotaging thoughts out of your mind! Write down something you can do for yourself this week and make a commitment to do it!

Focus on self-nurturing or self-loving activities such as getting a massage or buying flowers. Again, treating yourself well is part of living a full and healthy life. Often, I hear women say that buying themselves flowers is not the same as someone else buying them for you. While this is true, it does not mean that *different* is *less*. It is simply different. Try it, and you will see that flowers bring color and life into your day. They can help you feel appreciated whether someone else gives them to you or you give them to yourself.

Try to do something nice for yourself each day. Even if it is a small, small thing, it can make a big, big difference in how you see yourself. Make a small change, see how it feels and acknowledge your pleasure with a resounding, "I deserve this!"

$Today$ I will think of something to do that will be an act of self-nurturance. I will learn that I do not have to rely on another person to enjoy life and feel loved.

Psychotherapy refers to healing through talking. Psychotherapists make their living by doing psychotherapy. In some states, "psychotherapist" and "counselor" are used interchangeably. One of the most confusing things in choosing a psychotherapist is trying to decode all those letters after their names! There are various trainings and numerous courses of study, not to mention degrees, certifications and licenses. In looking for a qualified psychotherapist, do not become overwhelmed by titles, letters, etc. Below is a list of disciplines and designations and what they mean. If someone's credentials are not on this list, it does not mean they are not qualified, legitimate therapists. If you have any questions about someone's credentials, always ask.

M.D. – Medical Doctor. Can dispense medication. Internists, Pediatricians, Cardiologists are all M.D.s.

Psychiatrist – an M.D. who specializes in mental health, can prescribe medication and do psychotherapy.

Ph.D, Psy.D, Ed.D – Doctorate degrees. Have advanced training. Referred to as "Doctor", but does not have medical training and, in most states, does not have a license to dispense medication.

APRN – A Registered nurse with special training in psychiatric disorders who can dispense medication.

LCSW – Licensed clinical social worker. Social work master's degree specializing in psychotherapy.

MAP – Master's Degree, specializing in psychology.

MA or MS – Master's degree. Many different disciplines, usually with a specialty in counseling or related field.

MFTT – Master's degree in Marriage and Family Therapy.

CADC – Certified Alcohol and Drug Abuse Counselor. Specialized training in substance abuse. Certified by an independent board. May or may not have a Masters or Doctorate degree.

LADC – Licensed Alcohol and Drug Abuse Counselor. Same as above, but licensed through the state.

While education, certification, and licensing do not insure a perfect relationship, these qualifications let you know that your therapist has received adequate training to perform the work you are paying for. Don't assume they are credentialed or trained. In some states, you still do not need a license or proof of training to hang out a shingle that says "psychotherapist." Question your therapist regarding his/her training. If he/she acts insulted or offended, move on and find someone else!

Today I will not let choosing a therapist overwhelm me. I will pay attention to credentials and ask questions. It is part of advocating for myself. It also allows me to practice healthy assertiveness skills, which will benefit me in all my relationships! Finding someone I can work with may seem difficult to do, but having a therapist to guide, support, and offer me insight will aid in my healing.

When we are more physically active, our body needs more nutrients to keep it running more efficiently. It made sense to me that the same would be true in times when we were exerting ourselves emotionally. However, Pat Froberg, RD is a registered dietician in Avon, Connecticut, says there is no evidence to indicate that we need more food under emotional stress than at any other time. If we are eating a healthy diet, then it should sustain us through this difficult time. She offered some tips on easy ways to maintain a good diet without a lot of effort.

- Get most of our nutrition from food. Under stress, when we are running around and not planning good meals, we may resort to taking supplements to replace what we are not getting from food. The best way of making sure we are getting our nutritional needs met is by eating lots of fruits and vegetables, preferably fresh. Frozen is a second choice. Canned will have less nutritional value. She also suggested that by eating as many different color vegetables and fruit as we can, we insure that we are getting a broad range of nutrients.

- Americans are getting 2-2.5 times more protein than we need, so she wasn't as concerned about our protein intake. Carbohydrates are critical for brain functioning among other things. However, even though chocolate, cookies and chips are carbohydrates, they do not fulfill our nutritional needs and are merely empty calories. If the brain lacks carbohydrates, then it doesn't receive enough glucose, which is fuel for the brain. Carbohydrates are needed for concentration. Her suggestions for appropriate carbo foods included fruits, vegetables, whole wheat bread, and high fiber cereal.

- Under stress, many of us experience sleep difficulties. Eliminating caffeine, not just in coffee or tea, but in soda and chocolate, can help us sleep better. Ever wonder why everyone falls asleep after Thanksgiving Dinner? The tryptophan in the turkey is partly responsible. Other foods known to have high amounts of tryptophan include warm milk and yogurt.

- Beans, vegetarian chili, black bean soup, brown rice, and whole grain products will fill our need for fiber. They can also help reduce cholesterol, lower high blood pressure and control diabetes. While stress itself does not cause any of the aforementioned illnesses, if you are on the border, then stress can certainly kick you over that line. Eating fiber can help maintain a healthy balance and discourage those diseases from occurring.

- Some of us experience gastrointestinal stress. We may experience bouts of diarrhea. If you have a bout lasting two or three days, this is not a problem. Beyond that, you may want to consult your physician as the nutrients are not being properly absorbed into the body. If you find that stress results in lack of appetite and food simply looks awful, then it is okay to use a nutritional drink supplement. Of course, that is only for tough times. When possible, a healthy diet should be maintained.

Today I will look in my refrigerator and kitchen cabinets. What have I been eating since I began this process of separation/divorce? Am I nurturing my body or am I ignoring it? Am I having trouble concentrating or sleeping? Perhaps the answer is in what I am eating. I will take a few minutes to make a grocery list of healthy food and later I will stop at the store. Tonight I will make myself and my children something wholesome to eat. It is one more way that I can take care of myself.

Notes

Month Ten

... *And Becoming a Stockholder*

Sometimes when we meet someone, the chemistry is so strong that it intoxicates us. We refer to this as "love at first sight." It feels like we have found the perfect person for us; our soul mate, our one true love. We let the magic carry us away. We think we know all there is to know about this person. Some of us have felt this and rushed to the altar, sometimes, in a very short time.

Chemistry distorts our intellectual functioning and our belief system. We may believe that we will never fight or disagree. We may feel "As if I have always known him." We are a perfect match!

A belief system is about ideas and fantasies. It may or may not have anything to do with the facts. We imagine all the right components for a good relationship are there. Sometimes the belief system we created is so strong that we even deny evidence to the contrary. We do this by minimizing, rationalizing, or denying. We say things like, "Oh, that is not so bad," or "That will change when we are married," or "That is not so important."

We have bought stock in our fantasy and, like any stockholder, we really, really, really want our investment to work out. However, whether we are investing in the stock market or in fantasy, emotions can sometimes cloud good judgment. We hate to think that we made a mistake, so we hang in, even as our stock becomes worthless. Sometimes, we even invest more by getting engaged or married or buying a house together or having children. Did you want this so badly that you denied reality and kept your investment in your fantasy?

Do not waste time criticizing or blaming yourself. Rather, use this as an opportunity for self-growth. Why did you want this so badly? Why did you overlook what is now very obvious? And why did you keep investing more? Your insights are signs of growth. Get beyond the fantasy and consider ways to limit your losses. Until you admit there is a problem, there is no way to solve it. Use reality as your guide and you can begin to work toward debunking the fantasy.

Today I want to learn why I made such a huge investment, even in light of the evidence which was overwhelmingly obvious. What was it that I needed? What left me so vulnerable? Can I change that aspect of myself without becoming hard and cynical about future possibilities?

Day 2 Did Either of You Forget to Leave Mommy and Daddy?

Family of origin connection is vital in our lives. It offers support, a sense of our history, a rich network, and a community of love and acceptance. In order for a couple to build a solid unified marriage, both spouses must individuate from their family of origin. This doesn't mean they must sever ties with their families. It just means shifting priorities. It is almost impossible to maintain the same ties and loyalties to your family of origin and create a viable marriage. You need to re-prioritize and make your NEW family your primary focus.

As the American family continues to evolve and change, we see diverse family structures and connection. Some families all live in the same neighborhood, while others are spread across the country. Some families increase in size through divorce and remarriage; others, by having many children. Family structures, mores, and rules are as different and unique as each family itself. Throw into the mix the impact of different cultures on the family and you can see that there is no one "right" way to be a family. This richness of culture and variety is exciting, but can also lead to conflict when one spouse has more family connection than another. If you are from similar cultures, this may not be much of a problem. However, we often meet and fall in love with people of different cultures, religions, and geographic experiences. All these elements can create quite a challenge as you merge your life experiences and begin to sort out and establish on new priorities.

This problem is fairly prevalent in young couples.

Here is an example: Elaine met Jeff in college. They spent all their time together and married right after graduation. Both went to work full time. Then Elaine's mother became ill. She spent weekends with her ailing mother, who lived three hours away. At first, her husband was supportive, but in time, he became frustrated. This continued for a number of years. She refused to ask her siblings to help. Jeff spent his weekends with his friends, most of whom were still single. The couple rarely saw each other. Yet Elaine was shocked to find out that he had met someone else and wanted a divorce.

Other examples include: the woman who picked out her engagement ring with her mother, the wife who went car shopping with her father, or a husband who refuses to go on vacation without his parents. Then there was the bride who insisted her parents have final choice in naming their grandchildren.

Today I ask myself if we both made a commitment to make this relationship our priority. Did we fight over our parents' influence? What issues still need to be addressed with my own family of origin?

"Can we be friends through the process of divorce?"

This question often seems absurd, especially in cases where there has been domestic violence or abuse. Someone who hurts you is not your friend! Here are some thoughts on friendship for you to consider.

Friendship is not about always pleasing the other person. Many women are uncomfortable with assertiveness and try to minimize the opportunities for confrontation as much as possible. Sometimes this stems from messages that good girls do not get angry and that their role is to please everyone. Whatever family of origin messages were about confrontation, these will reemerge stronger than ever during your divorce.

Friendship is not just the absence of violence. If there was domestic violence, the notion of "friendship" may really be a code for keeping the peace and not making your husband angry. Divorce is adversarial by its very nature. Two people are fighting over money, property and custody of children. It is important to understand that one doesn't need to be aggressive to be heard, yet one should not be passive either. If you have trouble asserting yourself, be sure you hire an attorney who can advocate for you.

Friendship does not involve guilt. If you are the one who left the marriage, guilt can be the motivator for "friendship." Trying to take care of, or ease the burden and pain of the other is not friendship, it is guilt. It doesn't even help the other person; it is only an attempt to assuage one's conscience.

Friendship is the cornerstone of marriage. Basically if you were truly each other's friends, you probably wouldn't be getting a divorce.

Friendship does not need to exist for the sake of the children. You can be cordial and respectful when dealing with your kids. You don't even have to like each other to treat each other with dignity. Your children will learn what they see.

Today when I think about my friendships, I will notice that they are built upon trust, respect, and genuine caring. Friendship is a two-way street. Without reciprocity, it isn't friendship, it is merely being a caretaker! I will stop calling my relationship with my husband friendship. I will find a word that more accurately describes our relationship, knowing that it is changing and whatever it is today, it may not be that tomorrow.

Wendy Rosen, Ph.D of Cambridge, Massachusetts offers some thoughts for a married woman who has fallen in love with a person other than her husband and that person is a woman. Like all extra-marital relationships, reasons and circumstances vary from case to case. Here are two scenarios that illustrate some of the struggles and issues that arise from this complicated situation.

Jane had been in a long-term marriage in which she was somewhat happy. She loved her husband, but always knew something was missing: it didn't quite "click." She had been attracted to women in college, but had denied the attraction. Then she met Betty and found she was facing her sexual preferences head-on.

Glenda was also in a long-term marriage. She had no prior inkling that she might be attracted to women. She never felt attracted to other women, but suddenly she found herself in love with Grace.

As expected, both husbands felt betrayed by the affair, but absolutely stunned by the gender of their wives' lovers! When women leave marriages for other women, husbands feel absolutely powerless. There is nothing they can do to compete. This may make it easier for the husband to take the affair less "personally." That is, after his initial reaction, he may find he can more easily come to acceptance, knowing there was nothing he could do to remedy the situation. You may be able to maintain a relationship with your ex-husband because the same sex affair lifts it out of the personal for him and makes the issue exclusively yours.

Children, in this situation, deal with the same feelings of loss as they would in any divorce. The infidelity is more of an issue than the gender of the new person. The primary work for the child is of grieving the loss of the family unit as it once existed.

Aside from all the issues for your family, you are also looking at a new sense of self. Identifying and accepting yourself in a gay relationship will take time and effort. Here are some things to focus on:

- This is not about the "men."
- This marriage could not be saved.
- Deal with the feelings of guilt.
- Couples' therapy would not make a difference.
- Sexuality is a complex issue and there are no clear demarcations from straight to gay. Our sexuality exists more on a continuum.
- Seek support from a women's group or therapist.

Today I will be gentle and patient with myself, as so many things have changed in my life and in how I see myself. I will continue to honor my courage, while speaking gently, yet firmly, to my fear. I will be mindful of those I love. Their journeys toward acceptance will happen in their own way and in their own time.

For many kids, Halloween is one of the most important holidays of the year. The child of divorce is faced with choices and concerns. Who will take me treat-or-treating? Who will get my costume and dress me? Where will I trick-or-treat? The logistical problems for the single parent include:

- In two-parent homes, often one parent gives out candy while the other parent takes the child trick-or-treating. Now there is only one parent in the home. Do you stay and give out candy or do you go with your child?
- Parents often do not specify in their divorce decree who "gets" the child on October 31. If it falls on a visitation day, some children feel disappointed that they don't get to trick-or-treat in their own neighborhood with their friends. This is particularly true for the first Halloween, when new friends and acquaintances may not have been established in the new neighborhood.
- Halloween reinforces the reality of sharing your child with his other parent and that you will not share some of your child's experiences. In time, the child will grow comfortable with his two homes and it is likely he will enjoy the "doubles" of divorced families, such as two vacations, Christmases, and birthdays. But you may feel left out or cheated.
- Halloween is a peer driven event. Most children want to go trick or treating with their friends.

Parents should listen clearly to what their children want to do on Halloween. This does not mean "making them choose." It means paying attention to the child's comfort level and enthusiasm. Then make plans in a way that can meet the child's needs. Some things to keep in mind:

- The child should be allowed to trick-or-treat with friends in his familiar surroundings. If extended family members want to see the child dressed up, they should come to where the child is, rather than dragging the child around and taking him/her away from his/her peers.
- It can be a positive experience if both parents can be involved with the process. One parent takes the child out and the other stays back at the house giving out candy. Unlike other scenarios, this one will not give children the false hope of the parents reuniting. Rather it says to the child, "My parents can "rally" beyond their problems to do what is best for me."
- Limit candy intake. This is always important at Halloween, as kids are already pretty wired. This is especially so in a newly-separated/divorced family where there may be added stress or tension.
- Picture taking is important. The child should pose with each parent separately, again reinforcing the fact that while the parents are no longer a couple, they are both still involved with the child.
- If the choice of costume becomes an issue, let the parent who was responsible for costumes in the past make the decision/purchase this year. Next year you can begin to alternate that responsibility.

In the future, as the child becomes more comfortable in his new home and has made connections with children in that neighborhood, trick-or-treating can be alternated. There may be possibilities of trick-or- treating in both neighborhoods. Remember this is the child's holiday. Follow his cues on what he wants. The adults have plenty of other choices to make. This one belongs to the child.

Today Halloween *makes it clear that divorce impacts family members in many ways. I may feel sad that I will miss out on some activities in my child's life, but I can take comfort in knowing that the greatest gift I can give my child is two loving parents who can work together.*

Do you struggle with the question, "Is this really so bad?" When women start thinking about divorce, they are immediately hit with the reality of how many lives will be impacted by that one decision. Frequently, women's first concerns are for their children and the impact that divorce will have on their lives.

There is no doubt that living in a family that provides children with two loving parents is the best option. But in cases when that is not possible, children do better having two homes with each of those homes providing one loving, stable, happy parent. Divorce is not what hurts children. Fighting hurts children, as does inconsistency or the emotional or physical abandonment of a parent. When parents negotiate a respectful relationship with each other, and work to foster the other parent's ongoing relationship with the children, then the children will continue to thrive.

As a couple, you provide children with a model for what a marriage is supposed to be. Even if your spouse is a "good father," if he is a disrespectful and unreliable husband, the children suffer in this relationship. Many women say, "I tell my children all the time that their father's behavior is unacceptable." The problem is that by staying with a man who exhibits unacceptable behavior, your actions suggest acceptance. Children learn by what they see more than by what they are told. In speaking with adult children whose mothers stayed in unacceptable relationships for the sake of the kids, the following issues arose:

- Children lost respect for the mother for not leaving.
- Children often adopted one role or the other – either they behaved like the suffering Mom or were outrageous and hostile like the fathers. These were the only models they knew.
- Some of the children felt guilty, knowing the parents stayed together for their sake.
- As adults, their relationships with their parents often weren't particularly close.
- Adult children often distanced themselves from their unhappy parents.
- When parents divorced after the children were older, these children often felt resentful, knowing that the burden of caring for each parent would fall to them.

It is never an easy decision to stay or to go. If however, your decision is hinging on the welfare of your children ask yourself this question... *If this was my daughter's marriage and she came to me for advice, would I tell her to stay or go?*

Today I will consider the role model I am providing for what is acceptable behavior in marriage. I will consider the fact that if I choose to divorce, my children can still have two loving parents, without the negativity and fighting.

...and Other Creative Child Custody Options

When it is feasible, more and more parents are looking at the option of sharing physical custody of their children. This is possible when both parents are strong caretakers, positive models, and want to continue an active role in the children's lives. Joint custody involves a commitment by both parents to work together in harmony for the sake of the children. For the arrangement to be practical, it requires that the parents live in close proximity, usually in the same school district. Some creative custody agreements are:

- **Birdnesting** – The children stay in the home and the parents move in and out. Pro's: The children are in a stable, secure environment and never have to move. Con's: The parents are always moving and must share space with their ex. Can be costly (each partner needs another place to live) and lacks privacy and permanence. Can only succeed when there is a strong relationship of mutual trust, respect, and desire to work together. Often this is a good short-term solution, but isn't feasible as a permanent arrangement.

- **Monday and Tuesday /Wednesday and Thursday/alternate Friday, Saturday, Sunday schedule** – This works well for many families. For example, Mom has the children every Monday/Tuesday and Dad has them every Wednesday/Thursday and weekends are alternated. Pros: Longer stretches of time with each parent, a set schedule and frequent contact with each parent. Cons: Switches during the week can result in miscommunication and misplaced school supplies, sports gear and so on. This arrangement works well when the parents are willing to be flexible and work together.

- **Child alternates home by the week or month, with the other parent having visitation a couple of nights a week** – Pros: Stability for a period of time in each home. Cons: The switch can be difficult, as the child must change their role in the home, from visitor to occupant and then back again.

- **The traditional schedule** – Father has visitation on alternate weekends and one or two nights a week. Pros: Gives everyone a rhythm and schedule. Cons: Many fathers want to be more involved in their children's lives. This arrangement makes it difficult for fathers and children to feel as if they have enough time together.

Creating a visitation/joint custody schedule is a unique experience and should be tailored to fit the family's individual needs. Regardless of what schedule you ultimately work out with your ex, some key elements must be in place in order for it to be successful:

- A commitment to stick to the schedule.
- Flexibility.
- An ability to admit when you are wrong.
- An openness to review the schedule and modify it if it isn't working.
- A sense of humor.

Today I will consider if our schedule is working for all of us. If not, I will consider whether it is the schedule or our behavior that sabotages its effectiveness. I will try to address this with my children's father. Perhaps we can consider options that will better fit all our needs. If I work with him in this area we can create full and healthy environments for our children.

In most divorce situations, one or both parties experience a pang of doubt when they think, "Maybe we should try again." Frequently, this occurs after there has been a tender moment shared by the two of you, either relating to a memory, your children, or a shared experience.

Considering the potential for the relationship to work, most couples' therapists will inquire as to the time when the relationship was the best. When was your relationship the most solid? When were you both happy and in love? When was physical attraction at its height? When was emotional intimacy strongest? Often, when asked about the best time in their marriage, many women admit that it never felt quite "right." The questions then follow, why did you marry him and why did you stay married so long? Often women recognize they stayed not for what they had, but for the hope of what could be.

> Mira Kirschenman, in her insightful and wise book, *Too Good to Go, Too Bad to Stay*, says: "If it was never very good, then it never will be very good."

While this may feel like a strong statement, it is true in the large majority of cases. Marital therapy can not create what was never there. Ms. Kirschenman echoes the opinion of many marriage therapists: a marriage that never had that sort of connection is never going to have it.

If a couple shared a strong, positive energy and were once in love, then the therapist can assist them in trying to rekindle those feelings. Sometimes the feelings may have just dwindled under a heap of resentments and disappointments. Sometimes, when the pain is addressed and a couple finds different ways of relating, the fires are re-ignited. But the spark had to be there in the first place.

Today I may feel tenderness toward my spouse. In those minutes, I wonder if we should try again to make this marriage work. Then I ask myself to think about the relationship at its best. Was I ever really happy with him? Or did I just hope it would get better? Is my desire to try again an attempt to invent something that never existed? I need to sit with these hard questions and be honest with myself. When I am truly honest with myself, I am paying attention to the most important relationship: the one I have with myself.

Rashomon tells the story of a murder and the quest to find the killer. The play is divided into three acts and is staged in the courtroom. Three witnesses give their account of what happened. As they each testify, actors create the scene for the audience to witness. After the first Act, I was sure I knew the killer! In Act Two, another witness tells his story and the actors act out the story again, exactly the same way, only this time the stage is rotated slightly to give the audience another view of the event. After watching Act Two, I was no longer sure that I knew who the guilty party was. In Act Three, the same thing happened, again the stage turned slightly to shift the perspective. I was completely confused. How could I be witness to something and not be sure of what I was seeing?

Truth is greatly defined by perspective, and is not always black and white. *Rashomon* offers an important lesson in perspective. Depending on where you are standing, the events that play out look very different. We cannot imagine there is a truth other than our own. Only when we stand in someone else's shoes, can we really see their view of the situation. Can we at least concede that there may be another perspective? It may not be yours and it may not be to your liking, but it can exist. Acknowledging this can free you up from becoming arrogant and narrow-minded. This will keep you vital, flexible and creative. When you become absolute in your viewpoint, you can become closed, rigid and intolerant. Try this:

Imagine you are your estranged husband. Tell the story of your marriage from his viewpoint. What is his opinion of what happened in the marriage? How does he see the events? What would he say are your best attributes? What would he say was the hardest thing about living with you?

You are free to reject or accept his vision of the marriage. I ask only that you consider things from his vantage point. Consider it as a lesson in flexibility. It may make it easier to negotiate co-parenting issues. It will give you insight into his strengths and weaknesses, which can assist you in strategizing the best ways to deal with him. It may also help you understand who he really is, why you chose him, and why the marriage ultimately ended. Those are huge lessons to take with you into all future relationships.

Today I will explore my ability to see another person's point of view. It will not diminish or undermine my own experience. My experience is uniquely mine, as his is uniquely his. I will not abdicate my opinion for his. However, seeing his perspective can offer me a broader picture of the dynamics of the relationship.

Whether we are parenting our children, taking care of elderly parents or ailing friends, women in this culture are socialized to be caregivers. We are absolutely stalwart in our commitments to make sure everyone has what they need. Due to our unfailing sense of reliability and dependability, we rarely let anyone down. Except for one person. Ourselves. In some families, taking time for ourselves is seen as selfish. We may feel manipulated to put others' needs before our own. As a single person, you have to learn that it is okay to sometimes put your needs first. Often, we over-commit and then have no free time. Free time is important because it is when most women eke out a few minutes for themselves.

To combat this habit of not prioritizing your needs, make a date with yourself. Make a date with the same degree of commitment that you would when you make a date with another person. To help you accomplish this, try to:

- Write it down in your planner or on the calendar. Writing it down makes it real. Write it in INK.
- Make the date within the next seven days. Do this weekly. Don't procrastinate.
- Plan a specific event. Don't just block off the time and say, "I'll see what happens." Chances are, you will have difficulty sticking to the commitment because, without a plan, you are liable to fill that time doing something for someone else.
- Notify others you will not be available during that time. Line up a babysitter if necessary. Let your kids, boss, and parents, know that you have a "prior commitment" for that time and are unavailable.
- If you draw a blank about what you want to do, here are some ideas:
  - Get a massage.
  - Get a pedicure, manicure, facial.
  - Attend a seminar, workshop, a talk.
  - Go to the theater.
  - Take yourself out for lunch at a nice restaurant.
  - Hang out in the library.
  - Go to a fancy clothes store. Try on clothes that are different from your taste.
  - Take yourself out for an ice cream sundae.
  - Take a yoga class.
  - Learn to roller blade, ice skate, swim.
  - Try a trampoline.
  - Go to a museum, crafts fair, antique shop.

Plan something! Then allow yourself the excitement and anticipation of looking forward to your "date."

Today just when I start to think my life is all about courts, finances, children, and work, I will plan for my date. Even though it feels strange to do this, I feel somewhat energized by the prospect of "taking me out." I will commit to myself with the same enthusiasm as I do to others. This is a testimony to my self-value and a reawakening of my self-worth.

What are the three most important things in your life?

Without knowing the answer to that question, how can we live our lives with meaning? For example, if you say, "My family is the most important thing in my life," and yet you rarely spend time with them, then you are not living the life you truly want to live. Or if you say "My health is the most important thing in my life" and you smoke cigarettes, eat junk food, and never exercise, you are ignoring your own values. Many women who are leaving bad marriages complain that their husbands did not make them a priority or did not treat them with respect. However, when women do not live by their own value system, then they are treating themselves in the same way their abusive or neglectful husbands treated them.

When we know what is important in our lives and we begin to live our lives honoring those priorities, then we have the opportunity to be truly content.

Living your life following your priorities can give you peace. It feeds your self-esteem and sense of contentment. Life is more enjoyable because you are less stressed out, anxious, and uptight. The urgency to "get things done" so you can "get to the really important things" will diminish. You will feel less frustrated and harried when you pay attention to what is really important to you.

The point here is to bring joy into your life. If you know what is important to you and you live your life according to those priorities, then you will have fewer regrets and more joy.

Today I will think about what is really important to me. Do I make those things a priority? Just allowing myself to consider the possibilities brings me one step closer to living the life I really want.

After years of being someone's wife, women who are divorcing may find that they have lost touch with who they are. When asked, "Do you love yourself?" they often respond, "I don't know. I haven't ever even thought about it. I don't even know if I like myself."

Loving ourselves is not selfish, self-indulgent, or conceited. Loving ourselves means we know who we are and we accept ourselves. It means we treat our mind, body, and spirit with respect and dignity. We often love others unconditionally, but not ourselves.

Try this: For one day, listen to how you talk to yourself. How many times in a day do you criticize yourself? In the mirror, do you say things like "bad hair, fat thighs, and wrinkly skin"? Do you criticize your housekeeping? Decorating? Cooking? Do you find your mind going over things you said, but wish you hadn't? Do you spend time mentally kicking yourself? Do you doubt your ability? Do you compare yourself to other women? Listen to what your inner voice says about you. Do you notice any patterns? Are there areas where you seem more intolerant? Are there areas where you are more forgiving?

Why are you so hard on yourself? Our family culture instilled certain messages and the culture at large supported them. We tried valiantly to meet the expectations of others in order to be accepted and loved. We thought if we pleased people, then they would love us.

But what about pleasing yourself? It is when we are our authentic selves that we are the most loveable. That is hard to believe after years of people trying to change us. Some family members may have even withdrawn love and support when we did not act as they wanted. If we are being true to ourselves, the sting of disapproval is a lot less. However, when we act in a way that goes against our belief system, even if we get love and support from someone else, we feel hollow and fake inside, because we were not honest and loving with ourselves.

Today I will begin loving myself by stopping negative thoughts and replacing them with positive affirmations. This may feel tedious and time consuming at first, but if I practice daily, then positive affirmations will become a new habit, replacing the old habit of self-criticism. I will bring love into my life by treating myself in a loving way – this includes self-respect, self-acceptance and self-approval.

When does compliance change you from a peacekeeper into a victim? *Webster's Collegiate Dictionary* defines compliance as "a disposition to yield to others." Women are frequently so uncomfortable with confrontation, argument, or hurt feelings that we try to be as compliant as possible. Compromise is a sign of a healthy, mature attitude and is critical to the success of any relationship. Without compromise, we can become unreasonable and rigid, making relationships difficult, if not impossible, to maintain.

However, when our desire to maintain peace results in our constant compliance, then we set ourselves up for other to take advantage of us. We become victims. Women coming out of unhappy marriages were compliant in one form or another. Even those who were screaming mad, often realize, they were reacting to so many years of silent compliance.

"Whatever" is a word I hear frequently from women who have become so used to being compliant that they don't even realize it. "Whatever" is like hanging out a white flag saying "I surrender, I simply can't fight anymore. So, I comply." One of the biggest problems with all this compliance is, after years of silencing her own thoughts, opinions, dreams, expectations, and feelings, many women do not even know who they are or what they want anymore.

Compliance does not bring peace to the marriage; it only brings silence to a relationship. Your silence will definitely not bring you inner peace. The inner turmoil of withholding and denying your own reality will fester and grow. It will wreak havoc with your health, both physically and emotionally, and with your relationships with others, as well.

Today I begin to understand my need and my right to express my feelings and thoughts; I also begin to see that compliance impedes my growth. Going along with what everyone wants is a surrender of myself. When I am compliant, I am invalidating my own thoughts and feelings and telling myself that I have little or no worth. I will try to reconnect with the things in myself that are valuable, not only to others, but to myself. Compliance robs me and others, of my voice. I have something worth saying and I will begin to say it with conviction!

Regardless of whether the divorce was your choice or your husband's, the news that your former husband is dating again elicits some kind of response. You may experience the news as a small *ping!* in the solar plexus. Or you may feel the impact like getting hit by a bus.

When your children are introduced to the new person in their father's life, this can often result in your having feelings of self-doubt and insecurity. Will the children like her more than me? Will she replace me in their eyes? Can this new woman adequately care for my child?

If the new woman in your ex's life has children, this elicits other concerns. If your child is an only child, this may be especially true. Suddenly, he is part of a family with brothers and sisters, complete with two parents. You may fantasize about how perfect this new family is. You may feel left out and inadequate. Try to resist the urge to let your imagination run to those hurtful places.

Theresa has one son, Alan, eight. Her husband remarried soon after their divorce was final. The new woman, Melanie, has two daughters, six and ten. When Alan first began visiting this newly-formed family, Teresa was devastated by images of a perfect "Brady Bunch" family. This was compounded by Alan's coming home filled with stories about how much fun it was to have sisters. Teresa's ache was palpable as she mourned her marriage and longed for the children she did not have. When Alan was with his father's new family, she felt adrift and lonely. Her feelings of inadequacy continued to grow. She fantasized about this new family in vivid detail: Their dinnertime conversation, times huddled around the fire playing Clue and their joyful snowball fights. These images haunted her and diminished her sense of self. These thoughts kept her stuck. By focusing on the family unit she created in her mind, and how inadequate she was in comparison, she was doing some serious damage to her already-wounded self-esteem.

Teresa began to realize her focus on her "perfect family" fantasy was only hurting herself. She started to resist the temptation to revisit those painful illusions. Only after she got her thoughts under control was she able to see how much time and energy it took to keep the fantasy going. When she refocused some of that energy on herself, she was able to move forward. This refocus helped her reclaim her life and autonomy. Now she resists comparing the two homes. No longer threatened by Alan's new sisters, she welcomes them as a part of her son's life. Even though he has this new family, she and Alan are also a family. Her family is no less viable and valuable because they are a family of two and not five.

Today my imagination about my child's life with his father can get me into trouble. I will resist the temptation to create scenarios of life in that house. I will focus on what we have without comparison to other families. Family is defined by the love and connection, and not by the number of people. When I resist fantasies, I avoid self-inflicted pain.

A conversation with Holly about her divorced parents:

"My mother has no problem telling you exactly what she feels. She is very talkative and you always know where she stands. But I wish my Dad would talk more. He was never much for small talk and you never really know what he is feeling."

"Which parent was easier for you to talk to about serious matters in your life?"

"Oh, that is easy. My father is a wonderful listener. He listens without judgment and is very supportive."

A "good talker" is often mistaken for a good communicator. While Holly's mother talked up a storm, she could be very opinionated and aggressive. Her daughter didn't dare disagree with her. Holly's father, on the other hand, was an active and open listener. He encouraged his daughter to come to him by being an active listener. With him, she felt she could say what she wanted without fear of judgment or recrimination.

Both parents displayed attributes of good communication. Her mother could speak her mind without any problem and her father could listen actively. Good communication involves both of these skills. A good talker must be able to listen to the message being conveyed by others with consideration and respect. The converse is also true. The good listener must also develop skills to respond to what was heard. No wonder this couple got divorced! Both felt invalidated. There was no exchange of ideas. One talked, but didn't listen, and one listened but didn't talk, and so nothing was ever resolved.

In this scenario, the talker frequently becomes frustrated at the lack of feedback. They may talk more: repeating themselves, talking louder, losing patience. They hope that the non-verbal party will begin to respond. Sometimes talkers, out of sheer frustration, will actually pick a fight, to engage their partner in an exchange. However, the non-talker, when challenged in such a manner, may become overwhelmed and shut down or become frustrated and blow up.

The break-down in communication is not one person's deficit. When a couple struggles with an inability to dialogue in a healthy, constructive way, both need to take responsibility. Rather than blaming each other, they must work together to resolve what interrupts the flow of communication. Often, couples find that communication is so badly ruptured that there is enormous animosity. Resentment accumulates when you feel unheard and invalidated. Over time it is more difficult to establish new communication strategies.

Today when I think about my marriage, I look at how we communicated. What was our pattern? Do I find myself taking that same role in all my relationships? What are my communication strengths and what are my weaknesses? I will carefully consider my own style. Improving my communication skills can only strengthen my relationships, both present and future.

What can we do to stop the trend of escalating divorce? Two responses emerge. One is to make it harder to get divorced. The other is to make it more difficult to get married.

In 1999, Louisiana began offering the option of "Covenant Marriage." Couples sign a certificate making it more difficult to get divorced. To date, approximately 2 percent of Louisiana's marrying couples chose this option. Similarly, Minnesota has considered "Supervows." The idea is, if it is harder to get divorced, couples will work harder to stay married. In truth, to end these marriages, one only need establish residence in another state with easier divorce laws.

If we make it harder to get divorced, more women would be living with domestic violence. Most states have waiting periods to get divorced. As of this writing, Colorado is thinking of making that waiting period ONE YEAR. Forcing people to stay together is troublesome at best, dangerous at its worst. Four women a day die as a result of domestic violence. (Violence Against Women: A National Crime Victimization Survey Report, 1994) Furthermore, forcing people to stay married does not provide children with a happy home or healthy role models. Children often end up in marriages similar to the ones their parents had. A woman who stays in an abusive marriage, but tells her child, "This is unacceptable" gives a mixed message to her children.

Making it harder to marry may have some merit. How about a waiting period to get married? Premarital classes also sound like a good idea. But, who decides who is qualified to teach those classes and what the curriculum should be?

Perhaps a better way to encourage and support good marriages is to provide education in the schools and at home. Role modeling, conflict resolution and good communication skills for children would have payoffs in both their personal and professional lives. Teaching patience and impulse control may be a key. Children learn how to compete, but do they learn how to work together for a common goal? Couples end up competing with each other, bringing that need to win right off the soccer field and into their home. Teaching compassion would be a plus. We cannot teach people how to have a good marriage, but we can teach children how to be good people. If we teach them love, respect, patience, impulse control, and good communication skills, the rest will follow.

Today I will teach my children to be good human beings. That will take them far in their lives, in their marriages, choice of work and in their sense of self.

Sarah and Al divorced after forty years of marriage. Their divorce was messy and drawn out, with "all the trimmings"– including numerous attorneys, mediators and a trial. The couple was retired and did not have a lot of money. They spent most of their life savings on litigation. Instead of their being able to enjoy their "golden years" with flexibility and security, the only ones who profited from a lifetime of work, were their lawyers.

As the years went on, this couple continued to behave as acrimoniously as they ever had. They could not speak to each other at their daughter's wedding and have never been in the same room with their grandchildren at the same time. It is almost forbidden for their child to speak of one parent in the presence of the other. When this does happen, they become enraged and a litany of epithets is released. As if this wasn't enough, this couple felt it necessary to have a "mutual lifetime restraining order", barring them from being anywhere near each other. Now in their 80's, there seems to be no sign of the anger ebbing.

To hate this much, to actively work to perpetuate hostile feelings as strong as these, takes a great deal of energy. Why couldn't they let go of all this negativity and just get on with their lives? They are still bound together by their anger and have even formalized it with a restraining order. Sarah and Al have never gone through the process of letting go and truly experiencing a divorce from each other.

Keeping this connection through anger and even validating it with legal documentation, is a way to maintain a relationship. While these two people haven't seen each other in many years, their bitterness and animosity keeps them connected. It spills over into their relationships with their children and their friends, and affects their own health and well being.

Today do I use my anger to keep me connected? Am I afraid of what I will feel if I let my anger go? Has my anger become my constant companion? Does it keep me from entering into other relationships? I will remember that to feel my anger is healthy, but, as with most things, excesses can destroy.

Some separated women experience great apprehension as the weekend approaches, especially on those weekends when the children are off visiting with their Dad. For many women, this is the first time they have been alone for many, many years. The weekend, which once was couple time or family time, is the most difficult to adjust to. It is the time they feel the loss most profoundly.

Think about your weekends in your marriage – not just the ones that stand out as special, but about the majority of your weekends. Chances are, if your marriage ended in divorce, there were many weekends in the last few years of your marriage that were filled with anger and discord, or perhaps silence and awkwardness. In reality, you may have dreaded your weekends. It is important to be an accurate recorder of your life experiences. Very often, we create fantasies of what once was and then we suffer over the loss of the fantasy!

Sometimes we feel afraid of the "gained time." After years of taking care of others, many women experience this "gained time" when children leave home for college, when a spouse dies, or there is a divorce or retirement.

"Gained time" is just what it suggests – time made available by a change in circumstances.

I hear women talk about "killing time." Why would anyone think they have time to "kill"? Life is not infinite. Each moment comes once and never again. We never know how many moments we have. Would you "kill time" if this were the last night of your life? How would you spend this night? What do YOU like to do? What do YOU need for yourself? How can you help YOU through this time?

"Gained Time" is a gift. It is an opportunity to try something new. Even if you loved the way your weekends used to be, the truth is that they have changed. You can either adjust to the change, and use the time in a pleasurable, productive way, or you can sit around and mope about the "good old days."

Today I will think about what I want to do with my next weekend without the children. I will set time aside to get some errands and cleaning done, but I will make time to do something I like, just for the sheer pleasure of it. I will learn that when I am by myself, I can be with myself. I am GREAT company!

Sometimes, women are filled with resentment that they have to "share" the kids with their ex-husband. Many women say that their ex-husbands do not deserve to have a relationship with the children. You may be furious at your ex-husband, but punishing him by withholding visitation only damages your children and denies them access to their father. The children didn't do anything wrong – why should they be punished? Many men feel anguish about not seeing their children on a day-to-day basis. They feel unfairly treated by the courts as custody usually goes to the mother. You could argue that he should have thought about that before he left *them*. Very unhappy men stayed for the sake of the children only to find that they became very unhappy fathers. This is not helpful to the children.

Next to you, no one loves your children more than their father. And don't forget your children's rights here. They have the right to have two parents who love them and with whom they can spend time. Family is not defined solely by living under the same roof. Children go off to college, marry, and pursue their own careers. This does not end the relationship between parent and child. Think about your own parents – you no longer live with them, but this doesn't mean you don't have a relationship. Families do not stop functioning because they live in separate homes. They stop functioning because they treat each other badly.

If substance abuse or alcoholism or violence is present in your ex-husband's life, visitation may not be possible. This doesn't mean that the children will not love their father or vice versa. It means that the parent is too sick to be able to parent. In such cases, the children's safety is always a primary consideration. However, barring these complications, let your children go with their father with grace and enthusiasm. Encouraging that relationship will support your children in ways that will have a positive outcome in the future. Furthermore, it gives you time for yourself. Some women, when brutally honest with themselves, admit that their hesitancy to encourage a relationship between their kids and their Dad is due to their own fear of being alone and not knowing what to do with themselves. Learn to embrace this time for yourself. If you must, think of your ex as the best baby sitter your kids will ever have. Next to you, no one loves them more.

Today I do not want to do anything harmful to my kids and denying them access to, or being reluctant or negative about, their father just hurts them. I will make a conscious effort to support their time with their father. Then I will use my "down time" to recharge and relax.

Detachment is about letting go of your need to have things turn out a certain way. In detachment, we pay more attention to our own needs rather than trying to fix or run everyone else's life. In Buddhist tradition, detachment involves giving up an attachment to a certain outcome. In Alcoholics Anonymous literature, detachment is about "Letting go and letting God." When you detach, you are not absenting yourself from the other person, you are attending to yourself. When you begin to use detachment in your life, life gets easier and you feel a lot healthier. When you are no longer trying to control everyone's behavior, you are more available to listen without judgment or criticism. You are not all wrapped up in having that other person act in the way you think you need them to act. You become less anxious. Detachment is about accepting that you can't control things that, in reality, are beyond your control.

For example, you cannot control or change someone else's drinking... only they can do that. When you accept that, you can use all your energy to focus on other things that are in your control. You can look at the options you have and put your energy into exploring your choices, choosing wisely, and following through. Detachment gives you the opportunity to focus on yourself.

When you are in the early stages of divorce, your thoughts and feelings focus on the transgressions of your estranged partner. You may hold endless inner dialogues with him. As you begin to move through both the emotional and legal stages of divorce, you may be aware that your thoughts and feelings are shifting inward. You begin to focus on your own life as your detachment from him strengthens. Detachment is difficult. We are in a culture that teaches us we can have everything we want, but some things are beyond our control. One of those things is other people's behavior.

Today I will try to practice detachment. I will stay focused on my choices. I no longer need to control someone else's behavior in order to find my own happiness. When I try to control things that are beyond my grasp, I feel helpless and out of control. When I let go of the impossible, I suddenly see that choices abound.

Some of the most difficult and unexpected results of divorce are the peripheral losses we don't anticipate. These losses directly or indirectly result from the break-up of the marriage. Some are expected and some are not. The ones that we don't expect are the ones that hit us the hardest.

The losses we expect:
- A change in relationship with our in-laws.
- Change in financial status.
- Not having another "grown up" in the house.
- Taking over the other person's chores/responsibilities.
- Not having a "built-in date."
- Someone to lift stuff.

Some unforeseen losses:
- The division of friendships.
- The loss of someone who shares your whole marital history.
- The loss of marital status.
- The loss of the dream.

Each divorce, like each marriage, has its own characteristics and its own unique losses. We like to think that we have all our bases covered. We like to know exactly what we are in for. The truth is, we simply can't imagine or plan for everything that will happen. If only we had a crystal ball!

There are stories where the wife's family sided with the husband, the husband's best friend ran off with his wife, or the wife's best friend turned against her and sided with the husband. It doesn't happen often. But if it happens to you, it is one time too many.

There is no way one can prepare for all the possible things that can go wrong. In life, we can't prepare for the unforeseen. What we can do is work on our strengths, our self-esteem, and build confidence that we can recover from disappointment.

Today rather than focus on all the unknowns and things that can go wrong, I will focus on my strengths with the conviction that whatever disappointments befall me, I will find a way through them with courage and grace.

Day 22 *Helping is the Sunny Side of Controlling*

"Really, I am just trying to help."

How many times have we said that? How many times has some one said it to us? Giving advice, making suggestions, criticizing, belittling, insulting, making fun of, are all manipulative methods we employ to get someone to change their behavior. We think we know what is best for someone else. After all, we are the great nurturers. This is for "their own good!"

Think of the times you behaved in "helping" ways and your spouse (or children, friends, family, boss) acted insulted or annoyed. Imagine if the shoe was on the other foot, and someone said those exact words to you. You may be saying, "Well, I would be grateful if they cared enough to say something." Certainly, we want to hear that we have spinach in our teeth, or that yellow looks awful on us. Those aren't the things I am referring to. I am referring to unsolicited advice, disapproval, or criticism. Would we really want to hear *those* things?

Sometimes, especially with a spouse or family member, our desire to "help" is really about our desire to change something to *the way we want it to be*. In other words, we have an investment in the other person changing. It may not be what they want. It is what WE want. This kind of helping is no longer about enhancing their lives. This is about our getting *our* desired outcome. And that is when helping becomes controlling. When we are controlling, we are no longer trustful or respectful. We are not respecting their choices and opinions.

As women, we talk a lot about being loved for who we are, not for how we look or what we do or what we say. We need to follow our own advice and behave that way toward others. Do you find yourself advising, directing, and orchestrating events, people or places for YOUR desired outcome? Do you feel frustrated, angry or resentful when your desired outcome is not met through other people's behavior?

Today I need to look at my own behavior as part of my growth process. I need to see when I am too quick to step in and offer comments, advice, and criticism. I need to be aware that when I do that, my behavior is controlling and not helpful. I will be mindful of my goals when I offer to "help."

When a couple does not have children, well-meaning friends and relatives often say, "It is a good thing you didn't have kids." While it is true that divorce is "less complicated" without children, there is a certain finality to divorce of the childless marriage. Women who didn't have children, while grateful in some ways that they did not have to put kids through the divorce, sometimes feel sad. Children can serve as a testimony to the marriage having "value." Children also serve as a way of staying connected.

When a couple divorces and there are no children, there is simply no reason for them to stay in touch. Women often grieve this, as it feels unimaginable to them that this person with whom they shared such an intimate connection will no longer be a part of their life. Furthermore, a childless couple who divorces is more apt to lose the connection with extended family and friends. This can compound the feelings of loss.

Well-meaning family and friends are often not sensitive to this experience. It is your responsibility to ask for what you need, explaining to them that the issues, while different from the marriage with children, are no less painful. Furthermore, it is critical not to minimize your own experience by letting others' opinions distort your own grief.

Divorce is never easy, whether there were children or not. The issues are different, but placing judgment on which is "more difficult" undermines the process and invalidates the experience.

Today I will grieve for all the losses in my marriage, even if others have difficulty validating my experience. This was my marriage; my grief and pain are uniquely mine. I will ask for support from people who can accept my process without judgment or qualification.

The first divorce group I facilitated was back in the mid 1980's. This group was comprised of seven women between the ages of forty-five and sixty-five. Some had never worked outside the home. One woman didn't drive. Another had never written a check. One woman suffered from chronic migraines. All of the women had grown children and they had stayed home to raise their families. All of them had been left for younger women.

Pain, anger, bitterness, sorrow, devastation, and depression were some, but certainly not all, of the emotions these women felt. Weekly, they began to share their stories and their heartache. They comforted, consoled, and heard each other. They cried and even laughed.

Then something amazing happened. They began to share their experiences, not just of their marriages, but about their lives and their hopes and dreams. They became strengthened by each other's support. They pooled their talents. They mobilized. They began to plan outings. They had Christmas celebrations. They celebrated their first Father's Day as single women by going sailing. They grew stronger, wiser, and more confident.

The group met weekly, then bi-weekly, and finally monthly. After about three years, they knew they were ready to move on. The group ended, but the friendships did not. Now, many years later, I am still in touch with some of the women and many are still in touch with each other. They have seen each other through their ex-husbands' remarriages and, in some cases, their ex-husbands' funerals. Their children have married. They have grandchildren. Some of the women have remarried. They were brought together by tragedy and turned it into a victory. These were The Magnificent Seven.

I continue to run groups for women going through divorce. Each group is special. Each is electric with its own power and energy. When women come together to support each other, magical things can happen. We strengthen each other and we empower. We nurture and we applaud. We laugh and cry. And we help each other heal. Each group is magnificent in their own way!

Today I will think of how I am magnificent. I will listen for the magnificence in other women. Rather than feel jealous or envious, I will see my magnificence reflected in their being.

Day 25   The Brain Sees What the Heart Wants to Feel

Frequently, we struggle with the chasm between what exists in our marriages and what we want! We make excuses for inappropriate behavior. We deny, comply, ignore, rationalize, and minimize. We look the other way, and invalidate our own needs. We do this because we want to be loved. We want desperately for our relationship to work. Our investment is huge. The desire for our preconceived outcome drives us. So, we accept the unacceptable, we diminish our own needs, and we deny our truth. We let our feelings dictate to our intellect. We let our emotions run our thoughts and we surrender our power. And when we do this, we set ourselves up for disappointment.

When you chose this man to marry, what was happening in your life? Were you tired of being single? Were you pressured by family and cultural mores? Were you afraid you wouldn't meet anyone else? These fears cloud our judgment and distort our decision making process. Relationship choices made from fear are destined not to work.

"Why is it important now?" you may ask, "I am getting divorced from him, what difference does it make?"

It can make a huge difference. As you make decisions now in the uncoupling of your marriage, be aware of the role your emotions play. If you denied your needs in the marriage because of fear, be cautious not to do that again in your divorce. Learn to advocate for yourself, not based on fear, but from a sense of self-worth.

If anger is dictating how you proceed in your divorce, consider whether that is the best way to make a decision. Do not let your need for revenge push you into behaving badly or making impulsive decisions. You will regret this later. Learning how to deal with your feelings during your divorce will help strengthen all your relationships. And if you choose to remarry, the awareness of how your feelings impact your life will clear the way for smarter, healthier choices.

Today I will pay close attention to the way things really are. I will push through my desire to view them as I want them to be. I will allow my brain to work without interference from my heart. If I want to make good decisions, I know they must come from my head. I will talk quietly and gently to my fear and anger, but I will not give it the power to create chaos in my life.

From Ex-Wife to Exceptional Life

The following is an excerpt from the newsletter, *Harvard Women's Health Watch*, November 2001.

If you aren't recovering from a setback as rapidly as you'd like, your resilience may be impaired. Impaired resilience is one sign of depression, a condition that robs us of self-esteem, energy to meet challenges, and faith in life. Depression, which affects about 25 percent of women at some time in their lives can be successfully treated in 80 to 90 percent of cases. To a degree, resilience is inborn – resilient adults were often resilient in childhood. But it is possible to strengthen this trait. If you want to be more resilient, consider the following:

- **Let your true self shine through.** Authenticity is central to resilience. If you spent a lifetime cultivating a "face for the world" – perhaps to accommodate others or mesh with societal ideals – showing your true feelings may not be easy. Friends, support groups, or professional counseling can help.

- **Accept responsibility for your life.** Make decisions that affirm your values and standards. Recognize that while some things are beyond your control, you can still influence many situations. This helps counter resentment, fear, and the ability to forgive.

- **Stay connected.** Renew your interest in life and those around you. Keep abreast of political, cultural, economic, and technological developments so you understand and can adapt to the world we live in.

- **Accept Change.** It is a given. The variable lies in our response.

- **Practice your beliefs.** If your strength springs from religion, try deepening your involvement in your faith community, or spend more time in prayer or meditation. Take part in pursuits that uplift your spirit, whether that's the arts, outdoor activities, or something else. Explore opportunities to volunteer – helping others may be the best way of healing ourselves.

Today I will think of myself as a resilient woman. I will look at the above five areas of my life without judgment or blame and I will pick one to focus on today. I will think about it throughout my day.

If the children are still grieving the divorce, then dating when your children are with their father is a way to avoid flaunting your social life in their face. It is important eventually for children to see their parents having a social life, going out with friends or to classes or meetings. This gives children a sense of how a well-rounded adult manages her life. You role model balance for them: between being a mother and being a woman with your own interests. Some women feel guilty taking time for themselves when the children are with them. "I only have them with me part-time. Shouldn't I devote all my time to them?"

You are your children's primary role model and the messages you give them about parenting and women will resonate throughout their lives. Do you want your female children to grow up thinking that when they have children, they cannot pursue other interests? Do you want your male children to grow up thinking the women they marry should devote their life solely to raising a family? Of course not. We are raising tomorrow's parents, wives, and husbands. Our behavior is a primer for their expectations, philosophy, and behavior in their own relationships.

The converse is also true. Going out all the time provides a negative message and simultaneously deprives them of their much-needed time with you. Even older children and teenagers need the consistency and security of having you just be *there*.

Parenting is probably the most important job in the world and carries with it enormous responsibility. Equilibrium is never easy. As a single parent, it can be difficult to strike that delicate balance. Flexibility, awareness, communication with your children, and paying attention to your own needs are a few of the ingredients that can help you find what works best in your family.

Today am I doing the best I can to manage a balance between my children's needs and my own? Do I make time for myself? Or am I constantly at their beck and call, trying to "make up" for the divorce? Or am I out so much, whether for work, school, or social life that I am not as available as I need to be? I will consider whether my life feels in balance. After careful scrutiny, if I find things are out of kilter, I will not hesitate to work toward bringing them more into balance.

Are people telling you that you do too much?

All of life's challenges come with stress. While we can handle the challenges, most of us could do with a little less! So, just for today, lighten up! Everything that is pending can wait. Today, rather than adding something else to your plate to work on, or grow from, or gain insight from, I offer you laughter. Time to kick back, read a couple of great one-liners and then go out and share them with a friend. I have heard it said that the shortest distance between two people is laughter. Here are some tools to help you shorten the distance. Have fun!

"When women are depressed they either eat or go shopping. Men invade another country." – *Elayne Boosler*

"Behind every successful man is a surprised woman."– *Maryon Pearson*

"I never married because there was no need. I have three pets at home which answer the same purpose as a husband. I have a dog which growls every morning, a parrot which swears all afternoon and a cat that comes home late at night."– *Marie Corelli*

"I base most of my fashion taste on what doesn't itch."– *Gilda Radner*

"Sometimes I wonder if men and women really suit each other. Perhaps they should live next door and just visit now and then." – *Katharine Hepburn*

"In politics, if you want anything said, ask a man; if you want anything done, ask a woman." – *Margaret Thatcher*

"Nagging is the repetition of unpalatable truths." – *Baroness Edith Summerskill*

"If men can run the world, why can't they stop wearing neckties? How intelligent is it to start the day by tying a little noose around your neck?"– *Linda Ellerbee*

Today taking a time out from all my worries and stress cannot hurt me. In fact, it may help. Humor can help rejuvenate me with rest, renewed strength, and hope. It can infuse my being like a healthy dose of vitamins for the soul.

Births, deaths, christenings, bar mitzvahs, weddings and divorces are all rites of passage in our lives. They are significant events that we mark with family, community, and food. The wedding is the birth date of the marriage and divorce signifies the day it died. Both events have major significance in our lives and both events need to be acknowledged. Many divorced women feel ambivalent about these two dates as they grower nearer on the calendar.

As a woman having gone through divorce, your wedding date may be a sad and contemplative day. How does it impact you? Do you still count the years? Or do you merely acknowledge the day for a moment and move on? Or do you acknowledge the day of the divorce and ignore the wedding day?

However you deal with these two days, they are uniquely yours. Some women find the first year after the divorce is the most difficult one but with each year; the memories blur as does the pain.

If an anniversary occurs before the divorce is final, both parties can find themselves in an awkward situation. Do we send a card? Do we ignore it? While there is no right or wrong, it is probably healthiest to share your feelings with a person other than your soon to be ex-spouse. Do you have any expectations about how he will behave toward you? Remember that just because you have an expectation, does not mean another person can or will fulfill it. To continue to count on his meeting that expectation can set you up for even more disappointment.

Celebrate a new anniversary. Rather than saying "This would have been our __ anniversary if we were together," try saying it on the anniversary of the divorce.

"This celebrates my __ year as a single person." That may feel awkward at first, but looking at the glass as half full instead of half empty can have positive effects on how you see your life. It may take time. Rejoicing in what you have, rather than mourning what you had, will keep you filled with gratitude rather than regret.

Today I know that anniversaries serve as markers in my journey. When I think of my wedding anniversary, I will think of ways I can honor the marriage experience without sentimentalizing it. I will focus on learning how to rejoice for what **was**, but also how to enjoy and appreciate **what is**.

As they start to feel better and the roller coaster ride of emotions starts to level out, many women begin to look at how far they have come. New insight into themselves and their relationships give them a sense of strength and empowerment. However, even though they are feeling stronger, they are concerned that they may lose some of the ground they have gained. They are afraid they will lose their footing and regress.

Remember those exercises we did long ago in kindergarten to help us develop perspective? They were in every *Highlights* magazine. There would be a picture for us to study. Hidden in the picture would be all kinds of other objects, out of place and obscure, so we would have to search for them. Usually there would be a list: "look for the book, the cat, the umbrella, the boot," and so on.

I remember struggling to find those hidden objects. I would find the book, the cat, and the umbrella fairly easily. But then that boot, the elusive boot, I just couldn't find it! I would turn the page all different ways and then… there it was! I would be so excited, yet afraid that if I took my eyes off it, I wouldn't be able to locate it again.

But of course, I always could. Once we learn something, it is ours forever. Once we have the perspective and perception, we really can't lose it, even if we want to. As you develop insight, it becomes part of you forever. It is not something you forget. You own it.

Today I will cherish all my new insights, and rejoice in the knowing that they are mine to keep. No one can take them away from me.

Notes

Month Eleven

...then we continue to see the world through the eyes of a child."

— Anais Nin

Do you emotionally shrink at the thought of having to confront an authority figure? Does the idea of having to ask someone for help cause you to panic? Does the thought of complaining about a service or product make you recoil with anxiety? Why do competent, high-functioning women turn childlike in some situations? Consider the people who make you anxious. Often they are people whom you perceive as having more power than you do. When you ascribe traits of power to someone, you then see them as authority figures.

Some authority figures in our lives include:

- People older than we are.
- People whose opinion matters to us.
- People who can really make our life difficult.
- People who we want to like us.
- People we admire.
- People who intimidate us.

These can include parents, bosses, co-workers, family, friends, attorneys, therapists, car mechanics, hairdressers, neighbors, even our children. Anyone whom you feel has more power than you do, can intimidate! Think of the most intimidating person in your life. What power do they hold over you? The people whom we see as powerful are really people we give power to. In reality, it is our perception of them which enhances their power. We actually create our own intimidating experience.

We all want approval and validation. Most of us really hate confrontation. But what is our alternative? Not speaking up only reinforces a sense of powerlessness. If we have relationships in our life in which we will truly be hurt for speaking up, either physically or emotionally, then perhaps we need to reconsider the value of these relationships. Why do you stay in that kind of relationship? Why would you allow yourself to be victimized?

Today I will consider the relationships in my life that result in my feeling childlike. What can I do to change this? What am I afraid of? Is my fear really warranted? Can I practice my assertiveness and speak up? Or is it truly a relationship that threatens me with harm? If that is so, I still have choices about this relationship. I always have choices. I am an adult, and not a child. When I exercise my choice, I feel empowered and whole.

When is a difference of opinion really a problem? I have seen couples fight over things as trivial as how to fold socks or the "correct" way to make turkey stuffing.

If in your family of origin, you were not taught tolerance for ways different from your own, then you will find you probably have difficulty in most relationships. I do not mean to imply that all differences are acceptable! Certainly some things will be (and should be) unacceptable. While they may differ for each person according to their value system, there are some universal differences that are always problems in a marriage or relationship. These include violence, substance abuse, dishonesty, and disrespect.

You may have been too tolerant in your marriage, trying to dismiss differences that were substantial in a desire to keep your relationship intact. This may have led to your feeling devalued. Or you may have been very uncomfortable with even the smallest difference. Any departure from the familiar may have caused you discomfort.

If you are over-accepting, especially of unacceptable behavior, your work involves building your self-esteem and exploring why you have difficulty expressing and advocating for yourself. If on the other hand, you experience every difference as a problem, then your work involves learning tolerance, flexibility and facing your fears.

Today I will consider the things I found objectionable in my marriage. Did every difference between us create tension for me? Or did I continually accept everything without any regard to my own preferences? I will explore my own style. Doing this will help me clarify my own style in relationship and help me identify what is truly important to me.

Perhaps there is no symbol more laden with meaning for women than their wedding ring. Inevitably, when a divorce is imminent, the question arises – when is it appropriate to remove my ring?

The time to remove your wedding ring varies. Women who experience betrayal often feel the marriage ended at that moment. They may feel that to continue to wear the ring is hypocritical. Other women entertain taking it off when divorce papers are filed or served.

Still others feel married until the divorce is legally finalized. Others continue to wear their ring long after the divorce, especially if they did not want the divorce or if they feel that, for religious reasons, the divorce is invalid. Some women continue to wear it as a way to avoid questions at the office. It provides them with a sense of security and it wards off future suitors! Still other women continue to wear their ring, but transfer it to the other hand or wear it on a chain around their neck.

The point is that there is no "right" time to take it off. If the ring is an important symbol for you, then the act of removing it should mean something, as well. Do this mindfully, not in anger. Do it when there is acceptance and inner understanding. Do it as an affirmation of your single status. It doesn't have to just mark the end of the marriage; it can symbolize the beginning of your commitment to yourself, "to love, honor and cherish" yourself.

Today I will consider what my ring means to me and when it is appropriate to take it off. I will acknowledge it reflects the end of something, but that it also can symbolize my new single status. I will work just as hard to be a good companion to myself as I worked to be a good companion to my spouse. I know more now and I have more to offer myself than ever before. All the things I learned about myself through both my marriage and divorce will now provide clues and insight on how to "be" with myself.

Finding out that your ex is dating someone can elicit a number of conflicted feelings. From the outside looking in, it can seem as if, in this relationship, he is doing all the things that he could not, or would not do for you. Based on that assumption, you jump right to the next one, which goes something like this:

- Why can he do those things for her?
- She gets the best years of his life.
- Why wasn't I good enough?
- Now he is everything I always wanted.
- Maybe I made a mistake.

You create your own hell with all those assumptions. If you think back to the beginning of your relationship, it probably looked pretty much like this new one does. People are always at their best at the beginning. You are creating your own feelings of loss and inadequacy by:

- Comparing the end of a relationship with the beginning of a relationship. A new relationship doesn't begin unless it is good and an old one doesn't end unless it was bad!

- Assigning meaning to certain behaviors you see. The truth is, you probably do not have a lot of information about what the relationship is and you are assuming that your observations have a certain meaning.

- You are looking at your ex, who probably (like you) has lost weight and bought some new clothes through this process. He may have joined a gym with his new free time. He is looking good. Don't be fooled. (Because the outside changed, doesn't mean the inside has as well.)

Unless he took the time to figure out what went wrong and accept responsibility for his part of the divorce, his new relationship will eventually begin to resemble the old relationship. She isn't getting the improved model; she is getting the recycled one. There is the possibility that he is working on changing. Well, so are you. Rather than spend your time worrying about it, you have work to do. Learn what went wrong and how you might do things differently in the future. This will diminish the sting of divorce and create something strong and useful for you. Sometimes good people are bad for each other. Rather than denigrate yourself or spend your time obsessing, learn to refocus your mind on your own issues and self-awareness.

Today I must let go of creating scenarios in my head about my husband and his new relationship. That is simply not healthy for me. When I feel myself starting to ruminate about the two of them, I will refocus my energy on myself. When I think about him so much, I continue to give him too much power. I will learn to divorce myself from my own unhealthy thoughts.

Day 5   Memorial Day, Labor Day, and Fourth of July

Memorial Day, Labor Day and Fourth of July are holidays that celebrate different aspects of American culture. Memorial Day honors those who fought to defend our principles and ideals, Labor Day honors our work ethic, and Fourth of July honors our fight for independence. We don't consider them "Big Holidays." They are, for most of us, times to be outdoors, watch some fireworks, and eat lots of good food. They also give us an extended weekend.

For the newly-divorced woman, however, these holidays can take on great significance. You, too, have been fighting for your principles, working hard, and struggling with your newfound independence. No three holidays in our calendar reflect your struggle as these three do. Since we do not have a specific holiday that honors those who have been through the struggle of divorce, adopt these as your three days. Memorial Day honors your fight to preserve your ideals and principles. Labor Day represents your struggle to juggle all the roles and responsibilities in your life, and the Fourth of July, like divorce, is about freedom and independence.

You work hard to be your best and to have the best life you can. Our nation celebrates these ideals which are intrinsic to our culture. These days also celebrate each person's internal struggle. Our personal struggles may not feel grand to others, but if you are going through divorce, you know it can be hell. Honoring your struggle and your courage also honors your strength and your ethics. On one of these bright, fun-filled days of celebration, take a moment to honor your resolve and your growth. When you wave the flag, watch the fireworks, or attend the picnic, take a moment to remember your contributions to the world, our nation and in your own life.

Today my life may be changing in ways that are not completely clear to me. When I watch the fireworks, I will remember not only the sacrifices others have made for freedom, but also those I have made. I do this to insure a better life for myself and the ones I love.

Perhaps no day is more poignant after marital separation than your child's birthday. This day evokes memories of other birthdays and of the birth itself. Celebrating a child's birthday after a recent separation illuminates in a powerful way how much the family structure has changed. Once, this day was filled with a sense of closeness and connection between you and your child's father. The contrast can be drastic and harsh.

Often this is a day on which the parents' battle escalates. Each parent stakes their claim to the child and their entitlement to direct the festivities. The tension does have a negative impact on the child. Even if he/she is not directly exposed to the arguments, the tenor of your voice, the lack of patience, the slamming of doors, the pursed lips and the heavy sighing all cue your child into the conflict between the two people he loves most in the world. Not a great birthday gift, huh?

A good rule of thumb is that for the first year after separation, the birthday celebration be held in accordance with past traditions. So, if you always had a family party, do that. If you always had a child's party, do that. If possible, having both the father and mother present gives the child the message that the parents can get along for his sake. That is the best birthday present any child could have. This, of course, means that if the father has moved out, he now is coming back into the home as a guest. He should act cordially and polite toward you. You should maintain the air of a gracious hostess. To do any less would ruin your child's celebration. If you were the one who moved out, then you will be the guest in the father's house and roles will be reversed. If there is violence or so much acrimony that the two of you absolutely cannot be in the same room, then have two celebrations. No child feels it is a hardship to have two parties, two sets of presents, and two birthday cakes! Most children feel that two birthday celebrations is one of the best things about being from a divorced family.

The fairest way to manage this tug-of-war over birthdays is to alternate who has the child on the birthday. Have birthday celebrations on the weekends; one parent can hold the celebration the weekend before the actual birthday and one parent, the weekend after. No child is going to feel deprived by that schedule.

Today the best birthday gift I can give my child is the cooperation of his parents. He will remember how we behaved long after the toys are discarded and the cake is eaten. It is his day and I will not lose sight that this is my priority.

If you are the non-custodial parent, you may feel as if you are having difficulty connecting with your children in such limited time. Many non-custodial parents become "Disneyland" parents. They try to make the weekend into a vacation by minimizing discipline and boundaries. Many feel it is difficult to really "parent" in a short period of time so they treat their child like a "buddy." While this may feel easier and more comfortable, your child already has buddies and really needs his mother (and father)! Furthermore, if you spend all your visitation weekends catering to your children's whims, you may find that you resent those weekends as your children expect more and more.

Creating worthwhile bonding experiences is the key to connection. Problem-solving exercises are used in organizational psychology to create a more cohesive work team. This is also effective with the parent/child relationship. The bonding experience needs to be an activity that the child is invested in. Hanging curtains or going furniture shopping together may feel more like a chore than a bonding experience.

Experts recommend an "outward bound" kind of experience in which you are dependent upon each other to problem-solve against a common foe - in this case, nature. A wilderness trek puts you in a situation where you rely on each other out of necessity. The bonding comes naturally. You build mutual respect and positive memories. The experience also builds character, strength, and self-confidence.

Not every weekend needs to be a challenge of such immense proportions. However, every weekend cannot be about movies, candy, video games, miniature golf, and toy shopping. You can achieve a bonding experience by taking a camping trip, a long hike, or learning a sport together. Take up sailing or kayaking, or rent a canoe. Your child may groan and resist at first, but chances are he/she will get into it and the payoff for both of you will be enormous. For younger, or less able-bodied children, try an art project together.

Create a mobile or a mural in their bedroom. Build a sandcastle or a snow fort. Try cooking together. Challenge your child to use his intellect, to engage his problem-solving capabilities, to learn to work with you. Identify a mutually desired goal and work as a team. This will build a connection and a bond that will last a lifetime. It will also take the focus off of indulgences and discipline. It will involve you both in a way that will teach you about each other and yourselves.

Today I will consider what kind of bonding experiences I can create for myself and my child. I can consult books on parenting, ask a child therapist, or even the school counselor for some good ideas which fit both my budget and circumstances. I can be excited at the prospect of trying something new and fun.

"As I watched my children wait at the window for their father to arrive, I couldn't believe the flood of feelings I experienced," Julie, thirty-eight, a divorced mother of two boys, seven and nine, explained. "Their father is taking them to New York with his girlfriend. Her parents own a large summer house in the Adirondacks. She has six brother and sisters, all married with children. They are all coming this week for a family reunion.

As an only child raised in a large city, I never had this kind of experience. I am excited for my children that they can have all these new people in their lives. They will get the experience of a large family. I find myself wishing that I could give them such an experience. I wonder if they will love this new family more than they love me. Of course, I know this is not the case. But sometimes, I feel so insecure.

I guess I am also envious of their experience. In some ways, I wish I were going, too. Not to be with my ex-husband, but to have this wonderful family experience that I never had growing up. I also realize that the kids will share this experience and these memories with him and I will not be a part of it. It is hard not to feel excluded and left out. I even thought about not letting them go, but I know that would be based on my issues and not what is best for the children."

Julie eloquently describes what many divorced mothers feel: although no longer emotionally attached to their ex-husbands, they have mixed feelings as their children begin to have life experiences that do not include them. She feels threatened, envious, left out, a little angry, and a bit melancholy. She explores these feelings and then begins to shift her focus.

"I need this week to myself. The truth is that when we were married, I never got breaks like this. I could never have gone back to school while we were still together." Julie is working on her nursing degree, something she has always wanted to do. "This week gives me time to really study for the Boards. I also plan to have some down time. I don't know when the last time was that I had time to myself. Although I am sad every time my children's father picks them up, I am also relieved to have the time to myself. When my children are away, I get to focus on myself. I think, in the long run, it has made me a better parent. I have more patience and I am better able to focus on their needs. I don't feel as resentful as I once did, needing to put everyone else's desires and needs before my own.

I didn't always feel this way. I was wild when he left me. But in time, I learned that it was for the best and just as I began accepting that, BAM!, he found a girlfriend. Through the support of my friends and therapist, I was able to recognize that we are both moving on with our lives. His new girlfriend is wonderful with my kids and they have a great time with her. They adore having this big family that they didn't have with their father or me. I used to worry that they would forget about me. Now I see how silly that was. They are overjoyed to come home from their visits, no matter how much fun they have had. I know now that I am their Mom and that will never, ever change. When he left, I could never have imagined I would ever feel so good."

Today I feel so many emotions when my children go away with their father. They are experiencing things which I am not a part of. While that makes me sad, I am grateful for the opportunities they have to see and experience new things. In the meantime, I will treasure my downtime, focusing on what I need to do for myself.

Meeting the challenge of any crisis involves thinking about it in different ways, some of which may be considered a little, well, crazy. However some of the most creative minds in history earned the title of "Crazy"! Innovative thought is often eschewed or even condemned. When people see opportunities to do things a new way and others do not share their vision, they are often labeled crazy or eccentric.

Without imagination, some of the greatest inventions would not have occurred and some of the greatest discoveries would never have happened. Christopher Columbus was laughed at when he said the world was round. No one believed the Wright brothers would actually fly. Look to the ever-changing technological world of today for a myriad of astounding examples of vision becoming reality.

Creative thought does not just happen. One must train oneself to think creatively. Puzzles, art projects, and word games all help nurture our creativity. Being creative allows us to "think outside the box," to come up with options and solutions that may not occur to anyone else. Creative challenges also help us avoid becoming too rigid in our thinking. As we age, exercising our brain keeps our mind supple and flexible. Maintaining a flexible mind keeps us resilient, resourceful, and empowered.

Creative practice is necessary in finding unique ways of dealing with our problems. It also can be fun. Here's an example of a creative question you can use to stretch your imagination:

> If your husband were a car, what kind would he be? What color and what year would he be? Would he be fast or slow? Would he be shiny or rusty? Would the inside of the car be immaculate or would there be soda cans and candy wrappers everywhere? Would the engine be well-maintained?

Playing with the above image can help you develop your creativity and flexibility. It can help you see things a different way. It can help you relax and laugh a little.

Today When I am stuck in traffic, rather than get cranky and anxious or start worrying, I will see all the cars in the traffic jam as other women's husbands. As I drive along, I will look for the car that most resembles MY husband. How nice it is to take a break from all my obsessing and worrying! How refreshing to stretch my imagination and have some fun!

For years you may have thought of yourself only as "Wife" or "Mother." Sometimes we can lose sight of the person we are. One way to learn more about yourself is by writing a personal ad, but not to put on-line or in the newspaper (at least not yet!). Think about how you would describe yourself to someone who has never met you. The purpose of this exercise is to reconnect with who you are.

Try to keep it down to 100 words. Having trouble getting started? Then browse some ads in the newspaper or on-line to get the "feel" of this assignment. Start with the basics: age, religion, a brief physical description (yes, you can and WILL say nice things about yourself!). Then go on to describe the person you are, the things you like to do, and what things are important to you.

"What is the purpose of this?" you may ask yourself. It is important that you spend time thinking about yourself as an individual. Look at yourself as the individual you are and the individual you hope to be. Explore who you are and how you perceive yourself. Examine what you have to offer.

This is a good exercise to do with a friend. Read your ads OUT LOUD to each other. One of the goals is to get comfortable with yourself and build your confidence. Seeing and hearing your own words will help build confidence. Don't dwell on the negative, you probably know those aspects very well. Accentuate the positive. State your thoughts honestly and with care. What do you really like about yourself? What do you like to do? What are your strengths?

When you read your ad out loud, you may feel yourself embarrassed. Notice how it feels to say nice things; notice your friend's response. Part of the healing process is about reclaiming your self-worth. Divorce erodes our self-esteem and distorts our perspective. This exercise is about reclaiming those positive parts of yourself. Do this exercise periodically. When you look back on all past attempts, you will begin to see your confidence growing. Over time, the ad will reflect a more positive, confident you!

Today I may feel silly writing a personal ad, but it is fun and healing to be silly. I will approach my ad with light-heartedness and optimism. I will acknowledge this is difficult and enlist a friend for support in the process. There is a lot to be learned from trying new things. This is one of those opportunities.

Anna felt conflicted about being with family and friends when the decision to divorce had not yet been announced. She felt like a fraud having to maintain the posture that "everything was fine" and that they were "one big happy family." She and her husband decided to wait until after her sister's wedding to break their news. "I feel like such a hypocrite, but I really don't want to ruin my sister's wedding. I guess I have to just suck it up and make believe," Anna said.

Unfortunately, there is no convenient time to divorce. Most couples find there is a "lag time" between making the decision to divorce and announcing it. Often, family considerations, holidays, or celebrations are cited as reason for the delay. How do you manage this period and interact with family and friends without feeling the extraordinary weight of duplicity? No one wants to behave hypocritically. Feeling one way and acting another are very difficult. In fact, to do so is not healthy, either emotionally or physically. In waiting until after her sister's wedding to break the news of her divorce to the family, Anna was being very considerate. But is there a way to be considerate and still be authentic?

When asked how you are doing, there is no reason to have to lie and say, "Oh, we are wonderful and life is glorious." Why not say something like, "Well, this is a tough time of year," or "We are going through some difficult times now." In being more up front, you will find you have less of a struggle. After all, pretending is awfully hard work! Often, when we relax enough just to acknowledge how we feel, without the details, we can actually find this authenticity opens the way to glean some enjoyment and pleasure from our present situation. If pressed for details, you can simply say, "I am not comfortable getting into that right now. But thanks for your concern."

We can be true to our feelings and still honor our need for privacy. They are not mutually exclusive goals.

Today when I think about facing family and friends before I am ready to share my news, I will be mindful that I can be authentic with my feelings without sharing details. When I am authentic with others, I am more connected to them and to myself. I do not need to add the additional stress of disconnection and secrecy to my life.

What does it mean to love too much? It means that you put *all* your love, caring, thought, and time into another person. It means always putting his needs first. Listed below are some characteristics of women who love too much:

- May have come from a dysfunctional home where your emotional needs were not met.
- Having had little nurturing yourself, you try and fill this need vicariously by becoming a caretaker of another, usually a needy man.
- Having had emotionally unavailable parents, emotionally unavailable men feel "familiar" and "comfortable," while still causing you feelings of pain and rejection.
- Terrified of abandonment, you will do anything to keep the relationship from dissolving.
- Nothing is too much trouble. You give him money, buy him clothes, find him a job, find him a therapist, make excuses for his emotional abuse, give him possessions, and give him a place to live.
- Accustomed to not getting much in personal relationships, you are comfortable with waiting and hoping for change.
- You blame yourself for everything. You also take all the responsibility for the relationship and feel guilty a lot of the time.
- Your self-esteem is critically low.
- You mask your attempts at controlling men by being "helpful."
- By being drawn into the chaotic problems of others, you keep from focusing on responsibility for yourself.
- You find kind, stable, reliable men boring.
- You mistake chaos for passion.
- You have a tendency toward episodes of depression, which you seek to forestall with the excitement of an unstable relationship.
- You may be predisposed to abusing alcohol, drugs, and food.

Today I will consider the above list. Do I identify with some of the attributes/behaviors of a woman who loves too much? If so, I may have found the answer to my suffering. Just knowing that puts me on a path to healing. I know there are books, groups, therapists who can help me on my journey. For today, I will just work on acceptance and affirmation. Identifying myself as a woman who loves too much can help me understand my feelings and behavior. It is the beginning of a whole new way of being. When I make the effort to love myself as much as I love others, I will be confident and happy with my life, my choices, and myself.

In a frustrated voice, Kathy described her relationship with Jane.

> "My best friend and I have been very close for ten years. We spoke every day and shared all of life's ups and downs. She was like a sister to me. I know she is going through some bad times now. She and her husband are splitting up, but she never returns my calls. I am hurt and angry. I can't believe she dumped me." "Well," I inquired, "Have you tried speaking with her about what you are feeling?" "Oh, yes," she replied, in great pain, "I have called her repeatedly and she rejects all my invitations. Now I am so tired of asking her to do stuff that I simply refuse to call her anymore."

I thought about this for a moment and tried to imagine this conversation between two old friends, which continuously resulted in, one of them, maybe both of them, getting hurt.

> "What is it that you keep asking her?" I pressed on gently. "I keep asking her to do stuff. You know, go to the movies, or kayaking, or shopping. She keeps turning me down." "So you invite her out and she always declines the invitation. Have you told her how this feels for you?" "Of course not. How can I trust her with my feelings?"

Kathy, although well-intended, was simply asking the wrong question. What she wants is not really to *do* things with her friend, she wants reassurance that they *are* still friends. Her friend is going through a tough time, and may not be available to participate in activities. But she may be very much in need of a heart-to-heart talk with her friend. I was wondering if her friend also felt abandoned and betrayed.

Because we are afraid to ask the "real" question, we ask around it. Then we get an unsatisfactory answer. Frustration and misunderstanding take root and a chasm begins to grow. Lack of trust and fear of rejection inhibited Kathy from asking the right question. In trying to avoid a painful response, paradoxically, her inaccurate question elicited just that. Kathy explored what it was she really needed to ask. She recognized that she needed reassurance and a renewed sense of intimacy, not a kayaking expedition. Her insight freed her to ask the more appropriate question and the response from her friend was more positive. Jane had also missed their closeness and was feeling disappointed that she was receiving offers to "do something" not to "feel something." This cleared the air. The women found they were able to connect again and their friendship was strengthened by this experience.

Today if I ask the right question, there is a far better chance of my receiving what I need.

For many women, their greatest fear is of the unknown. Divorce always produces a state of apprehension, because there are so many unknowns. Sometimes we resist changes that are good for us because of our fear. Sometimes we want to make changes, but feel paralyzed by what feels like enormous effort.

Divorce shakes up our habitual way of being in the world. It shakes it up in a BIG way. Suddenly, everything is in flux and may seem out of control. Anxiety about our future escalates. The things we counted on to bring us solace and peace are disrupted or no longer have meaning. The predictability and dependability of our lives is in constant tumult. We become shaken to our core when we consider all the changes that lie ahead. The natural propensity may be to cling tenaciously to what is known, to become even more rigid. We fall into a slump, without even knowing it. We meander through our lives, going through the motions of chores and obligations, often without really having a sense of what we are doing.

Let's try to loosen things up a bit by making small, conscious changes. For example, try getting out of bed on the *other* side. Or, if you brush your teeth before you shower, try brushing them after instead. Try taking a different route to work, or wearing your hair in a different way. Notice how these changes feel. Notice your mind as it rebels against them. Notice how you long to revert to the familiar.

Some things feel uncomfortable to change, even if you have no attachment to them. It can even feel uncomfortable to change when you are changing for the better. By making small, conscious changes, your body and mind get comfortable with the notion of change. Making a few conscious changes every day, you become more flexible. As a result, changes will not be so frightening or upsetting. Try sticking to the same change for a number of days and see how long it takes for the change to be integrated into your routine.

Today I will make a few mindful, deliberate changes in my routine. I will notice my resistance without judgment. By doing this daily, I will increase my emotional flexibility and decrease my fear. I will learn that change is manageable and I will replace my fear with courage and grace.

Through our life, we encounter difficult people. We may argue with them, fall silent, comply or take distance. In a divorce, particularly an acrimonious one, difficult behaviors abound. No one is on their best behavior under this amount of stress. Figuring out how to cope with difficult behavior is a bit easier once we identify why the person behaves as he does and what he hopes to accomplish. Here is a list of the most common behaviors that frustrate us all, and suggestions for dealing with them:

The Bully – *uses temper tantrums to overwhelm you, makes insulting and cutting remarks. Needs to feel superior and not lose control of the situation. Wants to get his own way.* Stand up, listen, do not attack back, and take time-outs. Keep to the agenda.

The Complainer – *gripes about everything incessantly. Needs to keep looking like a victim, not take any responsibility, tries to bring others down to make himself look/feel better.* Listen. Try to pin down specific complaints. Offer no apology. Ask "How do you think we could fix this?"

The Silent Type – *the most response you get is "nope," "maybe" and "I don't know." Needs to punish, hurt and control. Also may be evading resolution as a way to maintain power.* Try a direct approach to the behavior. "I cannot read your mind, so there are things you need to tell me." Do not badger or nag. Set a time limit, and then walk away. Part of the reward for being silent is the constant attention and urging. Do not reward the behavior with this response.

The Promiser – *agrees with everything but then doesn't follow through on anything. Needs to be liked and accepted by everyone.* Try saying, "I really want to know what is on your mind."

The Wet Blanket – *finds something wrong with everything. Tries to deflate your optimism. "It will never work" is their battle cry. Wants power and control over your life. Is threatened when you feel good about something.* Do not argue. Do not get drawn into a power struggle. Do not ask for advice from this person.

The Staller – *afraid to make a mistake. They never can decide on anything. They stall a major decision until it is made for them. Their sense of self is often tied to getting approval from others.* Do not become irritated. Examine the facts and work on problem-solving. Let them talk about conflict in decision making.

The Big Shot – *the "know it all." Condescending, imposing and pompous. Sometimes doesn't know what he's talking about, but thinks he does. Seeks approval and respect. They build their self-esteem on knowing "the facts."* Do not correct or counter. Do not get involved trying to "out-expert" him. Listen and validate. Be sure to affirm their stance when they are right.

Here are some steps to help you cope and stop pulling out your own hair in frustration!
- Assess the situation. Is this really an issue you have to win?
- Stop wishing and hoping things were different. That sets you up to be blind-sided again – and again.
- Plan a strategy for getting your point across.
- Stick to your agenda. Do not be distracted by his techniques to infuriate or diminish you.
- Do the best you can and then let it go.

Today as I assess my situation and my husband's behavior, I will also look at my own style. While it is always easier to see his flaws, looking at my own behavior is where I can create real change.

Alimony is compensatory for the time you focused on family and put your own career on the back burner. It is for "services rendered" and opportunities missed. It can assist you in attending school or learning a trade. Alimony honors a woman's participation, value, and sacrifice. It is a just and important measure. But when alimony is rescinded if you remarry, then the message isn't so clear. If it is compensatory, then what difference should your present living situation make? When alimony ceases upon remarriage, the message is "Well, she has someone else to take care of her, so let her be his burden!" If alimony is truly compensatory, it should not stop upon your remarriage or co-habitating.

When alimony is doled out in weekly or monthly payments it leaves the woman dependent upon her ex-husband. He continues in his role of provider. She is left waiting for that check, hoping it is on time and that it doesn't bounce. It is demeaning and disempowering. She can't save. She can't get ahead. She remains a victim to her ex's support.

One just way to eradicate that inequity in power is to have alimony distributed, when possible, in a lump-sum settlement at the time of the divorce. This gives the woman economic freedom to make her own choices. She can invest in a home, stocks, or education. When she receives a lump-sum payment, her ability to make significant life changes escalates. Emotionally, a lump-sum payment helps sever her dependence so that other issues such as co-parenting can be addressed without the shadow of financial blackmail. Alimony would play no part in future relationships. If she chose to re-marry, she could do so without fear of financial setback.

Many men prefer lump-sum settlements. The amount paid may be "discounted." Their financial obligations to their ex-wife are severed, thus making it easier for them to deal with the ongoing issues in a more congenial and focused manner. If he remarries, he does not carry this debt into his new relationship.

Certainly, every situation is different. You may think that your husband doesn't have that much money to give you. With creative input from the attorney, an accountant, or a financial planner, there may be remedies to that situation. It can't hurt to ask!

Today with so much to pay attention to, it is difficult to think of all the possibilities. The more I know, the better choices I can make. I will continue to be open to new ideas and ask for help. When I begin to tire, I will rest rather than give up. I will remember that these decisions will affect me for the rest of my life.

There may come a day when you consider getting involved in another relationship. After swearing you would NEVER embark on another romantic endeavor, here you are thinking about it.

The question of trust always seems to be lurking. How can I ever trust again? How could I risk experiencing this level of pain again? How can I even trust that I know what a good relationship is about?

Sometimes when we are young, we trust the wrong people. Sometimes, even in light of glaring problems, we go ahead and commit. When we ignore the warning signs, we are not trusting ourselves. Denying our own reality is the first wrong turn on the road to a wrong relationship. If you have doubts, trust your radar.

Look for dependability. Is this a person who comes through, again and again? Is it someone who is able to honor commitments, such as being on time, getting to work, and paying his bills? Do other people see him as dependable? What do co-workers, family, and friends say about him? If they report he is not dependable, do not shrug off that information by thinking, "Well, he isn't that way with me." Chances are, with time, he WILL be that way with you, also.

Look for predictability. Does this person react consistently in similar situations, or are his reactions all over the place? While we don't want to assume we know everything about a person, predictability speaks to their ability to be consistent. Consistency supports trust. Knowing how someone reacts under pressure, or in an emergency, or in stressful times, will give you an idea of what kind of partner this person will be.

Do you experience this person as predictable and dependable in various situations and events? Has he behaved in a way that you can begin to rely on? Can you count on his reactions to certain life struggles?

If this is so, then you have begun to trust him. When we can rely and count on someone, then we have surrendered some of our doubt and defense and traded it in for some trust and connection.

Don't distort, minimize or rationalize certain responses so that he fits the criteria for trust. The single most important person you need to trust is yourself. Don't let yourself down by ignoring any warning signs. Trust in yourself to be your best protector and guide. And take your time.

Today I will trust myself to pay close attention to another person's behaviors. Promises, rationalizations, or denial will not sway me. I will have faith in my ability to pick someone worth my trust, but I have to be honest with myself.

Phyllis, a divorced woman in her forties, thought her relationship was going quite well. Her boyfriend of one year, Alan, felt it "lacked commitment." "Well, he thinks we should buy a house together. He feels we need a commitment of some type." Alan also urged her to open a joint bank account and to cut back their work hours so they could spend more time together. Her doing these things would, in his words, "Prove her commitment to him."

Financial and legal entanglements are very different from an emotional promise or vow. The difference can elude us as we look for ways to "insure" the continuation of a relationship. For example, a woman may get pregnant by her boyfriend with hopes that the child will solidify the commitment.

The entanglements of legal and financial issues, and even children, do not necessarily insure commitment. Those are the manifestations of the commitment and should not be mistaken for the commitment itself. Going through a divorce, you have experienced first-hand how those obligations have nothing to do with emotional commitment. Emotional commitment involves loyalty, trust, respect, and dedication. When these things are in place between two people, they begin to build their life together.

Obligation before commitment will not help foster closeness or commitment. In some ways, it may deter you from reaching that goal. Obligations can evolve into resentments fairly quickly. Joys of homeownership and children can quickly become issues of conflict to a couple with large obligations and minimal commitment. The stronger the commitment, the less likely that the obligatory pieces of life will stress and destroy the relationship.

Fortunately, Phyllis had learned some valuable lessons from her divorce. She was able to see that Alan was trying to "ensnare" her through obligation. Alan claimed he didn't "need" marriage, yet he was searching for some reassurance that she would not leave him. He was having trouble accepting that her love was her commitment. He wanted a guarantee that she was "In it for the long haul." While Phyllis loves him, she is concerned about confusing the two issues. Her plan is to discuss with Alan their definitions of commitment. Ultimately, she hopes he will begin to accept and trust her commitment without merging finances or buying a house.

Today I see that in my marriage, the boundaries between commitment and obligation might have blurred. Certainly, they overlapped at times. Was obligation stronger than our commitment?

In the 1980's, the television comedy, *Kate and Allie* introduced the idea of two divorced mothers pooling their resources to create a new living experience for themselves and their kids. The basic premise was that one Mom stayed at home, and the other worked outside the home. By moving in together, they were able to combine their talents and lifestyles in a way that supported and enhanced all concerned. Having two adults in the household made it easier for each of the women to parent, pursue their interests and have social lives.

For the children, having two adults present gave them different role models, additional support, and a more enriching home life. Sharing space with other kids also exposed them to working out living arrangements, conflict resolution, and additional companionship. It is surprising that more women aren't getting together to combine their resources in a way that enhances the family living situation. The options and benefits are endless.

Certainly, conflicts can arise. If you do consider joining households, make sure that you are clear on your expectations and that you share them with the other woman. This includes finances, household responsibilities, parenting responsibilities, and so forth. The more you define the roles and responsibilities prior to moving in together, the less likely there is to be conflict. And if conflicts do arise, having talked about your expectations ahead of time can diminish their impact.

The *Kate and Allie* model is not the only possibility for creating an innovative family life. Other options include renting a room to a college student and reducing the rent in exchange for babysitting or moving the lawn; or moving in with an elderly person who is desperately trying to stay in her home, but is overwhelmed by the maintenance. You and your children can pitch in and offer assistance, while they can offer your children a grandmotherly presence and living space for reduced rent. These suggestions are creative ways to upgrade your standard of living, save some money, bring some practical support into your life and create friendships that can last a lifetime.

Today when I start to panic about my financial situation or housing, I will remember that I am only limited by my imagination. Other women in similar situations may be looking to pool resources. I need to keep open to alternative ways of solving problems. I may be surprised at the connections and options that are available to me!

As you gradually move from being a couple to being a single, many of the small traditions and rituals which define your family change, either by desire or necessity. Often, we focus on the big changes such as holidays and celebrations. However, those small daily rituals are where you may feel the greatest loss. These are intrinsic parts of our everyday life and not just a once-a-year occurrence. Each family has those traditions: Who makes the coffee, who walks the dog in the morning, who locks the doors and shuts off the lights at the end of the day. These are traditions established by years of routine.

Do not minimize or deny these feelings of loss. They may lack the drama of the "big traditions," but they represent the security of routine. We may not even be aware of a specific absence, but recognize a malaise that permeates our mood.

Those absences are felt as much by the person who wants the divorce as by the one who doesn't. You may have wanted out of the marriage, but now find yourself grieving for those "little things." That may surprise you. Noting the absence of these things can help you be more aware of why your mood changes so quickly and without provocation. It can help you identify what you are grieving for, instead of feeling out of control and just wildly hysterical. The more mindful you are, the more your feelings, thoughts, and moods make sense. The more they make sense, the easier it will be for you to experience the changes. Your awareness will help you begin to replace these traditions with new ones.

Emma, recently divorced, used to sit down every Sunday morning to do the crossword puzzle in the newspaper. Now she finds that she can't even look at it. The thought of doing it makes her sad. Finally, it came to her that she and her husband did that puzzle together every Sunday morning for their entire marriage. After a busy week, doing the puzzle together reconnected them and gave them a problem-solving task to do together which they both enjoyed. Now the puzzle, far from being enjoyable, only emphasized her loss. For months, she didn't do the puzzle or even read the paper. Then, on one sleepless night, she took the puzzle to bed with her and, after a few minutes, found that it helped her sleep. Now, the puzzle is part of a new ritual. She keeps it by her bed stand and works on it a little every night, until she dozes off. The puzzle again brings her pleasure, but the purpose and ritual have changed to accommodate her new needs.

Today I will pay attention to those small, favorite rituals that are no longer part of my life. I will honor the loss. Then I will consider whether these rituals merit restructuring. If so, I will reinvent them in ways that bring me pleasure and contentment.

Often, we focus on our external obstacles. We concentrate on those circumstances we perceive as responsible for our not getting what we want in life. We rant and rave and wish things were different. We say "if only" and shake our head (and sometimes our fist) at those events or people that we see as responsible for our unhappiness. Yet external obstacles are just that. They are things outside of us over which we really have no control. Many of us are unaware of the internal obstacles that are really the source of most of our discontent.

Do you sabotage yourself? Are there aspects of your personality or behavior that wreak havoc in your life and keep you from actualizing your dreams? The following list includes some self-sabotaging behaviors, attitudes and ways of thinking. Read the list. Take your time and allow yourself to review these items without self-ridicule or denial. This is not an "evaluation" or test, but an opportunity to gain insight. Be gentle with yourself and stay open to the possibility of learning.

- Blame others
- Disorganized
- Trouble making decisions
- Overly cautious
- Lack energy
- Insensitive to others
- Preoccupied with what others think
- Lack self-confidence
- Follows the crowd
- Counts on luck, not ability
- Unobservant
- Fears success
- Doesn't plan ahead
- Expects to fail
- Lacks creativity
- Too rigid/too flexible
- Impulsive
- Unable to delegate
- Distorted thinking
- Live in the past
- Give up easily
- Take everything personally
- Surrounded by negative people
- Shy away from competition
- Uninformed
- Unprepared

To some degree, all of us engage in some of these behaviors or have some of these attitudes occasionally. We are more likely to achieve our goals if we can limit our self sabotaging ways. In order to create joy and contentment in your life, it is important to recognize how you sabotage yourself. Then you can begin to substitute healthy behaviors for those old roadblocks.

Today one of the ways to bring joy and contentment into my life is to reduce behaviors and attitudes that sabotage my happiness. I will do this with an open mind toward change and growth. Self-criticism is a form of sabotage. Self-exploration is a way to grow!

When the man has children from a previous relationship, the end of your marriage can signify the end of your relationship with your stepchildren. This is especially difficult if you have has no children of your own.

Stepmothers have a tough time in the best of situations. If they are attentive and involved, they can be seen as pushy and controlling. If they "wait and see," children can read that as cold and unaffectionate. It is difficult for stepmothers to find their role. To have it rescinded can be painful and frustrating. Biological children enjoy a bond secured by genetic, legal, historical, and emotional ties. The relationship with stepchildren has none of these bonds to support it. This is painfully apparent in court when the stepmother finds out that regardless of her emotional connection with her husband's children, she has basically no legal rights.

In a 1991 movie *Table for Five*, when the mother dies, the stepfather struggles to keep the children he has raised and loved for years. The biological father, who had little to do with the children, is awarded custody. This movie has a "happily ever after ending." The two men work out a compromise and agree to co-parent the children. But often this is not the case in the real world.

Regardless of the age of the children or how long you have known them, if the relationship was important to you (and to them), it needs to be honored. If you will not see the children after the divorce, it is critical for the children to have some closure to your relationship. Reassure them that the divorce was not their fault. Let them know how much they have meant to you. Stay "age appropriate." Do not divulge details of the marriage. Jenna and her 13-year-old stepdaughter, Leslie, together divided all the photos of the ten-year marriage into three picture albums; one for Leslie's father, one for Leslie and one for Jenna. This project affirmed their connection. It allowed them to reminisce about their years together. It was a way of closure for both.

Stepchildren sometimes refuse to talk with the stepparent after the divorce. Family loyalties emerge and kids take sides. Try not to take it personally. Children often see things in black and white. Older kids may feel angry or rejected and act out that wound by withdrawing. If there are on-going visits with the children, these may stop, if the father again remarries. The new wife may feel more threatened by your relationship with the children than by the biological mother.

Today I acknowledge that a step-relationship is held together by caring, affection, trust, and love. Sometimes that is not enough to withstand the acrimony of divorce. Just acknowledging this loss can help with my growth and healing process.

Approximately 50%-75% of the divorces filed are filed by women. Why are women leaving marriage at such an alarming rate? Is it that we have become too picky, or that men's ability to partner is declining?

We may think most women leave because of alcoholism, drug abuse or verbal or physical violence. Surprisingly women in those situations often have the hardest time leaving. Most women say they leave because they feel neglected and they are tired of putting everyone else's needs before their own. Many say the only time their husbands pay them any attention is when they want sex. They say they feel invisible.

Often when men are involved in an activity, it feels to their wife as if you could drop a bomb on them and they wouldn't respond. Women on the other hand, multi-task constantly. Rob Becker wrote and starred in the one-man show *Defending the Cavemen*, a funky, funny, yet accurate look at male-female relationships. Becker has a theory. He takes us back to the time of the cavemen, when the men were hunters and the women were the gatherers. The men's role was to provide food for the family. The task of hunting down a huge wooly mammoth with only a spear required extreme focus. This ability kept the men alive and the women and children fed. Women, on the other hand, stayed at the cave to tend the children, keep the fire going, gather food, and make clothing. Their roles were multi-faceted and required the ability to do many things at once. Fortunately, men and women both mastered the necessary skills and the human race survived.

Unfortunately, those differences in the way we operate in the world, often leads to the destruction of a marriage. The wooly mammoth has been replaced by Monday night football and women are not content to keep the home fires burning and tend the children. Today's woman wants partnership, connection and companionship. Marriage is no longer a necessity for survival as women are more able to take care of themselves. More and more women, especially those, who once were married are finding that single life is very rewarding. Perhaps, the species will again evolve to accommodate the changing needs of both sexes. Until then, we will read books, go to marital therapy, talk to our girlfriends and try and try to figure out how to bridge the gender gap.

Today when I think about how many women left their marriages, I do not feel alone. I feel validated in my need for more. Without emotional connection, marriage becomes an empty, unrewarding experience. I have the right to want more in my life.

Many women stay in bad marriages for years. When they think about divorce, some become overwhelmed with fear of the unknown. What will it be like to live alone? Will I have financial security? Can I be a good single parent? Will I ever have another relationship? Without answers to these questions, they settle for living in unhappy circumstances. Some rationalize that "at least we know what we have." Because of their fear, some even stay in abusive, violent situations.

In the movie *Kate and Leopold*, Leopold says "Brave is merely those with the clearest vision of what is before them." What a useful definition! What separates the women who proceed with their plans and take their life into their own hands, from those who stay in unhappy circumstances? The women who go ahead with their plans and leave their marriages are not necessarily the ones with less fear. They are the ones with, as Leopold said, "the clearest vision of what is before them." This includes having done their homework and knowing as much as possible about what their situation will be after the divorce. However, if getting a divorce required knowing the outcome in advance, no one would move ahead.

There are no absolutes, and a number of variables are at play – not just when leaving a marriage, but in any change you make. If you buy a new car, you may be trading in "known" problems for unknown ones. What if the car is a lemon? What if you lose your job and can't afford the payments? What if? What if?

Getting comfortable with unknowns is a challenge for all of us. Being in control and feeling safe are two major issues for most women. *Being* in control makes us *feel* safe. However, unknowns are a fact of life. If we never get comfortable with at least some amount of risk, then we will never grow. Bravery, or comfort with risk, also comes from experience. Where have you taken risks? Have they proved successful? If not, how did you remedy the situation? Consider those times when change may not have turned out as expected. You may find that the change led to something even better than you hoped. Focus on the risks you have made throughout your life that resulted in joy. If you have difficulty identifying your successful risks, it could be from years of negative thinking. Everyone has taken risks with positive outcomes! Find those risks and focus on them! Remember the joy you felt when your mission was accomplished. You can feel that again and again. *Try.* You are braver than you know!

Today I will create a vision of what I want my life to be and I will move toward that vision.

Creativity is about looking at something and seeing it in different ways. Many of us sabotage our own creativity. We say "I can't draw" or "I am tone deaf." In making such declarations, we deny our own uniqueness. We are creative daily and tend to deny it, ignore it, or not even be aware of it. Every time that you change a hair style, try a new recipe or rearrange your furniture, you are expressing your own unique way of seeing the world. Creativity is not just bestowed on a chosen few. We don't realize that we see the world from our uniquely individual viewpoint. That viewpoint is where our creativity is born.

Creativity can be healing in many ways. When we are creative, we are exercising our mind. We are seeing the world with a different perspective. When we change our perspective, we are open to different points of view. We have access to more information which results in our becoming more insightful.

Creative experience also builds self-awareness and self-esteem. When we express our unique vision of the world, we affirm our value by giving it voice. We also take the risk to be different and to stand up for our viewpoint. How can you develop your creativity?

- Create a new meal. Don't use a cookbook, just your imagination.
- Go into a big department store and try on clothes that you would never consider wearing in public.
- Try eating your breakfast for dinner and your dinner for breakfast (your kids will love this).
- Switch roles with your kids for a day. Let them be the grown-ups and you be the child! (Also a very creative activity for them!).
- Buy a hat. Wear it!
- Paint one wall in your home in your favorite color.
- Listen to foreign language tapes in your car and learn Spanish, Italian, Chinese, etc.
- Buy some flowers and arrange them in a vase.
- Put on your favorite music and dance.
- Make designs in your pancakes using batter tinted with food coloring.
- Carve a pumpkin.
- Wrap presents using something other than gift wrap.
- Take an adult education class in art, music, writing, journaling, scrapbooking, ice skating.
- Take a ride to some place you have never been before. Don't use a map!
- Try anything *new*.

Today I will explore my creative side, recognizing that the goal is to enjoy the process, not to create a perfect product. When I honor my creativity, it enhances my sense of self. Creative activities bring joy to my life as well as foster emotional healing and enhance self-confidence.

Weight and body image are concerns for most women. We worry whether we are thin enough, toned enough, healthy enough. During times of stress, our eating patterns may go awry. Some of us eat when we feel stressed; some of us completely lose our appetite. Some fluctuation in our eating patterns is normal.

When does an eating pattern become a disorder? According to Molly Hinchman, Ph.D of Cornwall, Connecticut, eating disorders fall into three categories. They are Anorexia, Bulimia, and Compulsive Overeating. All three have symptoms in common and there are symptoms that are unique to each one. Distorted body image and preoccupation with food are symptoms that are likely to be present in all three of the disorders. Induction of vomiting, use of laxatives and enemas, excessive exercise regimens, use of weight-loss medication, and fasting are found in anorexia and bulimia only. Bulimics also eat secretly, steal food, binge, and purge. Anorexics experience severe weight loss, rigid eating patterns, and excessive restriction of food. The symptoms of compulsive overeating include emotional eating, feeling out of control, regret, shame, remorse and eating when you are not hungry. Sneaking food, repeated attempts to cut back, tendency to binge on carbs, white sugar, salt and food cravings are also often present. Compulsive overeaters tend to be overweight.

Losing and gaining weight in times of stress is not abnormal. It is a coping response to difficult times. However, the major differences between eating disorders and periodic changes in regimen include duration, a desire to stop and some feelings of shame. The physical impact of these three disorders cannot be under-estimated. With anorexia, the severe weight loss can lead to cessation of menses, electrolyte imbalances and possible organ shut down. With bulimia, the binge and purge behavior results in electrolyte imbalance, rotting teeth and serious gastrointestinal problems. Compulsive overeating can lead to obesity, which is linked to heart disease, diabetes, and high blood pressure.

If you have concerns that you might have an eating disorder, then call your physician, a therapist, a nutritionist or eating disorder specialist. All three disorders can be successfully treated. Without treatment they can be fatal.

Today I will examine my eating habits. Is there something about the way I use food that is unhealthy? I will not minimize or deny that this could result in serious medical complications. I will seek help. When I ask for help, I am not being weak. When I confront a potential problem, I am being courageous and strong.

As a single person, it is easy to imagine the rest of the world is happily paired off, enjoying life in a way that you do not. However, over the past twenty-five years, the number of single people in the United States has rapidly grown. Being married was at one time the norm, but now that is not necessarily true. Many people are choosing to be single. Yet some see being single as what they "do" until they meet Mr. Right and marry.

Stella, in her early thirties, was a very attractive, successful young woman who was distraught because she had not met Mr. Right. Impeccably dressed and poised, she spent all of her money trying to look "just right" so she could attract the "right" man. She lived with her parents. She explained that if she moved out, bought a condo or a house, and then met someone and HE had a house, then she would have to sell it. Furthermore, if she bought furniture and then met someone and he didn't like her furniture, then she would have to get rid of it and start all over again. She didn't travel, either, her concern being that she didn't want the experience to somehow diminish the traveling she would do with her future partner. She was depressed, and no wonder! She was not living. She was waiting to live! She had put her life on hold.

As a divorcing woman, you know that marriage is not the panacea for everything. You do not have fantasies about the perfect married life. You know better. The key to being happily single is to be comfortable with who you are. Get to know yourself and like yourself. Bring love into your life by focusing on the things you love. Your work and your creativity can flourish. You can pursue relationships with like-minded people. You are free to spend your time as you wish. You can take better care of yourself and develop a broader range of interests and activities. While singles may need to do more planning and more reaching out than married folks, the up side is they can choose how to spend their time. Developing a positive attitude will improve the quality of your alone time and your time with others. Negativity does not attract healthy people. Without a positive outlook, you may struggle to find connection that is meaningful, supportive, and fun. Seeing the positive aspects of being single affords you the opportunity to live your life to the fullest. Now, back to Stella, who had put her life on hold.

She began to think of her single life as an opportunity. She began taking trips, first just little weekend jaunts, then she went to Paris. She came back so invigorated that she enrolled in a French class at a local college. That began her quest to pursue her Bachelor's Degree. Through her schoolwork, she met many like-minded people. Her social circle expanded. She received a promotion at work. When last we spoke, she had bought a house and was happily decorating it, the way *she* wanted. There was no Mr. Right, but now there was Ms. Right. She learned the key to life contentment was not in any other relationship, but in the one she has with herself. Today she is a happy, vibrant woman with many interests and friends. She would tell you that she has a wonderful life.

Today I will think about my biases about being single. I need to consider all the options I have now, that I did not have when I was married. When I focus on the positive, I become a positive person and a more content and approachable human being.

We are women. We are tenacious. That is both bad and good. When we want something, we really want it. One of the things we want is for people around us to change. Sometimes, it is our parents or our children. Often it is our partners. When women are going through divorce, they cry in frustration at the outrageous things their spouse is doing. They act surprised at certain behaviors.

"I can't believe he would do this!" "Why not?" I ask. "It is so outrageous, (mean, cheap, sneaky)" "Is this new behavior? Has he ever done this before?" "Oh, yeah. All the time. "So, why are you shocked?"

Why do you think things will change?

Divorce is a stressful time. None of us are at our best under stress. We fantasize that behaviors will change, simply because we want them to. When they don't, we get angry.

Our need to change people is a form of control. We want to change people so they can be the way we think we need them to be. We say things like "You need to stop yelling (drinking, working late, smoking, withdrawing)." What we really mean is "I want you to stop that so I can be happy and have things the way I want them." We can't change other people and they aren't going to change because we want them to. When the behaviors become intolerable and each person is not willing to work on THEMSELVES, then people divorce. At least one of the partners gives up hope that the other will change.

Rather than set yourself up to be outraged (disappointed, hurt, angry, betrayed) by your spouse's continuing bad behavior, try using it as a way to affirm that the divorce is the right thing to do. When going through divorce, we all have doubts. Now, when you see more of the unacceptable behaviors you saw in your marriage, try using them as an affirmation that you made the right decision. So, when you have doubts or fear, or even nostalgic moments, be grateful when your spouse acts badly. It affirms your decision.

"Ah, yes! THIS is why I am divorcing him!"

Today I will stop trying to change another person's bad behavior. I will use that energy to draw strength and affirmation that my decision, as hard as it was, was the right one.

More grandparents are finding it necessary to petition the courts for the right to see their grandchildren. This is due to the increase in divorce, as well as our increasingly mobile society. Extended families no longer live within walking distance of each other. Now, older adults frequently move when they retire, seeking milder climates or adult communities. Young families are more mobile due to professional considerations and increased financial flexibility. It is not unusual for today's grandparents to see their grandchildren a couple of times a year, on holidays or on vacations.

When divorce occurs in the family and there is acrimony, grandparents fear they will be cut off from having a relationship with their grandchildren. Sometimes grandparents panic and rush to petition the courts, before allowing anger and resentment to calm down. Many situations, given time, can be worked out amicably. The rush to court only escalates the adversarial climate. When that occurs, parents and grandparents may carry resentment at being "forced" into an agreement. If grandparents can be patient and allow the divorce process to evolve without panicking about their own issues, it will serve everyone's best interests.

The best thing the grandparents can do is support the divorcing couple and try to minimize the acrimony. In this way, they are supporting their grandchildren. Stirring the pot by bringing another act of litigation only causes more turmoil. When possible, non-custodial grandparents should work out visitation through the non-custodial parent. The non-custodial parent's time should be used to fulfill all family obligations on his side.

However, in cases where the non-custodial parent is not involved with the children – because he lives in another state, or does not have visitation rights – then the grandparents need to deal with the custodial parent. It is in everyone's best interest to try to keep the lines of communication open. The grandparents should be as neutral as possible, be supportive of the whole family and never badmouth either parent to the child. This kind of alienation only upsets and confuses the child, diminishes the relationship between parent and grandparent, and creates more hostility. Most importantly, as with all alienation, the effect on the children can be extremely damaging.

Today I will consider having a discussion with all the grandparents, asking them to be patient and not to choose sides. They have rights and concerns, but those will have to take a back seat to the needs of my children. Setting boundaries is one of the ways I continue to grow in strength, confidence, and competence.

Closure acknowledges the end of something important in our lives. Funerals are rituals to help us achieve closure. In the divorce process, closure is not attended to with any ritual. The final divorce decree is often delivered with less ceremony than the routine process of signing a credit card receipt. The actual court process offers us little in the way of closure. Most women report that going to court for that last time was somewhat anti-climactic.

Divorce closure takes place in many stages and in many venues. There is legal, financial, and even geographical closure. Emotional closure is more difficult to predict and even to identify because it happens in stages. We let go a little at a time. Our losses are not just limited to the loss of a partner. We lose another income, a co-parent, a companion, a best friend, a handyman, a built-in date, and a lover. We also lose the dream of happily ever after. Other losses may shock us: relationships with in-laws, friends, stepchildren, celebrations, and traditions are just a few of these.

Every woman has different losses and grieves them in her own unique way. Closure is the process of saying good-bye and grieving your losses so you can move on. Not letting go is like staying on the wrong train. It won't take you where you want to go. Until you get off and let it leave the station, there is no opportunity for another train to pull up to the platform. So you can't go on with your journey.

Below is one format for a divorce closure ceremony. Tailor it to fit your own needs. Address the following questions and discuss them with a friend or a therapist or with yourself in your journal:

- What will I miss most about my husband?
- What will I miss most about my marriage?
- What value did those things have to me?
- Say good bye to each of those separately. Say/write why it had value for you and what you will miss most about it.
- How has each of those things helped you grow as a person?
- Say good-bye to the roles you left behind (Joe's wife, Becky's daughter-in-law, etc). Say why you valued those roles and how you grew from them.
- Imagine your husband standing in front of you and you can say anything you want to him, but this is the last opportunity you will have to do this. What do you need to say?
- If you have anything else to say good-bye to, identify those things and say why you valued them.
- Again, imagine your husband standing there in front of you and imagine that you simply turn around and walk away from him, focusing on the feeling of leaving him behind. As you continue to walk away, focus on how you are feeling as you walk further away from him.
- Imagine yourself feeling calm and confident about the future. Write/talk about the feeling of being in charge of your own destiny.

Today saying goodbye is never easy, but it is a vital part of getting on with my life. When I am ready, I will prepare my closure ceremony with great care..I will include everything I need to honor my loss.

Notes

Month Twelve

Divorce is the end of a marriage. It is also the beginning of your life as a single person. It heralds opportunity for new experiences and adventures. After being a wife for many years, it can be difficult to adjust to single status. Many women worry that without a husband they cannot make it on their own. They worry about how they will manage financially, emotionally and practically. The demise of the marriage is usually accompanied by negative feelings about oneself. These negative feelings can lead to nagging self-doubt and make this new life phase even more difficult to deal with.

There is so much more to do now and to take care of that you wonder if you can get it done. Piled on top of all that is the added burden of the divorce business: the paperwork, litigation, stress, financial decisions, and courts. It is a time-consuming process. Then, there is all the emotional fallout: sadness, fear, loss, anger, betrayal, abandonment, and wretched self-doubt. If that sounds like a bleak picture, it really isn't. There is a silver lining; all of this passes. The litigation of divorce does not last forever! When it does end, it creates an enormous amount of time and energy for you to bring new, more positive things into your life.

You will make adjustments in terms of practical chores, houses and cars. Frequently, women choose to live in a smaller home and, rather than feelings of loss, they enjoy being unencumbered by a large home, lawn and mortgage. By downsizing, they simplify their life and a great deal of the stress begins to abate.

Some women return to school or work at this juncture. At first, this can feel overwhelming and harrowing, especially if you have not been in school or the workplace in many years. However, most women find that working, going to school, and making their own money adds to their sense of self-worth and accomplishment. Many are surprised at how much more secure they feel as they become the architects of their own lives.

It is difficult to predict how long this will take. For each woman, the journey through the transition into a comfortable, enjoyable single life varies. No matter how badly you may be feeling, remember that each day you are evolving. Changes are always occurring, even though they may seem indiscernible. One day, you will think to yourself, "Hey, this new life that I have created is pretty damn good!"

Today I will remember that "When one door closes, another one opens." There will be challenges, but there will also be great gifts and wonderful surprises. It will take time. I acknowledge how difficult it is to go through this process, but I also acknowledge that my future is not bleak and without joy.

Post-divorce is a period of adjustment. There are many changes for the newly-single woman. As you begin to gain comfort with your new life, consider which of the following areas may need some attention:

Economic issues:

Have you paid your attorney in full? Created a budget? Changed your credit cards? Notified the bank and other financial institutions of the divorce?

Housing issues:

Are you planning to stay in your home? What changes/repairs need to be made to the home in order to accommodate your life changes? If you are moving, have you hired a realtor? Gotten an appraisal? If you plan to relocate, have you begun narrowing your choice of area and type of housing? Have you discussed mortgage options with a financial institution? Do you have a good sense of what you can afford? If you are refinancing, have you begun searching out good mortgage rates?

Single parenting issues:

Have you developed a routine with your kids? Is visitation going smoothly? Have your children worked through their divorce related issues? Have you recently spoken with the school about their progress?

Emotional issues:

Are you crying less? If you have feelings of guilt, sadness, or remorse, are they lessening? How are you dealing with fear? Do you have anger at him? How do you deal with boredom, loneliness, alone time? Are you continuing to do things that support your emotional growth?

Work/school issues:

Have you begun to make appropriate moves to further your work/school situation? Are you able to focus on your work? Do you find work/school offers you emotional satisfaction? Are there things about your work/school situation that need to be changed?

Post-divorce issues:

Have you resolved conflicts, feelings and issues with your ex? If not, what needs work? How is your relationship with your in-laws? Have you written a will?

Personal issues:

Are you participating in events/activities that bring you pleasure? Do you have a network of people to do things with? Have you befriended other divorced/single women? Are you taking care of your health?

Today I will use these questions as guidelines. Each divorce requires different adjustments and attention to specific areas. These questions serve as a guide to facilitate my analysis of my life at this time. All of life is a process. I will focus on the areas that need work, while enjoying those areas of my life that are resolved and calm.

Lucy has been through a horrible divorce. Her husband is still being a bastard. Her adult children have pulled away. It has been a terribly difficult year. Recently, she mentioned that she is happy with her life. How does she manage to be so upbeat and positive?

"Well," she explained, "I imagine that I know no other life than the one I have now. I have a good job, which I love. I have strong family connections and deep, solid friendships. I am my own person and no longer ruled by someone else's whims and edicts. If I focus on what I DO have, I have a wonderful life that brings me peace and fulfillment."

Lucy is able to focus on the gifts of the present. So often, post-divorce women evaluate their lives in comparison to what they used to have, or what they thought they had. This continuing focus on what was lost leaves no room to rejoice in what is found. By focusing on what she has, Lucy is able to enjoy her life. She has optimism and gratitude. If we focus on what was lost, we do ourselves a huge disservice. The loss is embellished and a fantasy is created that looks very little like the life that truly existed.

Ask yourself this: If the memory of your marriage were suddenly and magically wiped out of your consciousness and your current life was the only life you knew, would it be so bad? You may realize that what you are grieving for is not something you even want anymore. You may find that your present life is fulfilling and enjoyable. When we stop comparing what *is* to what we think *should* be, then life gets far less complicated and far more pleasurable. If this is not the life you want, then what things can you do to improve your life? What actions can you take to move you closer to being happy?

Today I will stop focusing on what was and as I look at this new life I am creating, how do I feel about it? Can I take a moment to find gratitude in what I have without holding it up to the impossible standard of a fantasy or memory?

Some women find that divorce gives them the strength to stand up for themselves in a way they had not before. Bravo! Not letting others abuse you turns you into a survivor. Learning assertiveness skills and when to use them can create better relationships with others, while assisting you in getting what you need.

Sometimes, in an attempt to salve our anger or pain, we may become inflexible and unwilling to give in on anything. When we become that rigid, we cross the line into aggressive behavior. In doing so, we create additional problems for ourselves such as higher legal bills, increased acrimony with our ex, tension with our kids and more stress.

Rolling over and acquiescing to everything isn't the answer, either. Learn to choose your battles; it's old advice, but good advice. In reality, divorce is not about winning, it is about compromise. Let's look at some questions to ask yourself before you go to battle:

Do you really know what happened? So many times, we jump to conclusions or make assumptions and then are ready to "have it out" before we know all the facts.

How much does it really matter? Think long range - will this issue impact you a year from now or even a week from now? Sometimes we take a stand when it isn't really necessary or appropriate. We just feel so enraged at the moment!

Will it get you what you want? Sometimes, we take a stand on an issue with hopes that the victory will help us feel better about something else.

Do you just want to be heard? Do you really care about what you are fighting over or is it more about a need for validation?

What are your options? Are there things you can do to work this through on your own?

Do you want a positive outcome? Make sure your stand isn't just about "getting back" or venting your anger.

Have you thought it through carefully? What considerations are there in taking a stand on this issue?

Will you have regrets if you do nothing? Years from now, how will this feel?

What are the probable consequences? Are there any risks? For example, if you wage a war against your ex due to his infidelity or cheating on his taxes, will there be consequences to you when he fights back? Are there certain aspects of your behavior that you would rather not reveal? Know your own vulnerable spots before you begin something you might regret.

Will your being assertive make a difference? For example, if your husband truly has no money, going after him for lots of alimony is not going to prove fruitful. Be realistic about your goal and the possibility of achieving it.

Today when I think of all the assertiveness skills I have learned, I am aware that I can speak up for myself. However, I am also aware that I could misuse these skills in a way that would just create havoc and resentment in my life. As I go through this process, I am learning that having assertiveness skills is important, but using them appropriately is critical.

You may have said, "I will never do this again," meaning that you will never get involved in a relationship or get married again! The sense of betrayal, disillusionment, and abandonment are so enormous that the thought of getting into another relationship may feel terrifying. The idea of dating may seem daunting. You may feel as if no one would want you or that there is no one out there worth wanting.

There may come a time when you start to consider the possibility of another relationship. Often the acrimony has begun to wane and you have begun to acknowledge that NOT all men are like your ex. Your confidence may have grown since the separation and you may have made new friends. Many women lose weight, buy new clothes, and get new hairdos. Some begin working out regularly. Others begin therapy or join a support group. All of these things help you feel better about yourself. And as you feel better about yourself, you feel better about everything, including your ability to participate in another relationship. Then, of course, the day may come when you find you are actually attracted to someone!

How to tell if you are really ready?
- You feel comfortable with yourself.
- You enjoy many aspects of being on your own.
- Your anger is diminished.
- You feel you have something to offer.
- You understand why you chose your ex-partner.
- You have examined your part in the demise of the relationship.
- You understand how your parents' relationship impacted your choice of partner.
- You are not looking for someone to complete your life, but to enhance it.
- You aren't running from unhappiness, but moving toward another stage in your life.
- You like you.
- You know what traits you need in a partner.
- While you are willing to compromise, you will not settle.
- You know your bottom line.
- You are not trying to save anyone.
- You are not looking for someone to save you.
- The relationship you have with yourself is a good one--free of guilt, self-anger and self-doubt.
- You know what you want and need from another relationship.

Today I will consider how ready I am to try a relationship with another person. But I must be sure that I have a strong relationship with myself. Will I listen to my instincts? Will I pay attention to warning signs? When I am confident that I will honor my own needs, I will begin to think about being with another. If it is not today, it doesn't mean it will never be. I will try not to rush the process or act out of a sense of urgency.

The *Merriam-Webster Dictionary* defines autonomy as the "right or power of self-government." Independence is synonymous with autonomy and so are self-reliance and personal freedom. Not having to rely on another for permission or decision making is another way to think of autonomy.

Being single doesn't automatically make us autonomous, just as being married doesn't automatically mean you lose your autonomy. Often, particularly in unhealthy relationships, autonomy was compromised. How many of the following statements apply to you?

- When I am independent, I feel good.
- I am clear on the difference between dependence and closeness.
- I do not have to distance to feel independent.
- I am no longer emotionally dependent on my parents.
- When my mate is independent, I still feel loved.
- I know that the more independent I feel, the healthier my relationships can be.
- When I am independent, I feel more secure with myself.
- I am aware that I do not have to surrender my independence to be in a loving relationship.
- I don't miss feeling emotionally dependent on another person.
- I do not feel needy.

Feeling good about oneself and feeling independent doesn't detract from a healthy loving relationship. Quite the contrary, you bring a quality of "wholeness" to the relationship. A relationship built on choice rather than need will be less draining for both partners. Right now, as you concentrate on the relationship you have with yourself, you will know that this is true. When you feel more independent, you feel less needy, less fearful, and less insecure. You enjoy being you! Continue to foster feelings of autonomy and they will enhance your sense of competence. Whether you enter into a loving relationship with another or not, you will always work on the loving relationship you have with yourself. That is part of autonomy, as well. It is important not to forget yourself even when you love another.

Today my independence makes it easier for me to love, without being needy. Freedom to love myself or another without doubt, anxiety or insecurity is a challenge for me. I will work toward autonomy with joy and hope and know that all things are possible.

"I am in love with him, but I don't love him." The phrase "In love" usually refers to great passion and chemistry, while "Love" is mutual respect, shared history, tenderness and trust. Sometimes the chemistry is still strong and you still feel a pull toward him, and that feels like love. But those loving feelings may not even be about his being loveable. You may be in love with:

- What the relationship was at one time.
- What it could have been.
- Your fantasy of what it was.
- The idea of love.
- How everyone else sees him.
- His potential.
- The idea of the relationship.
- The sex.

Love is a word we use in many ways, to mean many things. Poets, songwriters and novelists spend lifetimes trying to express this feeling we call love. True love requires respect, admiration, trust, tenderness, and genuine regard. Ask yourself "What is loveable about this person?" I am surprised how many women claim to be madly in love, but cannot find a single loveable trait in the object of their affections. "Madly" becomes the operative word here. "Loving" someone who does not behave in a loveable way towards you *is* mad. I am not denying that you feel something, but let's be clear about what it is. When we delude ourselves into thinking we are in love with an unlovable person, then we create our own loss, heartache and pain.

Today I will consider the true meaning of love and if it does not fit my circumstances, I will relinquish any fantasy I may have. I will find another word that is truer in describing my feelings. That is one more step in being truer to myself.

Power is the ability to influence what goes on in your life and your relationships. It is not the same as control, which is when you try to impose your values, thoughts, feelings, and needs on another. Power is about figuring out what you need. Power is your ability to advocate for yourself, be assertive, and pro-act. When you have power, you live your life as a survivor rather than a victim. Consider the following statements as they relate to your personal power. Appraise your growth, assess your strengths, and note the areas that need work:

- I afford myself the same status that I do others.

- I think of power as positive.

- I feel powerful.

- I feel comfortable when I am powerful.

- I do not see my ex as more powerful then myself.

- I speak up on my own behalf.

- I am able to say no.

- I am able to ask for what I want.

- I draw power from being able to communicate.

- I am no longer intimidated by people I perceive as powerful.

Certainly, there are times when you feel more powerful than at other times. There are many reasons for this variation: mood, issue, place and person all play significant roles in your ability to feel powerful. Concentrate your efforts on those areas that feel problematic: where you feel minimized and powerless. Pay attention to when you confuse control and power. One of the ways you will feel your power is when you feel calm inside. The need for control will obliterate your peace and will cause you anguish. That is the result of surrendering your power.

Today I will take a moment to affirm how far I have come. I will embrace my growth and acknowledge how good it feels when I am powerful. When I look at those areas which "need work," I will do so with love and acceptance, rather than criticism or blame.

Some time has passed since this process all began. Usually in a few months, most women begin to feel some relief from their symptoms. They begin to sleep better and enjoy food again, have increased concentration and even begin to laugh. After a period of time, the anger begins to evolve. It becomes less intense and less frequent. Your feelings begin to change. Although it may still feel as if you are on a roller coaster, you are beginning to see some progress.

However, if you feel that you are in the same place emotionally as you were when this began and you have not experienced any changes in your emotional distress, it is time to examine what is going on with you. Your prism of emotion should have gentle movement. When moved ever so slightly, prisms reflect the light differently. This movement includes elements of insight, self-awareness, and growth. If you are reading this and saying, "No, I haven't changed at all. Nothing is changed, nothing is better," then it is time to figure out why that is so. After all, you don't want to feel this way forever, or do you? Sometimes, without even realizing it is happening, we begin to develop a very special relationship with our pain. It can serve us on other levels and we begin to hold it near and rely on it.

Some reasons women hold onto pain include:

- It may be a way of keeping other relationships distant.
- It may keep us from moving ahead, which can feel scary.
- It may give us attention.
- It may feel like revenge: "The more I hurt, the worse he will feel."
- It may keep us connected.
- It may be concealing some greater hurt which we do not want to face.
- It keeps us company and gives us "something to do."

If you are having difficulty moving on, ask yourself what you are afraid of. Fear is often the major motivator in keeping us "sitting in a dirty diaper." It sounds strange and hard to believe, because none of us willingly wants pain and anger in our life. However, your anger and pain are known entities. It may feel safer holding onto these known companions than risking the unknown that accompanies change.

Today am I having difficulty moving on? Is this pain becoming my companion? Could the pain serve to mask underlying issues? Can I imagine my life without my pain? What losses would I incur by giving up this familiar, yet uncomfortable companion? I will consider these questions as I go about my day and perhaps I will discuss them with a trusted friend or therapist.

Validation refers to affirmation. It supports your perception and experience of life. Below are some statements to help you look at validation and the role, either positive or negative, that it plays in your life.

- I trust myself.
- I take responsibility for things that have happened, without self-criticism.
- I take responsibility for myself.
- I am honest with myself.
- I am more secure with who I am.
- I validate my own changes.
- I no longer am dependent on his approval for validation.
- I validate myself more than anyone else does.
- When others disagree with me, I am not invalidated.
- I can admit to being wrong without feeling invalidated.
- I feel more like an equal in my relationships.

On any given day, our feelings of being validated change. Many factors affect these changes including situation, person involved and mood.

- Who are the people in your life who validate you?
- Do different people validate different things about you?
- What areas/circumstances of your life are most validating?
- Are there people/ areas/circumstances that offer little validation?
- How do you deal with those areas of your life that offer little or no validation?
- Are you able to validate yourself in those environments/situations?
- When you look back to one year ago, how was the issue of validation different for you?
- Where have you shown the most growth?
- What areas still need work?

Today I will explore the role validation plays in my life. I will recognize that each woman makes progress in her own way, and I will be careful to validate MY progress rather than minimize, diminish, or negate it.

Which is better? Is being married better than being single? Women can argue this point endlessly and with great passion. Like most things, there is good and bad in both. Loneliness seems to be the number one emotional concern of those re-entering the single life. However, most women agree that there is nothing lonelier than sharing a bed with someone you don't want to be with. Loneliness is a part of life, whether you are single or married. It is important not to confuse being alone with feeling lonely.

Unfortunately, married people are still awarded some benefits that singles do not have. For example, in many states, married people pay less for automobile insurance. Married people can be on each other's health insurance. Married people (or at least couples) seem to get the best seats in restaurants. In some instances, there are surcharges for traveling solo, as on cruises. At times, the world appears geared to couples.

There are other considerations, too. Single women worry about who will stand by them in times of illness or who will be their date at their child's wedding. They worry about being alone on holidays. They think that the world will judge them as unlovable or as LOSERS. They worry about not having access to safe, consistent sex. They worry that they are more vulnerable to crime. They worry about money.

On the other hand, married women envy their single sisters their freedom. Married women complain about not having enough time to take care of themselves, about constantly making concessions and compromises. They may feel financially secure, yet feel they have lost their own identity. They envy a single woman's lifestyle – being able to eat when you want, go where you want when you want, not having to take care of others, not having to consult with another, or ask another person for anything. Being single in mid-life, offers a woman the opportunity to experience independence differently than she did when she was younger. The experience and wisdom of the years opens up opportunities for self-growth that was not possible at age twenty.

Whatever your couple status is, for right now, it simply is. Choose to maximize the experience in every way possible because, as you already know, things can change very quickly.

Today rather than bemoan my marital status, I will consider the benefits of my situation and how to make the most of them. I will not wish for or long for something that I do not have now. If I spend my time mourning what I do not have, I will miss all the opportunities of what I do have.

In 1992, Faith slipped on some ice and broke her ankle very badly. At that time she had been divorced for two years and was living on her own, with a big dog as her only companion. The fall resulted in surgery, three days in the hospital and many hours of physical therapy. This was a life changing experience for Faith.

> She reminisces, "If someone had told me an hour before the fall that this would happen to me, I probably would have freaked out, obsessing about how to arrange for everything and worrying as to how my life would unfold." About one year after the accident, she confided to a friend, "This was the most significant thing that ever happened to me. I learned about life, friends, pain, control, asking for help, strength, courage, and a zillion other things." Her friend responded, "I hope you don't lose those lessons." "Oh, no, I definitely won't," she responded.

She had kept her x-rays and occasionally took them out and marveled at what science could do to reconstruct shattered bones. But another feeling surged through her as she examined those x-rays. It was a feeling of pride. Not pride about slipping on the ice, but pride about her courage and strength through that difficult time. She was proud of her resiliency and her tenaciousness. Three years ago, when the last of the hardware was removed from her ankle, she had the screws set into a Lucite block. It sits proudly on her desk as a constant reminder for all that she learned and all the pride that she feels. She calls it her "survival trophy."

Divorce is one of those life-changing events that warrant a survival trophy. Create one for yourself as a testimony to the difficult time and the lessons learned. When life gets challenging, it will serve as a reminder of your courage. Remembering what we have been through helps us face what lies ahead.

Some women have painted pictures or created collages; others have purchased vanity plates for their car. Planting a garden, building a tree house and sculpting, are some other creative ideas women have shared with me. Some women redesign their engagement ring and then wear it with great pride. The "survival trophy" is limited only by your imagination. The only rule is that it reminds you of the pride you feel for what you have been through, what you have learned, and how you have grown.

Today I will think about my "Survival Trophy" and what that means to me. I may not yet have an idea, but it will come to me. All I need to do is to stay open to the possibility. For now, just exploring the notion is creative, fun and offers a great distraction from any stress I feel.

It is through the difficult events in our lives that we learn the most about ourselves and our world. Let's explore your personal growth. The following statements can be considered in a number of ways. Take into account your emotional, intellectual, and spiritual growth. Use them to create a picture of your evolution through this difficult and challenging period of your life.

- I am taking chances.

- I am expanding my attitudes.

- I am enhancing my life.

- I do things for my self.

- I feel more comfortable with myself.

- I am less overwhelmed by adversity.

- I have changed my lifestyle to better fit who I am.

- I feel creative.

- I am continuing to develop emotionally.

- I am taking charge of things that cause me pain.

- I am less afraid.

- I am expanding my circle of people.

- I feel like I want to grow.

- I can acknowledge I have grown a great deal in the last year.

- I am excited about my infinite opportunities.

- I know I still have a lot of growing to do and I am looking forward to it.

If you find there is an area in which you need to do more work, ask a "how" question. For example, if you are not feeling particularly creative and want to work on this area, the question to ask yourself is, "How can I bring more creativity into my life?"

Today by looking at the areas of growth in my life, I can affirm how far I have come. I also become aware of what areas I wish to focus my energies. I do this with self-love and support, and I am careful never to minimize the great strides I have made.

You can do this exercise by yourself or with a trusted friend. Sit directly facing an empty chair or if you are doing this with a friend, have them sit across from you. Think about what you will miss the most, whether it is some aspect of your spouse or some aspect of the marriage. For example, you may miss his smile or his handiness at fixing things. You may miss his sense of direction or his family. Then, imagine you have the opportunity to say good bye to each loss. Say whatever you need to for closure. Say out loud what you are feeling. It is especially important to say it out loud. Not because someone else needs to hear it, but because YOU need to say it AND hear it! Your friend, the listener, is not to comment, only to encourage you to talk and to support your pain. She is not to offer advice or solutions, just comfort.

Following the exercise, describe what you feel to your friend. If you are doing this by yourself, write what you feel in your journal. Although you may cry during the farewell, afterward you will probably experience a feeling of lightness, release, or relaxation. Honor your loss by giving each the time you need.

Today I will think about how I will do this exercise. Will I ask a friend to be with me? Do I prefer to do it myself? I will make sure I plan enough time to express my feeling and thoughts. I will also make sure I allow the time I need to grieve when I am done. I may be fearful of doing this, but I know that when I say good-bye to the past, I am stronger and more ready to face the future.

Day 15   When Is It Appropriate to Begin Dating?

Like most issues in divorce, there is no definitive answer to the dating question. It depends on the couple, how much pain there is, and the age of the children. Each woman handles this differently. And in each family, members will react to the news you are dating in ways as varied and unique as they are.

Many women feel their husbands haven't waited long enough to begin dating. When I ask, "What is long enough?" most are unclear, but can only say he didn't give it enough time. When I press the matter, no one seems to have a definitive answer. Some things I have heard include:

- **When the divorce is final.** Many divorces drag on for years and it is not uncommon for one or both parties to begin to date before it is final.
- **When I am ready for him to date.** Sorry. But that is not your decision anymore.
- **When he asks me for permission.** Ditto.
- **When the children are ready.** Same answer. A parent's choice to date should not be dictated by his/her children's approval.
- **When I am dating someone.** Life is not fair. He doesn't have to wait until you are happily recoupled to begin dating.

This may seem frustrating. You may be wondering if there are any guidelines at all. There are certain civilities and common courtesies that people should afford each other. And by all means, while your children don't dictate your social life, you can certainly be sensitive to their needs. Here are some good rules of thumb to follow:

Be discreet. Don't flaunt your dating to hurt your ex. That just makes you look really mean. A new partner who is worth anything is not going to find that an endearing characteristic.

Be sensitive to your children's needs. Your new partner may make you go weak in the knees and give you a new purpose for living. However, your children are probably not going to see it that way. The new person represents a reality that their parents' marriage is over. It also means that they will have to share you with someone else.

Check out your own level of readiness for dating. Are you really ready? Can you devote time and energy to a relationship? Do you feel you have sufficiently mourned your marriage? Do you know what mistakes you made in the marriage and are you aware of what things you need to change?

Check out your own motives. Are you dating because you are lonely? Are you dating to get back at him? Are you dating because you are afraid if you don't hurry up and get moving, you will never meet anyone?

Today I recognize that each of us may be ready to date at different times. It isn't a race. Being an adult includes learning to be on my own and to make conscious decisions about my life. I have no control over his choices, but I can manage my own life in a way that will empower me. I will behave in a way that fosters my self-confidence and, at the same time, be mindful of my children's needs.

A few of you, maybe many of you, can think of a number of less than flattering things to call your ex-husband. You can call him whatever you want , for as long as you want, but do it in silence. As time goes on, social situations will present themselves when you might need to introduce him to others. Sometimes this happens in front of the children. "My ex-husband" is, I suppose, accurate enough. But how do you feel being introduced as someone's "ex?" It seems to have connotations of being disposed of or discarded.

Referring to your ex as "my children's father" is a more positive and more accurate description. It says nothing about your relationship to each other, either positive or negative, except in relationship to the children, which is all anyone needs to know. When your children hear "my children's father," it reinforces for them that the divorce does not disturb their relationship with their Dad. It also respects and validates their ongoing relationship, as it shows support.

This issue may seem insignificant to you. That may change when one or both of you are re-married. Example: you are both remarried and, with your new spouses, attend a function at your children's school. All four of you are there. How does introducing your first husband as your "ex husband" impact on your current spouse? Even the term "ex-husband" indicates a prior relationship in which your current husband gets to be "second." He doesn't need to be reminded constantly and in public of his "second" status. Furthermore, others may feel uncomfortable as "ex" can be interpreted as having undertones of hostility.

Today I will consider what I want him to call me. "My ex?" By my first name? "Hey, you?" How would I like to be addressed? Do some labels hurt me while others validate me? I will think about my needs around this issue and perhaps I will even discuss this with my children's father.

Counseling for the divorcing couple may facilitate a peaceful parting. Conflict and acrimony pits once loving, committed adults against each other, creating an environment which discourages cooperation. The divorce process can easily escalate into out-and-out war. Divorce therapy focuses on:

- Acknowledging and accepting responsibility.
- Making sense of conflict.
- Developing new communication tools.
- Avoiding unnecessary litigation.
- Sparing the children inappropriate involvement in the process.

Divorce therapy can bring about the following results:

- Understanding, which can reduce anger.
- Positive parenting.
- Enhance future relationships.
- Diminish the misuse of the attorney as therapist.

During the divorce process, it is easy for people to lose their integrity, dignity, and self-worth. A deteriorating marriage usually brings out our worst side and divorce is just an extension of that behavior. A peaceful parting can help facilitate a more amicable divorce. The goal is healing through communication and activity with each other. In divorce therapy, this is accomplished by:

- Emphasizing co-parenting strategies.
- Developing a contract for positive relations throughout the divorce proceedings.
- Remembering the positive aspects of the relationship.
- Implementing a strategy for parting.

This agenda can usually be accomplished in six to eight sessions. Unlike marriage therapy, the couple does not need to reach compromise and resolution of the issues. They only need to accept that resolution is *not* possible with regard to marital issues. However, that does not mean the couple cannot or should not be able to communicate, compromise, and resolve future divorce issues and parenting objectives. Divorce counseling is not used to convince the other person you were right, to punish him, or as a forum for your anger. It is important to note, that if there are issues of abuse, domestic violence or if you are fearful of your estranged spouse, this is not a recommended strategy.

Today I can see the value of participating in a program of this nature. These insights can be helpful in future relationships. Am I comfortable with my ability to stay focused and not use this venue for revenge? If so, I will consider seeing if my spouse would be interested, as well. This could help us transition from spouses to co-parents.

Many of us actually prefer to stay home on New Year's Eve or spend the night with friends rather than get all dressed up to trudge through snowy, icy weather, only to eat and drink too much! Yet, the fantasy of this night still seems to hold many women captive. The notion of "being alone" on New Year's Eve makes an otherwise strong, capable, independent woman feel like a 13-year-old wallflower! A woman can be spending New Year's Eve with friends, family, and children, but without a date, she may say, "I am alone." If this is your first New Year's Eve without your spouse, then this is your first New Year's Eve single. This is a New Year and a new beginning, and it is worth celebrating! Here are some ideas to get you thinking about your options.

- A quiet night at home with videos, take-out food, and your kids.
- A girl's night in. Have a couple of friends sleep over--give each other pedicures and facials.
- Going out with girlfriends, celebrating friendship with dinner and a good movie.
- A progressive dinner. Each house makes a different course of the meal and you move with your friends from house to house.
- A house party, where each of your single friends brings another single friend. A good way to network with safe people.
- A get-together with single Moms and their kids.
- Journal about all the things you learned in the old year and all the things you hope for in the New Year.
- Go away skiing or take a cruise. Look for last minute travel deals on the Internet.
- Check into the local Marriot or Holiday Inn with your kids. The big hotel chains often offer package deals and kids love the big indoor pools.
- Ignore the whole thing and go to bed early after eating a pint of chocolate chip ice cream and watching *Sleepless in Seattle*.

You have options that you may have not had before. Try something new. It will make you feel adventurous and that will help you feel more confident! Most importantly, take a few moments at the start of this New Year to feel gratitude and hope. Don't forget to praise yourself for getting through a really tough year!

Today I know I am in charge of my life. I am in charge of what I choose to do for New Year's Eve. I can choose to do nothing, which is different than just letting "nothing happen."

Frequently, women are incredulous at their husband's behavior during divorce. Why do we expect men to be on their best behavior during divorce? Do we behave any better? If you were anxious during your marriage, you are probably more anxious now. Conversely, if he was controlling during the marriage, he is probably considerably more controlling now.

Divorce is not a catalyst for us to act our best. Under stress, people do not communicate more effectively. Our foibles, weak spots, and least attractive characteristics often get called into play. Women tend to give others the benefit of the doubt. We want to believe that people will act in a harmonious manner. We do not desire conflict and confrontation. We have expectations that he will "get it" (understand how we feel) and that the transition from married to single will go smoothly.

Think about this rationally. If he (and you) were able to "get it," would you even be getting a divorce? If he couldn't make the changes, take the high road, communicate effectively during the marriage, what makes you think he will be able to do it now? Thinking this way sets you up for disappointment and this results in your feelings being hurt. The best predictor of future behavior is past behavior. It is true that people can change but the divorce process does not encourage change for the better. During divorce, our negative traits are amplified, especially in the eyes of our spouse. It might be helpful for you to consider your own behavior. Are you acting differently? Are your best traits shining through? Probably not.

Refocus your emphasis; while you can't change anyone else's behavior, you can change your own. So, if you were passive and compliant, work at being more assertive. If you had a tendency to control, explore ways of relaxing that control. If you screamed a lot, try practicing restraint.

People only change if they want to, not because WE want them to. We can change ourselves, but that does not occur without insight, desire, and effort. By focusing on his behavior, you set yourself up for hurt and disappointment. By looking at your own behavior, you work on awareness and self-growth.

Today I will look at my own behavior and try to be honest about what I can work on. I do this for myself, because when I behave in a way that is healthy, I feel better about myself. Expecting him to change is really just a way to avoid looking at myself. I will decide to put my thoughts and feelings and energy into myself, because I want peace in my life.

A pre-nuptial agreement is a contract made between two people, prior to their marriage, in which they agree how their property will be disposed of in the event of death or divorce. The contract only goes into effect if the marriage occurs. If you signed a pre-nuptial agreement and are considering a divorce, now is the time to find it and bring it to your attorney. If you have moved to another state since you signed the agreement, you will want to check it to see if it stipulates what state will have jurisdiction over the document. Make sure you choose a lawyer from the appropriate state. There are times when pre-nuptials can be over-ridden and there are times when they are upheld. According to Atty. Laurie DeNigris of New Britain, Connecticut, they are usually upheld if:

- Each party had adequate time, prior to signing the agreement, to consult with an attorney.
- You entered the agreement voluntarily; there was no duress.
- There was a fair amount of time prior to the wedding for you to review the document.
- It is fair at the time of enforcement.
- Full financial disclosure was given prior to signing.

If you are beginning to date again, then pre-nuptials may be on your mind, especially if your divorce was a nasty and financially-devastating event. Often, couples who experience very acrimonious divorces find themselves considering a pre-nuptial agreement when they re-marry.

There are pro's and con's to having a pre-nuptial agreement. The pro's are: it gives you a framework in which to dispose of property and assets if the marriage should deteriorate; it protects children from previous marriages; it maintains family assets such as a family business or inheritance.

The con's are: you don't know if it will be fair at the time of the divorce. Frequently, women do not take enough time to carefully review the document and consider their rights. Some pre-nuptial agreements are presented right before the wedding and the woman may feel that she hasn't much choice. She may feel pressured to sign it or her wedding will be called off.

In short, get advice from an attorney in your state before signing any legal document. Like most things, there are pluses and minuses. Only with careful consideration and good counsel should you move ahead with any important decision.

Today I am again reminded that getting solid and knowledgeable feedback will empower me. Then I can move ahead in ways that will protect and benefit me and my children.

All of us have the desire to be loved unconditionally. Ideally, parental love gives us this experience. However, some of us may not have felt this unconditional love as children. As adults, we may seek unconditional love in our romantic relationships. Clearly, we all want to know we will be loved (and not left) when we get old, if we get sick, or if we lose our job. If we define those kinds of events or life passages as the criteria for unconditional love, then that is healthy. It is what we have the right to expect in a loving committed relationship. We want someone who is in it for the "long haul."

However, when unconditional love becomes license to treat another person badly, that is not acceptable. In truth, unacceptable behavior is not love at all. When a partner lies, cheats, betrays, and deceives, then they are not acting with love.

All relationships have conditions, which are really rules. Without rules, all relationships would be impossible. For example, your relationship with your therapist is one of unconditional positive regard. However, it has rules: you show up at a certain agreed-upon time and your session ends at a predetermined time. You pay a certain fee for service. Other rules may include you don't smoke in the office and the therapist doesn't fall asleep while you are discussing your deepest thoughts and fears. The rules are the framework that contain the relationship. Imagine for a minute what would happen if suddenly your therapist stopped halfway through the session and said, "You know, I don't feel like doing this today. Come back another time," or "You were kinda boring today, I think you should pay me double." You wouldn't be able to sustain a caring relationship with that person. They would be acting inconsiderately and disrespectfully.

Without certain rules to define the relationship and without adherence to those rules, the relationship would quickly deteriorate into one that is filled with chaos, confusion and lack of trust. This is true of any relationship, including a marriage.

Today did I expect unconditional love from my spouse, even if my behavior was not loving? This may be difficult to objectively confront, but keys to why my marriage deteriorated may be found in my behavior. The converse is also true; did my spouse break the rules of respect, trust, and loyalty and then act totally surprised at my withdrawal from the relationship? Learning to accept rules as part of relationship doesn't diminish the possibility of love, it only can serve to strengthen the love and deepen the commitment.

Mary experienced a terribly acrimonious divorce. She and her husband fought about everything! They had lawyers and therapists and accountants. Their children had lawyers and therapists. It went on for seven years! Finally, the couple had divided nearly all their possessions, but could not agree on one final item. It was a whistling teapot. Not a fancy one, but the basic chrome model available at any discount store. It was the principle of the matter, each exclaimed. It had been given to them by Mary's Aunt Martha, who, it turned out, was also her husband's fifth grade teacher. Each felt a claim to Aunt Martha and her teapot. It cost them over $600 in legal fees before the attorneys could convince one of them to just go buy a new whistling teapot.

Today I will think about the wisdom of choosing my battles carefully. Sometimes winning is losing and vice versa.

Often a second marriage is approached with the notion that one can "do it right this time," or "make up for all of the mistakes of the first marriage." Before you get any deeper into the fantasy of a blissful second marriage, let's discuss the realties of remarriage. Two-thirds of all divorced people remarry. The national average for time between marriages is three years for men and five years for women. Of those second marriages, approximately sixty-six percent will end in another divorce, which is slightly higher than the divorce rate of first marriages.

A second marriage is nothing like a first. In a first marriage, when we vow to stay together until "death do us part", we never even entertain the thought that divorce relates to us. In a second marriage, we have experienced that sense of disappointment. We have learned that just because we want something doesn't mean it will happen.

In a first marriage, our goals are usually congruent. The children are planned for, the first house is purchased together, and perhaps you support each other's professional growth and individuation from families. In a second marriage, there may already be children. Usually, homes have been bought and careers established. Goals of the couple in the second marriage may be different and on different timelines.

In a second marriage, pre-nuptial agreements may be an issue. Rarely is this the case in a first marriage, usually because there may not be a large accumulation of assets and because the trust is easier. After a divorce, particularly an acrimonious one, one or both partners may be less willing to enter the holy union without some financial protection. Also, the presence of children has a profound impact on a second marriage. It affects the new couple financially, practically, emotionally, legally and historically.

Does this sound as if second marriages are filled with mistrust, skewed goals and bitterness? I don't think so. It is just a more realistic picture of what can go wrong. Couples are more aware of the hard work involved. The pitfalls that perhaps were fueled by idealism and naiveté in the first marriage are diminished.

Today I am beginning to realize that there is only one first marriage. That doesn't mean a second marriage cannot be fulfilling, loving, and healthy, as long as I am willing to let my fantasies go. As is the case with most things, if I reach for the impossible, I miss what is possible. What do I want from a second marriage? In what ways has my first marriage taught me how to be a better person, partner, and friend?

Emily is a 22-year-old medical student. Her parents divorced when she was ten years old. Like most children, Emily has very specific memories of that difficult time. She remembers in vivid detail the event that precipitated her father moving out. She describes with poignancy the conflict of being caught up in a custody battle. Time, distance, and maturity have given her insight into much of what happened. Today, she is close with both parents, but there were years of difficulty. Dish-throwing and yelling were rationalized. Her mother told her, "Couples fight, it is normal." So she withdrew from the fights without much concern.

Now, she knows this behavior was not normal. She tends to shy away from conflict. She tries to accommodate and please, as do many children who experience parental violence. Prior to her father's leaving the house, there was an incident when the police were called. Afterwards, she ruminated about the incident. An attempt to rewrite history, to attach meaning to a single event, and to see it as the cause of the divorce is fairly common for children.

The most difficult aspect of the divorce was her mother's bad-mouthing her father. She believed her mother when she said that her father was irresponsible with money. Emily acted like a little parent, worrying about his finances and trying to protect his feelings. When he moved away after the divorce, she was devastated by his absence, and fearful she would not see him again. She did visit him every vacation and holiday. Even though she enjoyed her time with him, this schedule was a struggle for Emily. Spending her vacation time with her father meant being away from her friends during "downtime." She feels that impacted her skill at making friends. He moved many times and she did not develop friends at these second homes. Also, he acted more like a friend than a parent.

When she considers how she grew from the experience, Emily feels the divorce made her more introspective and taught her to respect "how she works." It also facilitated her really getting to know her parents as people. Her advice to parents going through divorce is to spend lots of time with their kids and never fight in front of them. Don't even fight when they are in the house. Do everything you can to fix your marriage, but if it isn't going to work, don't think waiting until the children are older helps. It doesn't. Don't drag it out.

Today I know every child's story is different, but many elements remain the same. I will be aware of how my own behavior will impact my children for many years to come.

Question to a divorce attorney: "If there was one thing you wish women knew about the divorce process before entering into litigation, what would that be?"

Answer: "I wish women could understand that this system is not set up to help them get what they want."

I was taken aback, as I thought the system did help women. Then I realized that she was referring to a woman's need for revenge or justice. The law would not support her sense of hurt and betrayal and would not compensate her for her pain. The law is an unemotional vehicle used to establish division of property and protect children's rights. The system is not designed to work out your emotional stuff.

Countless women try to use the legal arena as an opportunity for justice for their emotional pain. Rarely do they feel adequately compensated. Sometimes, they feel abused again. First, the man they love let them down, and now they feel the legal system did the same.

The truth is, the system did not let them down. These women misinterpreted the role and power of the system. In their pain and panic, they desperately sought ways to salve their hurt. When they looked toward the legal system for this remedy, they set themselves up for being let down. It isn't that the system is unfair. It's that the system is not designed to heal a broken heart.

Using the court system and perpetuating litigation to deal with your anger will cost you thousands of dollars, not to mention a horrific amount of time, energy, and stress. Discuss with your lawyer what your expectations are about your settlement. Be clear on what is possible and what is not. Know the limits of the legal system. Be realistic. Divorce is the "business" of dissolving a marriage. Find other venues such as therapy, support groups, and friends to work out your emotional pain.

Finally, look forward. See what other opportunities there are in your life. Use this life-changing event to explore other options. Get to know yourself: what makes you tick and what you want from life. Divorce closes one door, but as with all other major life events, it opens others.

Today am I able to separate my emotional issues from my legal situation? Do I expect the court system to punish him and take care of me? These are difficult questions, but awareness is critical for my well being. I will carefully consider my expectations so I do not set myself up to feel betrayed and abandoned yet again.

Divorce creates havoc in a woman's life, but there is a bright side. Divorce gives you an opportunity to explore who you are and what you want. Many of us have not had this opportunity for years. Some may never have had the chance. This is, as all the books and movies purport "your time." How do you figure out who you are and what you want?

There is no easy answer. It is a process, one that is rewarding and affirming if you are gentle, yet insistent with yourself. One way to begin to explore this question is to create a vision of what you want. Imagine how you would like your life to be 10 years from now, or five years from now or even one year. When you allow yourself time to imagine, things will begin to come into focus.

- Where do you want to live?
- What kind of work do you want to be doing?
- What would you like your lifestyle to be like?
- What does your life stand for?
- What values do you hold most dear?
- What kind of life do you envision for your children?
- If you only had one month to live, how would you spend it?
- Who do you look up to and what characteristics do you most admire?
- If you won ten million dollars, what would you do with it?
- If you could have three wishes come true, what would they be and why?
- When people talk about you, what do you want them to say?
- How do the values of your parents and your values differ? How are they the same?
- What things do you most like about yourself?
- What things would you like to change?

These questions require more than simple and quick answers. Keeping a journal can help you hone your answers. Focus on just one of the questions to give yourself a gentle nudge. Your thoughts will start to accelerate. Let your imagination carry you. No desire is too big or impossible. Let your desires give you a framework for the inner work that you need to do.

- Join a support group, a cooking class, a spiritual circle, or a volunteer committee. Through exchange and reflection with other women, we crystallize our vision of ourselves. We can see our uniqueness and also our sameness.
- Try new things by yourself. Go to a museum, shopping, or on a road trip. Be with yourself. Begin to connect with your joys and sorrows, your likes and dislikes, your passions and aversions.
- Spend time in quiet solitude. Learn to listen to your inner voice. This ability to listen inward will illuminate your path to self-knowledge and awareness.

Today I do not know everything about myself, but I do know that I want to know more. I am committed to living the life I want and deserve. That can only be attained through self-awareness. I will begin my journey today, in a small way, knowing that all journeys begin with a single step.

Taking the focus off of others and refocusing that energy onto one's self may feel selfish. It can even feel like loss of control. Women have nurturing instincts. As small girls, we were given dolls, dollhouses, and kitchen sets. We were read fairy tales of selfless lovely maidens being rewarded with "happily ever after." We learned that we are rewarded for "good behavior" with positive attention and when we are "bad," we are punished or ignored. We learn early in life what skills and behaviors are loveable and we take those lessons into the world.

Many of us were taught that "conceit" and "selfishness" were bad traits. To feel good about yourself and to say out loud, "I am smart (or pretty, or funny)" was considered an unattractive way to behave. We know now that confidence in oneself and one's abilities leads to self-esteem. And self-esteem leads to better experiences in life. Studies show girls who play sports have more self-confidence, which leads to better self-esteem. These girls are less likely to use drugs, become teenage Moms, or drop out of school.

When we tried to take care of ourselves, stood up for what we believed in, or simply refused to be compliant, we were often labeled "difficult", "uncooperative", "aggressive." Over the years, we learned to silence our opinions and our needs. That behavior became a habit. So now, the idea of putting ourselves first or feeling good about ourselves may feel completely foreign to us. Any time we make a move toward taking care of ourselves, we may feel as if we are doing something wrong. The "tapes" of the old teachings lie deep within us and sometimes we aren't aware just how loud the volume is. Movies, books, and music all carry messages that support those old tapes of self-sacrifice.

The first step in changing these patterns is to *know what we need*. Knowing oneself is a lifelong process, not achieved by reading a self-help book or attending a workshop. Self-awareness grows from learning to listen to yourself and paying attention to your needs. Therapy or counseling can help. A trained therapist can offer you a reflection of yourself; a mirror into your inner wants, hopes, and dreams.

Today I know that good help is available to me regardless of my financial resources. In researching my options, I am beginning to acknowledge that I am worth the time and worth the effort. I am beginning to take care of me already!

You may be feeling nostalgic for "the good old days." Perhaps you are remembering certain events, special days, and celebrations. When a relationship ends, we grieve for the loss of what there once was, as well as what could have been. Often, we grieve for something that disappeared a long time ago. Many women say, "I grieve for the way it was in the beginning."

We have a kind of amnesia, it seems, where we selectively eradicate the awful times and hold on to a highly edited, positive version of our relationship. These fantasies are creations of our own mind; by creating them, we create additional pain and grief.

Ask yourself this question: "If I were to attend a party tonight and a friend were to introduce me to a man who was just like my husband, and she were to fill me in on what this man has been doing for the last five (ten, twenty, thirty) years, including how he treated his wife and family, is this someone I would be interested in getting involved with today?"

Today I will look at him as he is now – not who he was, or who he could be. I will let myself feel loss based on the reality of who has become, rather than the fantasy I created.

One evening, maybe when you are feeling a bit lonely, bored, or nostalgic, you will take out the photo album of your wedding and sit down on your couch. Perhaps you will pour a glass of wine and listen to some favorite old songs. Slowly, you will turn the pages and stare into the faces of a young bride and groom, and you will wonder, "Who are those young people and what happened to them?"

Even though you are the same person shown in the photos, you are also a completely different person. Life changes us all, for better or worse. As you scrutinize photos of him, maybe you look for some sign you missed of the man he would become. There are, of course, no physical signs. However, signs of who you both would become did exist. In hindsight, you can see them now. There were those times he drank too much and you dismissed it as immaturity, or the time he lost his temper and you attributed it to stress. Maybe he cheated on an exam, or even cheated on you. The point is that everyone makes mistakes growing up and it is hard to tell which are the trials and tribulations of growing up and which are big, flashing warning signs.

You really couldn't have known. Don't blame yourself. You were different then, also. Given who you were and what you knew about the world, you did your best. It does no good to critique old behavior with new eyes. It only leads to feelings of regret and self-recrimination. The fact that you would do things differently today is evidence that you have grown, and if you are growing, you are on the right path, no matter how many twists and turns that path make take.

You may look at the pictures of yourself and think the same thing: who is that person? You will see the mistakes and transgressions of the past with the eyes of a more mature, worldly person. Hopefully, you will be gentle and accepting of yourself. That is part of the process of evolving. That is part of the process of living.

Today I will try to make sure I learn as much as I can about this chapter in my life. But the book is far from finished. There is much to say and think and do. I will make mistakes that with hindsight will again seem obvious or avoidable. But this awareness illustrates my growth. I will rejoice in the person I am becoming.

It has been one year since you opened this book. As you look back on this year, could you have imagined so many challenges? Whether your legal divorce is final or not, you have moved significantly closer to your independence. The legal divorce, as you now know, is only part of this whole process. There is the emotional divorce as well. You may not be completely there either, but you are probably a lot closer.

Often, when we finish a book, we close it and put it up on a shelf or pass it on to a friend. You may want to continue to use this book, to work on issues and areas of your life that are not as fully evolved as you wish. Or you may want to go back and reread some of the things you wrote, to affirm how far you have come. This book is a record and testimony to your one-year journey from being married to learning to be with yourself. Like all journeys in our life, much of the challenge is in the process. Continue to be mindful of all you have learned along the way. It has been a year of transitions. Hopefully it has also been a year of growth that will bring you closer to being the person you want to be.

Today is a day to revel in your successes over this past year. As you have learned, no success is too small or insignificant to affirm and celebrate. Growth is a painful and arduous process: sometimes in its midst, we aren't even sure anything is happening. It is like waiting for your hair to grow after a really bad haircut. It seems that nothing is happening. Daily you tug on that hair, mousse it, gel it, ponytail it, clip it, and it seems forever unruly and unmanageable. Then one day, like a miracle, it starts to look a bit better and then suddenly, as if it happened overnight, the bad haircut is no longer an issue. This process, called divorce, is just like that awful haircut. We can't see the progress when we are in the process.

Now a year has passed and you are not the same person you were a year ago. Hopefully, you like yourself more – have more confidence and more joy in your life. Hopefully you look toward the future with optimism, curiosity, and wonder. Hopefully, you have learned to honor yourself, your thoughts, your values, and your feelings. Hopefully, you have learned to surround yourself with people who do the same. Hopefully, you have made peace with the hurts and disappointments of the past. Hopefully, you have a sense of closure and some distance from the tough times. Hopefully, you have learned to love and accept yourself fully. This book is merely a chapter in your life. You will have many more chapters in your lifetime.

May you continue on a path that brings you joy, laughter, health and peace. These are my wishes for you.

Selected Bibliography

Books:

Alberti, Roberti and Michael Emmons. *Your Perfect Right*, 1995. San Luis Obispo, CA. Impact Publishers.

The Dalai Lama and Howard Cutler, MD, *The Art of Happiness*, 1998 NYC, NY. Riverhead Books.

Gray, John, *Men Are From Mars, Women Are From Venus*, 1992. New York, New York. Harper Collins Publications.

Hay, Louise, *You can Heal Your Own Life*, 1999. Carlsbad, Ca. Hay House.

Kirschenbaum, Mira, *Too Good to Go, Too Bad to Stay*, 1985. Los Angeles, CA Penguin Books.

Dr. Reinhold Niebuhr, *The Serenity Prayer*, Union Theological Seminary, NYC, NY Composed 1932. AA records. 1950.

Ruiz, Miguel. *The Four Agreements*, 1997. San Rafael, CA. Amber-Allen Publishers.

Journal Articles:

K. Bruinsma and D.L. Taren, *Chocolate: Food or Drug,* Arizona Prevention Center. University of Arizona, College of Medicine. Tucson, Arizona 85719, USA.(Journal of American Diet Association, October 1999: 10), pp 1249-1256.

Manuals:

Diagnostic Criteria from DSM-IV. American Psychiatric Association. Washington, DC. 1994. pp 162

Miscellaneous:

Neibur, Reinhold, M.D. *The Serenity Prayer* (for Alcoholics Anonymous). 1932. New York: Union Theological Seminary.

Newsletters:

Harvard Women's Health Watch. November 2001. Cambridge, Massachusetts.

Reports:

National Center for Health monthly Vital Statistics Report. Advance Report of Final Divorce Statistics, 1989 and 1990. April 18, 1995. Vol. 43, No. 9

U.S. Census Bureau Reports. *Numbers, Timing and Duration of Marriages and Divorces,* 1996. Rose M. Krieder and Jason M. Fields for Current Population Reports, February 2992:18.

U.S. Department of Justice. *1994 Violence Against Women: A National Crime Victimization Survey Report,* Washington, D. C., January 1994.

Website Articles:

Robert Friar, *The Science of Love – Your Brain's Love Cocktails,* Ferris University, Michigan, (discoveryhealth.com) paragraph 3.

Peter Orli, Ph.D, *Seven Myths of Divorce,* www.divorcesource.com/CA/DS/peter.html

Gary Spink, *The Chemistry of Love,* www.Monash.edu.au/pubs/moash-96-01/lovedrug.html

Readings:

Alberti, Robert and Micheal Emmons, 1995. *Your Perfect Right*. Impact Publishers, San Obispo, CA

Anderson, Carol & Susan Stewart. 1994. *Flying Solo: Single Women in Midlife*. W.W. Norton and Company, NY.

Beattie, Melody, 1998. *Co-Dependent No More*. Hazelden, MN, Hazelden Publishing and Educating Services.

Black, Claudia, Ph D. 1991. *It Will Never Happen to Me*. Colorado: Ballantine Books.

Connell, Cowan M.D. & Melvyn Kinder, M.D. 1985. *Smart Women: Foolish Choices*. NY, Clarkson N. Potter.

Cousins, Norman. 1991. *Anatomy of an Illness*. NYC: Bantam Books

Evans, Patricia, 1996. *The Verbally Abusive Relationship*. Avon, MA, Adams Media Corporation.

Fischer, Bruce, 1981. *Rebuilding: When your Relationship Ends*. San Obispo, CA. Impact Publishers.

Goldhor-Lerner, Harriet, 1985. *The Dance Of Anger*. NY: Harper & Row.

Jacob, Gregg, PhD., 1996. *Say Good Night to Insomnia*. New York: Holt and Company.

Kirschenbaum, Mira, 1985. *Too Good to Go, Too Bad to Stay*. Los Angeles, CA: Penguin Books.

Kuschner, Harold. 1983. *When Bad Things Happen to Good People*. NYC: Avon Publishers

Love, Patricia, 1990. *Emotional Incest*. NY: Bantam Books.

Norwood, Robin, *Women Who Love Too Much*. 1998 NY: Jeremy P. Tarcher, NY.

Ricci, Isolina, Ph D.1980. *Mom's House, Dad's House*. NY: MacMillan.

Trafford, Abigail, 1992. *Crazy Times*. NY: Harper Collins Publisher.

Trafford, Abigail, 2004. *My Time*, NY: Basic Books.

Wallerstein, Judith, PhD. & Blakeslee, Sandra, 2003. *Raising Your Children Before, During and After Divorce*. NY: Hyperion.

For Further Information...

Videos:

About Divorce—
Mrs. Doubtfire (children)
Kramer v Kramer
The War of the Roses
The First Wives Club
Starting Over
Good Friends

About Substance Abuse—
My Name is Bill W.
When a Man Loves a Woman
Clean and Sober
28 Days

About Step-families—
Table for Five
Stepmom

Organizations and their Phone Numbers:

Alcoholics Anonymous 1 (800) 800-4398
Al-Anon 1 (888) 425-2666
Gamblers Anonymous 1 (213) 386-8789
Cocaine Anonymous 1 (800) 800-NOCAINE
YWCA 1 (888) 993-2463
National Domestic Violence Hotline 1 (800) 799-7233 (TTY) 1 (800) 787-3224

Websites:

www.divorcesource.com
(Information related to all aspects of divorce)

www.NDVH.org
(National Domestic Violence Hotline and information)

www.AA.org
(Alcoholics Anonymous information)

www.Alanon,alateen.org
(Al-anon and Ala-teen information)

www.Gamblersanonymous.org
(Gamblers Anonymous Information)

www.webmd/mentalhealth.com
(Resource for questions and issues pertaining to mental health)

Index

Index

Control
helping is the sunny side of
controlling, 321
seeds of, 196
Cooperation, 92
Coping mechanisms, 231, 357
Corelli, Marie, 327
Cosby, Bill, 87
Costanza, Mary Lou, 212
Counselors. *See* Therapists
Couples' therapy, 134, 187, 380
Court. *See* Divorce court
Cousins, Norman, 132
Covenant Marriage, 315
Creativity, 135, 356
Credit cards, 28
Crisis, Chinese symbol for, 106
Crisis, meeting the challenges of, 340
Custodial parents, 232
Cutler, Howard, 20, 180, 256

D
Dalai Lama, the, 20, 180, 256
Dating. *See also* Husbands dating; Learning
to be single again; Relationships
appropriate time to start, 378
coed divorce groups and, 105
before the divorce is final, 28
holding off on, 119
jumping to conclusions about
your ex, 335
pre-nuptial agreements, 383
social norms, 286
SPADs (Single Parent Again
Dating), 261
when you have children, 326
David (Michelangelo's), 41
Day planners, 113, 219
Debts, 284

Decisions
child custody, 217
concerning alimony, 60
concerning reconciliation, 14
the coroner, 264
dealing with during the divorce, 324
dealing with pain, 239
fact-based *versus* wish-based, 109
fear of filing, 17
impulse, 22
making healthy, 98
Too Bad to Stay, Too Good to Go
(Kirschenman), 307
"what if" dilemma, 109
when to end the marriage, 20, 174
Defending the Caveman, 354
Denial
about drug/alcohol use, 50
but he doesn't think he has
a problem, 270
of abuse, 100
ah, yes!, 359
I knew we had problems, 222
DeNigris, Laurie, G., 151, 383
Department of Children and Family
Services, 115
Depression
childhood, 276
clinical, 259
medications, 259
minimalization, 46
SAD-Seasonal Affective Disorder, 215
two steps forward and one step
back, 204
Detachment, 319
Diet, maintaining a healthy, 297
Differences, problematizing, 333
Dillard, Annie, 237
Disappointment, 46
Discipline, kids and, 275
Disneyland Dad, 92

Index

Index

Index

Index

Victim, 115, 186
Video recommendations, 396
Violation of trust, 37
Violence. *See also* physical abuse
   anger without, 13
   against women, 163
Violence by Intimates (U.S. Dept. of
      Justice), 163
Visitation issues
   birdnesting, 306
   exploring, 232
   positive viewpoint, 318
   reducing stress in exchanges, 273
   your child's other family, 313
Visiting parents, 232
Visual imagery, 19
Volatility, 248
Volunteer work, 220

W
Wallerstein, Judith, 58
Websites, 15, 396
Wedding anniversaries, 328
Wedding photos, 193
Wedding rings, 334
Weddings, 112
Weekends, 162, 317
Well being, 31
Wet blankets, 346
Williams, Robin, 63
Winston, Liz, 63
Winters, Shelley, 63
Wisdom, inner, 120
Women. *See also* Learning to be single
      again; Relationships
   leaving the marriage for another
         woman, 303
   role of, in marriage, 44, 51
   turning to after betrayal, 71
   who love too much, 343
   why they are leaving, 354
Women's shelters, 100

Worries, reason for, 127

Y
Yoga, 180
You Can Heal Your Life (Hay), 290
Your Perfect Right (Alberti; Emmons),
      54, 149
Your personal ad, 341

Notes

Notes

Notes